Threat Finance

I dedicate this book in loving memory to my late father Professor Dennis Keene,
scholar, poet, translator and philosopher

Also a wonderful father, mentor and my dearest friend
and an epitome of all in life that is pure and good.

Thank you.

Until we meet again…

Threat Finance

Disconnecting the Lifeline of Organised Crime and Terrorism

DR SHIMA D. KEENE

Routledge
Taylor & Francis Group
LONDON AND NEW YORK

First published in paperback 2024

First published 2012 by Gower Publishing

Published 2016 by Routledge
4 Park Square, Milton Park, Abingdon, Oxon OX14 4RN

and by Routledge
605 Third Avenue, New York, NY 10158

Routledge is an imprint of the Taylor & Francis Group, an informa business

Publisher's Note
The publisher has gone to great lengths to ensure the quality of this reprint but points out that some imperfections in the original copies may be apparent.

British Library Cataloguing in Publication Data
Keene, Shima D.
Threat finance : understanding and countering the finance of organised crime and terrorism.
1. Terrorism – Finance – Prevention. 2. Terrorism investigation.
I. Title
363.3'2517–dc23

Library of Congress Cataloging-in-Publication Data
Keene, Shima D.
Threat finance : disconnecting the lifeline of organised crime and terrorism / by Shima D. Keene.
p. cm.
Includes bibliographical references and index.
ISBN 978-1-4094-5309-3 (hbk. : alk. paper) – ISBN 978-1-4094-5310-9 (ebook)
1. Terrorism – Finance. 2. Organized crime – Finance. 3. Commercial crime – Prevention. I. Title.

HV6431.K385 2012
363.325–dc23

2012019100

ISBN: 978-1-4094-5309-3 (hbk)
ISBN: 978-1-03-283743-7 (pbk)
ISBN: 978-1-315-55099-2 (ebk)

DOI: 10.4324/9781315550992

Contents

List of Figures and Table

Figures

Table

List of Cases

Ahmed Ali Yusuf and Al Barakaat International Foundation v Commission [2005] T-306/01

Ahmed and others v HM Treasury [2010] UKSC 2

Al-Ghabra v HM Treasury [2010] 4 All ER 829

Al Rajhi Banking and Investment Corporation v Wall Street Journal Europe SPRL [2003] EWHC 1776 (QB)

A v HM Treasury [2010] UKSC 2

A v HM Treasury [2010] 4 All ER 745

A v HM Treasury [2010] 2 WLR 378

A v HM Treasury [2010] All ER (D) 179

A, K, M, Q and G v HM Treasury [2008] EWHC 869

A and others v HM Treasury [2008] EWCA Civ 1187

Federal Insurance Company, et al., Petitioners v Kingdom of Saudi Arabia, et al. [2008] (06-0319 (L)) United States Court of Appeals for the Second Circuit

HM Treasury v Ahmed [2010] All ER (D) 40

HM Treasury v Ahmed [2010] UKSC 5 (SC)

Yassin Adbullah Kadi v Council and Commission [2005] T-315/01

Kadi v Council of the EU and the Commission [2008] c-415/05P 3 CMLR41

Kadi v EU Council and another; Al Barakaat International Foundation v EU Council and another [2010] All ER (EC) 1105

Kadi v European Commission [2010] All ER (D) 79 (Oct) T-85/09

Kadi v European Commission (supported by EU Council and others, intervening) [2011] 1 CMLR 697

Kadi v European Commission (supported by EU Council and others, intervening) [2011] All ER (EC) 169

Marfouz v Ehrenfeld [2005] EWCH 1156 (QB)

R v Allsop and others [2005] EWCA Crim 703

R v Aurora [2010] T2010/0359 (Croydon Crown Court)

R v Ajit Arora & 1 Other [2010] T2010/0358 (Croydon Crown Court)

R v Cuthbertson [1981] AC 470

R v Cuthbertson [1980] 2 All ER 401
R v E [2004] EWCA Crim 1243
R v Gold [1988] 2WLR 812 (HL)
R v Gokal [1999] 97 04132S2
R v Governor of Brixton Prison, Ex parte Levin [1997] Crim LR 891
R v Governor of Brixton Prison [1997] 3 All ER 289
R v Governor of Brixton Prison [1997] 3 WLR 117
R v Governor of Brixton Prison [1998] 1 Cr App Rep 22
R v Governor of Brixton Prison [1997] UKHL 27
R v Governor of Brixton Prison [1997] AC 741
R (on the application of M) v HM Treasury and other actions [2008] UKHL 26
R (on the application of Secretary of State for the Home Department) v E [2009] EWHC 597 (Admin) PTA/2/2007, PTA/11/2007, PTA/8/2008
R v Secretary of State for the Home Department Ex p. Simms [2000] 2 AC 115 (HL)
R v Smart and Beard [2002] EWCA Crim 772
R v Tsouli [2007] EWCA Crim 3300
R v Tsouli [2008] 2 Cr App Rep (S) 247
R v Tsouli and others [2007] All ER (D) 277 (Dec)
R (on the application of Youssef) v HM Treasury [2010] UKSC 2
United States of America v Usama bin Laden et al. (2001) 538 F.3d 71
United States v Royer (2008) 549 F.3d 886
United States v $4,255,625.39 (1982) 551 FSupp 314

List of Statutes and Statutory Instruments

Al-Qaida and Taliban (UN Measures) Order 2006
Anti-Terrorism, Crime and Security Act 2001
Asset-Freezing Act 2010
Computer Misuse Act 1990
Counter Terrorism Act 2008
Criminal (International Co-operation) Act 2003
Criminal Justice (International Co-operation) Act 1990
Criminal Justice Act 1987
Criminal Justice Act 1988
Criminal Justice Act 1993
Data Protection Act 1998
Drug Trafficking Act 1994
Drug Trafficking Offences Act 1986
EC Regulation 2580/2001
European Convention on Human Rights 1950
Executive Order 13224 (US)
Extradition Act 1989
Financial Services Act 1986
Financial Services and Market Act 2000
Freedom of Information Act 2000
Human Rights Act 1998
Intelligence Services Act 1994
Interception of Communications Act 1985
Misuse of Drugs Act 1971
Money Laundering Regulations 1993
Money Laundering Regulations 2003
Prevention of Terrorism Act 2005
Proceeds of Crime Act 2002

Regulation of Investigatory Powers Act 2000
Regulation of Investigatory Powers (Maintenance of Interception Capability) Order 2002
Security Service Act 1989
Security Service Act 1996
Serious Organised Crime and Police Act 2005
Terrorism Act 2000
Terrorism Order 2006
Terrorism (UN Measures) Order 2001 (SI 2001/3365)
Terrorist Asset Freezing Act 2010
Theft Act 1968
United Nations Security Council Resolution 1371 (2001)
United Nations Security Council Resolution 1373 (September 2001)
United Nations Security Council Resolution 1452 (2002)
USA PATRIOT Act 2001

About the Author

Shima Keene is a security advisor and scholar practitioner specialising in Threat Finance, advising and working closely with numerous government departments, the military, law enforcement and judiciaries around the globe. She also advises and provides high level security related education to numerous private sector organisations in a variety of industry sectors to include finance, aviation, oil and gas, insurance and telecommunications. In addition, Shima is a Subject Matter Expert to international defence and security organisations such as NATO, the Organisation for Security and Co-operation (OSCE) and the Council of Europe, and serves as an Expert Witness to the Crown Prosecution Service on matters relating to the financial aspects of organised crime and terrorism.

Through her work to date, she observed that a common problem in relation to countering terrorism and organised crime was, and continues to be, the disjointed knowledge base of those attempting to combat the threat. As a result, much of her recent work has been designed not only to bring together the existing knowledge base in the field, but to further enhance understanding and to develop an innovative multidisciplinary 'tool kit' for the broader stakeholder community with which to combat the threat. She has been strongly encouraged by colleagues in both the practitioner and academic communities to write and publish her work, which has served as the main incentive for writing this book.

Shima began her career in the City of London as a corporate financier in the Mergers and Acquisitions (M&A) department of the Japanese financial conglomerate, Nomura International. She remained in the City for over 10 years, working for various investment banks such as Goldman Sachs, Daiwa Capital Markets Europe and Dresdner Kleinwort Benson in a variety of roles including corporate strategy, industry analysis, securities trading and sales, project finance and project management.

In addition to her investment banking career, she served as a reservist in the British Army for six years. Much of her military career was spent in the Royal Army Medical Corps with attachments to 10 Coy, 4th Battalion, the Parachute Regiment as company medic, battlefield first aid instructor and physical training instructor. Her military work resulted in her increasing interest in the field of security and following the events of 9/11, she decided on a change in career direction to attempt to utilise her knowledge and experience in 'high finance' in the field of counter terrorism, and left the City to focus on researching the financial aspects of terrorism.

Between 2004 and 2008, Shima was based at the Defence Academy of the United Kingdom, Shrivenham, as Research Officer within the Defence Management and Security Analysis Department at Cranfield University, where she conducted research into Islamic terrorism. During this time, Shima was also Director of the Security Technology Executive short course at the Cranfield Forensic Institute and Senior Research Fellow and Adviser to the Advanced Research and Assessment Group (ARAG), based at the Joint Services Command and Staff College (JSCSC), Shrivenham, where she developed the concept of asymmetric financial warfare. More recently, she was Special Advisor to the MoD, based in Whitehall, responsible for the development of Fin COIN strategies in Afghanistan.

Shima is currently the Director of the Threat Finance Programme at the Institute for Statecraft, London. She is a former Senior Research Fellow at RAND, and is an adjunct professor and visiting lecturer at several academic institutions where she lectures on a variety of subjects including terrorism, financial crime, international criminal law, security risk management and maritime piracy. Shima holds a PhD in International Criminal Law, MPhil in Defence and Security Studies and a BSc (Hons) in Business Studies.

Acknowledgements

I would like to express my gratitude to all my colleagues who have supported my work in recent years. In particular I would like to thank my mentors Professor Barry Rider and Chris Donnelly, whose wisdom and insight never cease to amaze me. I feel extremely fortunate to have been mentored by such extraordinary intellects and cannot begin to express how grateful I am for their invaluable guidance and support.

Given the nature of my work undertaken in recent years, in particular with the Advanced Research and Assessments Group / Research and Assessments Branch, MoD, it is not possible for me to express appreciation for the support I have received other than to the institutions as a whole. Of equal significance is the assistance I have received from colleagues in other UK government and law enforcement agencies with whom I have collaborated and have been seconded. I would also like to thank my colleagues from around the world including those in the FBI, US Treasury, US Department of State, UN, OSCE and NATO.

I would also like to thank the numerous private sector organisations in various sectors including finance, law, defence and security, oil and gas, airline and telecommunications, who have been supportive of my work. I am especially grateful to the numerous individuals who are too many to name individually, who shared their experiences, information and challenges to an extent that gave me not only the broad spectrum of understanding necessary to tackle the complexity of the subject, but inspired me to develop a multidisciplinary approach in countering existing security challenges.

Reviews of *Threat Finance*

Dr Shima Keene has shed fresh light on and deepened our understanding of a subject critical to international security. Despite broad consensus that countering the finance of organised crime and terrorism represents both a vital requirement and a tremendous opportunity, few understand the nature of the problem or how to act against it. Keene's comprehensive, accessible, and compelling book should be the new standard text on the subject for policymakers, intelligence officials, law enforcement officers, and anyone responsible for combating terrorist organisations and transnational organised crime networks. Dr Keene's recommendations for improving financial intelligence, developing comprehensive counter-finance methods, adapting law enforcement organisations, and crafting options to target criminal and terrorist financial streams should be adopted with urgency. Dr Keene argues that improving understanding of the basic concepts of terrorist and criminal finance is essential; reading her book is an excellent starting point in that connection.

Brigadier General H.R. McMaster, U.S. Army, former commander of Task Force Shafafiyat (Transparency) in Afghanistan

This book provides a lucid education on the often inconvenient realities of serious economic crime and identifies with clinical precision the reasons why it sometimes seems beyond the practical capabilities of the law to deal with it. What makes it so important, however, is Dr Keene's ability to mobilise the difficult thoughts that need to be thought if modern democracy is to survive the corruptive threats of crime and terror and their ability at the more sophisticated levels to exploit the modern accommodations of international finance and cyberspace with apparent impunity. The challenge, so vividly described here, can appear overwhelming; but the lasting influence left by this seminal work is the conviction that it will be more adequately met if some of the current cosy thinking on this subject in relevant fields of influence can be turned on its head.

Kenneth Murray MA CA, Head of Forensic Accountancy, Scottish Crime and Drug Enforcement Agency

Interdicting tainted wealth is perceived by many as if not a cure for the ills of our time as at least a logical and meaningful strategy against enterprise criminals. Indeed, so persuasive is the logic, that similar laws and techniques have been adopted against terrorists. Dr Shima Keene, who comes at all this, from the refreshing perspective of someone who has worked in the defence establishment and has real knowledge of the way such criminal and terrorists operate, subjects the application and operation of the legal, regulatory and intelligence regimes to searching and critical analysis. She pulls no punches and identifies where a lot more thought and effort is needed to achieve anything like what was hoped for. This is a unique and challenging analysis that no one who looks after other people's wealth can afford not to consider – very carefully!

Barry Rider, Professorial Fellow, Centre for Development Studies, University of Cambridge UK

It is generally recognised that, without a sound economic basis, no programme of human action will be viable in the long term. It is surprising, therefore, that the economic aspects of threats to our national security posed by terrorism and organised crime have received relatively little attention from those charged with ensuring our security and countering the threats. In her thorough, penetrating and highly original study, Dr Keene makes it clear why this has been the case, she explains the nature of the problem with admirable clarity, and she presents eminently sensible, realistic recommendations as to how the problem should be tackled.

Were these the only things to be learned from Dr Keene's ground-breaking work, it would still be the most important research- based publication on national security issues to appear in recent years. However, much more can be drawn from this volume. Firstly, Dr Keene identifies how criminals and terrorists have been able to react to and exploit the rapid changes in the international security environment, whereas our governmental institutions have failed to keep pace with those changes and adapt accordingly. Our laws, our intelligence processes, our enforcement agencies, not only need radical reform –

they need to become capable of continuous change and adaptation if they are to remain effective and deal with the rapidly-evolving problems so starkly described by Dr Keene.

Secondly, an all-of-government approach will be needed to cope with the problem. The traditional agencies are no longer sufficient. Dr Keene's work shows that Finance Ministries and private sector financial institutions are now every bit as important as Defence Ministries, Police Forces and Intelligence Agencies as front-line players in the fight for our national security. But, alas, the significance of this has not yet been realised by governments and a strategic approach is sorely lacking.

Thirdly, Dr Keene identifies the need for us to develop a new generation of people who can see things differently and who can understand and cope with the real complexity which characterises today's security environment. Changing peoples' mindset will be the most important – and the most difficult – challenge we face in coping with the changing nature of conflict as epitomised by terrorism and organised crime. The best tools and mechanisms are useless if we do not have sufficient people with the skills to employ them effectively.

Consequently, Dr Keene's book is not just important for law-enforcement and intelligence officers. It should be required reading for anyone interested in national and international security. Through her examination of 'Threat Finance', she exposes many of the failings in our whole national security process.

Chris Donnelly, Director, The Institute for Statecraft, former Senior Fellow of the Defence Academy of the United Kingdom and former Special Adviser to the Secretary General of NATO

This is a remarkable work on a complex and little understood subject which has long deserved the level of forensic examination Shima provides. It acts as an exceptionally useful reference for those engaged in the fight against organised crime and terrorism in both the public and private sectors, and especially in the security and compliance departments of international banks.

Karl Barclay, Chairman Stirling Assynt International Group Limited and former Head of Global Security and Fraud Risk for the HSBC Group

Introduction

> *... It is in the areas that we have been discussing that the real war on serious enterprise crime and terrorism will likely to be fought over the next few years. Sadly, I am not convinced that we have even started to frame the right questions yet, let alone devise answers. Success, however it is judged, will be achieved not merely by passing more or even better laws, or by pouring more resources in to the battle –but by a thoughtful and measured balancing of our response to the real threats.*[1]
>
> *Professor Barry Rider*

Overview

National governments and decision-makers in the twenty-first century face a new security environment which has emerged as a result of globalisation accompanied by the ever increasing speed of technological advancements. One consequence is that the historic national security paradigms that once formed the basis of geographically based security strategies have become irrelevant.[2] Furthermore, the existing security environment poses a new set of security dynamics that is increasingly spawning a variety of asymmetric threats.[3] In addition, the scale of global changes poses a serious challenge not only to stable, traditionally well-run democracies such as the United Kingdom (UK), but presents far greater challenges to fragile states.[4] This in turn has a direct impact on the UK and other nations.

---

1 Barry A.K. Rider, 'Law: The War on Terror and Crime and the Offshore Centres: The 'New' Perspective?' in Donato Masciandaro (ed.), *Global Financial Crime: Terrorism, Money Laundering and Offshore Centres* (Ashgate Publishing, 2004) 92.

2 K.G.L. Webb, *Managing Asymmetric Threats to National Security Terrorist Information Operations* (Australian Research Council Project Report, August 2007).

3 M. Evans, 'From Kadesh to Kandahar: military theory and the future of war' (2003) 16(3) *Naval War College Review* 132.

4 W.M. Hall, *Stray Voltage: War in the Information Age* (Naval Institute Press 2003).

Terrorism remains a key concern in relation to national security, both in terms of the threat of a physical terrorist attack, as well as its economic ramifications. Countering this threat takes place in many forms, one of which is through the law. The UK is fortunate relative to many other jurisdictions in that its terrorism laws are well established owing to its history with Irish terrorism.

In terms of tackling terrorist finance, the targeting of financial, and perhaps more importantly, the economic base of an organisation, will impact not only the operational capability of that organisation, but ultimately lead to its destruction. The importance of tackling the finances of adversary organisations has long been recognised. However, despite the existence of relevant legislation and regulation, the current environment continues to favour the terrorist. Some economists have calculated that less than 1 per cent of terrorist finances have been captured to date.[5] One contributory factor has undoubtedly been the emergence of the single financial global market place which began with financial market deregulation in the 1990s. As a result, criminal money[6] is able to move around the globe with relative ease, irrespective of geographical boundaries.

This raises the question as to the extent of the efficacy of geographically confined legal and regulatory intervention against terrorist funds and associated criminal property. A further concern is the acknowledgement by practitioners in the law, that cases involving finance and/or information technology generally do not have successful outcomes.[7] In order to appreciate the successes and failures, as well as the limitations of current legal counter measures, an appropriate level of understanding of the nature of the threat is vital. Furthermore, it is equally important to obtain that understanding in the context of the overall threat environment where both those who are the perpetrators of the threat, as well as those who attempt to mitigate it, are forced to coexist.

Terrorism and the Asymmetric Threat Environment

From time immemorial, terrorism has served as one of the most common expressions of man's inhumanity to man. It is a tool used intentionally by individuals, groups and state actors to create a climate of extreme fear in order

5 Loretta Napoleoni, *Modern Jihad: Tracing the Dollars behind the Terror Networks* (Pluto Press 2004) 170.

6 To include terrorist finance.

7 Kenneth Murray, 'The uses of irresistible inference: protecting the system from criminal penetration through more effective prosecution of money laundering offences' (2011) 14 *Journal of Money Laundering Control* 7.

to obtain realistic or imaginary political, social, economic and strategic goals. However, despite its long history, it was the simultaneous attacks on the World Trade Centre and the Pentagon on 11 September 2001 (9/11) by al-Qaeda that served as a major turning point in the history of terrorism. 9/11 is not only regarded as the most devastating terrorist attack in modern history, but brought terrorism to the top of the political agenda. Furthermore, the attacks symbolised a new age of terrorism, marked by different motivations, actors and sponsors. In addition, greater ambitions and lethality were highlighted, no longer confined by geographical boundaries, representing an upward shift to a new level of global threat, previously unseen and unknown.

The reaction to this new threat was the so-called 'Global War on Terror' (GWOT), coined by the United States (US) government under the Bush administration. It is a term disliked by many, owing to what is regarded as being a representation of an over-aggressive stance taken by the US. Critics argue that as the threat is based on ideology, a physical response based on firepower alone is counter-productive. Instead, many suggest that a more diplomatic approach may prove more successful.[8] It is undoubtedly true that military action taken since 9/11 in the name of GWOT, despite good intensions, have exacerbated the threat by helping to fuel the *Jihadist* cause. This view is shared by many experts including Eliza Manningham-Buller, the former Director General of the Security Service in the UK, during the Chilcot Enquiry in July 2010.[9]

However, the US views the 9/11 attacks not merely as an act of terror on US soil, but as an act of war against the US. As such, the US justifies its use of the term 'war' as well as the military action that followed since 2001 including the 'assassination' of Osama bin Laden on 2 May 2011 in his compound in Abbottabad, Pakistan.[10] Therefore, an understanding of counter-terrorism strategies within a military context is appropriate. Recent developments in modern warfare recognise the fundamental shift that has occurred on the battlefield. Military strategists acknowledge that recent developments in

8 Michelle Gallant, 'Promise and perils: the making of global money laundering, terrorist finance norms' (2010) 13(1) *Journal of Money Laundering Control* 175.

9 Deborah Orr, 'Manningham-Buller was right about the Iraq war', *Guardian* (London, 22 July 2010).

10 The legality of bin Landen's 'assassination' has been heavily debated. The US Attorney General, Eric Holder, argues that the act was not an assassination but an act of national defence. See BBC "Bin Laden death not assassination". [Online]. Available at: http://www.bbc.co.uk/news/mobile/world-us-canada-13370919 [accessed: 15 June 2011].

technology, economics, culture and communications are enabling a rapid pace of globalisation and have led to the development of an asymmetric battlefield.

In response, a number of irregular warfare strategies have been developed, such as Effects-Based Operations (EBO) and Fourth-Generation Warfare (4GW).[11] 4GW derives its name from the assertion that modern war has unfolded in a series of phases, each of which was rooted in a particular combination of technologies, organisations, tactics and strategies.[12] The first generation of modern warfare was dominated by massed manpower and culminated in the Napoleonic Wars. The second generation, which was quickly adopted by the world's major powers, was dominated by firepower and ended in World War I. In relatively short order, during World War II, the Germans introduced third-generation warfare, characterised by manoeuvre. Fourth-generation wars have now evolved, taking advantage of the political, social, economic and technical changes since World War II.[13]

The significance of 4GW is that the battlefield has changed beyond recognition compared with the previous generations of warfare. After three generations of marginalisation, the non-state actors that form the global network of terrorist organisations, to include associated criminal organisations, corrupt governments and indifferent or uninformed individuals or corporations, take centre stage. The state now faces an enemy where the asymmetry is such that concepts such as 'civilian' and 'military or even 'legality' become obsolete.[14] This is the reality of countering terrorism in the twenty-first century. The net result is the decline of the state, where there can be no purely military solution to overcome the adversary.[15] 4GW can be described as an evolved form of insurgency,[16] which utilises all available networks including political, economic, legal, social and military, to convince the enemy's decision-makers that their strategic goals are either unachievable or too costly for the perceived

11 Albert A. Nofi, 'Recent Trends in Thinking about Warfare' CRM D0014875.A1/Final, Defense Technical Information Center, September 2006. [Online]. Available at: www.dtic.mil [accessed: 10 December 2009].

12 William S. Lind, Keith Nightengale, John F. Schmitt, Joseph W. Sutton and Gary I. Wilson, 'The changing face of war: into the fourth generation', *Marine Corps Gazette* (Oct 1989) 22.

13 Nofi, 'Recent Trends in Thinking about Warfare' (n.11).

14 Harold A. Gould and Franklin C. Spinney, '4GW is Here!', *Center for South Asian Studies Newsletter* (University of Virginia 2001). [Online]. Available at: www.virginia.edu/soasia/newsletter/Fall01/warfare. html [accessed: 10 October 2009] and http://www.smallwarsjournal.com/documents/ 4gw. htm [accessed: 10 October 2009].

15 Martin van Creveld, *The Rise and Decline of the State* (Cambridge University Press 1999) 4.

16 Thomas X. Hammes, 'Insurgency: modern warfare evolves into a fourth generation' *Strategic Forum* 214, Jan 2005. [Online]. Available at: http://www.ndu.edu/inss/strforum/SF214/SF214.pdf [accessed: 20 October 2010].

benefit.[17] As such, 4GW introduces a financial/economic dimension in terms of its strategic goal as well as its tactical approach in achieving its overall goal of defeating the enemy.[18] A key component of such asymmetric strategies is the potential use of counter finance strategies.

Countering Adversary Finances: The Achilles Heel

9/11 not only brought terrorism to the top of the political agenda for the US and its allies, but highlighted the importance of tackling terrorist finance, which was acknowledged as being the lifeblood of terrorism. The counter-terrorism community recognised that by severing the terrorist funding supply chain, it was possible to mitigate and possibly even prevent further terrorist attacks. However, as the interest in terrorist finance intensified, so too did the realisation of its complexity, and the requirement for specialist expertise, which was not widely available. As a result, the initial enthusiasm was soon to be replaced by a temporary loss of interest in the subject, despite its potentially vital role in the fight against terrorism. It was only recently in 2009, eight years after the 9/11 attacks, that the UK renewed its interest in the subject, which now forms a key part of its counter-terrorism strategy.

However, the full potential of the UK counter-terrorist finance (CTF) strategy is still far from being realised.[19] Despite improvements in the general understanding of terrorist finance since 9/11, the covert nature of the subject continues to be a challenge for the wider CTF community. For example, despite interest from academia in the subject, the lack of access to data for the majority has proved to be problematic. As such, most academic analysis has been based on incomplete and often unreliable data, making the research output only partially useful.

Various misconceptions surrounding the subject of terrorist finance have also been noted. Some have described the task of detecting terrorist finance as attempting to 'look for a needle in a haystack' or even to 'look for a needle in a haystack of needles'.[20] This paradigm of inexpensive terrorism temporarily

17 Thomas X. Hammes, '4GW: our enemies play to their strengths' (2004) *Armed Forces Journal* 40.

18 Thomas X. Hammes, *The Sling and the Stone: On War in the 21st Century* (Zenith Press 2004) 208.

19 Peter A. Sproat, 'Counter-terrorist finance in the UK: A quantitative and qualitative commentary based on open-source materials' 13(4) (2010) *Journal of Money Laundering Control* 315.

20 Deputy Assistant Commissioner Janet Williams, Head of Intelligence and Covert Policing, Specialist Crime Directorate, speaking at the CONTEST conference, Defence Academy of the UK,

placed the subject into the 'too difficult to deal with' category. In addition, as the depth of understanding increased, it became clear that the subject of terrorist finance cannot be looked at in isolation. For example, the relationship between organised crime and terrorism needed to be better understood.

As a result, the subject of terrorist finance has evolved. Misleading terms such as the 'nexus' of organised crime and terrorism have been discarded to be replaced by 'threat finance'.[21] It is absolutely right that the various components of 'threat' finance be tackled in relation to one another, as opposed to as independent subjects in isolation, as terrorist and criminal networks do not organise themselves along the lines of individual silos. To this end, various cross-government agencies have been established to attempt to better understand, detect and interdict threat finance as a whole.

Countering adversary finances take place either within the traditional criminal justice system or through other 'disruption' strategies. Ultimately the two are interrelated and impact one another as the intended target, either from a prosecution point of view or a disruption point of view, is either the same individual, in this case the terrorist, or a part of that terrorist network. Financial intelligence obtained for disruption purposes may be presented in court as secret evidence, the legality of which may be scrutinised as will be discussed later. However, irrespective of which component of the counter terrorism community one belongs to, the actions and limitations are governed by terrorism legislation. As such, it is necessary to provide a general overview of recent legislation relating to terrorist finance.

UK Terrorist Finance Legislative Overview

The current anti-money laundering (AML) and CTF regime is based mainly around five legal sources, namely the Terrorism Act (TA) 2000; the Anti-Terrorism, Crime and Security Act (ATCSA) 2001; the Proceeds of Crime Act (POCA) 2002; the Money Laundering Regulations; as well as various Orders in Council, which implement UN Security Council Resolutions. In terms of legislation relating to terrorist finance, robust legislation was already in place in the UK prior to 9/11 in the form of the TA 2000. The principal offences relating to

Shrivenham, September 2004.

21 Threat Finance is a term coined by the US government and comprises five key elements, namely terrorist finance, organised crime, proliferation finance, narcotics trafficking and human trafficking.

the financing of terrorists, fund raising, use and possession of terrorist money, funding arrangements and money laundering, are contained in Sections 15–18 of the TA 2000. For example, Section 15 states that it is unlawful to invite someone to give money, receive money, to provide or process money or other property with the intention or belief that it will be used for the purposes of terrorism. Similarly Section 16 makes it an offence to use money or other property for the purposes of terrorism or to possess such a thing intending that it should be used, or has reasonable cause to suspect that it may be used, for the purposes of terrorism.[22]

The Act also contains offences of failure to disclose, belief or suspicion of an offence under Section 19 and, for the regulated sector only, failure to disclose knowledge or suspicion of terrorist money under Section 21A.[23] In addition, the TA 2000 provides powers to seize cash at the border on suspicion that it was to be used for terrorist purposes or was part of the resources of a proscribed organisation and a power to order forfeiture of seized cash, on the civil standard of proof of the balance of probabilities, as well as powers to freeze a country's assets, if that country was acting to the detriment of the UK economy.[24]

In 2001, the government further strengthened domestic measures to CTF through the ATCSA 2001, which extended the provisions for the seizure and detention of cash on suspicion that it was to be used for terrorist purposes or was part of the resources of a proscribed organisation to anywhere in the UK,[25] and re-iterated a power to order forfeiture of seized cash on the civil standard of proof of the balance of probabilities. ATCSA 2001 also facilitated the disclosure of information between government bodies[26] and imposed more stringent demands on those in the regulated sector to report suspicions that funds were destined for terrorism.[27] Furthermore, it provided the police with powers both to force financial institutions to monitor accounts and to obtain financial information.[28] It also authorised the restraint of funds at the outset of any investigation rather than having to wait until a criminal charge was laid.[29]

22 The latter should be distinguished from Sections 17–18 which contain offences covering more indirect financial involvement and money laundering.
23 Sproat, 'Counter-terrorist finance in the UK' (n.19) 441.
24 Gallant, 'Promise and perils' (n.8) 175.
25 Section 1.
26 Sections 17–20.
27 Section 3 and Schedule II, Part III.
28 Schedule II amending Section 38 and Schedule VI Terrorism Act 2000.
29 Schedule 2.

In addition, ATCSA Section 4 allowed the Treasury to freeze the assets of foreign individuals and groups, as well as whole countries; where there were reasonable grounds to suspect that they posed a threat to the UK economy, or the lives or property of UK nationals. However, in practice, the freezing of assets is achieved by the use of the Terrorism (UN Measures) Order 2001 (SI 2001/3365), which restricts the making available of funds and financial services to terrorists, and provides HM Treasury with powers to freeze accounts of suspected terrorists pursuant to United Nations Security Council Resolution (UNSCR) 1373 of 2001. In certain circumstances, the Treasury issues directions under ATCSA Article 4 to freeze the assets of persons, who are subsequently also listed by the UN al-Qaeda and Taliban Sanctions Committee. Here, it is also worth noting that the European Union (EU) adopted Council Regulation (EC) No 2580/2001, which gives effect to UNSCR 1373 (2001) in Community Law. Targets listed by the EU are deemed to hold a 'community-wide' threat as The European Communities Treaty does not provide the EU with the legal competency to enforce measures against the 'domestic' terrorists of member states.[30]

ATCSA 2001 essentially consolidated and strengthened existing criminal confiscation powers, introduced a new power of civil recovery, extended investigation powers and tightened up existing money laundering legislation. Terrorists may be involved in organised crime generating unlawfully earned wealth or may have committed an offence which brings them within the scope of the powers contained in the Act. Either way, law enforcement and the Assets Recovery Agency[31] was provided with an extended range of powers at their disposal to investigate the proceeds of crime and to seek their confiscation in criminal proceedings or their recovery in civil proceedings.

In terms of the legislation relating to AML, the main money laundering offences of concealing, arranging and possessing property are contained in Sections 327, 328, 329 of POCA 2002 respectively. Additionally, Sections 330, 331 and 332 impose a duty to report suspicion of such offences upon anyone in the regulated sector and nominated officers outside the regulated sector. Section 333 makes it illegal for anyone to 'tip off' those who are the subject of a money laundering investigation and Section 342 outlaws prejudicing an investigation. The Money Laundering Regulations impose additional

30 Ibid.

31 The Asset Recovery Agency was disbanded in 2008 and ceased to exist as an independent agency. On 1 March 2008, the transfer of the Director and staff of the Assets Recovery Agency, its property, rights and liabilities to SOCA and the National Policing Improvement Agency began in anticipation of the Agency's abolition on 1 April 2008.

administrative requirements on organisations undertaking specified regulated activities, listed in Reg 2(2), including Know Your Customer (KYC) rules, which will be examined in more detail later.

Other requirements include maintaining records for five years, establishing reporting procedures and training staff. Failure to comply is a criminal offence, which can be prosecuted by the Financial Services Authority (FSA) in addition to the Crown Prosecution Service (CPS).[32] The 2003 version of the legislation further strengthens the ability of the authorities to combat terrorist finance by adding various types of business dealing in financial transactions, such as *Hawala*.[33]

However, despite the existence of established legislation with respect to terrorist finance and money laundering, a gap between the law and the law in practice exists. It should also be noted that most charges relating to terrorism manifest themselves in the form of conspiracy charges as opposed to using relevant sections of the legislation relating to terrorist finance owing to the inadequacies in obtaining the necessary forensic finance trail, which will be discussed in later chapters. Furthermore, the various obstacles that impact the efficacy of the law is numerous and far ranging. Legislative challenges include the impact of non-terrorist-related legislation, such as human rights law, where convictions achieved to confiscate 'terrorist' assets, for example, may be overruled, as will be examined further in Chapter 7.

The tendency for the court to shy away from cases of a financial nature is also problematic. This problem is not limited to cases involving terrorist finance but also to financial crime in general, such as money laundering. The current use of financial experts such as forensic accountants is inadequate in that their main use is limited to providing an expert opinion to the court. Instead, their role should be to go further to provide and interpret the evidence to prove the heart of the matter in a way that a jury is able to draw an inference.[34] Without professional interpretation of existing evidence, there is a concern that the knowledge within the judiciary is inadequate to be able to properly digest the material in such a way that justice can be served.

The need to further develop an understanding of criminal finance including terrorist finance is not confined to the judiciary. The failure by the

32 Schedule 2.

33 *Hawala* is an informal value transfer system. See Chapter 4.

34 Kenneth Murray, 'Dismantling organised crime groups through enforcement of the POCA money laundering offences' (2010) 13 *Journal of Money Laundering Control* 7.

British government to invest in sufficiently skilled law enforcement personnel or regulators to police its large financial sector has also been noted.[35] In addition, the problem is not limited to law enforcement, but also applies to the wider CTF community. In addition, a number of practical challenges need to be addressed. Specific challenges affecting the private sector include issues surrounding account opening procedures and financial profiling, exacerbated by 'cultural' issues that affect both the private and public sectors. Cultural issues range from a variety of practical issues such as the lack of understanding of non-Western cultures which undermine existing counter finance strategies, as well as issues of an organisational nature including the cultural[36] distrust amongst organisations leading to a silo mentality. Additionally, given that the threat is global, the international dimension comes into play where national challenges are aggravated within the global context.

The Need for a New Approach

The need for high quality interdisciplinary research in the field of terrorist finance and associated economic crime has been articulated by numerous sectors of the counter terrorism community. The appetite currently exists within both academic and practitioner audiences to develop an in-depth understanding of the subject. Many recognise that the historic approach, that of single-focus expertise, is no longer adequate in meeting the existing challenges of the new security environment in the twenty-first century. In response, the emergence of numerous cross-departmental agencies further illustrates the willingness to attempt to break down silos and embrace a multi-disciplinary approach.

This appetite has emerged partly in recognition by many of the general lack of success to date in tackling terrorist finance and associated criminal assets.[37] The importance of the subject of tackling adversary finance has already been stated. However, despite the resource and effort devoted to tackle the problem, results have been disappointing. Measuring success in this field is also challenging. However, one broad measure which can be used is to compare terrorist funds and assets seized against a guesstimate of global terrorist funds in circulation.

35 Nick Kochan, *The Washing Machine: Money, Crime and Terror in the Offshore System* (Duckworth 2006).

36 The term 'culture' has been used in an organisational context, referring to the set of shared attitudes, values, goals, and practices that characterizes an institution, organisation or group as opposed to geographically based nationalistic culture.

37 Sproat, 'Counter-terrorist finance in the UK' (n.19) 315.

Between September 2001 and June 2002, approximately $115 million of alleged terrorist assets were intercepted worldwide. By December 2003, the amount interdicted reached $138 million and by December 2004 the total was $147 million.[38] By October 2010, around £140,000 was frozen in the UK.[39] In comparison, it is estimated that the global terrorist network has an annual turnover of approximately $1.5 trillion,[40] which equates to twice the Gross Domestic Product (GDP) in the UK, which in turn accounts for 5 per cent of world GDP.[41] If these calculations are correct, this equates to the fact that only an estimated 1 per cent of terrorist finance has been captured. Furthermore, the situation could be far worse as the figures relate only to those that are known.

The reasons for this failure to date are numerous. Observations of the existing statement of the problem, developed predominantly over the last 10 years through the author's own work with numerous UK government departments, law enforcement agencies, the judiciary, the private sector and academia involved in the field of CTF, have highlighted insufficient understanding of the subject. This is a view that has been strongly and universally supported by public and private sector organisations alike.

A further concern is that some fail to see the relevance of tackling adversary finances. The reason historically was due to the myth of inexpensive terrorism, which continues in some circles to this day. However, more recently, with specific reference to finances relating to al-Qaeda, the continuing war in Afghanistan with the Taliban has redirected key finances from al-Qaeda to the Taliban.[42] Some practitioners believe that as finance, and more specifically the lack of it, is already an issue for al-Qaeda, they do not see the value in devoting resources to combat the problem. However, this sadly illustrates the lack of understanding of finance as a weapon in the fight against terrorism.

Terrorist finance is not simply about following the money and attempting to disrupt and confiscate financial and other economic assets. Instead, it is a multifaceted weapon that can be used in a number of ways. For example, it is a

38 Robert Hall, 'On the Money Trail' (*The World Today*, May 2005). [Online]. Available at: www.theworldtoday.org [accessed: 14 October 2009].

39 Mr Mark Hoban, Financial Secretary to the Treasury, speaking in Parliament on the subject of the Terrorist Asset-Freezing etc. Bill [Lords] 15 Nov 2010. [Online]. Available at: http://www.publications.parliament.uk/pa/cm201011/cmhansrd/cm101115/debtext/101115-0002.htm [accessed: July 2011].

40 Napoleoni, *Modern Jihad* (n.5) xv.

41 George Magnus, 'Introduction' in Napoleoni, *Modern Jihad* (n.5).

42 NATO–Ukraine Joint Working Group on Economic Security: Workshop Kyiv, Ukraine, 14–15 May 2009 'The Economic and Financial Dimension of the Fight against Terrorism.'

weapon of influence which may be deployed as part of psychological operations as well as a forensic tool, which provided that the financial evidence is collected and presented appropriately, may be effective in securing convictions in a court of law.

However, this is not currently the case with reference to both terrorist finance and financial crime in general. The lack of familiarity with the basic concepts of how funds are raised and transferred is proving to be problematic in court when dealing with such cases.[43] Unless the level of understanding of the subject can be improved throughout the judicial system,[44] there is concern as to whether justice can be achieved in the courtroom. This also raises questions as to whether existing investigation and detection methods, coupled with the way in which the evidence is presented in court, are adequate. Furthermore, the weakness of the judicial system in addressing cases of a complex financial nature also needs to be addressed.[45]

In order to understand the inability to effectively counter adversary finances to date, a comprehensive understanding not only of the adversary, but the operational environment that makes the battlefield hostile to the counter-terrorism community, together with an honest inward self-reflection in terms of the counter finance response, is necessary. As long as this situation is allowed to continue, the existing asymmetric environment will favour the criminal and terrorist. The weaknesses of current methods and systems need to be addressed, which can only be achieved through the comprehensive understanding of a variety of interrelated subjects.

Therefore, a vacuum currently exists in terms of knowledge and understanding of terrorist finance and related financial crime. As such, there is a requirement for in-depth, original research containing innovative thought processes which can only be achieved through a multidisciplinary approach in order to be relevant to the wider network of stakeholders. These stakeholders consist of not only those directly involved in the fight against terrorism and organised crime, namely the intelligence agencies, law enforcement and the judiciary, but also all those affected by it. The wider network includes financial institutions, insurance companies, global corporations, law firms, various government departments – the list goes on. As a result, informed literature must exist that adequately educates at both an individual and an organisational level,

43 *R v Aurora* [2010] T2010/0359 (Croydon Crown Court) Observation as Expert Witness.

44 To include judges, the prosecuting and defending barristers, as well as the jury.

45 Murray, 'The uses of irresistible inference' (n.7) 7.

without compromising sensitive information. It must also be in a language that is not overly technical, as the literature must serve as a bridge between the various disciplines represented by the various stakeholders.

Conclusions

Al-Qaeda, with its commitment to implement mass atrocities, continues to threaten the Western world. Moreover, it is likely that this threat will continue for the foreseeable future. Terrorism is a complex, multi-causal problem where many of its components are interrelated. To counter it requires a multidisciplinary approach, which equally applies to terrorist finance. The countering of the finances of adversary organisations has the potential to be extremely effective, but only if the subject is understood fully and the appropriate strategy and tactics are adopted by all of the stakeholders in the community. The existing situation is that despite the effort invested in the countering of adversary finances, success to date has been limited. Success in incremental small measures is no longer adequate. Advanced research with a high level of sophistication is needed to understand the reasons for this lack of achievement to date and present innovative recommendations as to how the situation can be reversed. This publication aims to serve as a vital first step in achieving that aim.

1

Understanding the Threat Environment

> *... the financing of terrorism is a sub/terranean universe governed by secrecy, subterfuge, and criminal endeavours; but also a good measure of sophistication and an understanding of the global financial system. It is best described as an octopus with tentacles spreading across vast territories as well as across a wide range of religious, social, economic and political realities.*[1]
>
> *Dr Nimrod Raphaeli*

Overview

The threat environment in relation to terrorism and related organised crime may be broadly described as falling into one of two broad categories. The first is in relation to the threat posed by the adversary. As such, the first part will provide an analysis of the adversary in terms of its motivation, modus operandi and capability, which in turn has a direct impact on the understanding of its financial requirements. Another important element that requires closer examination is the environment in which these adversaries, as well as those who attempt to counter them, operate within. In the second part, an assessment of the broader 'threat environment' will be provided, with special focus on key issues such as the impact of globalisation, cultural asymmetries and technological advancements.

---

1 N. Raphaeli, 'Financing of terrorism: sources, methods, and channels' (2003) 15(4) *Terrorism and Political Violence* 59.

Adversary Analysis

The adversaries examined in this section will include terrorist organisations with special focus on al-Qaeda and associated organisations as elaborated in Chapter 1.

ISLAMIC TERRORISM

Islamic terrorism, also referred to as *jihadist* terrorism, falls under a dimension of terrorism referred to as 'new' terrorism, a term broadly accepted by the academic community to include terrorism relating to Islamic extremism.[2] 'New' terrorism differs from 'modern' terrorism in that the latter is used to describe an era between 1967 and 1990 referring to politically motivated terrorism.[3] The recognition of the start of this period is marked by the upsurge of political terrorism by the Palestine Liberation Organisation (PLO) founded in 1964,[4] and led by Yasser Arafat.

The term 'modern' terrorism is also used to describe other terrorist organisations, during the same period, such as the Irish Republican Army (IRA), the Basque Fatherland and Liberty (ETA) in Spain, the Abu Nidal Organisation (ANO), also known as Fatah Revolutionary Council, Arab Revolutionary Brigades, Black September and the Revolutionary Organisation of Socialist Muslims, as well as ideological based terrorist groups such as the Red Brigades in Italy.

'New' terrorism, on the other hand, is marked by different motives, actors, sponsors, greater lethality and generally flatter hierarchical structures.[5] According to Amir Taheri, the exportation of the fundamentalist Islamic revolution from Iran in 1979 had started the 'new kind of terrorism'.[6] Whilst past terrorist movements were politically driven, these 'new' Islamic terrorists would be insulted if their actions were described as 'political' violence, as their

2 Martha Crenshaw, 'The psychology of terrorism: an agenda for the 21st century' (2000) 21(2) *Political Psychology* 405.
3 Thomas Copeland, 'Is the "new terrorism" really new?: an analysis of the new paradigm for terrorism' (2001) 21(2) *Journal of Conflict Studies*.
4 Intelligence Resource Programme FAS. [Online]. Available at: http://www.fas.org/irp/world/para/plo.htm [accessed: 2 October 2009].
5 Michael Jenkins, 'Foreword' in Ian Lesser, *Countering the New Terrorism* (RAND Corporation, 1999) 9.
6 Amir Taheri, *Holy Terror: Inside the World of Islamic Terrorism* (Adler & Adler 1987) 9.

ultimate aim is global domination in that the movement aims to convert all mankind, through choice or force, to the teachings of Muhammad.[7]

In addition, the National Commission on Terrorism also found that the main motivation of 'new' terrorism is fanaticism, as opposed to political interests, and that terrorists are more unrestrained than ever before in their methods.[8] Earlier concerns about alienating people from supporting the cause are no longer important to many of today's terrorist organisations.[9] Rather than focusing on conventional goals of political movements, today's religiously motivated terrorists seek destruction and chaos as ends in themselves.[10]

Although the al-Qaeda network of international terrorists is a prime example of 'new' terrorism, Islamic extremism is not the only form of apocalyptic and catastrophic terrorism. Aum Shinrikyo, the Japanese religious cult responsible for the first major chemical attack on a Tokyo subway in 1995, as well as the bombing of the Alfred P. Murrah Federal Building in Oklahoma by right-wing American militants, provides other examples of 'new' terrorism.[11] However, the central focus of this publication is on 'Islamic' terrorism, otherwise referred to as '*jihadist*' terrorism. As such, it is important to understand the concept of *jihad* which is its key driver.

THE CONCEPT OF JIHAD

The Islamic term '*jihad*' is frequently used in the media and is arguably the most recognised Islamic concept by the West. The term *jihad* is widely understood to mean 'holy war'. However, the word '*jihad*' in reality means 'struggle' or 'striving' in the way of Allah or to work for a noble cause with determination. It should be noted that the word 'war' in Arabic is *harb* and 'holy' is *muqadass*. Therefore the true meaning of the term *jihad*, also referred to as the 'sixth' pillar of Islam, is frequently not well understood.[12]

---

7 Michael Kometer, *The New Terrorism: The Nature of the War on Terrorism* (US Air University Press 2004) 10.

8 National Commission on Terrorism, *Countering the Changing Threat of International Terrorism: Report on the National Commission on Terrorism* (Washington, GPO, 2000).

9 Crenshaw, 'The psychology of terrorism' (n.2) 405.

10 Matthew J. Morgan, 'Origins of the new terrorism' (2004) *Parameters US Army War College Quarterly* 30.

11 Ibid.

12 Michael G. Knapp, 'The concept and practice of jihad in Islam' (Spring 2003) *Parameters US Army War College Quarterly*.

Throughout history, even Muslims themselves have disputed the meaning of *jihad*.[13] In the Qur'an, it is normally found in the sense of fighting in the path of Allah and was used to describe the warfare against the enemies of the early Muslim community or *ummah*. In the *hadith*, the term *jihad* is used to mean armed action, and most Islamic theologians and jurists in the classical period[14] of Muslim history understood this obligation to be in a military sense.[15]

In classical Islam, the world is divided into two parts: *dar al-harb* meaning the house or abode of war, and *dar al-Islam* meaning the house of Islam. Muslims have an obligation to convert *dar al-harb* into *dar al-Islam*. In fact, *dar al-harb* and *dar al-Islam* were considered to be in a permanent state of war unless a truce or treaty had been agreed.[16] Over time, the jurists have articulated that *jihad* can be qualified in four ways: *jihad* of the heart, tongue, hands and sword. *Jihad al-sayf*, the *jihad* of the sword, is always understood to mean fighting although the word for fighting is *qital*. In addition, there is a *hadith* that reveals a distinction between the greater and lesser *jihad*. The greater *jihad* is deemed to be *jihad al nafs*, the struggle against oneself, relating to the daily and never ending struggle to overcome one's baser instincts. The lesser *jihad* is considered to be the *jihad* against the enemies of Islam.[17]

The relevance to counter terrorist-finance (CTF) is to understand that *jihad* does not necessarily refer to a physical act of war. *Jihad* can be achieved in numerous ways whether it is through communication, achieved through the use of propaganda ultimately leading to the recruitment of those to carry out terrorist acts, as well as to identify sponsors for the attacks. Assisting in the 'cause' through raising finances for terrorist purposes and assisting in the transfer of those funds is also considered to be a form of *jihad*. A full understanding of *jihad* will encourage lateral thinking in relation to CTF and counter-terrorism in general.

AL-QAEDA: A HISTORIC OVERVIEW

> *We – with God's help – call on every Muslim who believes in God and wishes to be rewarded to comply with God's order to kill the Americans and plunder their money wherever and whenever they find it. We also*

13 Ibid.

14 The first three centuries.

15 Bernard Lewis, *The Political Language of Islam* (University of Chicago Press 1988) 72.

16 H. Kruse, 'The Islamic doctrine of international treaties' (1954) *Islamic Quarterly* 152.

17 Marc Sageman, *Leaderless Jihad: Terror Networks in the Twenty-First Century* (University of Pennsylvania Press, 2008).

> *call on the Muslim ulema,*[18] *leaders, youths, and soldiers to launch the raid on Satan's US troops and the devil's supporters allying with them and to displace those who are behind them so that they may learn a lesson.*
>
> *Declaration of War by Osama bin Laden, together with leaders of the World Islamic Front for the Jihad against the Jews and the Crusaders,Afghanistan, 23 February 1998.*

Al-Qaeda was established by the late Osama bin Laden in the late 1980s to bring together *Jihadists* who fought against the Soviet Union in Afghanistan. Despite the death of bin Laden in May 2011,[19] the ambitions of al-Qaeda remains unchanged under the new leadership of Ayman al-Zawahiri.[20] Its aim continues to be to establish a pan-Islamic Caliphate throughout the world by working with allied Islamic extremist groups to overthrow regimes it deems to be 'non-Islamic', and to expel Westerners and non-Muslims from Muslim countries. Al-Qaeda issued a *fatwa* under the banner of 'the World Islamic Front for Jihad against the Jews and Crusaders' in February 1998 proclaiming that it was in the duty of all Muslims to kill US citizens, civilian or military, and their allies everywhere.[21]

Al-Qaeda is the first truly global terrorist group of the twenty-first century and it confronts the world with a new kind of terrorist threat. Since the contemporary wave of terrorism began in the Middle East in 1967, no groups resembling al-Qaeda have previously emerged. The organisation has moved terrorism beyond the status of a method or technique of protest and resistance and turned it into a global instrument with which to compete and challenge Western influence in the Muslim world. It is a worldwide movement capable of mobilising a new and hitherto unimagined global conflict.[22]

Since 9/11, al-Qaeda has become a radical Islamic phenomenon held together through its global network of communities, whether it be a virtual community that is Internet-based or a physical network. In some instances a

18 Meaning community.

19 Osama bin Laden was 'assassinated' by US Navy Seal Team 6 in his compound in Pakistan on 2 May 2011. See Nima Shirazi, 'Disregarding Law, Redefining Justice: The Legality of Killing Osama' 28 May 2011. [Online]. Available at: http://www.foreignpolicyjournal.com/2011/05/28/disregarding-law-redefining-justice/ [accessed: 2 June 2011].

20 Al-Qaeda announced Dr Ayman al-Zawahiri as its new leader on the 16 June 2011. See Frank Gardner, 'Ayman al-Zawahiri appointed as al-Qaeda leader' (*BBC*, 16 June 2011). [Online]. Available at: http://www.bbc.co.uk/news/world-middle-east-13788594 [accessed: 27 June 2011].

21 US Dept. of State, Patterns of Global Terrorism 2001 (Washington, May 2002).

22 Rohan Gunaratna, *Inside Al Qaeda: Global Network of Terror* (Hurst & Co. 2003) 1.

local command and control structure may exist, but in many cases this is not the case. The networks are united by a simplistic hatred of the West, based on the perception of victimisation of the Muslim community and the thirst for revenge through non-negotiable, religiously legitimised violence. *Jihad* is portrayed to many vulnerable young Muslims as a romantic struggle against the evil powerful West.

The leader and the first key financier of al-Qaeda was Osama bin Laden. Osama bin Muhammad bin Laden was born in Riyadh, Saudi Arabia on 30 July 1957[23] and was the seventeenth of 52 children of the Saudi construction magnate Muhammad bin Awdah bin Laden. He attended the Abdul Aziz University in Saudi Arabia where he became inspired by tape recordings of sermons by Abdullah Azzam, a Palestinian and a disciple of Qytb.

It is interesting to note that Bin Laden's influence which led to his leadership and iconic status in international terrorism was as a result of money. He was conspicuous among the Afghan volunteers not because he showed evidence of religious learning but because he had access to some of his family's fortune. Although he took part in at least one actual battle, he became known chiefly as a person who generously helped fund the anti-Soviet *jihad*,[24] highlighting yet again, the significance of money.

Bin Laden understood better than most of the volunteers, the extent to which the continuation and eventual success of the *jihad* in Afghanistan depended on an increasingly complex, global organisation. This organisation included a financial support network that came to be known as the 'Golden Chain', put together mainly by financiers in Saudi Arabia and the Persian Gulf States. Donations flowed through charities or other non-governmental organisations (NGOs).[25] April 1988 brought victory for the Afghan *jihad* when Moscow declared that it would pull its military forces out of Afghanistan within the following nine months. As the Soviets began their withdrawal, the *jihad* leaders debated what to do next. Bin Laden and Azzam[26] agreed that the organisation successfully created for Afghanistan should not be allowed to dissolve. They established what they called a base for foundation, 'al-Qaeda', as a potential headquarters for future *jihad*.

23 Ibid., 16.
24 9/11 Commission Report, 55. [Online]. Available at: http://www.9-11commission.gov/report/911Report.pdf [accessed: 14 October 2009].
25 Ibid.
26 Dr Abdullah Yusuf Azzam, PhD (1941–1989) also known as Shaikh Azzam was a central figure in the global development of the militant Islamist movement.

Pre-9/11, bin Laden was not only the ideological inspiration behind al-Qaeda, but continued as its key financier. As part of the bin Laden family, bin Laden is believed to have inherited between $25–30 million, although various intelligence sources provide other figures which are much greater.[27] For example, the Swiss believe he inherited between $250–500 million, the Australian government a sum over $250 million, and the British estimate is between $280–300 million. Whatever the figure, bin Laden is believed to have invested most of his wealth from his father's fortune abroad, which he then used to develop a global economic and financial empire consisting mainly of legitimate businesses in numerous sectors. These included engineering, agriculture, manufacturing, finance, forestry and medical equipment and research, which will be detailed in Chapter 3.

It is also important to note that financiers are not only individuals who provide finance personally, but also those who are financial facilitators, in that they have the necessary contacts and networks to enable funds to be raised and transferred as necessary. Bin Laden's personal financial situation was clearly important, especially at al-Qaeda's inception. However, even more significant is his access to the wider financial network which he obtained partly through his family business connections, enabling not only access to new funds, but also the ability to move those funds across the globe.

In terms of al-Qaeda's financial policies, according to the 'Declaration of *Jihad* against the Country's Tyrants, Military Series', recovered by Manchester police from the home of Nazihal Wadih Raghie on 10 May 2000, al-Qaeda has five security principles relating to finance. The first is that funds should be divided between those individuals who invest for financial return; the remaining balance, operational funds, should be saved and spent only on operations, namely terrorist attacks. The second principle is that operational funds should not all be put in one place. Third, that only a few of the organisation's members should know the location of its funds. Fourth, whilst carrying large amounts of money, precautions should be taken and finally, money should be left with non-members and spent only when needed.[28]

These principles are clearly important for those involved in countering the finances of terrorist organisations, and taken together with other financial information, such has been outlined above, may help guide policy formation

---

27 Gunaratna, *Inside Al Qaeda* (n.22) 19.

28 'Declaration of Jihad against the Country's Tyrants, Military Series', recovered by Manchester police from the home of Nazihal Wadih Raghie, 10 May 2000' see Gunaratna (n.22) 63.

and day to day action. The only note of caution is that it is likely that the five security principles relating to finance were written by bin Laden under the advice of al-Qaeda's finance committee. Bearing in mind that post-9/11, the finance committee no longer exists, coupled with al-Qaeda's decentralised franchise structure; it is difficult to assess just how closely these principles are adhered to today.

AL-QAEDA: THE LONG-TERM STRATEGY AND ITS SIGNIFICANCE

The lack of successful large-scale al-Qaeda attacks in the West coupled with setbacks to the position of its regional affiliate in Iraq, as well as the steady drip-feed of terrorism-related arrests in Europe and the US since 2005, has led to speculation that the threat from al-Qaeda is on the decline.[29] However, this should not be taken that its global ambitions have been altered or that the *jihadist* movement is losing emphasis in any way.[30] For example, there is evidence that adversity has been exploited by re-deploying the talent and experience of Iraq veterans in other *jihad* theatres. Compared to the early years of this decade, al-Qaeda is now present and concentrating its efforts in insurgencies in North Africa, East Africa, the Middle East and South Asia. Training camps have been re-established in these areas, which have already produced capable operatives. Sooner or later, this will enhance al-Qaeda's ability to mount attacks in Western countries and expand its operations in the Islamic world.[31]

However, questions remain over al-Qaeda's capability as attacks against the West are disrupted at early stages. Nonetheless, al-Qaeda's nature to think in the long-term must also be taken into consideration. It is only when its overall strategy is understood, that the effectiveness of al-Qaeda's strategy and tactics, can be assessed effectively. Despite al-Qaeda's highly decentralised organisational structure, especially at an operational level, all parts are working within a cohesive framework with the ultimate aim of restoring the Islamic Caliphate (Khilafa) by 2029.[32]

The plan as conceived in 1999 represented an evolution of al-Qaeda's original strategic goal, to evict Western forces from the Holy Lands and liberate

29 Colin Flint, Steven M. Radil, 'Terrorism and counter-terrorism: situating al-Qaeda and the global war on terror within geopolitical trends and structures' (2009) 50 *Eurasian Geography and Economics* 150.

30 Marc Sageman, 'Confronting al-Qaeda: understanding the threat in Afghanistan' (2009) 3(4) *Perspectives on Terrorism* 4.

31 Stirling Assynt, *Al-Qaeda's Strategic Plan: An Overview* Assynt Report, 30 November 2009.

32 Ibid.

Jerusalem. Rhetoric has continued to focus on these points, but the refined plan consisted of four phases, each seven years long, as illustrated in Table 1.1. Al-Qaeda recognised the importance of strategic attacks at a number of levels. First, by bringing the West into persistent conflict, this would provide an engine for *jihad* in terms of recruitment for those fighting for a common cause. Secondly, the conflict would provide excellent operational experience and enable these recruits to become battle-hardened and to keep their skills current.

Phase two of the plan speculates that the constant conflict would eventually exhaust the West, both economically and politically. Once this was achieved, the transnational and committed *jihadists* could then be used as a cadre to overthrow Governments in their home countries. Al-Qaeda uses the term 'creative chaos' to describe the process whereby regional power bases will eventually be connected by undermining or overthrowing unstable regimes around and between them.

Table 1.1 Al-Qaeda's four-stage strategic plan (2001–2029)

Phase 1	Phase 2	Phase 3	Phase 4
The Awakening (al-Sahwa) 2001–2008	The Mobilisation (al-Nafeer) 2008–15	The Liberation (al-Tahreer) 2015–22	The Caliphate (al-Khilafa) 2022–29
Raise awareness of the need for *Jihad* in the Islamic world.	Raise forces of liberation across all Islamic regions. By the end of this period, corrupt regimes in the Islamic world should be under pressure, and the West should be losing the will to support them.	The dissolution of the corrupt regimes.	The unification of the newly liberated states into a powerful, united organisation.

Source: Stirling Assynt

The various elements of the plan were first released by Jordanian journalist Fouad Hussein[33] in 2005. Although some have criticised the plan as being retrospective and unreliable, the plan is generally regarded as being valid.

33 Fouad Hussein is a Jordanian journalist and author of the 2005 Arabic-language book *Al-Zarqawi: The Second Generation of al-Qaeda*. It is based on interviews with senior Islamic militants, including Abu Musab al-Zarqawi, the late leader of al-Qaeda in Iraq, and Saif al-Adel, a high-ranking member of al-Qaeda and Islamic Jihad. Hussein first met Zarqawi and Zarqawi's mentor Abu Muhammad al-Maqdisi in 1996 in a Jordanian jail. At the time Hussein was being held as a political prisoner. Since its release Hussein's book has garnered heavy

In terms of its reliability, as the alleged source was Saif al-Adel, an al-Qaeda leader currently imprisoned in Iran, his word was considered to have been compromised in the eyes of most *jihadists*. Furthermore, as his revelations came after the overall shape of al-Qaeda's campaigns was already clear, they were viewed by some as a retrospective explanation to fit events. However, the fact that the strategic plan originated in 1999, shows that this is not the case. In addition, several clear statements from the senior leadership in early 2009 indicated that they perceived al-Qaeda to be in transition to the second of four seven-year strategic phases, further validating the strategic plan.

One such statement was in January 2009, when bin Laden announced that the *jihad* was moving into a 'new phase', adding that the Mujahideen had fought the US and its allies for seven years and would fight them for 'another seven years and another and another'. The next month, in February, al-Qaeda's then deputy leader Ayman al-Zawahiri announced that 'now is the time for young Muslims who want to join the Jihad to heed the Nafeer'.[34] In a separate message, leading ideologue Shaikh Attiyattolah gave the most explicit public articulation of the strategy to date, stating that al-Qaeda is working to a plan based on seven-year phases. He added that the first phase was complete and the second would begin in 2009.[35]

INTERIM ASSESSMENT

In order to provide a meaningful assessment on al-Qaeda's overall long-term strategy, an evaluation of the implementation of the first phase of its strategy is appropriate. During the 'Awakening' phase indicating the period between 2001[36] through to 2008, the number of global *jihadists* has increased dramatically. Al-Qaeda has largely achieved its aims for this phase, with Iraq the major driver, especially with regards to finances. Many commentators see this as good fortune for the organisation, but the strategic context indicates that al-Qaeda planners understood the course that events would take and devised their approach accordingly.

However, the rapid success of the US and the Northern Alliance in Afghanistan in late 2001 was not foreseen and this represented an almost fatal

press coverage and analysis in Iran. [Online]. Available at: http://www.search.com/reference/Fouad_Hussein [accessed: 10 October 2010].

34 Stirling Assynt, *Al-Qaeda's Strategic Plan* (n. 31).

35 Ibid.

36 When 9/11 occurred.

setback.[37] Nevertheless, some saw this as akin to the Prophet's flight from Mecca, and therefore drew strength from it. Furthermore, the initial concept of 'fixing' the Americans in Afghanistan eventually came to pass once the West's strategic focus shifted to operations in Iraq, allowing *jihadist* elements time to consolidate and regroup. Consequently, the West can be seen to have not only helped al-Qaeda recruit but also missed an opportunity to eliminate it in its heartland.

In terms of alliances, the Taliban remains al-Qaeda's main ally and Afghanistan has seen a pronounced rise in violence.[38] Larger suicide attacks have been mounted by foreign fighters, either from Iraq or trained in newly re-established and well-run camps in the Afghan/Pakistan border region.[39] Foreign fighters have provided expertise and innovation to the Taliban, including the transplantation of effective tactics from the Iraqi theatre.

The very fact that the militant resurgence in Afghanistan was to a large degree boosted by the controlled export of fighters from Iraq, provides positive evidence of the organisation's central strategic direction, despite a great deal of operational autonomy. As described above, a key objective is gaining wider acceptance of methods and getting all *jihadist* groups to adopt a common purpose. The development of franchise groups such as al-Qaeda in Iraq or in the Islamic Maghreb takes this to its ultimate logical level, but success in integrating others is also shown by the increasing adoption of al-Qaeda's rhetoric by other groups. Local issues are increasingly being subordinated to the global campaign.

CAPABILITY ASSESSMENT

In order to assess the credibility of any strategy, the intent must be realistic in terms of the capability to deliver that intent. Whilst al-Qaeda's intent is clear, there is doubt over its current capability to deliver. There is speculation that frustration at the lack of a successful attack by late 2008 may be driving a shift in tactics. For example, on 14 April 2009, the design for a compact but potent chemical weapon known as al-Mubtakar al-Farid[40] was posted on a *jihadist* website. The device itself was designed and tested in Afghanistan 10 years ago.

37 Sageman, 'Confronting al-Qaeda' (n.30) 4.
38 Patrick Porter, 'Long wars and long telegrams: containing Al-Qaeda' (2009) 85(2) *International Affairs* 285.
39 Thomas H. Johnson and M. Chris Mason, 'Understanding the Taliban and insurgency in Afghanistan' (2007) 51(1) *Orbis* 71.
40 Meaning 'the Unique Innovation'.

However, there is now a real concern that the potential for the use of such a device has significantly increased.

Al-Qaeda's existing capability is also affected by several factors which may be viewed as key constraints in the ability to deliver its strategic ambitions.[41] Despite its successes in Afghanistan, al-Qaeda has suffered some setbacks which need to be considered.[42] First, its failure to land further blows on the West or other targets coupled with excessive Muslim casualties in some operations has led to a crisis of credibility for the organisation.[43] This loss in credibility has contributed to a crisis in funding worsened by the global economic recession. Despite these setbacks, al-Qaeda has proved itself to be extremely resilient. This organisational resilience has been noted by the US Director of National Intelligence who has described its ability to absorb losses, and the promotion of capable people in line with an effective succession plan as 'amazing'.[44]

At the same time, a low standard of operational security has also been observed, which has hampered recent plots reflecting the lack of experience of newer operatives as well as a lower standard of training than prior to 2001. Nevertheless, the organisation still has very many capable elements and has the ability to anticipate the West's moves. As a result, there is a need for continued pressure to keep al-Qaeda off-balance, a task which will become more challenging as al-Qaeda manage to secure further safe havens of operation.

AL-QAEDA IN THE TWENTY-FIRST CENTURY

Al-Qaeda has been referred to as the new brand of terrorism using 'high tech' means to inflict mass fear and destruction.[45] This has helped open the eyes of the world to the negative aspects of globalisation. One significant enabler of globalisation has been the Internet and the rapid expansion of cyber space.

The role of the Internet is vital in the way that it has enabled anonymous communication between terrorists, aided recruitment through global chat

41 Porter, 'Long wars and long telegrams' (n.38) 285.

42 Sageman, 'Confronting al-Qaeda' (n.30) 4.

43 Andrew Phillips, 'How Al Qaeda Lost Iraq', paper presented at the annual meeting of the APSA 2008 Annual Meeting, Hynes Convention Center, Boston, Massachusetts, 28 August 2008. [Online]. Available at: http://www.allacademic.com/meta/p280690_index.html [accessed: 25 October 2009].

44 Stirling Assynt, *Al-Qaeda's Strategic Plan* (n.31).

45 John H. Sandrock, 'Topics in Terrorism: Toward a Transatlantic Consensus on the Nature of the Threat'. A Compendium of papers presented at the conference on 'Topics in Terrorism' held on 29–30 November 2004, published July 2005 (vol. 1), the Atlantic Council of the US.

rooms, encouraged the sharing of knowledge, as well as playing a significant role in the spreading of propaganda. In terms of the terrorist threat to the Western democracies from al-Qaeda, it is important to note that al-Qaeda is a network of terrorists and terrorist organisations. Whilst some of these organisations are highly structured, others operate as loosely knit cells. The behaviour of networks and loose cells, however, is more difficult to predict, partly because the strong leadership that contributes to the predictability of structured organisations is missing.

Traditionally, terrorists have relied on the old saying, 'Kill one and frighten ten thousand'. Today's terrorists understand that with the impact of the media they are able to kill or injure thousands and frighten millions, as was the case in 9/11. More recently, the attack on the Japanese oil tanker the M Star in the Strait of Hormuz on 28 July 2010[46] is interesting in terms of the handling of the media. The Japanese authorities have been applauded by key individuals within the British counter-terrorism community for its low-key handling of the incident as the lack of media attention is precisely what the terrorists do not want.

In terms of the threat, the potential lethality of attacks continues to be a key concern, including the possible use of weapons of mass destruction (WMDs) as well as the continued use of simultaneous multiple suicide bombings.[47] In order to successfully implement an act of terrorism, much preparation is required. With more sophisticated attacks such as the use of chemical, biological, radiological and nuclear (CBRN) weapons, considerable expert knowledge is required. This, needless to say, costs money in terms preparation, especially if specialists are to be involved, as they may need to be bribed, incurring yet more expense. Additionally, access to materials in some cases can be challenging and implementation even more so.[48]

Again, further finance is required for relevant access and to buy technical know-how for implementation. Despite several attempts for al-Qaeda to obtain nuclear weapons, they have failed to do so to date; seemingly as they have not yet acquired the necessary connections, expertise or funding. Less sophisticated methods technologically, such as suicide bombing, continue to be

46 Adam Schreck, 'Japanese oil tanker "attacked" in Gulf' *Arab News* (28 July 2010). [Online]. Available at: http://arabnews.com/middleeast/article92066.ece [accessed: 12 October 2009].

47 Brent Ellis, 'Countering complexity: an analytical framework to guide counter-terrorism policy-making' (2003) 6(1) *Journal of Military and Strategic Studies*. [Online]. Available at: http://www.jmss.org/jmss/index.php/jmss/article/view/235/250 [accessed: 10 October 2009].

48 Robin M. Frost, 'Nuclear and Radiological Terrorism' (2005) 45 Adelphi Paper no. 378.

a preferred method.[49] However, contrary to belief, suicide bombing operations are far more complex and costly than is commonly understood.

The finance required for such an operation is not simply the cost of the suicide belt, as many seem to believe. The location of the attack plays a significant part in terms of cost; however, every operation requires recruitment, training, intelligence gathering and coordination of the attack itself. Additionally, after the attack has taken place, payments are made to the suicide terrorist's family. Another factor to take into consideration is the multiple simultaneous attacks which has become a hall mark for al-Qaeda attacks. Such synchronised attacks are not only more complex to plan and execute, but incur additional costs at all stages of the process.

PRESENT THREAT TO THE UNITED KINGDOM

According to the British Security Service, MI5, there are approximately 2,000 individuals who pose a direct threat to national security and public safety, and a further 2,000 who are actively plotting but not individually known to the authorities. It is thought that the UK faces 30 known plots, and the Security Service is monitoring in excess of 200 networks.[50] The threat was described by the Director General of the Security Service, Jonathan Evans[51] as:

> *... the most immediate and acute peacetime threat in the 98-year history of my service.*

Evans also observed that recruits are getting younger and that international influences are now much more diverse with links not limited to Pakistan.[52] According to some sources, al-Qaeda has recently entered a phase of development when 'clean skins' or 'grassroot *jihadis*',[53] are acting as independent cells in order to deliver their attacks without drawing attention from the security and intelligence agencies.[54] In a public speech delivered by Eliza Manningham-

49 Sageman, 'Confronting al-Qaeda' (n.30) 4.

50 Andrew Sparrow, 'Brown Unveils National Security Strategy' *Guardian* (19 March 2008). [Online]. Available at: http://www.guardian.co.uk/politics/2008/mar/19/terrorism.uksecurity1 [accessed: 12 October 2009].

51 Jonathan Evans, Deputy Director General MI5 since 2007. [Online]. Available at: https://www.mi5.gov.uk/output/director-general.html [accessed: 15 October 2009].

52 *Guardian*, 'MI5 chief's warning' 5 November 2007. [Online]. Available at: http://www.guardian.co.uk/terrorism/story/0,,2205608,00.html [accessed: 20 October 2010].

53 Who have not been identified by the security forces and are not coming up on their radar.

54 David Rubens, 'Police expect Mumbai-style attack on city' *Sunday Times* (London, 20 December 2009).

Buller, Director General of the Security Services on 9 November 2006, on the terrorist threat facing the UK, she announced that:

> *... today, my officers and the police are working to contend with some 200 groupings or networks, totalling over 1600 identified individuals (and there will be many we don't know) who are actively engaged in plotting, or facilitating, terrorist acts here and overseas.*[55]

and that:

> *... tomorrow's threats may include the use of chemicals, bacteriological agents, radioactive materials and even nuclear technology. Today we see the use of home-made improvised explosive devices; tomorrow's threat may include the use of chemicals, bacteriological agents, radioactive materials and even nuclear technology.*

The threat is real and spreading with characteristics not dissimilar to a controlled virus. The challenge is clear but the concern is whether it is realistic to expect the intelligence and law enforcement agencies alone to contain and control the problem. Any investigation needs to be intelligence led, however, the source of that intelligence needs to be genuinely 'all source' and mechanisms put in place to be able to make better use of 'open' and 'commercial source' intelligence.

Analysis of the Broader Threat Environment

Understanding the global threat from international terrorism from a systemic perspective denotes understanding that its very nature is derived from a series of political, economic and technological realities that are all interconnected. According to Capra:

> *Terrorism is always a weapon of the politically disempowered, who feel that they are unable to voice their grievances through conventional political processes. In order to combat them effectively, we need to understand clearly the terrorists' frustration.*[56]

55 Terrorist threat to UK – MI5 chief's full speech, *Times Online* November 10, 2006. [Online]. Available at: http://www.timesonline.co.uk/tol/news/uk/article632872.ece [accessed: 20 October 2009].

56 Fritjof Capra, 'September 11: True Security – We cannot fight terrorism effectively without understanding its roots' *Resurgence* 211. [Online]. Available at: http://www.resurgence.org/resurgence/issues/capra211.htm [accessed: 17 October 2009].

The terrorists' frustration in the case of al-Qaeda can be attributed partly to international politics and the foreign policies of Western governments. In order to combat terrorist financing, which is part of the wider counter-terrorism strategy, it is important to examine these issues, to attempt to comprehend the drivers not simply for terrorists, but for their supporters to include financiers.

INTERNATIONAL POLITICS AND FOREIGN POLICY

Currently, al-Qaeda's terrorism is directed principally against the US and its allies. As such, it is appropriate that the attempt to understand the origin of the hostility begins with an observation of the image of the US around the world. This image is multifaceted, consisting of many positive aspects of Western society such as individual liberty, cultural diversity and economic opportunity, as well as great enthusiasm for technology, fashion, sport and entertainment. On the other hand, the US is also seen by many as the driving force behind a new form of global capitalism, supported by military force, that is often socially unjust and environmentally destructive as well as damaging to moral values and standards.

To understand the political context of the recent terrorist attacks, the situation in the Middle East must also be appreciated. The Western assumption is to regard the US as peacemaker in the region. However, in other parts of the world, and especially in the Muslim world, the view is to the contrary. There is widespread anti-American sentiment based on a number of concerns. Resentment against the US exists regarding its uncritical support for Israel, in particular Israeli occupation of Arab land, as well as for the dispossession of Palestinians and for state-sponsored assassinations.[57]

Additionally, US support for undemocratic and repressive Arab governments, in particular that of Saudi Arabia, coupled with 10 years of sanctions and military attacks against Iraq, which have allegedly resulted in the deaths of half a million children, have also been met with much criticism and hostility. These perceived grievances have contributed to the rise of a large number of radical Islamic movements.

The American quest for natural resources around the world has resulted in the US government's continual effort to 'stabilise' various regions and, in doing so, the US has often supported undemocratic and repressive regimes.

57 Steven Simon, 'Price of the surge: how U.S. Strategy is hastening Iraq's demise' (2008) 87 *Foreign Affairs* 57.

Ironically, the US has at times supported hardline Islamic movements. Indeed, some of the most notorious Islamic terrorists, including followers of Osama bin Laden, were originally trained by the CIA.[58]

To understand the motivation of al-Qaeda and other Islamic extremists, it is important to pay special attention to the US relationship with Saudi Arabia. This relationship is based on an extraordinary bargain, concluded in 1945 between President Roosevelt and King Ibn Saud, according to which Saudi Arabia grants the US unlimited and perpetual access to its oil fields, containing 25 per cent of the world's known oil reserves, in exchange for protection of the Saudi royal family against its enemies, both external and internal.

This bargain has shaped American foreign and military policy towards the Middle East for almost half a century, during which the US has protected a totalitarian regime in Saudi Arabia that blatantly disregards basic human rights and tramples over democracy. Some argue that the main purpose of the Gulf War in 1991, originally code-named 'Desert Shield', was not to drive Iraq out of Kuwait, but to protect Saudi Arabia from a possible attack and to guarantee US access to the Saudi oil fields. Since then, the US has maintained and steadily expanded its military presence in the Gulf. In addition, it also defends the Saudi regime against its internal enemies. The Saudi Arabian National Guard, which protects the royal family, is almost entirely armed, trained and managed by the US.

One of the goals of al-Qaeda is to drive the US out of the Gulf region and to replace the 'corrupt' Saudi regime by what they consider an 'authentic' Islamic state. Such a state would be modelled on that of the fundamentalist Taliban in Afghanistan, which was many times more repressive than the current Saudi regime, especially in its barbarous treatment of women. Nevertheless, as long as the US continues to support the totalitarian system in Saudi Arabia, it will fuel anti-American hatred. However, it is ironic that much of the funding sources for *Jihadist* terrorist originate from Saudi Arabia, a subject that will be explored further in Chapter 3

The relevance to CTF is that the roots of discontent are frequently exacerbated and manipulated in order to raise financial support for terrorism.

58 'The CIA trained Osama bin Laden and other Arabs in the techniques of terrorism'. [Online]. Available at: http://www.futurepower.org/paz/cia_trained_bin_laden.htm. See also Adel Darwish, 'A New Anti-US Terror Base in Afghanistan' (1998).[Online]. Available at: http://mideastnews.com/Laden.htm [accessed: 15 October 2009].

In order to mitigate future terrorist acts, it is necessary for the US, the UK and their allies to re-examine their foreign policies and to accept that some past as well as current actions by the allies may be fuelling terrorism at every level. The systemic understanding of the background of extremist Islamic terrorism calls for a multifaceted anti-terrorist strategy. Since the extension and scope of this 'new' terrorism is global, it requires sustained international police and intelligence work, based on extensive and widespread cooperation among the international counter-terrorism community.

TERRORIST ORGANISATIONS VERSUS ORGANISED CRIME GROUPS

The relationship between organised crime and terrorism has been a hotly debated subject in recent years. Although this is a subject that requires further research, evidence to date suggest that the so-called 'nexus' of organised crime and terrorism is misleading in that the term suggests the coming together of the two organisations, whereas in reality the relationship can more accurately be described as one serving as part of the other's logistical supply chain.

Another argument put forward in terms of justifying the existence of the so-called 'nexus' is that terrorist organisations frequently turn to criminal means in order to sustain themselves economically, and as such can be described as being an organised crime group in its own right. However, this is quite different from the implied merger of major established organised crime groups, such as the Russian mafia, the Chinese Triads or the Japanese Yakuza, with terrorist organisations such as al-Qaeda. Indeed, many terrorist organisations have become almost indistinguishable from organised crime groups as Professor Rider observes:

> *... there has been a tendency to label terrorists as almost a sub-species of organised crime. Terrorists have stooped to ordinary crime to raise funds and secure their objectives and, of course, most terror networks would have the characteristics of a continuing criminal enterprise.*[59]

However, whilst the objectives of most terrorists can be stigmatised as 'criminal', they are generally not acquisitive. Another key difference is motivation in that the end goal is political and the use of criminal means to achieve those goals are considered to be interim measures necessary to achieve that end

59 Barry A.K. Rider, 'Law: The War on Terror and Crime and the Offshore Centres: The "New" Perspective?' in Donato Masciandaro (ed.), *Global Financial Crime: Terrorism, Money Laundering and Offshore Centres* (Ashgate Publishing 2004) 67.

goal, whereas for traditional organised groups, the end goal is profit. There is also evidence that where possible, terrorist groups prefer to obtain funding through legitimate needs, namely donations. While the giving of property for the purpose of committing serious criminal acts might effectively 'criminalise' the property in question, it is not necessarily of illicit and thus tainted origin.

However, where legitimate sources are unavailable, terrorist organisations secure their funding from criminal activity, whether it be narcotics trafficking or fraud, they will have the same needs, in regard to the treatment of the proceeds of their crime, as traditional organised crime groups. However, their need for security and secrecy is probably more compelling in most cases, compared to Organised Crime Groups (OCGs) as their stakes are somewhat higher. Perhaps to a greater extent than most forms of organised crime, terrorists with a political agenda will require funds for a wider agenda. They will wish to maintain individuals and perhaps their families and networks, even when they are not directly pertinent to the prosecution of terror. They will also need to create secret money that can be easily accessed by operational units.[60]

The reality of the relationship between organised crime and terrorist organisations will be illustrated through the use of case studies in the next section. Three case studies will be examined, first, Piracy in Somalia, second, al-Qaeda in Iraq (AQI) and finally the Taliban in Afghanistan, as an illustration of the collaboration between al-Qaeda and organised crime models to enable further understanding of the relationship between traditional crime models and terrorism.

CASE STUDIES: PIRACY, SOMALIA; AL-QAEDA, IRAQ; TALIBAN, AFGHANISTAN

The case of maritime piracy in Somalia is of interest for two reasons. First, the group's motivation is currently economic as opposed to political or religious, therefore falls under the banner of OCGs. The second is its link with militant Islam which again appears to be based purely on 'business' at this moment in time, as opposed to a sharing of ideology as such, although the hatred for the West, albeit for different reasons, is worth monitoring. Somali piracy has become big business in recent years involving approximately 1,500 pirates, with

60 Ibid. 68.

seven syndicates controlling separate but linked enterprises largely financed and brokered from Kenya, Dubai, Lebanon, Somalia, Russia and elsewhere.[61]

In 2009, pirates attacked a total of 217 ships[62] with 47 successful hijackings and the collection of more than $60 million in ransom payments. In 2010, there were 445 pirate attacks representing a 10 per cent increase from 2009.[63] Since 2005 there has been a significant increase not only in the number of pirate attacks off the Somali coast, but also the number of hostages taken, as well as the duration of their captivity and the ransoms paid for their release. The average ransom paid has increased from $150,000 in 2005 to $5.4 million in 2010.[64] Somali piracy has become such a profitable business that piracy investment exchanges exist around the world for investors who are able to enjoy a significant return on investment. For example, the pirate 'stock exchange' in Haradheere, Somalia, is open 24 hours a day where locals can commit funds or arms to one or more of 72 'maritime companies' hosted by the exchange.[65]

Pirates are generally unemployed young men from two of Somalia's clans; many of whom are ex-militia from the internal wars of the south attracted to piracy by the opportunities for economic gain that piracy has revealed.[66] The justification for the crimes is illegal foreign fishing and alleged toxic dumping. Whether or not those claims are correct, they are believed locally and a prominent narrative of victim hood is widely accepted.[67] The theme of 'victim hood' is a factor that not only unites this group with terrorist organisations such as al-Qaeda but the perception of abuse by the West contributes directly to its support. The second reason for interest is due to the fact that Somalia has been identified as being one of the areas of focus highlighted by al-Qaeda's strategic plan. Although existing knowledge in terms of the extent of the relationship between al-Qaeda and the Piracy crime groups is limited, according to Stirling Assynt:

---

61 Robert I. Rotberg, 'Combating maritime piracy: a policy brief with recommendations for action' (World Peace Foundation policy brief #11 26 January 2010).

62 This figure should be viewed in the context of overall traffic in the region amounting to 22,000 ships passing through the Gulf of Aden alone.

63 Acturial Profession Report. [Online]. Available at: www.safety4sea.com/article.php?id=1563 [accessed: 20 March 2011].

64 Maritime Sun, 'No to arms despite piracy' 24 February 2011. [Online]. Available at: www.maritimesun.com/news/no-to-arms-despite-piracy/ [accessed: 20 March 2011].

65 Tom Minney, 'Somali pirates stock exchange finances sea ventures' (*African Capital Markets News*, 28 April 2010). [Online]. Available at: http://www.africancapitalmarketsnews.com/402/somali-pirates-stock-exchange-finances-sea-ventures/ [accessed: 31 January 2011].

66 Peter Lehr, 'Somali piracy: the next iteration' (2009) 3(4) *Perspectives on Terrorism* 26.

67 Rotberg, 'Combating maritime piracy' (n.61).

> *... Al-Shahab in Somalia is increasingly becoming a core part of al-Qaeda, embracing its global vision. Somali links have particular potential to deliver plots in the West, and there is at least one camp established in the country.*[68]

What is known is the existing 'economic' relationship between Somali pirate groups and Al-Shahab. A further example of the cooperation between al-Qaeda and Somali pirates can be seen in the indictment of Al-Adel for his part in the 1998 US embassy bombings in Africa. According to the indictment, al-Adel is a member of the majlis al shura of al-Qaeda and a member of its military committee, and he provided military and intelligence training to members of al-Qaeda and Egyptian Islamic Jihad in Afghanistan, Pakistan and Sudan, and to anti-UN Somali tribes.[69] It is also possible that his trainees included the Somalis of the first Battle of Mogadishu. It is now known from captured letters that al-Adel established the al-Qaeda training facility at Ras Kamboni in Somalia near the Kenyan border.[70]

The relationship between the two organisations is clearly synergistic. As legitimate funding sources for terrorist organisations become more scarce, criminal resources will become increasingly valuable. The focus should be not only to combat the attacks at sea, but at examining the proceeds of crime inland and how it is laundered through the piracy exchanges, the financial centres as well as through real estate.[71] The relationship between piracy and terrorism is also important in relation to the payments of ransoms in that once the relationship is acknowledged, the payment of ransoms will be deemed as funding terrorism, and as such, a criminal offence. This will have significant economic ramifications on maritime trade and may result in the region becoming a 'no-go' zone requiring further re-routing of cargo, further adding to the expense caused by maritime piracy in Somali waters.

Criminality within terrorist organisations can be clearly demonstrated in the case of AQI. Kidnap and ransom (K&R), for example, is not only used by Somali pirates, but served as one of the main sources of funding for AQI, especially during the reign of the late al Zarqawi. The case of AQI is interesting

68 Stirling Assynt, *Al-Qaeda's Strategic Plan* (n.31).

69 Eugene Kontorovich, 'An empirical examination of universal jurisdiction for piracy' (2010) 104 *American Journal of International Law* 9.

70 [Online]. Available at: http://www.search.com/reference/Saif_al-Adel [accessed: 2 November 2009].

71 Petrus C. van Duyne, Melvin R.J. Soudijn, 'Hot money, hot stones and hot air: crime-money threat, real estate and real concern' (2009) 12(2) *Journal of Money Laundering Control* 173.

as K&R was not only a criminal means of obtaining money, but also served as a propaganda tool.[72] For example, there have been instances where AQI have bought hostages from criminal organisations so that their execution could be televised. In this case, the use of hostages is clearly not financial.[73]

The case of the Taliban is also relevant in terms of the relationship between criminality and legitimacy in relation to its business funding model. Similar to AQI, the Taliban uses K&R to raise funds when other sources of income are scarce.[74] The main difference between AQI and the Taliban is that the latter's use of K&R to date has been mainly for economic as opposed to political gain. As with al-Qaeda, Taliban funding is derived from both external and internal sources.[75] External funding includes Arab donors, the Afghan and Pakistani Diaspora, Pakistani businesses and charities. Additional income is derived from the laundering of narcotics originating from Afghanistan through reinvestments in property, businesses and car dealerships operating in Afghanistan, Pakistan and the UAE. Internal sources of funding include the domestic narcotics trade, locally collected taxes, extortion and proceeds of local crime such as kidnap ransoms.

Terrorist organisations on the whole prefer to obtain funding where possible through legitimate means.[76] In the case of the Taliban, legitimate sources, namely charitable giving, is usually provided to the higher levels of command within the Taliban.[77] The lower tiers of operational command eventually receive funding filtered through from the higher levels of command, although much of it has been siphoned off on route. As a result, the lower levels of operational command are forced to raise the rest of the funding to meet their operational budget through criminal means. This is a source of great frustration for the Taliban local command, as it detracts from its hearts and minds objectives of

72 Judith Tinnes, 'Counting lives in a theater of terror: an analysis of media-oriented hostage takings in Iraq, Afghanistan, Pakistan and Saudi Arabia' (2010) 5(5) *Perspectives on Terrorism: a Journal of the Terrorism Research Initiative* 3.

73 See Chapter 5.

74 Muhammad Amir Rana, 'Taliban insurgency in Pakistan: a counterinsurgency perspective' (2009) *Pakistan Institute of Peace Studies* 9. [Online]. Available at: http://www.humansecuritygateway.com/documents/PIPS_TalibanInsurgencyPakistan_CounterinsurgencyPerspective.pdf [accessed: 30 October 2009].

75 Ashley J. Tellis, 'Beradar, Pakistan, and the Afghan Taliban: What Gives?' (2010) Policy Outlook, Carnegie Endownment for International Peace. [Online]. Available at: http://www.carnegieendowment.org/files/after_beradar.pdf [accessed: 25 October 2009].

76 Fotini Christia, Michael Semple, 'Flipping the Taliban: how to win in Afghanistan' (2009) 88 *Journal of Foreign Affairs* 34.

77 Antonio Giustozzi (ed.), *Decoding the New Taliban: Insights from thee Afghan Field* (Columbia University Press 2009).

the Afghan people, albeit often by force. Criminal action against the people tilts the scale of hearts and minds in favour of the Western alliances, which is precisely what the Taliban does not want.

A further point of interest in terms of the relationship between criminality and legitimacy is the concept of legality. For example, narcotics forms a major part of economic trade in Afghanistan at all levels, not just in relation to the Taliban.[78] In the West, narcotics is illegal, therefore any funds relating to the narcotics trade must also be illegal. However, Western concepts of 'money' and legality cannot be applied in such environments. Afghanistan is a country where several currencies co-exist. It should be noted that opium and hashish serve as recognised currencies alongside the US Dollar, Pakistani Rupees, Iranian Rial and the Afghani. Therefore by Afghan standards, the concept of narcotics being illegal is somewhat alien. This naturally follows that any related concepts such as money laundering is also difficult to comprehend. Furthermore, for the Afghan government to simply pass legislation making narcotics illegal is also unlikely to be effective as a huge paradigm shift in terms of the cultural attitudes and behaviour towards narcotics needs to occur first, which clearly cannot take place overnight.

This is the challenge of tackling financial crime in general. The problem of definition has been highlighted by numerous experts. However, the problem goes much deeper than definition alone. Criminality and what is considered to be legal and illegal behaviour is shaped by the culture and moral standards of that country. This explains part of the reason for the failure of attempting to impose Western standards upon others. At the same time, financial crimes relating to terrorism and organised crime, tend to be global in nature. Therefore, it is appropriate that the subject of globalisation and its impact on terrorism and organised crime is elaborated upon.

THE IMPACT OF GLOBALISATION

It has been suggested that globalisation has had an important impact upon the development of 'new' terrorism as well as crime in general. As such, it is important to examine the phenomenon of globalisation in some detail. Globalisation can be defined as a continuous decline in the economic importance of national political borders and an unprecedented intensification of economic relations and interactions, up to the point where the difference

78 Peter A. Sproat, 'Counter-terrorist finance in the UK: a quantitative and qualitative commentary based on open-source materials' (2010) 13(4) *Journal of Money Laundering Control* 315.

between domestic and foreign transactions becomes insignificant or even non-existent. According to Held, McGrew et al.,[79] globalisation is characterised by four types of change.

First, it involves a stretching of social, political and economic activities across political frontiers, regions and continents. Second, it suggests the intensification, or the growing magnitude of interconnectedness and flows of trade, investment, finance, migration, culture and so forth. Third, the growing extensity and intensity of global interconnectedness can be linked to a speeding up of global interactions and processes, as the evolution of worldwide systems of transport and communication increases the velocity of the diffusion of ideas, goods, information, capital and people. Fourth, the growing extensity, intensity and velocity of global interactions can be associated with their deepening impact, such that the effects of distant events can be highly significant elsewhere and even the most local developments may come to have enormous global consequences. In this sense, the boundaries between domestic matters and global affairs can become increasingly blurred.[80]

In other words, Held and McGrew describe globalisation as the widening, intensification and ever increasing speed of worldwide interconnectedness, whereby all key areas of human activity are linked. This is true, not just in terms of the global economy, but equally applies to the illegal economy relating to organised crime and terrorism, and explains in part the development of closer working relationships between the various networks of terrorists and organised crime groups around the globe. Dicken takes the issue of definition a stage further by drawing a distinction between internationalising processes and globalising processes.

According to Dicken, the differentiation should be made in order to understand the 'contemporary global economy'. Dicken defines the internationalising processes as involving:

> *The simple extension of economic activities across national boundaries. They reflect, essentially, quantitative changes that lead to a more extensive geographical pattern of economic activity.*

Whereas globalising processes involve:

79 D. Held, A. McGrew, D. Goldblatt and J. Perraton, *Global Transformations: Politics, Economics and Culture* (Polity Press 2000).
80 Ibid.

> *Not merely the geographical extension of economic activity across national boundaries but also – and more importantly – the functional integration of such internationally dispersed activities. They reflect essentially qualitative changes in the ways economic activities are organised.*[81]

What Dicken is referring to is the cultural impact of globalisation on organisations, which can also be seen in terrorist and organised criminal groups. Globalisation does not simply mean that these groups are operating across the globe – the significance is that the modus operandi of these groups has become increasingly integrated as they set aside previous cultural differences that may have existed in the past, and increase their cooperation with one another, learning from each other's mistakes and successes.

It is often said that the world is getting smaller. While this is not true in a literal sense, what is meant is that advancement and diffusion of technological innovation, especially in the fields of transportation and communication, have helped to link the world more closely together. Technological innovation has contributed to globalisation by supplying the infrastructure and means for trans-global world connections and networks. In particular, developments in transport, communications and data processing have allowed global links to become more dense, faster, more reliable as well as much cheaper.[82] What is important to note is that all of the benefits of globalisation have had a major impact on the everyday lives of people around the world including terrorists and criminals.[83]

Communication is a key factor in understanding the changing modus operandi of terrorist organisations. Communication can be achieved through many means: the first is face to face communication. The terrorist is no longer restricted to a localised geographical region as the growth in the ease of travel, especially air travel coupled with low cost flights, means that he or she can travel with great ease and speed to meet a fellow terrorist half way round the world.

A second method of communication is telecommunication. The growth of cellular telephony has had an impact on terrorists and counter-terrorism for

81 Peter Dicken, *Global Shift: Reshaping the Global Economic Map in the 21st Century* (Sage Publications 2003) 12.

82 Ibid. 12.

83 Michelle Gallant, 'Promise and perils: the making of global money laundering, terrorist finance norms' (2010) 13(2) *Journal of Money Laundering Control* 175.

many reasons. Cellular telephony, more commonly known as mobile phones, can be purchased on contract or on a 'pay-as-you-go' basis. Where there is a contract, law enforcement investigators can obtain itemised phone bills more easily, enabling the identification of numbers called, therefore assisting in the establishment of terrorist networks. However, with the pay-as-you-go system, there is evidence that terrorists and organised criminals are increasingly using mobile phones for single use, after which the handset is discarded. The main attraction is anonymity and the difficulty in proving ownership, especially if communication is between two pay-as-you-go phones. Another method of communication is the Internet, which will be analysed in detail in Chapter 2.

One key component of globalisation is deregulation and liberalisation, as well as privatisation of the public sector. The significance of deregulation and liberalisation to CTF is that it has led to an explosion of activity around the globe, making regulation and governance an increasing challenge. The sheer volume of activity has led to a lack of transparency in many cases, despite the existence of regulation, and has led many industries including finance to be more susceptible to abuse by terrorist and other criminal organisations. Understanding globalisation and its effects is vital to understanding the development of modern terrorist groups and terrorist financing.[84] Advancements in communication, transport and technology, as previously mentioned, have enabled terrorists to change and improve their modus operandi compared to the terrorists of the 1960s and 1970s. As such, a new set of security challenges confront the CTF community to attempt to keep up with the adversaries of the twenty-first century.

A further challenge is the increasing volume of global financial transactions resulting in the difficulty of identifying suspicious activities possibly relating to terrorism. World financial flows have grown considerably since the 1970s. The volume of cross-border transactions has increased considerably and transactions operating within the 24-hour global financial markets are almost instantaneous.[85] The speed and global reach of these transactions arguably lead to less transparency despite the existence of internal monitoring systems put in place by compliance departments as part of the requirements set by regulatory authorities.

84 Ibid. 175.

85 The Global Transformations Website [Online]. Available at: http://www.polity.co.uk/global/summary.htm#organized [accessed 28 April 2011]

One further challenge of cross-border transactions is the variation in regulatory requirements from country to country in that some countries may be compliant with international standards, whilst others may not be.[86] It is important to remember that for financial institutions, although reputation is an important issue, they are, at the end of the day, commercial organisations which are driven by profit, and terrorists and organised criminals are able to take advantage of any vulnerability that may exist as a result.

Economic globalisation is also of significance to CTF as it refers to the change in the relationship between states and markets. Although the global economy as a single entity is by no means as highly integrated as the most robust national economies, the trends point towards intensifying integration within and across regions. The shift towards markets and private financial institutions as the 'authoritative actors' in the global financial system, reinforced by financial liberalisation poses serious questions about the nature of state power and economic sovereignty. Alongside financial integration, the operations of multinational corporations integrate national and local economies into global and regional production networks. Under these conditions, national economies no longer function as autonomous systems of wealth creation since national borders are no longer significant barriers to the conduct and organisation of economic activity. Thus, the distinction between domestic economic activity and worldwide economic activity is becoming increasingly difficult to sustain. These developments are of interest to CTF as terrorist and other criminal organisations have developed in the same way and also operate in a borderless parallel criminal economy.

The explosion in the volume of trade refers not simply to financial transactions, but also to international trade in general. Central to the organisation of this new global capitalist order is the multinational corporation (MNC). In 1999, there were over 60,000 MNCs worldwide with 500,000 foreign subsidiaries, selling $9.5 trillion[87] of goods and services annually across the globe. Today, transnational production considerably exceeds the level of global exports and has become the primary means for selling goods and services abroad. It is not difficult to see how the development in the physical movement of goods and services, mentioned above, has impacted upon the way in which terrorist and organised criminal groups operate. The only difference is

86 Jun Tang, Lishan Ai, 'Combating money laundering in transition countries: the inherent limitations and practical issues' (2010) 13(3) *Journal of Money Laundering Control* 215.

87 [Online]. Available at: http://www.polity.co.uk/global/summary.htm#organized [accessed: 14 November 2009].

that terrorist and organised criminal groups offer goods and services which are generally illegal as well as legal. This illegal economic power has had an enormous impact on the modus operandi of the various terrorist and organised criminal groups, whereby differences in culture or long-term objectives are superseded by economic imperatives and they are able to cooperate with one another.

In addition, as previously mentioned, the globalisation of economic activity exceeds the regulatory reach of national governments while, at the same time, existing multilateral institutions of global economic governance have limited authority.[88] Although the criminal elements of the business activities of terrorist and other criminal organisations are of course not governed by regulation, they are naturally able to take advantages of weaknesses in the legitimate economy and abuse the system accordingly.

UNDERSTANDING THE ASYMMETRIC BATTLEFIELD

Efforts to disrupt terrorism and organised crime are frequently referred to as warfare.[89] As one enters the asymmetric battlefield of 4GW, the distinction between military and civilian becomes unclear, both in terms of the adversary as well as those who counter that threat. The interdependent relationship between globalisation and the asymmetric battlefield is worth revisiting and exploring further as part of the overall analysis on the threat environment. Nofi in his paper on the '*Recent Trends in Thinking About Warfare*',[90] describes the nature of the asymmetric battlefield as containing seven key characteristics, namely global, pervasive, granularity, vulnerability, technology, media and network.

First, Nofi argues that modern technologies and economic integration have enabled small actors to become effective in global operations. Second, that the environment has become pervasive in that the decline of nation state warfare has forced all open conflict into the 4GW mould. Third, the granularity is highlighted by the multiplication of many extremely small viable groups and a broad variety of reasons for conflict. Fourth, open societies and economies offer many vulnerabilities and targets of opportunity, while allowing the free

88 Antoinette Verhage, 'Supply and demand: anti-money laundering by the compliance industry' (2010) 12(4) *Journal of Money Laundering Control* 371.

89 See Introduction.

90 Albert A. Nofi, *Recent Trends in Thinking about Warfare*, CRM D0014875.A1/Final September 2006 Defense Technical Information Center. [Online]. Available at: www.dtic.mil [accessed: 20 January 2010].

movement of individuals. Fifth, the advance of new technologies to include automatic weapons, cell phones, the Internet, GPS, chemical and biological weapons, has dramatically increased the capability of small groups of warriors. Sixth, global media saturation through not only the press, but television, Internet, cell phone, all provide an extraordinary propaganda reach and lends itself to facile manipulation of public opinion. Finally, the world has become networked as never seen before as improvements in technology enable better and faster learning, adaptation to knowledge as well as increasing the ability to survive and to operate effectively.[91]

Furthermore, the goal of modern warfare is becoming increasingly less about geographical domination but increasingly concerns itself with the ability to dominate psychologically. Morale is a key factor in that its principal objective is not the destruction of the enemy's force, but of his will to continue the fight.[92] It follows, therefore, that victory must be won in the moral sphere. The aim of 4GW is to destroy the moral bonds that allow the organic whole to exist, namely cohesion.[93] The concept of 4GW is applicable not simply to the military battlefield, but also extremely relevant to all the stakeholders in the general fight against terrorism and organised crime. The adversary is not a single recognisable entity that can be fought on a physical battlefield and must be understood in the context of the global threat environment. These concepts are particularly relevant in the context of CTF as they jointly impact not only on the financial basis of support, but also upon the ways in which terrorist organisations obtain that support, raise funds and distribute those funds.

The theme of the global threat environment is continued in the next chapter by specialising on the cyber environment by examining the challenges caused by emerging technologies such as the Internet and mobile telecommunications, which have not only furthered 'globalisation' by eliminating borders, but also dramatically changed the way people live and communicate, and the modus operandi of terrorists and criminals alike.

---

91 John Robb, '4GW', *Global Guerrillas*, 8 May 2004.[Online]. Available at: http://globalguerrillas.typepad.com/globalguerrillas/2004/05/4gw_fourth_gene.html [accessed: 20 February 2010].

92 Nofi, *Recent Trends in Thinking about Warfare* (n.90).

93 Robb, '4GW' (n.91).

2

Emerging Threats: Security and Legal Challenges in the Cyber Environment

I do not really understand what a website is.[1]

Judge Peter Openshaw, Woolwich Crown Court, Trial of Younis Tsouli, August 2007[2]

The speed of technological advancement in recent years has been a key factor that has not only contributed to globalisation, but has had a fundamental impact on the modus operandi of the adversary. The growth of the Internet and with it, the significance of the cyber environment as a whole, pose a variety of new security threats and associated legal challenges which deserves further attention.

One concern relates to the inability for the judiciary to keep up to speed with emerging technologies. One extreme case can be highlighted by the comment made by Judge Openshaw in the fifth week of the trial of Younis Tsouli in 2007.[3] Throughout the trial, the judge struggled with many of the fairly basic concepts relating to the Internet, such as a website. In this particular case, the defendant was sentenced to 10 years in prison. However, the question is whether the decision was reached on the basis of a fair trial which requires a sufficient understanding of the evidence presented. Furthermore, the judge's comments and questions regarding the Internet is of concern in that anything more technical would have proved beyond the understanding of the

1 *R v Tsouli* [2007] EWCA Crim 3300 [2008] 2 Cr. App. R. (S.) 45.

2 Frances Gibb, 'Judge halts terror trial to ask: what's a website?' *The Times* (London, 18 May 2007).

3 'What's a website, asks judge at internet trial' *Daily Telegraph* (London, 18 May 2007).

courtroom, bringing into question the ability of the courts to understand the crime committed, yet alone its ability to serve justice.

However, a further concern is that the Tsouli example is not an isolated case. Although most members of the judiciary would be familiar with the concept of a website, the lack of knowledge of Internet related subjects is not uncommon. Practitioners and academics have identified two specific areas where understanding is grossly lacking, namely in the field of information technology (IT) and finance.[4] The gap between the non-expert and the expert[5] is such that many believe that this is the reason why the adversary has the upper hand.[6]

A further concern relates to why there have been so few successful prosecutions involving cases of relative financial complexity to include terrorist finance and financial crimes in general. This can partly explained by the fact that the whole legal process beginning with the initial investigation, the presentation of that material in court, and the understanding of the relevance of that evidence is so poor that many cases simply do not even get to court. Another contributory factor is the aforementioned inability to keep pace with technological advancements as well as the inadequate and inappropriate use of expert witnesses, which will be expanded upon in Chapter 7.

Furthermore, as there is a close link between finance and the Internet, it is essential that a better understanding is achieved in this field for the purpose of CTF. As a result, this chapter aims to highlight the challenges posed by ever advancing technologies in the cyber environment, and the need not only for new legislation and regulation in this field, but also to increase understanding in the subject and its relevance to terrorist finance. In the previous chapter, the discussion on globalisation highlighted that the Internet has changed the way in which people communicate. The introduction of email and other communication methods such as Skype[7] has resulted in low cost and instantaneous as well

4 R.E. Bell, 'The prosecution of computer crime' (2002) 9(4) *Journal of Financial Crime* 308.

5 Such as the forensic computer expert and the forensic accountant.

6 Roderic Broadhurst, 'Developments in the global law enforcement of cyber-crime' (2006) 29(3) *Policing: An International Journal of Police Strategies & Management* 408.

7 Skype is a proprietary voice-over-Internet protocol service and software application originally created by Niklas Zennström, and owned by Microsoft since 2011. The service allows users to communicate with peers by voice, video, and instant messaging over the Internet. Phone calls may be placed to recipients on the traditional telephone networks. Calls to other users within the Skype service are free of charge, while calls to landline telephones and mobile phones are charged via a debit-based user account system at very competitive rates compared to other telephony service providers.

as relatively secure communication across the globe. The impact for terrorist organisations is that they have also benefited from stronger global networks directly as a result of technological advancements such as encryption, which has resulted in the ability for terrorists to communicate with one another not only quickly, but in relative safety from being intercepted by government agencies. The next section will examine the relationship between terrorism and the Internet, more specifically the Internet as target, al-Qaeda's use of the Internet, methods of target selection and recruitment, its use for information and psychological operations, the use of the Internet for the purpose of fund raising and its benefits to the terrorist in terms of its anonymity.

Terrorism and the Internet

It is often said that the world is getting smaller. While this is not true in a literal sense, what is meant is that advancement of technological innovation, especially in the fields of transportation and communication, has helped to link the world more closely together. Technological innovation has contributed to globalisation by supplying the infrastructure and means for trans-global world connections and networks. In particular, developments in means of transport, communications and data processing have allowed global links to become denser, faster, more reliable and much cheaper. What is important to note is that all of the benefits of globalisation have had a major impact on the everyday lives of people around the world including terrorists and criminals.[8]

Communication is a key factor in understanding the changing the modus operandi of terrorist organisations. Communication can be achieved through many means: the first is face-to-face communication. The terrorist is no longer restricted to a geographical area as the growth in the ease of travel, especially air travel and low-cost flights, means that he or she can travel with great ease and speed to meet a fellow terrorist half way round the world, something that was not possible 50 years ago. Another form of communication is verbal or written. The aforementioned introduction of email and other communication methods such as Skype has resulted in low cost and instantaneous and secure communication across the globe which can also be utilised by terrorist organisations. The advancement in technology including encryption has meant that terrorists can communicate with one another not only quickly but in

8 Michelle Gallant, 'Promise and perils: the making of global money laundering, terrorist finance norms'. (2010) 13(2) *Journal of Money Laundering Control* 175.

relative safety from being intercepted by government agencies as new methods and technologies are continuously developed and introduced.

The Internet has also served as a powerful propaganda and recruitment tool for terrorist organisations, as chat rooms are increasingly used to create virtual communities to unite those with a common interest.[9] Internet chat rooms and websites are difficult to monitor and as the Internet has no boundaries,[10] they are difficult to control and shut down in some instances. In addition, the speed of the Internet enables information to be available instantaneously to a mass audience which can be used to incite hatred with obvious advantages to the terrorist. As a result, electronic media has become a key weapon to terrorists making the physical war less important compared with the media propaganda war.[11] The furore over the Danish cartoons portraying the prophet Muhammad is a case in point. The media has become a key tool for terrorists especially as it has emerged into an entity that is not only easily and widely accessible but uncontrollable in many aspects for which the Internet has had a significant role to play.[12]

Technological advancements have resulted in the wide ownership of mobile phones incorporating video recording devices. As such, 'news' reporting is no longer restricted in the domain of the official media. Anyone with a phone is a potential reporter who is able to easily post their personal video recordings and accompanying commentary on cyberspace with no form of quality control. The uncensored video footage is then able to easily convince and mislead audiences as to the reality of the situation. The power of the media propaganda war is such that in many ways the physical war becomes less significant.

Another key component of terrorism is finance. No organisation is able to operate without financial support. The Internet plays a key role in that first, it is used to target potential donors through a variety of means ranging from propaganda videos, chat rooms to gaming, in order to attract interest and support.[13] Second, websites allow users to provide account details so that

9 Anne Stenersen, 'The Internet: a virtual training camp?' (2008) 20(2) *Terrorism and Political Violence* 215.

10 David H. Gray, 'The Importance of the Internet to the post-modern terrorist and its role as a form of safe haven' (2009) 25(3) *European Journal of Scientific Research* 396.

11 Hsinchun Chen, Wingyan Chung, Jialun Qin et al., 'Uncovering the dark Web: A case study of jihad on the Web' (2008) 59(8) *Journal of the American Society for Information Science and Technology* 1347.

12 Ibid.

13 Shima D. Keene, 'Terrorism and the Internet: a double edged sword' (2011) 14(4) *Journal of Money Laundering Control* 359.

donated funds can be transferred to the terrorist organisations' bank accounts instantaneously. With the increasingly popular use of Internet banking, terrorists and organised criminals can also use methods such as phishing to steal money from victims' accounts or to use the system legitimately to transfer money to the accounts of terrorists in their organisations.[14]

INTERNET AS TARGET

The Internet can be a terrorist target in its own right and is referred to as 'cyber terrorism' which can be defined as the unlawful destruction or disruption of digital property to intimidate or coerce people.[15] Much of the concern in recent years relating to terrorism and the Internet has focused on the threat from the cyber terrorist, which must be differentiated from the use of the Internet by terrorist groups. The cyber terrorist specifically targets the Internet as a target for disruption and even possibly destruction, whereas the latter utilise the Internet as a tool to achieve their aims.

One example of a cyber terrorism attempt in the United Kingdom was in 2005 when the Security Service foiled a terrorist plot by al-Qaeda to try to bring down the Internet. The terrorist plot was to destroy a high-security Internet exchange in London which would have brought Internet traffic in the United Kingdom to a standstill and caused chaos across the nation. Raids by the Metropolitan Police resulted in the arrests of a number of terror suspects, and the discovery of computer files detailing the complex Internet destruction plan. The terrorists involved in the gunpowder plot were targeting the main building of Telehouse Europe,[16] which houses many large computer servers and acts as the main Internet hub serving British Internet Service Providers (ISPs).[17] Although cyber terrorism may be part of the terrorist agenda in terms of attacks it wishes to carry out, the main attraction of the Internet is predominantly for operational and planning purposes as opposed to purely as a target for terrorist attack. There is much evidence that the Internet has been used by al-Qaeda for this purpose.[18]

14 G. Merlonghi, 'Fighting financial crime in the age of electronic money: opportunities and limitations' (2010) 13(3) *Journal of Money Laundering Control* 202.

15 P. Daukantas, 'Government Computer News via Infowar.com' (2001). [Online]. Available at http://www.infowar.com [accessed: 15 January 2011].

16 Telehouse Europe is the office of the *Sunday Times*.

17 'UK foils terrorist plot to kill the internet Main server hub targetted in bomb plot' *pcplus*. [Online]. Available at: available at http://www.pcplus.co.uk/news/home_news/uk_foils_terrorist_plot_to_kill_the_internet [accessed: 15 January 2011].

18 F.N. Baldwin, 'The financing of terror in the age of the Internet: wilful blindness, greed or a political statement?' (2004) 8(2) *Journal of Money Laundering Control* 127.

AL-QAEDA AND THE INTERNET

Al-Qaeda's use of the Internet to plan operations for 9/11 was brought to light when computers seized in Afghanistan revealed that al-Qaeda was collecting intelligence on targets and sending encrypted messages via the Internet, as well as using Internet-based phones. Further investigation revealed the existence of various al-Qaeda websites. These include alneda.com,[19] containing encrypted information to direct al-Qaeda members to more secure sites and assam.com[20] serving as a mouthpiece for *jihad* in Afghanistan, Chechnya and Palestine. Other sites include jihadunspun.net, 7hj.7hj.com, aimed at teaching visitors how to conduct computer attacks,[21] aloswa.org, featuring quotations from bin Laden tapes and religious legal rulings that 'justified' the terrorist attacks,[22] as well as jehad.net, alsaha.com, and islammemo.com, all of which have posted al-Qaeda statements on their websites.[23]

In terms of further evidence regarding al-Qaeda's use of the Internet, several cases have been brought to court in relation computer fraud involving members of al-Qaeda. In January 2010, two American citizens Wesam El-Hanafi, a 33-year-old American citizen, and Sabirhan Hasanoff, 34-year-old dual citizen of the US and Australia, were indicted for conspiring to modernise al-Qaeda by providing computer systems expertise and other services.[24] According to Preet Bharara, US attorney for the Southern District of New York, the indictment charged that the two men had assisted al-Qaeda since at least November 2007.[25] The court document revealed that in late 2007, Hasanoff was paid $50,000 and was engaged in discussions about joining the organisation. The following year, El-Hanafi went to Yemen where he met two members of al-Qaeda who instructed him on operational security measures and directed him to perform tasks for the group. El-Hanafi later bought a subscription to a software program that enabled him to communicate securely with others over

19 Also featured international news on al Qaeda, and published articles, *fatwas* (decisions on applying Muslim law), and books.

20 Believed to be linked to al Qaeda (originally hosted by the Scranton company BurstNET Technologies, Inc.).

21 J. Kelley, 'Militants Wire Web with Links to Jihad' *USA Today*, 10 July 2002.

22 Y. Melman, 'Virtual Soldiers in a Holy War' *Ha'aretz*, 2002. [Online]. Available at: http://www.haaretz.com [accessed: 25 January 2011].

23 H. Trabelsi, 'Al-Qaeda Wages Cyber War against US' *Middle East Times*, Dubai, 27 June 2002, rpt. in CNO/IO Newsletter, 1–7 July 2002.

24 J. Williamson, 'Two US men indicted for giving tech support to al Qaeda', *Top News*, Washington, 1 May 2010. [Online]. Available at: http://www.topnews.in/usa/two-us-men-indicted-giving-tech-support-al-qaeda-24280 [accessed: 25 January 2011].

25 Ibid.

the Internet. Each man was charged with one count of conspiracy to provide material support to a foreign terrorist organisation.

Another example is the case involving the son of a Moroccan diplomat, 23-year-old Younes Tsouli,[26] an IT student living in Shepherd's Bush, West London. In 2005, Tsouli became an administrator for the web forum al-Ansat, used by 4,500 extremists to communicate with each other, sharing such practical information as how to make explosives and how to get to Iraq to become a suicide bomber. Tsouli, operating under the name 'Irhabi 007',[27] worked with al-Qaeda leaders in Iraq to help Islamist extremists wage a propaganda war against the West.[28]According to Peter Clarke who was then serving as the Head of the Metropolitan Police counter-terrorism operations: 'It was the first virtual conspiracy to murder that we have seen.'[29]

Tsouli's capture led to the arrest of several Islamic terrorists around the world, including 17 men in Canada and 2 in the US as well as associates in the UK. His 10-year jail sentence was later increased to 16 years.

The Internet has also been used as a platform for communication, both overt and covert, as well as to profile potential candidates for radicalisation and recruitment. Additionally, it has served as a tool for command and control as well as to provide training, and has also been utilised for fund raising purposes. The terrorist use of the Internet can be broadly divided into five distinct areas: target selection, recruitment, information operations, psychological operations and fund raising, all of which are interrelated and will be examined in turn.

TARGET SELECTION

The Internet is used by terrorists to gather information on potential targets.[30] Terrorist targets can fall into one of three broad categories. First, the enemy, which from the terrorist perspective is any individual or organisation

26 *Daily Mail*, 'British Muslim computer geek, son of diplomat, revealed as al Qaeda's top cyber terrorist', 16 January 2008. [Online]. Available at: http://www.dailymail.co.uk/news/article-508543/British-Muslim-geek-son-diplomat-revealed-al-Qaedas-cyber-terrorist.html [accessed: 15 January 2011].

27 "Irhabi 007" combines the James Bond reference with the Arabic for terrorist.

28 Videos he posted included messages from Osama bin Laden and images of the kidnapping and murder of hostages in Iraq such as American Nick Berg. *Daily Mail*, 'British Muslim computer geek'.

29 Ibid.

30 D. Brown, J. Dalton and H. Hoyle, 'Spatial forecast methods for terrorist events in urban environments' (2004) 3073 *Intelligence and Security Informatics* 426.

operating in the counter-terrorism community, as well as the wider community considered to be *dar-al-harb*. Second, the targeting of potential new recruits and third, supporters of their cause with an emphasis on those who will provide financial support.

All three categories are inter-dependent and interrelated, therefore each category needs to be examined individually in turn. In terms of 'enemy targeting', the website operated by the Muslim Hackers Club reportedly featured links to sites in the United States that purport to disclose sensitive information such as code names and radio frequencies used by the United States Secret Service. The same website also serves as an education and training site by offering Internet specific crime tutorials to include the use of viruses and hacking techniques.[31]

In addition, free generic imaging software such as Google Earth, available to anyone with an Internet connection, can also allow terrorists to view counter-terrorist activities at a target site. An al-Qaeda computer seized in Afghanistan contained engineering and structural architecture features of a dam, enabling al-Qaeda engineers and planners to simulate catastrophic failures.[32] The usefulness of such imaging software cannot be overstated in that it allows terrorists to conduct a detailed reconnaissance exercise without the need to physically be at the location. Tracing the route of their activity is particularly difficult.

The relevance to terrorism and terrorism finance is that it eliminates the need for terrorists to physically conduct reconnaissance, which is not only reduces the risk of being compromised drastically, but also cuts down on the operational cost of a terrorist attack. The Internet provides terrorists a place to plan without the risks normally associated with cell or satellite phones. The Internet can also be used to construct profiles to identify potential recruits and donors.[33]

RECRUITMENT

Images and video clips serve terrorist organisations as tools of empowerment, which can lead to radicalisation of the viewer, which in turn may lead to recruitment into the terrorist organisation. Individuals with sympathy for a

31 M. Hosenball, 'Islamic Cyberterror,' *Newsweek*, 20 May 2002.
32 B. Gellman, 'FBI Fears Al-Qaeda Cyber Attacks' *San Francisco Chronicle*, 28 June 2002, 1–10.
33 Brown et al.

cause can be converted by the images and messages of terrorist organisations, and the addition of digital video has reinforced this ability. There is also evidence to suggest that Internet chat rooms are virtual meeting points for individuals to come together not only to enrol in the cause, and be further radicalised and recruited into the terrorist organisation.

The Internet provides a truly global reach in that a terrorist recruiter is able to communicate with potential recruits irrespective of location. In addition, this global reach is further strengthened by technology in that the challenge of languages can also be overcome through web browsers, including Netscape and Internet Explorer. Current versions support JavaScript functions allowing Internet servers to know which language is set as the default for a particular client's computer. Hence, a browser set to use English as the default language can be redirected to a site optimised for publicity aimed at Western audiences, while one set to use Arabic as the default can be redirected to a different site tailored toward Arab or Muslim sensibilities. This allows recruiting to be audience and language-specific, enabling the web to serve as a recruiter of talent for a terrorist cause.

INFORMATION AND PSYCHOLOGICAL OPERATIONS

Information Operations, also known in its abbreviated form as Info Ops, may be defined as the use and management of information in pursuit of competitive advantage over an opponent. It may involve the collection of tactical information, validation, dissemination of propaganda, as well as disinformation. According to an al-Qaeda training manual recovered in Afghanistan in 2003:

> *Using public sources openly and without resorting to illegal means, it is possible to gather at least 80 per cent of all information required about the enemy.*[34]

The Internet may also be used for disinformation purposes in that benign threats may be deliberately posted on the Internet or disseminated via cell phones to mislead law-enforcement officials. Info Ops is closely related to Psychological Operations, also known as Psy Ops. The latter aims to influence a target audience's value systems, belief systems, emotions, motives, reasoning, or behaviour. Psy Ops is also sometimes referred to as Political Warfare, Hearts and Minds, and Propaganda.

34 *Inside Defense* "Citing Al Qaeda Manual, Rumsfeld Re-Emphasises Web Security" 15 January 2009. [Online]. Available at: http://www.insidedefense.com [accessed: 15 January 2011].

One example of the use of the Internet for the purpose of Psy Ops occurred immediately after 9/11, when al-Qaeda operatives used the Internet to fight for the hearts and minds of Muslims around the globe. Al-Qaeda used two websites, alneda.com and drasat.com, to discuss the legality of the attacks on 9/11. The websites were used to justify the attacks and to gain support as well as to attempt to discredit any opposition. For example, several internationally recognised and respected Muslims who questioned the attacks were criticised as being hypocrites. The websites argued that Islam shares no fundamental values with the West and that Muslims are committed to spreading Islam by the sword. As a result of the commentary, several Muslim critics of al-Qaeda were silenced and withdrew their prior condemnation.[35]

Militant Islam justifies its actions by portraying its attacks not as an unprovoked act of terrorism on innocent people, but as a war with collateral damage as a result of a counter-attack of an ongoing war between the Western world and the Islamic World. The same argument has been applied to every subsequent attack since 9/11. The reality is that the perception of the clash of cultures is largely exaggerated in an attempt to bring Islam to war with the West. To take the bait, as the Bush administration did so wholeheartedly, is unfortunate, as this has the effect of playing directly into the hands of militant Islam. Instead, such simplistic perceptions should be challenged at an intellectual level, not only by non-Muslims, but by Muslims who also share this view. As such, the involvement of independent Muslim scholars and other 'thinking' Muslim men and women are essential. It is a concern that existing counter measures to combat al-Qaeda's philosophies seem inadequately challenged in the cyber environment.

Cultural differences clearly exist around the globe. Equally, cultural differences exist within a single country and even within different organisations in a single town. In many ways it is human nature to be tribal. However, this does not mean that warfare is the answer to resolving any possible difference in opinion. A civilised society should have the ability to resolve its differences in ways other than warfare. At a fundamental level human beings are not dissimilar. Their needs are essentially the same irrespective of race, culture, sexual orientation or class. As Maslow's theory of the hierarchy of human needs[36] suggest, the need for physical survival is followed by economic survival.

35 P. Eedle, 'Al-Qaeda takes fight for 'hearts and minds' to the Web", (2002) *Jane's Intelligence Review*, 5 August 2002.

36 One of the best-known theories explaining the actions of people is that of Dr Abraham Maslow. See A. Maslow, "Motivation and Personality" (Harper and Row 1954). Dr Maslow hypothesised that people are motivated by a hierarchy of needs. The hierarchy he described

Once these basic needs are met, mankind is motivated by higher needs that are related to social success and self-actualisation. Equally, negative experiences that lead to anger include the sense of injustice and humiliation. Instead of focusing on the differences, if the similarities can be explored further, this will undoubtedly lead to the realisation that the militant Islamic representation of the two enemies is simply not a reality.

As previously mentioned, the survival of any individual or organisation depends upon the ability to sustain itself economically, which requires funding. As finance is so key to its survival, terrorist organisations apply numerous methods to raise funds to be able to operate.

FUND RAISING

Information operations and psychological operations are relevant to terrorist funding is that both are used to persuade potential donors to support their cause by providing financial support.[37] The application of psychological tactics to obtain funding has also been recognised. There is evidence that the Internet has played a key role in the fundraising for terrorist organisations. Websites are used which give the appearance of legitimacy to deceive the donor into giving money for what they believe to be a humanitarian cause. These donors are frequently unaware that they are funding terrorism.

In other cases, the 'humanitarian' card continues to be played, but for the purpose of justifying '*jihad*'. Such websites are typically looking to raise funding for a humanitarian cause, such as for the victims of conflict in regions such as Chechnya, Afghanistan and Bosnia or simply for the promotion of Islam. The website usually states that it desires to do so by peaceful means. Supporters are encouraged to assist the effort either through monetary support, scholarly verdicts, encouraging others to support *jihad*, or a combination of all three. Relevant bank account information is provided on the website in order that

---

may be drawn as follows: 1. Physiological (physical survival such as needs, food, water, sleep, warmth). 2. Safety (the need for safety such as physical safety, economic security, freedom from threats, comfort and peace). 3. Social (Social needs such as acceptance, group membership, affection). 4. Self-esteem (the need for self esteem such as recognition of strength, intelligence, prestige and status). 5. Self-actualisation (opportunities for innovation and creativity and learning at a high level).

37 L. Valeri and M. Knights, 'Affecting trust: Terrorism, internet and offensive information warfare' (2000) 12(1) *Terrorism and Political Violence* 15.

online donations can be made easily. One such example is the German site, www.explizit-islam.de, which continues to operate to this day.[38]

The Internet has also been used to profile potential donors. Internet user demographics enable terrorists to target users with sympathy toward a cause or issue, and to solicit donations if the right 'profile' is found. Usually a front group will perform the fundraising for the terrorist, often unwittingly.[39] In addition, portals offering anonymous fund transfers frequently provide other services to terrorists such as the issue of new identities and official passports which take 'fund raising' into a criminal dimension.[40] Terrorists have also been known to fund their activities through the Internet via credit card fraud. According to one of France's anti-terrorism investigators, Jean-François Ricard, many Islamist terror plots in Europe and North America were financed through such criminal activity.[41]

ANONYMITY

Anonymity is a key requirement for those involved in any criminal activity, terrorist or otherwise.[42] The Internet offers a number of ways in which the identity of the communicator can be kept anonymous. For example, speech compression technology allows users to convert a computer into a secure phone device and network accounts can be deleted or changed as required. In addition, anonymous logins are possible for many of the thousands of chat rooms on the net. If desired, the user can access cyber cafes, university and library computers, or additional external resources to further hide the source of the messages.[43]

The Internet can also be used to send hidden messages. The practice of steganography involves hiding messages inside graphic files, and is widespread among criminal and terrorist elements. Hidden pages or nonsensical phrases can be coded instructions for al-Qaeda operatives and supporters. For example, al-Qaeda frequently uses prearranged phrases and symbols to direct its agents. An icon of an AK-47 can appear next to a photo of Osama bin Laden facing one

38 *FBIS* (2009) 'Sunni Extremist Group Hizb al-Tahrir Promotes Ideology on the Internet', 5 February 2002 available at http://199.221.15.211.

39 P.S. Tibbetts, 'Terrorist Use of the Internet and Related Information Technologies', School of Advanced Military Studies, Fort Leavenworth, Kansas, June 2002, 20.

40 C.E. Manin, 'Terrorism and Information Communication Technology' *La Tribune*, April 2002, 112.

41 M. Elliot, 'Reeling Them In' *Time*, 23 September 2002, 33.

42 Valeri and Knights, 'Affecting trust' 15.

43 Tibbetts, 'Terrorist Use of the Internet and Related Information Technologies', 7.

direction one day, and another direction the next. The colour of icons can also be changed to signify command for action. In addition, messages may be hidden on pages inside sites with no links attached to them, or alternatively placed openly in chat rooms.[44] Encryption is another way is another cost effective way in which a message can be anonymous. Al-Qaeda's use of PGP[45] to encrypt its messages is well documented.

TERRORISM AND THE INTERNET: CONCLUSION

One significant enabler of globalisation has been the Internet and the rapid expansion of cyber space. Although the Internet has been a target of terrorist attack by al-Qaeda, it also serves as an invaluable tool to carry out a wide variety of functions to enable terrorist activity. In addition, the Internet has helped to unite militant Islamists from around the globe in terms of the ideology as well in practical terms. The role of the Internet together with other technological advancements has been vital in enabling anonymous communication between terrorists, aided recruitment through global chat rooms, encouraged the sharing of knowledge, as well as playing a significant role in the spreading of propaganda and serving as a vehicle to raise and transfer funds, without which it could not operate.

In order to counter the threat from the terrorist phenomenon al-Qaeda, a full appreciation of the ways in which cyberspace is utilised is essential. The extent of the use of the Internet is such that to some, the task at hand may seem daunting. However, for every known problem, there is a solution. At the root of the al-Qaeda ideology is the concept of justice built on the perception of injustice and the existence of a war between Muslims and non-Muslims. This is essential in justifying its actions and is fundamental to its continued existence. The reality is that the world is not black and white. However, such simplistic interpretations of complexity of real life can be marketed in a way that is appealing to young Muslim men and women looking for a purpose and an outlet for everyday frustrations exacerbated by observations of various injustices around the world.

44 M.T. Welch, 'Accumulating Digital Evidence is Difficult' *The Post Standard*, 11 September 2002, 9.

45 304th MI Bn OSINT Team (2008) 'Pretty Good Privacy (PGP)', supplemental to the 304th MI Bn *Periodic Newsletter* 'Al Qaeda-Like Security and Communications Guidance', 9 June 2008. [Online]. Available at: http:// www.orgsites.com/va/asis151/AQ_like_security_guidance2%5B1%5D.pdf [accessed: 25 May 2011].

The simplistic ideology becomes particularly attractive if the target audience do not have the benefit of a rounded education that enables them to hear and understand both sides of the argument making them susceptible to indoctrination. The Internet exacerbates the problem by further exploiting and galvanizing existing prejudices and misconceptions. In addition, search engines and Internet chat rooms are able to seek out vulnerable targets and manipulate undeveloped minds by providing one sided arguments to give the illusion of purpose and justice. In reality, the doctrine does not have the interest of the individual looking for answers but merely wishes to absorb that individual into its own network for its own purpose. The use of religion has also served as a powerful tool in capturing its potential pray, a technique used by numerous organisations not exclusive to terrorist organisations to attract, recruit and retain the pawns of that organisation.

As such, attempts must be made to provide a counter argument for dogmatic statements made that do not reflect the truth. At the same time, an attempt must be made not to give a counter view that is also guilty of 'Western' indoctrination. A balanced view is what is required. The greatest gift we have is free will. The greatest weapon against indoctrination is to sow the seed of doubt so that an individual is able to form a balanced opinion and choose what he or she knows to be right on the basis of truth as opposed to propaganda. If Internet technologies can be used effectively to this end, there may be a chance that the threat from militant Islam may be mitigated.

The increase in the importance of the role that the Internet plays in terrorism at various levels is such that it is necessary to assess the efficacy of the law in tackling e-crime. As the proceeding sections will highlight, numerous challenges exist in relation to tacking e-crime.

E-Crime and the Law

The international nature of e-crime inevitably leads to certain conflicts of the law. To begin with, the definition of crimes, or their key elements, may vary dependent on jurisdiction.[46] The inconsistency of substantive laws may also be accompanied by differences between investigative techniques, which are also governed by national or local law. Furthermore, differing societal views as to

46 Tyler Moore, Richard Clayton and Ross Anderson, 'The economics of online crime' (2009) 23(3) *Journal of Economic Perspectives* 3.

what constitutes 'criminal' behaviour, as well as the perception of the extent of the 'seriousness' of that crime, may prove to be problematic.[47]

In addition, a number of practical challenges exist. For example, where the location of the alleged perpetrator is in a different country to that of the victim, there may be difficulty in attempting to establish the identity of the wrongdoer and of obtaining enough evidence to support a conviction. The art and process of pursuit can be further complicated by other matters such as the rapid pace of technological change which can present the e-criminal with an advantage. The reactive nature of law enforcement inevitably results in a game of 'catch up' as in-house technological expertise and resources take time to come up to speed.[48] In addition, legislative bodies also require time to create new laws or to adapt the existing law to clear a path for the prosecution of the new e-criminal activities.[49] As Yee Fem Lim observes:

> *The communication of a hacker or other criminal may pass through as many as a dozen (or more) different types of carriers, each with different technologies (for example, local telephone companies, long-distance carriers, Internet service providers (ISPs), and wireless and satellite networks). The communications must also pass through carriers in a number of different countries, each in different time zones and subject to different legal systems. Indeed, each of these complications may exist within a single transmission. The phenomenon makes more difficult (and sometimes impossible) to track criminals who are technologically savvy enough to hide their location and identity.*[50]

It should also be recognised that investigative techniques such as the forensic examination of cellular phone records and physical tracking through telephonic means may well come into conflict with the laws of privacy and be subject to legal challenge. Moreover, jurisdictional problems can arise where, for example, the investigations relate to communications on a satellite-based network where the earth based gateways are located in another country. In such a situation, the information sought by the investigators, such as the content of

47 Steven Philippsohn, 'The dangers of new technology-laundering on the Internet' (2001) 5(1) *Journal of Money Laundering Control* 87.

48 A recent study, commissioned by the all party e-commerce lobby group, EURIM, reported that there is a huge backlog of e-crimes and a serious shortage of skills to deal with them. See 'Police need more e-Crime skills' *BBC online*. [Online]. Available at: http:/news.bbc.co.uk/go/pr/fr/-/1/hi/technology/3725305.stm [accessed: 2 February 2010].

49 Paul Hunton, 'The stages of cybercrime investigations: bridging the gap between technology examination and law enforcement investigation' (2011) 27(1) *Computer Law & Security Review* 61.

50 Yee Fen Lim, *Cyberspace Law: Commentaries and Materials* (Oxford University Press 2002) 26.

the communications and the identities of the callers and the recipients, together with the rules and procedures concerned with access to and seizure of it, will often be governed by that county's laws.[51]

Data preservation and retention is another issue. Traffic data, which can be defined as 'any data possessed for the purpose of the conveyance of a communication on an electronic communications network',[52] may be crucial to an e-criminal investigation. However, it is possible that the relevant ISP's system may not generate such information. Even if it does, that information may either not be recorded by the system, or may only be retained for a short period of time. The legal powers relating to the access and scrutiny of such data will be considered in more detail later. In the meantime, it should be noted that in English law, there is a general, statutory rule that 'personal data processed for any purpose or purposes shall not be kept for longer than is necessary for that purpose or purposes'.[53]

Furthermore, the Regulation of Investigatory Powers Act (RIPA) 2000 did not impose a duty upon communication providers to retain communications data. However, it did empower senior officers to require disclosure of it in the interests of the detection and prosecution of crime. It might also be noted that, in the aftermath of 9/11, the Home Secretary was given the power to draw up a code of practice which specifies periods of time during which communications providers can be required to retain communication data.[54]

Jurisdiction

Given that crimes will often involve trans-border data flow and be extra-territorial in nature, some difficult jurisdictional issues may arise. The e-criminal is not restricted by national or international boundaries, which in fact may serve more as an advantage, rather than a disadvantage. One advantage is that the cyber environment offers a greater global reach of potential victims in terms of both geographical coverage and volume. Technology also enables the criminal to maintain physical distance from his or her victims as well as maintaining relative anonymity, making detection more challenging.[55]

51 Charles Wild, Stuart Weinstein and Neil MacEwan, *Internet Law* (Old Bailey Press 2005) 186.
52 Article 2(b) Communications Data Privacy Directive 2002/58/EC.
53 The Fifth Data Principle, as stated in Sch 1 Data Protection Act 1998.
54 Anti-terrorism, Crime and Security Act 2001, s102.
55 Hunton, 'The stages of cybercrime investigations' (n.49).

Even once the location of the e-criminal has been discovered, this may simply mark the first significant step on the investigative trail, as the necessary evidence of the e-criminal activity may sit in a separate remote location. If the data is, in fact, found to be stored locally or nationally, then the investigation may have little difficulty in obtaining and executing a search warrant. However, if this is not the case, the legitimacy of such a warrant may be questioned in another jurisdiction. Furthermore, it must not be forgotten than in countries which have a federal structure, such as the US, the laws of states may be different in respect of the alleged e-criminal activity. For example, the online behaviour in question may be criminal in one state but not in another where the investigative trail leads to. Alternatively, the laws of that other state may prohibit the trans-border execution of a search warrant, requiring instead that the warrant be sought in the courts of the state, or district, where it is intended to be executed.

In recognition of this issue, the Law Commission proposed in 1989 that the concept of joint jurisdiction be woven into the statutory fabric of the then forthcoming Computer Misuse Act 1990.[56] This recommendation was accepted and the territorial scope of the offences under the Act was duly addressed in ss4 and 5. In essence, the legislation states that any jurisdictional claim must be based upon proof of a 'significant link' with domestic jurisdiction. For the purpose of an offence under s1 of the Act,[57] a domestic court will establish jurisdiction if the accused was in the home country when he caused the computer to perform the criminal function, or alternatively, if the computer to which he or she secured, or intended to secure unauthorised access was in the home country. For the purposes of an offence under s3 of the Act,[58] the 'significant link' with domestic jurisdiction will be established either where the accused was in the home country when the act which caused the authorised modification of the computer material, or where the unauthorised modification itself took place on a computer in the home country. Thus, in essence, jurisdiction will be established when either the accused or the victim computer was located in England or Wales at the time of the alleged criminal activity.[59]

The criteria for claiming jurisdiction in relation to an s2 offence, that of hacking with intent to commit or facilitate the commission of further offences are somewhat more complex. The Act[60] states that a domestic court may claim

56 See Law Commission Report No 186 (1989) para 4.2.

57 A basic hacking offence.

58 The offence of unauthorised modification of computer programmes or data.

59 Computer Misuse Act 1990. [Online]. Available at: http://www.legislation.gov.uk/ukpga/1990/18/contents [accessed: 1 December 2010]. See also Wild et al., *Internet Law*, (n.17) 188.

60 Computer Misuse Act 1990.

jurisdiction in any of the following three circumstances. First, where all aspects of the conduct take place in the country. Second, where the further offence referred to in s2 is intended to take place in this country.[61] Third, where the 'significant link' requirement can be established[62] and further, intended offence(s) will be committed (either wholly or in part) in another country (or countries), and as such conduct would be an offence under the law in that other country (or countries).

The territorial scope of inchoate offences related to the offences in the Act is detailed in ss6 and 7. Offences such as computer fraud or computer forgery, which are not attacking the integrity of systems but, instead, are using computer technology as a means to achieve specific criminal ends, are covered by Part1 Criminal Justice Act 1993.[63] The Council of Europe's Convention on Cybercrime[64] contains similar jurisdictional provisions. Therein, art. 22 provides that a member state will have jurisdiction in respect of offences committed within its territory, or in respect of offences committed by any of its nationals outside its territory where the conduct is criminal in the place where it is committed, or in the event that the offence is committed outside the jurisdiction of any state.

Given that the e-criminal activity will often be international, its investigation will regularly involve liaison between, and the mutual assistance of, law enforcement agencies from different nations.[65] This is facilitated by the Criminal (International Cooperation) Act 2003. In addition, the Convention on Cybercrime promotes general principles relating to 'international cooperation'. Naturally, even when the investigators have gathered sufficient evidence for a prosecution, jurisdiction may have to be claimed and, if the suspected e-criminal is abroad, a request for his extradition put before the courts. In order to succeed in an extradition procedure, the applicant must establish that the accused's actions amounted to a criminal offence of sufficient seriousness in both jurisdictions. This is sometimes referred to as the 'double criminality' principle. Under s2 Extradition Act 1989, the offence must be punishable by a minimum of 12 months' imprisonment.

61 Note that here there is no need to establish the usual 'significant link' requirement for the unauthorised access component of the offence. See also s4(3).

62 See s5(2).

63 Under s2(3), jurisdiction can be claimed in the light of a 'relevant event' occurring in England and Wales. Under s2(1), a 'relevant event' is defined as 'any act or mission or other event (including any result of one or more acts or omissions), proof of which is required for conviction of offences.

64 Council of Europe, Convention on Cybercrime, Budapest, 23.XI.2001. [Online]. Available at: http://conventions.Coe.int/Treaty/en/Treaties/Html/185.htm [accessed: 1 December 2010].

65 Hunton, 'The stages of cybercrime investigations' (n.49).

This requirement is mirrored within the Council of Europe's Convention on Cyber-crime.[66] Therein, art. 24 states that extradition should be made available for any of the offences established under the Convention, as long as a custodial sentence of at least one year could be imposed in both of the relevant states.

R v Governor of Brixton Prison, Ex parte Levin,[67] although unrelated to terrorism, serves as a good illustration as to some of the jurisdictional and extraditional issues which can arise in e-criminal cases. The accused, a Russian national located in St Petersburg, used his skills as a computer programmer to gain unauthorised access to the computer of a bank located in the US and to divert funds from that bank's customer accounts to accounts controlled by his accomplice at another US bank. However, the scheme was discovered and the relevant accounts were frozen. At the request of the US government, the accused was arrested and detained in England.[68] At the committal hearing, the magistrate found that the US government had made out a prima facie case on 666 criminal charges, including theft, false accounting, forgery, unauthorised access to a computer and unauthorised modification of computer material. Consequently, he ordered that the accused be committed to custody to await extradition.[69]

The accused applied for a writ of *habeas corpus* on the principal ground that the records of the instructions and transfers contained in the computer printouts were hearsay evidence and, therefore, not admissible. His council also argued that one of the offences cited by the extradition applicant had not been committed, in the light of the decision on *R v Gold*.[70] In addition, the jurisdictional claim was challenged. Levin's council claimed that the criminal activity had occurred in Russia, not in the US. Specifically, it was argued that the fraudulent transfers were instigated when Levin pressed the keys on his computer keyboard in St Petersburg and that therefore, Russian law applied. In response, it was argued that the place where the changes to the data occurred was the Citibank computer in Parsipenny, US. This argument was accepted by the court, based on the reasoning that the effects upon the data at the US bank when Levin pressed his keyboard in Russia were instantaneous. Beldam LJ explained that:

66 Council of Europe, Convention on Cybercrime (n.64).
67 *Regina v Governor of Brixton Prison, Ex parte Levin* [1997] Crim LR 891; [1997] 3 All ER 289; [1997] 3 WLR 117; [1998] 1 Cr App Rep 22; [1997] UKHL 27; [1997] AC 741.
68 In execution of a warrant under s1(3) Extradition Act 1989.
69 Wild et al., *Internet Law* (n.51) 189.
70 [1988] 2 WLR 812 (HL).

> *The applicant's keyboard was connected electronically with the Citibank computer in Parsipenny; as he pressed the keys, his actions, as he intended, recorded or stored information, for all practical purposes, simultaneously on the magnetic disc in the computer. That is where the instrument was created and where the act constituting the offence was done.*[71]

The Divisional Court dismissed the application, confirming that the magistrate had rightly committed Levin to custody to await extradition to the US.[72] However, Citibank was only able to recover $240,000 of the $10.7 million worth of illegally transferred funds and the consequences for Citibank's business reputation were considerable.[73] However, many have evaded detection and punishment.[74] As such, it is of paramount importance that the necessary evidence can be collected and presented in order that a successful prosecution can take place.

Evidence

By its very nature, electronic data is vulnerable as it can be destroyed, deleted or modified with ease. As such, the task of gathering evidence on e-crimes is more complex than it may initially appear. The data must not only be retrieved, but must be preserved before and after retrieval. The authenticity and cogency of that evidence must then be established. A further challenge is that electronic evidence will often include both the details of the core criminal activity as well as the informational records of communications, which may complicate its status as 'evidence' in court.[75]

The dramatic development of Internet and communication technologies (ICTs) in recent years has prompted governments and legislatures to reassess the legal powers relating to the interception of electronic communications.

71 *R v Gold* [1988] 2 WLR 812 (HL).

72 Wild et al., *Internet Law* (n.51) 190.

73 Russell G. Smith, 'Cross-Border Economic Crime: The Agenda for Reform' (2001) Australian Institute of Criminology: Trends and Issues in Crime and Criminal Justice 202. [Online]. Available at: http://www.aic.gov.au/documents/5/6/E/%7B56E66958-05A3-4C6D-9048-64D5FB7B9175%7Dti202.pdf [accessed: 7 July 2011].

74 R.G. Smith, M.N. Holmes and P. Kaufmann, 'Nigerian advance fee fraud', (1999) Australian Institute of Criminology: Trends and Issues in Crime and Criminal Justice, 121. See also Smith (n.73).

75 Hunton, 'The stages of cybercrime investigations' (n.49) 61.

In the UK, the RIPA 2000[76] empowered the Secretary of State to authorise the interception of communications where he or she considers it to be necessary for any of the following reasons. First, if it is in the interests of national security, second, if it is for the purpose of preventing or detecting serious crime, third, for the purpose of safeguarding the economic well-being in the UK, or finally, its purpose is to give effect to international mutual assistance agreements in connection with the prevention or detection of serious crime.

The Act[77] recognised the differences between voice and data traffic. In a report produced for the Home Office, the increasing diversity in the range of technologies being used for access to the Internet had been noted. It was also pointed out that 'a selected subscriber will utilise Internet services, such as a single email account, using multiple access technologies.[78] Moreover, the report referred to a number of anonymous communications services which subscribers could exploit to access Internet services, such as pre-pay mobile phones and Internet cafes. In the light of these facts, it was recommended that interception would be cheaper, more straightforward and more effective at the premises of the ISPs.

Consequently, s12 (1) of the Act provides that the Secretary of State may place obligations on, amongst others, ISPs to assist with interception warrants. Furthermore, under the Regulation of Investigatory Powers (Maintenance of Interception Capability) Order 2002, the Secretary of State may require those companies which provide a telecommunications service to more than 10,000 customers to maintain a capability to intercept communications.[79] In addition to, or instead of, actual interception of electronic communications, investigators may seek to access the data which flows from them. As previously noted, RIPA 2000[80] empowers a senior police officer to require a communications provider to disclose any communications data in its possession in the interests of the prevention and detection of crime. The term 'communications data' includes both traffic and location data but not, it seems, the content of any communication.

76 Which replaced the Interception of Communications Act 1985.
77 Investigatory Powers Act 2000.
78 Home Office, *The Technical and Cost Issues Associated with Interception of Communication at Certain Communications Service Providers*. [Online]. Available at: http://www.homeoffice.gov.uk/oicd/techcost.pdf [accessed: 2 February 2010].
79 Wild et al., *Internet Law* (n.51) 191–2.
80 RIPA 2000, S12.

Encryption is another issue which has caught the legislative eye. Encryption can be used by e-criminals to conceal their communications. Its attraction is that even if the encrypted communication is intercepted, it cannot be understood unless, or until it is deciphered. However, s49 RIPA 2000 does provide for the imposition of discloser requirements upon owners of encryption keys or any third parties to hold copies of them. Furthermore, where an encrypted message has been unlawfully intercepted, a person can only be required to disclose the cryptographic key[81] under the following circumstances.

First, where there are reasonable grounds for believing that a key to the protected information is in their possession. Second, that the forced disclosure is necessary in the interests of national security. Third, for the purpose of preventing or detecting crime. Fourth, in the interests of economic well-being of the UK and fifth, for the purpose of ensuring that public authorities effectively exercise their statutory powers or properly perform their statutory duties that such an imposition is proportionate to what is south to be achieved by it; and that it is not otherwise reasonably practical to obtain possession of the encrypted information in an intelligible form.[82] A further challenge as to what data can be presented as evidence in court relates to the debate concerning the tensions between the effective detection of crime and the protection of personal privacy.[83]

The balance to be struck between these two important positions is simply one of the many legislative challenges of the electronic age. However, once the investigations of e-crime have successfully obtained legal permission to access and seize potential evidence, it can then be scrutinised through the use of computer forensics.[84] Computer forensics is a highly specialist subject. However, some basic insight into the processes as well as the challenges is helpful.

---

81 Or a copy of the information in decrypted format.

82 See also Policing and Crime Act 2009 (c. 26), ss. 112, 116, Sch. 7 para.; Serious Organised Crime and Police Act 2005 (c. 15), ss. 59, 178; The Police, Public Order and Criminal Justice (Scotland) Act 2006 (Consequential Provisions and Modifications) Order 2007 (S.I. 2007/1098), arts. 1(3), 6, Sch. para. 4(8) and Serious Crime Act 2007 (c. 27), ss. 88, 94, Sch. 12 para. 19; S.I. 2008/219, art. 2(b).

83 Fletcher N. Baldwin Jr., 'The rule of law, human rights and proportionality as components of the war against terrorism: is the US judiciary in self-imposed exile?' (2004) 7(3) *Journal of Money Laundering Control* 218.

84 The rules governing the granting, service and exercise of search warrants are found in the Police and Criminal Evidence Act 1984, the Computer Misuse Act 1990, Copyright, Design and the Patents Act 1988.

Computer Forensics

Computer forensics plays a key part in the evidence relating to e-crime. There are several common computer forensic techniques. First, the computer hardware must be seized.[85] Next, the computer itself should be photographed in situ, the cabling and any separate, and external means of data storage must be accurately labelled. Computers that are running at the time of the raid must be safely shut down, and the time at which this happens[86] must be separately logged. Finally, an exact copy[87] must be made of every hard disc.

This is referred to as 'legal imaging', which is a process whereby the computer is booted from the floppy drive with a minimal, simple operating system. That system has drivers which instruct the computer to recognise an external storage device. The image which is recoded on the external device is an exact replica of the computer's hard disc(s). However, one of the real benefits of the process is that it records not only those files which would usually be visible on the computer but also those parts of the disk(s) which hold other useful information, such as file names/sizes and date/time stamps.[88]

In addition, other revealing pieces of information can be recovered from the 'bit copy', such as fragments of previously deleted files. Subsequently, attempts to reconstruct such documents can be made. Furthermore, deleted files can be recovered by simply 'undeleting' files thanks to modern computer operating systems which have built-in safety facilities to guard against accidental deletion. This means that although a file may have been marked for deletion, the contents of it will not disappear until the specific, spatial area which it occupied has been taken up by newer files.[89]

Clearly, such evidence-gathering operations can be more problematic where the investigation leads to corporate premises. In a large company there will usually be many computers which are extensively networked, either within specific localities of the organisation and/or across the company as a whole. The potential ramifications of seizing computer equipment in these circumstances are more serious and wide-ranging as employees, customers and creditors may

85 Joseph Migga Kizza, 'Computer crime investigations: computer forensics' (2010) 978 *Computer Science* 263.

86 As recorded by the computer's internal clock.

87 It is usual practice for two copies to be made, with one acting as a control.

88 Bhanu Prakash Battula, Kezia Rani, Satya Prasad and T. Sudha, 'Techniques in computer forensics: a recovery perspective' (2009) 3(2) *International Journal of Security* 27.

89 Wild, Weinstein Neil MacEwan, *Internet Law* 194–5.

all be affected.[90] Indeed, depending upon the nature and scale of the seizure, the whole business could be stopped in its commercial tracks. In such a situation, the investigators may, instead, seek out an individual who works in that organisation, who is beyond suspicion and has sufficient technical knowledge of the computer system to assist with the 'imaging' process.

In addition, if, as is often the case in e-criminal investigations, some of the evidence is Internet-based, it could be stored either on the suspect's computer(s) or at remote sites.[91] Consequently, differing forensic techniques may have to be used. In addition to the suspect's own computer, potential sources of the evidence would include the communications data records of his or her chosen ISP, data held at remote sites, as well as the dialling data kept at the telephone company.[92] Furthermore, personal computers hold files which record Internet activity. Examples include files which log incoming and outgoing email, subscriptions to newsgroups and, possibly, access to Internet Relay Chat (IRC) sessions.[93]

In addition, computers 'cache' recently used data in case it needs to be reused again in the short term. This is a particularly useful process when used in relation to the Internet as the cache files store copies of websites as they are visited. These files are often retained for weeks or months afterwards. Consequently, time is saved as a webpage can be retrieved from the Internet browser cache file without the need to revisit the website itself. This in turn means that traffic on the Internet is reduced.

The advantage given to investigators through this process is that some browsers and specialist software can be used to view cache files and also associated 'history' files which retain some date-and-time information. Thus, it is possible to determine what the users of a specific computer have been viewing and, to a limited extent and after careful interpretation, when.[94] Despite the various techniques computer forensic experts can utilise to obtain evidence, the evidence is meaningless unless it can be used effectively to achieve a conviction in a court of law. As such, the way in which the evidence is presented in court is of vital importance.

90 Battula et al., 'Techniques in computer' (n.88) 27.
91 Hunton, 'The stages of cybercrime investigations' (n.49) 61.
92 Wild et al., *Internet Law* (n.51) 195.
93 It should be noted, however, that these types of files can be deleted by the user.
94 P. Sommer, *Digital Footprints: Assessing Computer Evidence: Cyberspace Crime* (Ashgate 2003) 545.

Presentation of E-Crime Evidence in Court

The presentation of e-crime evidence in court may be problematic for several reasons. The first challenge is with reference to difficulties which have flowed from the interpretation of the aforementioned term 'communications data' within s22 RIPA 2000. The Home Office has stated that:

> *It is important to identify what communication data does include, both equally important to be clear about what it does not include. The term communications data does not include the content of any communication.*[95]

This distinction has also been made in the piece of legislation which RIPA 2000 replaced.[96] The significance is that the content of communications can only be used for investigative purposes and is not admissible in court. This legal distinction is not readily found in other jurisdictions which are similar to that of the UK. A further, practical problem arises when it comes to Internet-based communications. In the digital world, the technical means for collecting both forms of data, either 'communication' or 'content' are often the same. As such, separating the two from each other can sometimes be difficult.[97]

Even where the investigators are confident that they have uncovered enough evidence for a conviction, a final hurdle which the prosecuting authorities may encounter is the lack of understanding of IT within the courts system.[98] Some real problems concerning practice and procedure in the courts and the police service for dealing with computer evidence were identified by the Computer Evidence Task Group.[99] It found that criminal courts are generally unfamiliar with the subject of computer evidence and regularly underestimate the technical complexity of cases that involve it.

It was also reported that the mishandling of computer evidence 'quite frequently' leads to prosecutions having to be abandoned. It is perhaps for these reasons, together with those discussed above relating to the task of gathering evidence of e-crimes; that the following has been said:

---

95 The Home Office, *Consultation Paper on a Code of Practice for Voluntary Retention of Communications Data*, March 2003.

96 Interception of Communications Act 1985.

97 Wild et al., *Internet Law* (n.51) 196–7.

98 Hunton, 'The stages of cybercrime investigations' (n.49) 61.

99 Sommer, *Digital Footprints* 549.

> *Most successful prosecutions rely on more than one stream of computer-derived evidence. What is needed is a multiplicity of independent streams of evidence, both computer ad non-computer derived, which corroborate each other. Any single stream may fail, either because of intrinsic inadequacy or because the courts find it too difficult to understand.*[100]

Although in these situations, a subject matter expert is usually called upon as an 'expert witness', there are several concerns relating to the way in which experts are utilised in court. This subject will be revisited in Chapter 7 under the heading of 'Addressing Key Challenges'. In the meantime, this chapter will continue on the theme of e-crime by examining the counter e-crime effort in the UK.

Counter E-crime Effort in the UK

Law enforcement in the UK has attracted criticism for what was seen as insufficient recruitment of officers with the requisite technical knowledge to effectively combat e-crime. In an effort to tackle this criticism, The National Hi-Tech Crime Unit (NHTCU) was created in 2001 at a cost of £25 million.[101] The unit came into operation in April 2001 and was the first UK national law enforcement organisation tasked to combat serious and organised computer-based crime.[102] As a multi-agency unit, the unit drew skilled and experienced staff from the National Crime Squad, Her Majesty's Customs and Excise, and the military, as well as the intelligence agencies.

The organisation investigated serious and organised crime committed over the Internet, such as hacking, virus-writers, Internet fraud and other hi-tech crimes involving the use of computers and telecommunications equipment. Its work was broadly divided into five key disciplines: tactical and technical support; crime reduction; intelligence operations; and digital evidence recovery.[103] Since its launch, the NHTCU has been involved in a broad spectrum of computer-related crime investigations, including fraud, hacking, viruses and denial of service attacks, software piracy, online child abuse, extortion and drugs trafficking.

100 Ibid.
101 June Wei, Lai C. Liu, Kai S. Koong, Yi Li, 'A risk assessment model for information security' (2011) 5(2) *International Journal of Business and Systems Research* 158.
102 NHTCU. [Online]. Available at: http://www.nhtcu.org/NOPSurvey.pdf [accessed: 12 October 2009].
103 Ibid.

However, despite some successes,[104] NHTCU ceased to exist on 1 April 2006 bringing into question the effectiveness of the unit. Consequently, many of its staff and duties were transferred to the e-crime unit of Serious Organised Crime Agency (SOCA),[105] which is also due to be replaced by the National Crime Agency (NCA) by 2013. The move marked the third major revamp of organised crime policing in 13 years and was presented by the Home Secretary Theresa May as a response to the general criticism by the government's green paper on the future of policing published in July 2010, which noted that a large number of national policing units had emerged over time:[106]

> *The overall picture is now confusing and cluttered. And the public accountability for the activities of some of these units is, at best, opaque.*[107]

This latest reorganisation aims to bring together many of the disparate units and streamline police operations in relation to crime and other forms of serious organised crime and border controls.[108] However, despite good intentions, the continuing restructuring of law enforcement units involved in e-crime has left the fight against cyber-crime somewhat in an indeterminate state.

One law enforcement agency affected by the announcement was the Police National E-Crime Unit (PCeU) which is part of the Specialist Crime Directorate of the Metropolitan Police Service in London, dedicated to combating e-crime

---

104 In May 2004, a gang of 'phishers' was exposed. It had posed online as a bank and e-mailed customers to lure their banking details from them. Computers, passports, chequebooks, bank cards and crack cocaine were seized during raids on several premises in London from which the gang was operating. In July 2004, following a joint operation with police in St Petersburg, members of a Russian gang were arrested and charged with offences relating to extortion and money laundering after they had threatened online bookmakers with denial of service attacks. Furthermore, a recent NHTCU investigation, dubbed Operation Blossom, led to the successful prosecution of several individuals for conspiracy to defraud a Japanese bank, through its London offices, of £220 million.

105 *Out-law News*, 'NHTCU disappears into SOCA', 4 April 2006 http://www.out-law.com/page-6810 [accessed: 17 October 2010.

106 Home Office, *Policing in the 21st Century: Reconnecting Police and the People* (2009). [Online]. Available at: http://www.homeoffice.gov.uk/publications/consultations/policing-21st-century/ [accessed: 25 August 2010].

107 Ian Grant, 'Policing green paper leaves cybercrime fighters in limbo', *Computer Weekly* (London, 27 July 2010). [Online]. Available at: http://www.computerweekly.com/Articles/2010/07/27/242097/Policing-green-paperleaves-cybercrime-fighters-in-limbo.htm [accessed: 25 August 2010].

108 Danny Shaw, BBC, National Crime Agency details outlined by Theresa May, 8 June 2011. [Online]. Available at: http://www.bbc.co.uk/news/uk-13678653 [accessed: 15 June 2011].

in England, Wales and Northern Ireland.[109] The unit has a national remit, and was created in April 2008[110] to centralise the efforts of all police forces in the UK with the exception of Scotland, to fight all forms of e-crime. It also set up a Virtual Task Force that included the financial sectors, academia and ISPs to tackle the 'constantly evolving threat'. The government recently withdrew £1m from the PCeU funding and it is now unclear as to whether the unit will also be incorporated into the NCA.[111]

However, looking forwards, the newly established NCA's role will be to lead in the fight against organised crime and the protection of the borders of the UK:[112]

> *It will harness and exploit the intelligence, analytical and enforcement capabilities of the existing Serious Organised Crime Agency (SOCA), but better connect these capabilities to those within the police service, HM Revenue and Customs, the UK Border Agency and a range of other criminal justice partners.*[113]

The statement perhaps suggests recognition of existing criticisms regarding its ineffective use of intelligence, analytical and enforcement capabilities. However, the establishment of a new agency will not necessarily lead to the elimination of existing problems. As was the case when the NHTCU and NCIS were absorbed into SOCA, if the staff remain predominantly unchanged, the organisation also remains unchanged. Peter Sommer, e-crime expert and professor at the London School of Economics, has expressed concerns regarding the effect the latest reorganisation in terms of its impact on staff morale:

> *What, if any, new structures will emerge? And what is this likely to do the individual officers, who presumably will now have to divert their*

109 The unit is housed within the Specialist Crime Directorate (SCD6) part of the Metropolitan Police Service based in central London. However the unit works closely with the SCDEA in Scotland and international law enforcement. The PCeU has a seat at the table at both Europol and Interpol cyber workstreams.

110 Metropolitan Police Website. [Online]. Available at: http://www.met.police.uk/pceu/index.htm [accessed: 18 October 2010].

111 The PCEU has 30 staff, 20 of these investigative.

112 The Agency will be led by a senior chief constable and encompass a number of 'commands', including organised crime and border policing. The Agency may also take responsibility for other national policing functions, including some of those presently carried out by the National Policing Improvement Agency, which will be phased out.

113 Home Office, *Report on Policing in the 21st Century*.

attention to their own immediate careers and to producing yet more strategy papers?[114]

For any effective, positive change to take place, the system itself much be questioned and the culture that underpins the organisation must be challenged. The nature of e-crimes is very often international. As such, the counter e-crime efforts at the domestic level alone are insufficient. The next section will examine recent international cooperation and the move towards the harmonisation of e-criminal laws.

International Cooperation and Harmonisation of E-crime Laws

Historically, criminal law was predominantly driven and shaped by national interests in that the policies, procedures and protective measures enshrined in the law of individual states were mostly home-grown. However, E-criminal activity has forced changes to this traditional approach. Although long standing cooperative relationships continue to exist between countries in relation to the investigation of crime, problems may arise where the investigation extends to requests for searches of premises and seizures of items in another jurisdiction.[115]

Moreover, the issue of extradition can be problematic where there is a marked legal disparity between the countries in question and, for example, the criminal activity which is being investigated is not covered under any bilateral agreement between them. In some situations, a country may refuse a request from a foreign law enforcement agency for legal permission to conduct a search and seizure operation within its borders, perhaps because equivalent powers would not be available to domestic investigators in the same circumstances. A lack of dual criminality[116] can also present an insurmountable hurdle when it comes to jurisdictional and extraditional issues, particularly where any mutual assistance treaty makes it a pre-requisite for cooperative measures.[117] In the light of these facts, the importance of a process of international harmonisation

114 Grant, 'Policing green paper leaves cybercrime fighters in limbo' (n.107).

115 Angela Brungsa and Rodger Jamieson, 'Identification of legal issues for computer forensics' (2010) 3(2) *Journal of Digital Forensic Practice* 140.

116 Where the conduct is under investigation is recognised as criminal behaviour under the laws in both the host and visiting states.

117 Wild et al., *Internet Law* (n.51) 199.

of substantive criminal laws and procedures cannot be overstated.[118] It has been recognised that:

> *... although bilateral cooperation is important in pursuing investigations concerning unlawful conduct involving the use of the Internet, multilateral efforts are a more effective way to develop international policy and cooperation in this area. The reason for this stems from the nature of the Internet itself. Because Internet access is available in over 200 countries, and because criminals can route their communications through any of these countries, law enforcement challenges must be addressed on as broad a basis as possible, because law enforcement assistance may be required from any Internet-connected country. That is, even if two countries were able to resolve all the high-tech crimes issues they faced, they would still (presumably) only be able to solve those crimes that involved their two countries. Multilateral fora allow many countries to seek solutions that will be compatible to the greatest extent with each country's domestic laws.*[119]

In recognition of these challenges, the Group of Eight (G8) countries have been proactive for some time on this issue, forming a principled agenda and action plan nearly seven years ago. Following a meeting in Washington between the interior and justice ministers of Britain, Canada, France, Germany, Italy, Japan, Russia and the US, a set of initiatives were announced, all of which were aimed at combating e-crime. The particular areas of focus were paedophilia, drug trafficking, electronic fraud such as money laundering and cyber-piracy, as well as industrial and state espionage. Recommendations included increased training for law enforcement officers and prosecutors, in addition to encouraging further cooperation on the legal and procedural aspects of extradition, together with a greater movement towards parity of computer forensics standards. Of particular note was the establishment of the 24/7 High-Tech Point-of-Contact Network, directly linking e-crime experts from around the world with each other.

Within Europe, there have also been a number of initiatives launched in the last few years in the fight against e-crime, which have come from both the EU and the Council of Europe. For example, in March 2000, the Lisbon European Council urged the main legislative bodies of the EU to implement

118 Catherine Everett, 'Who is responsible for policing the Internet?' (2009) 9(5) *Computer Fraud & Security* 5.

119 Yee Fen Lim, *Cyberspace Law: Commentaries and Materials* (Oxford University Press 2002) 274.

a cohesive strategy towards e-crime. In response, the European Commission released a Communication which contained a number of proposals entitled: 'Creating a Safer Information Society by Improving the Security of Information Infrastructures and Combating Computer-related Crime'. This led to an analysis of the weaknesses in network security and the recommendation of a coordinated approach to network and IT security.[120]

The Commission also recognised the need to harmonise the substantive criminal laws of the member states within the EU. However, the Commission's decision did not concern itself with so-called content-related or computer-related offences but simply considered attacks against the integrity of the systems. For example, arts 3–5 promoted the criminalisation of obtaining, or attempting to obtain illegal access to information systems. The same was proposed in relation to illegal interference with information systems. Moreover, it was recommended that secondary participation in such criminal behaviour should also be rendered illegal.[121] It should also be recognised that these efforts are in fairly early stages of development and that much more needs to be done before e-crime can be tackled effectively not only within the EU but around the globe.

The Virtual Dimension

The significance of e-crimes not just in relation to terrorism but the wider 'crime' environment as a major threat has long been recognised.[122] [123] [124] However, whilst areas of e-crime such as hacking, online child pornography, identity theft, phishing and Internet fraud, have received much attention, crime relating to virtual worlds in cyberspace continue to be neglected. Part of the reason can be explained by the perception that virtual worlds are simply gaming environments in cyberspace. However, there is increasing evidence to suggest that virtual environments have a number of different applications that support

120 Council Resolution (EC) [2001] OJ 2002 C43/02.

121 Wild et al., *Internet Law* (n.51) 200.

122 SOCA. UK National Threat Assessment. [Online]. Available at: www.soca.gov.uk/.../54-the-united-kingdom-threat-assessment-of-organised-crime [accessed: 14 April 2011].

123 In recognition of the seriousness of the threat, the Home office announced in February 2011 that a further £650m will be allocated to the Serious Organised Crime Agency (SOCA) and the Metropolitan Police Central e-Crime Unit (PCeU) to tackle the problem.

124 T. Espiner, 'Cybercrime policing to get £63m boost', *Security ZDNet UK*, 16 February 2011. [Online]. Available at: http://www.zdnet.co.uk/news/security/2011/02/16/cybercrime-policing-to-get-63m-boost-40091830/ [accessed: 10 April 2011].

'real' life activities. In addition, there is evidence to illustrate that actions in the virtual world have very real implications and consequences in the real world.

Several cases have come to light in recent years concerning crimes in 'online' virtual worlds involving both property offences as well as crimes against the person.[125] The virtual world is not only an environment where such crimes can be committed, but may also be used as a vehicle to mask a variety of 'real' world crimes. Virtual worlds rely on the Internet to be able to exist and operate. As such, virtual worlds are also referred to as 'online' environments owing to the fact that one needs to be connected to the Internet to be able to access it. It therefore follows that the opposite, 'offline', refers to the real world. (Both terms will be used interchangeably with 'virtual' and 'real' throughout the chapter.) The main focus of this section is on the virtual or 'online' environment, although the real interest is how criminal activities conducted in such environments have direct implications and consequences in the real world.

An appreciation of virtual worlds and its potential use by terrorists and criminals alike is essential if a proactive approach to counter financial measures is to be adopted. As other methods and vehicles for committing such financial crimes become well known by law enforcement as well as its potential victims, coupled with counter measures taken to combat such crimes, those vehicles increasingly become a hard target. As the environment becomes more hostile for the criminal, the criminal will naturally turn to other vehicles which are softer targets. This will be an environment less known and understood, unregulated and unmonitored, where unsuspecting victims exist and the lack of a suitable guardian from crime enables crimes to be committed with relative ease. The virtual world is currently such an environment.

VIRTUAL WORLDS

Arguably, the best known example of a virtual world in cyberspace is Second Life.[126] Second Life is a Massively Multiplayer Online Role-playing Game (MMORG) which was created by the US company Lindenlab in 2003[127] and

125 G. Kirwan, 'Presence and the Victims of Crime in Online Virtual Worlds', Dun Laoghaire Institute of Art, Design and Technology, Ireland. [Online]. Available at: http://astro.temple.edu/~tuc16417/papers/Kirwan.pdf [accessed: 7 April 2011].

126 D.E. Jones, 'I, avatar: constructions of self and place in second life and the technological imagination' (2006) *Journal of Communication, Culture and Technology*. [Online]. Available at: http://gnovisjournal.org/ files/Donald-E-Jones-I-Avatar.pdf [accessed: 12 January 2011].

127 D. Kushner, 'My avatar, my self' (2004) 107(3) *Technology Review* 50.

reached almost 14.5 million users by July 2008.[128] Second Life employs 3,000 personnel, generating revenues of over $60 million per annum.[129] Although Second Life is viewed purely as a 'gaming' environment by many, its activities are far from being restricted to gaming alone. Legitimate global organisations such as MTV, Coca-Cola, Sun Microsystems, Intel and Warner Brothers, had all established a Second Life presence by 2006 for non-gaming purposes. For example, IBM and Reuters have built virtual facilities designed to host scientific and business meetings involving hundreds of avatars. The importance of virtual business can be seen by the announcement of the recruitment of a full-time Second Life reporter, Adam Pasick in October 2006, by the global press agency Reuters, to cover Second Life exclusively with a focus on virtual business and its related economy.[130]

In addition to virtual businesses, virtual worlds are increasingly playing a key role in education and training. Approximately 85 universities, colleges and schools worldwide have reconstructed part of their campuses in Second Life. Examples include the Harvard Extension School, which offers a distance education course in Law at the Court of Public Opinion, where students' avatars meet once a week to engage in group work,[131] as well as the Royal Institute of Technology in Stockholm, which has opened a virtual architects office 'LOL architects', as part of its 'Production of Architecture' course.[132] The Harvard Law School's Berkman Center has also built a large collaborative environment in Second Life, which it uses as a vehicle for holding regular seminars.

In terms of training, various software applications are enabling medical students to conduct 'virtual' medical training whilst first responders are being trained to react to a 'virtual terrorist' attack in order to prepare for the possibility of a terrorist attack in the real world.[133] The latter is an interesting development

128 Second Life Statistics. [Online]. Available at: http://socialmediastatistics.wikidot.com/second-life [accessed: 6 April 2011].

129 C.R. Ondrejka, 'Collapsing geography second life, innovation, and the future of national power' (2007) 2(3) *Innovations: Technology, Governance, Globalisation* 27. [Online]. Available at: http://ssrn.com/paper=1023493 [accessed: 24 December 2009].

130 *BBC Online* 'Online world to get news bureau: Reuters has opened a virtual news agency in the Second Life online world', 16 October 2006. [Online]. Available at: http://news.bbc.co.uk/1/hi/technology/6054352.stm [accessed: 16 October 2010].

131 *CyberOne* (2006) CyberOne: law in the court of public opinion. [Online]. Available at: http://blogs.law.harvard.edu/cyberone/ [accessed: 7 April 2011].

132 D. Oswald, 'Should planners start playing computer games? Arguments from Simcity and Second Life' (2008) *Planning Theory & Practice* 209.

133 B. Mennecke, E.M. Roche, D.A. Bray, B. Konsynski, J. Lester, M. Rowe and A.M. Townsend, 'Second Life and Other Virtual Worlds: A Roadmap for Research', (11 December) 28th International Conference on Information Systems (ICIS), 2007. [Online]. Available at: http://ssrn.com/abstract=1021441 [accessed: 7 April 2011].

as computer simulation models have traditionally been used for the purpose of planning practice, such as crisis planning and disaster management training.[134] However, such models have limitations regarding the prediction of human behaviour in such scenarios. This is where gaming is believed to be able to provide a more realistic alternative to computer simulation alone.[135] As such, academics have conducted research into the possibility of using Second Life as a platform to model human behaviour. As the existing trend in technological advancement is more about technology fusion, where existing technologies are adapted and integrated to create new functionality and applications, it is conceivable that the gaming environment could be combined with existing software to make training scenarios more realistic, making it a more effective training tool.

This view is supported by the US National Defense University (NDU), which has acquired four 'islands' in Second Life for this purpose. In March 2008, NDU's Information Resources Management College opened its first island, consisting of a Welcome Centre, Conference Centre and Crisis Centre.[136] In addition, a secure virtual environment known as OLIVE (Online Interactive Virtual Environment) was developed by the National Security Division of Forterra Systems specifically for government use. OLIVE focuses on the key areas of inter-governmental collaboration, medical treatment, education, continuity of operations and training[137] and currently forms the basis of the Asymmetric Warfare Virtual Training Technology, (AW-VTT), which has already been used to train troops for checkpoint duties in Iraq.

In addition, Forterra is in the process of developing other OLIVE applications for the US Navy, the National Institutes of Health, the Army's Medical Research Command, as well as several intelligence agencies, who are interested in using virtual worlds as an environment for 3-D, collaborative visualisation of data.[138] In addition, the US Department of Defence has also established a military presence in Second Life. According to General William S. Wallace, commander of the US Army Training and Doctrine Command (TRADOC), the Army Second Life effort consists of two virtual islands both serving as a vehicle for recruitment. One island is a Welcome Centre with an information kiosk and the means to contact a recruiter, whereas the other island

134 Blue light services refer to the emergency services, namely police, ambulance and fire service.
135 Oswald, 'Should planners start playing computer games?' 209.
136 M. Peck, 'Second-Life Training: Virtual Worlds Bring Benefits' *Defense News*, 2 June 2008. [Online]. Available at: http://www.defensenews.com/story.php?i=3558033 [accessed: 7 April 2011].
137 Ibid.
138 Ibid.

offers various virtual military experiences such as parachuting, designed to entice the individual into joining the real military.[139]

To operate in Second Life, there are only three basic requirements. First is access to a computer, second, fast Internet access and third, an account. To establish an account, a name, date of birth and an email address must be registered. However, the name and date of birth can be fictional. Furthermore, email accounts can be set up easily without need for any due diligence procedures, which in itself raise concerns regarding anonymity. It can be argued that once an avatar becomes economically active, the necessity to use credit cards will provide the necessary means of identification. However, if the credit card is stolen or compromised without the knowledge of the account holder, it is possible that transactions may go unnoticed and unreported for some time. This is due to the fact that the amount of the individual transaction is likely to be fairly small. As such, the credit card holder may decide that the amount of the loss does not warrant reporting it to the credit card company, as the procedures for reporting suspicion transactions can be time consuming and cumbersome.

From the criminal's perspective, it is not the value of the individual transaction but the sum of the total illegal transactions which makes the crime profitable and worthwhile. In addition, technologies can be implemented to automate processes, so that the same illegal action can be carried out repeatedly without any further effort. The smaller transactions also have an added benefit in that it is more likely to fall under the radar of various electronic surveillance systems developed to detect suspicious transactions in the real world.

Once an account is set up, an avatar can be created.[140] An avatar is a three-dimensional figure visible to the player and is a resident of Second Life. Each avatar has the ability to construct objects, ranging from clothing to real estate. These objects then form the basis of a virtual social life within the virtual world. In order to understand how financial crimes can be committed in the virtual environment, it is essential to understand how the virtual economy operates.

139 N. Shachtman, 'Army Builds Fantasy Island in Second Life', 3 December 2008. [Online]. Available at: http://www.wired.com/dangerroom/2008/12/the-armys-new-f/ [accessed: 7 April 2011].

140 P. Ernstberger, 'Linden Dollar and Virtual Monetary Policy', University of Bayreuth Working Paper, 23 January 2009.

VIRTUAL ECONOMY

Residents in Second Life pay 'real' money for virtual objects or property to enhance their virtual lives.[141] The money is paid via credit card on websites in the real world, and the goods are delivered virtually, inside the game.[142] Virtual money can be purchased in the form of the Linden dollar, which in turn, is connected to a whole series of economies inside virtual worlds. The vibrancy of the virtual economy can be illustrated by the fact that since 2007, at least US$1 million has been spent every 24 hours.[143] In addition, an increasing number of Second Life residents are leaving their real-life employment to make their living entirely within Second Life's economy.[144]

Furthermore, the income obtained within Second Life had become sufficiently reliable, coupled with the stable exchange rates between the Linden dollar and the US dollar, that enterprising businessmen in poorer areas of the world such as Mexico or China, have set up 'virtual sweatshops' where employees work at their PCs, working in virtual worlds to make gold and other items to sell for a real world salary. For example, a 'virtua'[145] worker can earn up to $100 per day, which is a higher wage than almost any career opportunity in rural China. To provide an indication of the scale of the virtual economy, the equivalent of nearly US$50 million each month is traded in user-to-user transactions. The Second Life economy is on an annual run rate of more than half a billion US dollars, where its residents create more than 250,000 new virtual goods every day. There are now more than 270 terabytes of content in Second Life which is growing by approximately 100 per cent every year.[146]

In terms of its relevance to the real-life economy, the crossover between virtual and real economies was first noted by economist Edward Castronova in 2001. Professor Castronova of California State University observed that virtual world residents were selling virtual items for real money on eBay. In his 2002 study on Virtual Economies, he examined the economy of EverQuest, which

141 E. Castronova, D. Williams, C. Shen, R. Ratan, L. Xiong, Y. Huang and B. Keegan, (2009) 'As real as real? Macroeconomic behavior in a large-scale virtual world' *New Media & Society*. [Online]. Available at: http://dmitriwilliams.com/EconVW.pdf [accessed: 2 January 2010].

142 *Net Imperative Digital Business Intelligence*, 'Net Virtual worlds come of age: Second Life users trade over a billion real-world dollars', 24 September 2009. [Online]. Available at: http://www.netimperative.com/news/2009/september/virtual-worlds-come-of-age-second-life-users-trade [accessed: 5 February 2011].

143 Oswald, 'Should Planners Start Playing Computer Games?' 209–6.

144 Ibid.

145 The term 'virtua' such as 'virtua fighter' is used to describe a virtual character in a gaming environment.

146 *Net Imperative Digital Business Intelligence*.

was then the second largest virtual world in existence. He discovered that it had a real, consistent US dollar exchange rate, which put the average wage of each player at the equivalent of $3.42 per hour. One EverQuest platinum piece, he found, was worth approximately 1 cent, equating to more than 1 yen or 1 lira. Castronova then calculated the virtual world's gross national product to be $135 million and concluded that EverQuest had per-capita GNP[147] of $2,266, which was greater than the GNP in India, Bulgaria or China.[148]

The inter-linkage of virtual and real economies can be further illustrated by the rapid move by leading 'brick and mortar' companies such as Sears, Circuit City, Reuters and IBM to set up shop within Second Life for the purpose of inter-linking the 'in-world' virtual economy with the 'real-world' economy. For example, a member can purchase virtual goods in the Circuit City virtual store. However, when a product is chosen, the member is taken to the 'real' e-commerce site for the actual purchase. As such, the growth of the 'virtual' economy has a direct impact on the 'real' economy.[149]

Economic Motivation in the Virtual World

Incentives for production are given through the implementation of a fully functioning economy with its own currency, the Linden dollar.[150] Land is a key commodity within Second Life. Land ownership is optional and can be conceptualised as being similar to obtaining a personal website in that it requires storage space on the main server. As such, land ownership equates to renting server space at Linden Lab, for which a fee is paid. Each piece of land takes up a certain amount of dedicated storage space with larger spaces of virtual land requiring extra space, and additional 'storage' or computer memory required to maintain virtual property, further adding to the cost of storage, which is a

147 Gross national product (GNP) per capita is the dollar value of a country's final output of goods and services in a year, divided by its population and reflects the average income of a country's citizens. In other words, GNP per capita shows what part of a country's GNP each person would have if this GNP were divided equally. Countries with a GNP per capita in 1998 of $9,361 or more are described as high income, between $761 and $9,360 as middle income, and $760 or less as low income. Knowing a country's GNP per capita is a good first step toward understanding the country's economic strengths and needs, as well as the general standard of living enjoyed by the average citizen. See World Bank Website. [Online]. Available at: http://www.worldbank.org/depweb/english/modules/economic/gnp/index.html [accessed: 28 May 2012].

148 T. Guest, *Second Lives* (Arrow Books 2008) 25.

149 Mennecke et al., 'Second Life and Other Virtual Worlds'.

150 P. Rosedale and C. Ondrejka, 'Enabling player-created online worlds with grid computing and streaming', 2003. [Online]. Available at: http://www.gamasutra.com/view/feature/2805/enabling_playercreated_online_.php?page=1 [accessed: 2 January 2010].

key factor in determining the price of virtual land and property.[151] Wealth can be created much in the same way it can through real land and property, with the added benefit that it cannot only be enjoyed in Second Life but also in the real world by converting Linden dollars back into real currency.[152]

One example of success in creating personal wealth in the real world through virtual land and property is the case of Anshe Chung. In 2006, Ailin Graef, alias Anshe Chung, made the cover of *Business Week* by becoming the first millionaire in the 'real world' through her 'virtual' property development business in Second Life. Ailin, a 33-year-old Chinese woman living in Germany, began buying and selling virtual land in July 2004. By November that year, Chung's Second Life Property and virtual cash holdings, not including her company's real world assets, had a total worth in excess of $1 million.[153]

The business model consisted of buying large plots of newly available virtual land, separating the areas into lots, and then either selling or renting the property at a profit.[154] By November 2006, her territory known as 'Dreamland' covered 36 square kilometres representing approximately 10 per cent of the total land area of Second Life.[155] Chung's virtual property success has provided inspiration for those who regard the virtual world as unconquered territory with the potential to create great personal wealth. However, where there is wealth, inevitably there is crime.

VIRTUAL CRIME

Although motivations for committing financial crimes in the virtual environment are similar compared to the real world, the concept of what constitutes a crime and how those crimes are committed differ. The ambiguity surrounding the issue of what constitutes a crime has also resulted in the general absence of legislation and regulation governing activity in virtual worlds. The result has been the materialisation of various types of crime with real-life ramifications.[156] One category of crime relates to those committed within virtual environments involving theft or destruction of virtual property. In response, virtual private

151 *Second Life* website. [Online]. Available at: http://secondlife.com/land/faq/ [accessed: 12 April 2011].

152 Ondrejka, 'Collapsing geography second life, innovation, and the future of national power'.

153 Guest, *Second Lives* (n.148) 332.

154 Ibid. p. 178.

155 E. Castronova, 'Virtual economies, virtual goods and service delivery in virtual worlds' (2010) 2(4) *Journal of Virtual Worlds Research*.

156 A. Salifu, 'The impact of Internet crime on development' (2008) 15(4) *Journal of Financial Crime* 432.

security providers have emerged, perhaps more aptly described as virtual mafia organisations. This is in many ways similar to the situation in Russia in the period after the collapse of the Soviet Union.[157]

Mafia and organised crime groups differ in that the mafia is an agency that deals in protection whereas organised crime seeks simply to maximise its financial gains as quickly as possible, using any means possible. The mafia banks on the inefficiency of the state in supplying efficient protection to legal transactions. The more confused the legal framework of a country, the more incompetent the police and the more inefficient the courts, the more the mafia will thrive. Conversely, by establishing law and order in such environments, the 'demand' for protection would fall, eliminating the need for such organisations. This is indeed the situation that can be witnessed in the virtual world.[158]

In Second Life, virtual mafias use its virtual muscle to perform many of the services one might expect from a bona fide crime family.[159] Services on offer range from mediation to a virtual hit, referred to as a 'Moe Green', which eliminates a virtual character from the game completely. Elimination of a virtual character or an object of virtual value represents time, which can be translated into money; therefore the crime of assassination is essentially that of financial theft, as opposed to what would be regarded as murder in the real world. In addition to the 'protection' and 'elimination' businesses involving virtual 'wet' work, virtual mafias mimic the modus operandi of real-world crime groups by running sports spread-betting, and back-door card craps games in virtual VIP casinos, with the virtual equivalent of about $4 as minimum bet. As in the real world, legitimate businesses such as website hosting and design, are run alongside illegitimate businesses, such as real estate extortion, protection and bribes.[160]

The concept of crime in virtual worlds is somewhat ironic in that one of the key attractions of Second Life is the supposed ability to escape from the negative aspects of real life.[161] The perception is that by entering the world of virtual reality, that one can be freed from personal problems such as one's appearance, financial debt, relationship problems, as well as from broader

157 J. Leitzel, C. Gaddy and M. Alexeev, (1995) 'Mafiosi and matrioshki: organised crime and Russian reform' (1995) 13(1) *The Brookings Review* 26.
158 D. Bell, 'Learning from Second Life' (2009) 40 *British Journal of Educational Technology* 515.
159 Mennecke et al., 'Second Life and Other Virtual Worlds'.
160 Guest, *Second Lives* (n.148) 116,117,119.
161 K. Bellman and C. Landauer, (2000) 'Playing in the MUD: virtual worlds are real places' (2000) 14(1) *Applied Artificial Intelligence* 93.

issues such as global warming and crime. However, this utopian virtual society also serves the criminal well in that he or she can also escape from the usual concerns including being brought to justice for crimes committed, both online and offline. For some users, the draw to Second Life lies in the ability to act without the restrictions of the law.[162]

Virtual crime in Second Life can be placed into two broad categories. The first is economic crime. As previously mentioned, most 'virtual' crimes such as virtual assassinations or theft are essentially financial as the motivation is financial and the act of violence does not involve injury to an actual person. However, there is also a second category which deserves a mention. These crimes relate to non-economic crime where the motivation is not financial but to satisfy some deviant criminal act. Examples include child abuse and child pornography or an act of violence in real life as a reaction to a situation that occurs online. The concern for both types of crime stems from the intersection between offline and online environments, as the next sections will highlight.

FINANCIAL CRIME AND THE CONCEPT OF PROPERTY

Virtual worlds such as Second Life are considered to be high-risk environments with the potential to commit various types of financial crimes such as fraud and money laundering. According to the Fraud Advisory Panel, set up by the Institute of Chartered Accountants in England and Wales, legal loopholes were exposing virtual world users to a growing risk from theft and deception.[163] Members of the panel have highlighted their concern regarding its potential use by gangs to commit credit card fraud, identity theft and tax evasion.[164]

A key challenge to tackling virtual crime is that the concept of crime is yet to be defined.[165] According to the Seoul Police Cyber Terror Unit,[166] virtual objects are deemed to have no legal value. If an object has no value, it naturally follows that a crime of theft cannot occur. For example, if a seller of a virtual

162 E. Castronova, 'The right to play' (2004) 45 *New York Law School Law Review* 185.

163 S. Adams, 'Online communities face money-laundering', *Daily Telegraph*, 14 May 2007. [Online]. Available at: http://www.telegraph.co.uk/news/uknews/1551482/Online-communities-face-money-laundering.html [accessed: 15 December 2010].

164 Ibid.

165 C.T. Clarke, 'From criminet to cyber-perp: toward an inclusive approach to policing the evolving criminal mens rea on the Internet' (1996) 75 *Orlando Law Review* 191.

166 The Cyber Terror Unit in Seoul had originally been established to tackle hacking attempts mainly by North Korea to attempt to disrupt South Korean business and government. The remit of the unit was extended to include virtual crimes. However, by 2008 over half their workload was related to online games.

item did not receive payment from a buyer, it is deemed that no crime has been committed as the virtual item is not perceived to have value.[167] However, there is a strong case that virtual property replicates many of the incidents of real world property and satisfies the normative demands made by the major theories justifying property.[168] The argument, in essence, is that the fact that this new virtual property is created and protected by computer code does not disqualify it from being property.[169]

In terms of modus operandi, online financial crimes can be conducted through a variety of mechanisms. Hackers are able to exploit bugs in the virtual world's programming, and by illicitly running software known as 'bots' to perform repetitive point-and-click operations to steal virtual artefacts. Although the scams are usually short-lived, as bugs are detected and fixed resulting in the closure of the bots, the scammers simply move on to discover another programming loophole which they exploit until they are discovered again. The cycle continues as the identities of the scammers remain unknown.[170] Another method of conducting financial crime in virtual worlds is through the use of a 'CopyBot' which enables users to copy objects and creations of other users, instead of paying for them.

One example of online theft occurred in 2007 in the Habbo Hotel in Second Life, where Dutch teenagers allegedly stole €4,000 worth of virtual furniture by tricking other users into divulging their passwords,[171] resulting in the offline arrest of at least one teenager. However, the challenge is that if the value of the stolen object cannot be easily quantified, the theft may not be definable as a real offence, and offline authorities may not be able to identify a clear course of action. Another example is the case of a resident known as 'There', who repeatedly sold virtual property that he did not own. The proceeds were then converted into real currency which could then be enjoyed in the real world.[172]

Other examples include the case of the Chinese exchange student living in Kagawa prefecture, southern Japan. In September 2005, the student designed and programmed an automated virtual character, a criminal virtual robot,

167 P. Hunton, 'Cyber crime and security: a new model of law enforcement investigation' (2010) 4(4) *Policing* 385.

168 Hunter and Lastowka, 'The Laws of the Virtual Worlds' (2004) 92(1) CAL. L. REV. 56.

169 J. Grimmelmann, 'Virtual worlds as comparative law' (2004) 49 *New York Law School Law* Review 147.

170 [Online]. Available at: http://www.shaviro.com/Othertexts/MMOs.pdf.

171 *BBC Online* (2007), "Virtual theft' leads to arrest". [Online]. Available at: http://news.bbc.co.uk/2/hi/technology/7094764.stm [accessed: 14 April 2011].

172 Guest, *Second Lives* (n.148) 112.

which logged onto Lineage II, and automatically attacked and robbed passers-by for the their most valuable virtual possessions. Items stolen were typically rare and valuable in that they gave special virtual abilities to their owners in the virtual environment. These items were then sold on a Japanese auction site in exchange for yen. He was arrested by the Japanese police, although no virtual charges were brought against the virtual robot. Another example was in November 2006, when 23-year-old Chinese student Wang Yue Si was arrested in Japan for selling virtual weapons and currency online, earning real-world income in contravention of his student visa. Police estimated Wang Yue Si's earnings at ¥150 million, equating to approximately US$1.3million.[173]

The relevance of virtual crimes in terms of consequences in the real world is that recent cases show not only that actions in virtual worlds are punishable in the real world, but can also lead to real-life crimes. Examples of real-life convictions include the case of a woman in Delaware, who was charged with plotting the real-life abduction of a boyfriend she met through Second Life and a 16-year-old boy in Tokyo, who was charged with stealing the ID and password of a fellow player in order to swindle virtual currency in an online game.[174]

There have also been cases where acts on injustice in virtual worlds have led to real-life murder. In September 2006, 45-year-old Thomas Montgomery of New York, shot and killed his co-worker Brian in as a result of jealously over a female avatar.[175] Another example was in 2005, when gamer Qiu Chengwei in Shanghai, China, stabbed and killed Zhu Caoyuan as a result of the 'virtual'

173 *Playsquad*, 'Chinese student arrested after making 150 million yen selling items for online RPG'. [Online]. Available at: http://playsquad.commongate.com/post/Chinese_student_arrested_after_making_150_million_yen_selling_items_for_online_RPG [accessed: 2 February 2010].

174 *Guardian*, 'Japanese woman faces jail over online 'murder''. Associated Press, Guardian.co.uk, 24 October 2008. [Online]. Available at: http://www.guardian.co.uk/world/2008/oct/24/japan-games [accessed: 1 May 2011].

175 In the spring of 2005, 45-year-old Thomas Montgomery of New York had created an online persona for a gaming site, as an 18-year-old Marine named "Tommy." Tommy met a 17-year-old from West Virginia named "Jessi" becoming obsessed, and began making plans to leave his wife. However, Tommy's wife discovered the affair and wrote to Jessi exposing Tommy's age and real identity. Jessi then found Brian, a 22-year-old co-worker of Tommy's online, who confirmed Tommy's wife's information. Brian and Jessi struck up an online relationship, and taunted Tommy in chat rooms. His jealousy spiralled out of control in September 2006, when he shot and killed Brian (his co-worker) in the car park of their workplace. When police in West Virginia went to Jessi's residence to inform her, they found Mary, a 45-year-old married mother of two. Jessi was her daughter, whose online identity Mary had been using the entire time. See N. Labi, (2007) 'An IM Infatuation Turned to Romance', *Wired Magazine* Issue 15.09 Politics: Law, 21 August. [Online]. Available at: http://www.wired.com/politics/law/magazine/15-09/ff_internetlies [accessed: 1 May 2011].

theft of a 'dragon saber' which Caoyuan had sold on eBay for 7,200 (US$ 900). In this instance, it was the refusal of the police to recognise that any crime had been committed that led to the fatal attacked on Zhu, for which Chengwei is currently serving life in prison.[176]

These cases raise the question as to whether the concept of 'virtual' property should be considered more seriously. Furthermore, the willingness of some jurisdictions to recognise virtual property as real property, making theft of virtual property an punishable offence, but for others not to follow suit, further results in a sense of inequality and injustice, which may lead to frustration leading to acts of vengeance in the real world. An additional challenge is that the legal status of virtual trespass has yet to be established.

However, the need to examine the broader legal issues in virtual worlds was recognised by lawyers attending the 'State of Play' conference[177] 'Law, Games and Virtual Worlds' in 2003.[178] Delegates agreed that virtual items clearly do possess real value, which can readily be converted into real-world currencies, representing real income derived from virtual sources which is not taxed. Furthermore, historical events have shown that where there is no legislation and regulation, the vehicle can become a magnet for financial crime and urged authorities to acknowledge virtual worlds as a real threat in terms of financial crime.[179] In 2007, the Fraud Advisory Panel (FAP) produced a report warning that online residents could fall victim to fraud in virtual worlds,[180] and expressed additional concerns over possible money laundering activity in virtual worlds by organised criminals and terrorist organisations.[181]

176 *Naked Law* (2010), '5 Real Life Crimes Stemming From Virtual Worlds' November 15, 2010 Bizarre, Crime, Technology. [Online]. Available at: http://nakedlaw.avvo.com/2010/11/5-real-life-crimes-stemming-from-virtual-worlds/ [accessed: 1 May 2011].

177 State of Play is a conference series put on by the Institute for Information Law & Policy at New York Law School which deals with the intersection of virtual worlds, games and the law. The interdisciplinary conference on virtual worlds examining the state of play at the time in an effort to understand the phenomenon of digital games and the virtual worlds they create, creating a discussion the complex social, psychological, and legal issues to which they give rise.

178 13–15 November 2003.

179 Hunton, 'The stages of cybercrime investigations' (n.49) 61.

180 Reuters, 'UK panel urges real-life treatment for virtual cash', 14 May 2007. [Online]. Available at: http://secondlife.reuters.com/stories/2007/05/14/uk-panel-urges-real-life-treatment-for-virtual-cash/ [accessed: 12 April 2011].

181 Adams, 'Online communities face money-laundering' (n.163).

MONEY LAUNDERING IN SECOND LIFE

The potential for online money laundering is a primary concern, and has been flagged up by numerous experts including World-Check, an organisation that tracks the assets of terrorist and other adversary organisations worldwide. World-Check has specifically expressed its concern over the unmonitored flow of money through virtual worlds such as Second Life, urging action to be taken.[182] Virtual environments continue to be an ideal environment for criminals to launder money, as there are very few checks to ensure whether financial transactions are legitimate.[183] Furthermore, criminals are able to hide behind the anonymity of the avatars they create, making identification difficult. In the virtual world there is negligible means of monitoring financial activity, sparse due diligence, paltry customer identification rules, nor any mandated forms or reports to complete. The virtual realm is currently completely unregulated and a voluminous means of money movement.

Online financial transactions have also been compared to the *hawala* or *hundi* value transfer systems, which are considered to be 'high' risk from an anti-money laundering (AML) and counter-terrorist finance (CTF) perspective by many authorities, primarily owing to its low level of regulation. In comparison, its virtual equivalent represents an even higher risk as a possible vehicle for money laundering and other financial crimes, compared to any informal value transfer system in the real world.[184]

There are several ways in which money laundering could take place in Second Life. First, numerous separate virtual accounts, all using fictitious or counterfeit identification, could be set up. The accounts are funded either with the proceeds of an organised crime sports betting operation, or with cash obtained from the sale of narcotics, all patiently deposited at the available ATMs by Smurfs. Smurfing, also known as structuring, is the practice of executing financial transactions, such as the making of bank deposits, in a way to avoid the creation of certain records and reports required by law in relation to suspicious financial transactions.

---

182 *Alphaville Herald*, 'Is Second Life Being Used for Money Laundering?' 1 March 2007. [Online]. Available at: http://alphavilleherald.com/2007/01/is_second_life_-2.html [accessed: 12 April 2011].

183 *Second Life*, 'Tipping and Money Laundering in Second Life', 22 November 2009. [Online]. Available at: http://secondlifee.wordpress.com/2009/11/22/tipping-and-money-laundering-in-secondlife/ [accessed: 12 April 2011].

184 Ibid.

Structuring includes the act of parcelling what would otherwise be a large financial transaction into a series of smaller transactions to avoid scrutiny by regulators or law enforcement and has been associated with money laundering, fraud and other financial crimes. Typically each of the smaller transactions is executed in an amount below some statutory limit that normally does not require a financial institution to file a report with a government agency. Criminal enterprises often employ several agents (smurfs) to make the transaction.[185] The launderer can then make purchases in the virtual world to and from himself by using those accounts as if he were purchasing assets from other residents.[186] Subsequently, the proceeds are transferred to an account where funds can be drawn either from the bank or using an ATM, making it difficult to trace the source of the funds.[187] Given the ease with which money can be transferred between the virtual and real world, it is advisable for authorities to consider the regulation of entities that serve as a bridge between the two environments.

THE VIRTUAL DIMENSION – CONCLUSION

Virtual worlds such as Second Life can no longer be considered purely in terms of a virtual gaming environment. Governments and businesses also utilise online environments for a number of different purposes to complement real world activities. This has resulted in a blurring of online and offline environments with potentially dangerous consequences. As a result of the interconnectivity between the two worlds, actions in virtual worlds have consequences in the real world. However, unless the boundaries are well defined, the lack of clarity can result in what should be considered 'virtual' and what should be considered as 'real' referring to actions that have real world consequences. The lack of clarity is particularly relevant when tackling crime. Furthermore, virtual worlds can currently be defined by their lack of financial monitoring or reporting requirements, sparse due diligence and paltry customer identification rules. The concern is that historical events have shown that where there is no legislation and regulation, a vehicle can become a magnet for financial crime.[188]

185 The term 'smurfing' is derived from the image of the cartoon characters the Smurfs, having a large group of many small entities. Miami-based lawyer Gregory Baldwin is said to have coined the term in the 1980s.

186 *Alphaville Herald,* 'Is Second Life Being Used for Money Laundering?' (n.182).

187 P. Shuteyev, 'WoW and Second Life are still used for Money Laundering. How?', 8 December 2009. [Online]. Available at: http://www.massmailsoftware.com/blog/2009/08/wow-and-second-life-are-still-used-for-money-laundering-how/ [accessed: 12 April 2011].

188 Hunton, 'The stages of cyber crime investigations' (n.49) 61.

There are various aspects of virtual crime which need to be considered. The main focus of this section concerns itself with financial crime which can be further divided into crime that is committed online with offline implications. For example, the proceeds of crime from fraud and other crimes conducted online can be easily converted into real money. Second, the potential use of virtual worlds to mask crimes committed in the real world such as money laundering should also be considered.[189]

It seems appropriate that measures be taken to make virtual worlds an environment in which it is less easy for criminals to operate. This could be achieved in a number of ways. First, clarification as to what constitutes an offence is required. Furthermore, the defining of boundaries between 'virtual' and 'real' worlds is necessary. In addition, measures need to be put in place to identify the vehicles that serve as a gateway through which the proceeds of crime transit. Furthermore, these high-risk entities, once identified, such as currency exchanges, that serve as a bridge between the virtual and real economies should not only be identified but also registered, and be required to provide suspicious activity reports to the relevant authorities. Further study is required to identify other vulnerabilities and to see how best these can be monitored and managed.

Anonymity was previously highlighted as a key issue in virtual environments and monitoring can only be achieved if the identity of the individuals is known. The technical ability to monitor 'virtual' activity, financial or otherwise, exists through the use of IP addresses.[190] IP addresses are unique to most Internet connections and, coupled with the monitoring of credit cards used for purchases and financial transactions between in-world residents, would make most identities clear. The introduction of relevant regulations together with the compulsory reporting of suspicious activities will no doubt result in higher transparency and the ability to detect financial crime conducted through virtual worlds.

---

189 D. Heider (ed.), *Living Virtually: Exploring New Worlds*, Peter Lang Publishing (2009).

190 An Internet Protocol address (IP address) is a numerical label assigned to each device such as a computer or printer, participating in a computer network that uses the Internet Protocol for communication. An IP address serves two principal functions: host or network interface identification and location addressing. Its role has been characterised as follows: 'A name indicates what we seek. An address indicates where it is. A route indicates how to get there.' Source: DOD Standard Internet Protocol (January 1980) 2011. [Online]. Available at: http://tools.ietf.org/html/rfc760 [accessed: 5 February 2011].

However, it is of paramount importance that a unified global approach is adopted to tackle this threat. The attempt by individual countries to tackle the problem alone will inevitably result in the criminal simply using the 'weaker' jurisdictions as a vehicle to conduct their illegal operations. An added problem given the global nature of finance is that once illegal funds have entered the global financial system, it is virtually impossible to detect. The nature of financial crime is that its perpetrators will always endeavour to find a weakness in the system to exploit. Unless appropriate measures are put in place, virtual worlds will continue to serve the criminal as a vulnerability to be exploited.

The future of crime, in particular financial crime, will utilise ever evolving technologies in the cyber environment. In order to tackle the threat effectively, the implications of emerging technologies must be understood and embraced as opposed to feared or ignored. The inability to do so will result in its continued use by criminals to mask their crimes and to place them in an advantageous position. This situation must be changed so that the technology can be used as a weapon again criminals to obtain asymmetric advantage over the adversary. Having explored the cyber environment, it is also necessary to examine the 'physical' environment to explore the sources of terrorist funds, which originate from both legitimate and illegitimate sources, which is the subject of the next chapter.

3

Terrorist Finance

> *Intelligence and security services worldwide, including the CIA and MI6, have never before encountered a global terrorist financial network as sophisticated as al-Qaeda's. Comparisons with other such networks reveal that al-Qaeda has built the most complex, robust and resilient money generating and money moving network yet seen. No network resembles al-Qaeda's ...*[1]
>
> *Rohan Gunaratna*

Despite the fact that counter terrorist-finance (CTF) has become recognised as being a key component of the overall counter-terrorism effort, its full potential is far from being realised and the understanding of the subject remains limited. As such, this chapter aims to address this issue through the analysis of the modus of the sources of funding for terrorist purposes, which are derived from both legal and illegal sources. In addition, key misconceptions such as the paradigm of inexpensive terrorism will be elaborated upon.

Terrorist Financial Networks

Prior to the existence of al-Qaeda, Western countries mostly dealt with terrorist structures that were either simple and disorganised local entities, or State-sponsored entities such as Hezbollah. Al-Qaeda as a terrorist organisation is unique in its complexity and global reach.[2] It exists in an age characterised by globalisation and advancements in technology, which is reflected in its modus operandi as well as its financial structures. The perception of al-Qaeda's financial networks is that they are flexible, resilient and impenetrable.

---

1 Rohan Gunaratna, *Inside Al Qaeda – Global Network of Terror* (Hurst and Coy, 2003) 61.

2 Robert E. Kelly, 'From the "global war on terror" to containment: an opinion brief' (2008) 2(4) *Perspectives on Terrorism*. [Online]. Available at: http://www.terrorismanalysts.com/pt/index.php/pot/article/view/34/html [accessed: 2 February 2010].

Al-Qaeda's financial network is global, with a presence in an estimated one hundred countries.[3] Gunaratna further noted that many of its methods for raising, storing and transferring money are not particularly innovative, and that it uses models used by other terrorist organisations and organised crime groups. What Gunaratna is pertaining to, therefore, is that at a macro level, the network itself is unique and complex; however, at a micro level, many of the methods used within those networks are also used by other groups. This is encouraging as the lessons learned from other terrorist groups and organised crime groups can be used in combating finances relating to al-Qaeda.

However, it must also be pointed out that al-Qaeda is unique in that it is the first terrorist organisation to embrace modern technology, in particular the use of the Internet as the previous chapter highlighted.[4] According to John Arquilla,[5] al-Qaeda and its affiliates:

> *... have understood that both time and space have in many ways been conquered by the Internet.*[6]

Until recently, al-Qaeda's use of the Web appeared to be centred on communications involving preaching, recruitment, community-building and broad based incitement. However, there is increasing evidence that al-Qaeda and its affiliate organisations are also using the Internet for tactical purposes, especially for training new adherents, as well as for obtaining and transferring funds.[7]

Part of the aforementioned lack of understanding of terrorist finance is exacerbated by the existence of numerous myths that undermine not only CTF efforts but counter-terrorism as a whole. Therefore, it is of vital importance to highlight where these myths and misunderstandings exist and to understand the reality of the situation in order that effective counter measures can be put in place. One such myth is the paradigm of inexpensive terrorism.

3 Josh Meyer, 'Cutting money flow to terrorists proves difficult', *Los Angeles Times* (Los Angeles, 28 September 2003).

4 Mike Taylor, 'The McDonaldization of Jihad: A Strategy for Combating the Franchise Operations of Global Corporate al Qaeda', prepared for the 2009 Meetings of the Georgia Political Science Association November 11–14, 2009. [Online]. Available at: http://my.gcsu.edu/~dataylor/papers/McDonaldization.pdf [accessed: 1 March 2010].

5 John Arquilla is a naval postgraduate school professor who coined the term 'net-war' in the 1990s.

6 Steve Coll, Susan B. Glasser and Julie Tate, 'Terrorists turn to the web as base of operations', *Washington Post* (9 August 2005). [Online]. Available at: http://www.crimeresearch.org/articles/Terrorists_Turn/ [accessed: 21 March 2010].

7 See Chapter 2.

Disputing the Paradigm of Inexpensive Terrorism

There has been a general tendency to portray terrorism as 'inexpensive'. For example, with reference to the 7 July 2005 bombings in London, ABC News reported[8] that the 'London bombings were inexpensive,'[9] The BBC also reported that the London bombings cost no more than a few hundred pounds to carry out.[10] However, the official government report on the London bombings states that the costs were £8,000.[11] Another example is the 9/11 attack, which was initially estimated to have cost between $400,000 and $500,000[12] although the real figure is now believed to be considerably higher.[13]

With reference to the Madrid bombings on 11 March 2004, some reports, including one from the BBC, claimed that the cost of the operation was under $10,000.[14] However, Spanish law enforcement, who carried out the investigations claim that the cost of the operation alone was likely to have been between 41,000 euros and 55,000 euros.[15] One may argue that these differences are insignificant when examined in the broader context of the overall damage caused in terms of economic cost, and the more significant and immeasurable human cost. However, from a CTF perspective, the tendency to underestimate the cost of terrorist attacks should be noted.

Suicide bombing operations, for example, are also described as costing very little. Bruce Hoffman, Director of the RAND Corporation in Washington, D.C., claims that suicide bombing operations, 'aside from the cost in human life, are cheap to carry out' and estimates the cost 'to be between $50 and $150'[16]

---

8 Tariq Panja, 'Analysts say London bombings inexpensive: security analysts say London bombings were relatively inexpensive costing about $2,000', *ABC News* (3 January 2006). [Online]. Available at: http://abcnews.go.com/International/Terrorism/wireStory?id=1466463 [accessed: 21 March 2010].

9 Loretta Napoleoni had estimated the cost to be $2,000.

10 Michael Buchanan, 'London bombs cost just hundreds' *BBC News* (3 January 2006). [Online]. Available at: http://news.bbc.co.uk/go/pr/fr/-/2/hi/uk_news/4576346.stm [accessed: 21 March 2010].

11 House of Commons, *Report on the Official Account of the Bombings in London on 7 July 2005* (The Stationery Office, 11 May 2006) 23.

12 9/11 Commission Report.

13 Shima D. Keene, *Al-Qaeda: Financing Terror* (Airey Neave Trust Report, 2005).

14 'Al-Qaeda sanctions ineffective', *BBC* (London, 27 August 2004). [Online]. Available at: http://news.bbc.co.uk/go/pr/fr/-/1/hi/world/americas/3603862.stm [accessed: 23 March 2010].

15 The Jamestown Foundation, 'The Madrid attacks: results of investigations two years later' (2006) 4(5) *Terrorism Monitor* 3.

16 Justin Rood, 'Al Qaeda suicide bombings in U.S. unlikely, expert says' CQ (2004) *Homeland Security Congressional Quarterly*. [Online]. Available at: http://page15.com/2004/09/al-qaeda-suicide-bombings-in-u.html [accessed: 23 February 2010].

per operation. What Hoffman describes, is perhaps the cost of the suicide belt or an improvised explosive device (IED). However what he has perhaps failed to incorporate into his calculation is the cost of the support infrastructure necessary to carry out a suicide bombing operation, as well as the cumulative cost of the multiplicity of attacks as witnessed in recent years in Iraq and Afghanistan, which has come to symbolise militant Islam.

The paradigm of inexpensive terrorism has been derived from the fact that terrorist devices, such as IEDs, can indeed be relatively inexpensive to manufacture. However, the main cost of deploying such a weapon is not simply the sum of the cost of component parts. Security measures can be a costly affair in that only trusted individuals can be deployed for the purpose, often with specialist expertise. As the activity is high risk, a premium is often demanded to undertake such activities, all of which add to the terrorist organisation's expense budget. Another factor is the cost of security to the logistical supply route to ensure the safe delivery of the supply of component parts.

Other key costs include the updating of technology in an effort to keep up with counter-IED measures. This requires constant research and development, from the terrorist's perspective, updating the modus operandi of attacks and training in an effort to maximise the effectiveness of the terrorist attacks. It is for this very reason that the targeting of the financial network for the dependents of suicide bombers has been a key strategy of the Israeli government.

However, the concept of relatively inexpensive terrorism has proven to be correct when dealing with simple structured organisations, such as the Palestinian organisations in the 1970s and Algerian organisations in the 1980s.[17] The idea is also true in relation to al-Qaeda relating to operational costs, where local national cells, which are mostly dormant, exist in modest conditions. However, to apply that idea to the entire al-Qaeda network, to quote Brisard:

> *... is not only irrelevant but simply turns to an end the war against terrorism financing.*[18]

As such, it is essential to understand the difference between the costs of an operation versus its infrastructure support costs. The operational cost of a

17 Jean-Charles Brisard, *Terrorism Financing: Roots and Trends of Saudi Terrorism Financing* (Report prepared for the President of the Security Council, United Nations 19 December 2002, New York) 6.

18 Ibid.

single terrorist act may be small relative to the damage caused; however, a differentiation must be made between the cost of executing a single terrorist act to that of financing terrorism in general. It should further be noted that most of the CTF efforts to date have focused on operational costs neglecting the equally, if not more significant infrastructure costs, which constitute the large majority of the costs for terrorist groups.

Al-Qaeda itself makes a clear distinction between its organisational funds and its 'operational funds' in various documents, including its training manual. For al-Qaeda, operational funds have two main objectives, the first is to invest in projects that offer financial return to maintain local cells, and the second is to carry out terrorist operations. Reflecting upon these various distinctions, Brisard observes that:

> *... Apart from the operational level, one must not confuse the requirements of al-Qaeda in terms of daily logistics and the super-structure level, which is the real innovation introduced by Osama bin Laden. Al-Qaeda is not only a combatant organization, it is also and most of all a confederation of militant organizations around the world. The first purpose of money for al-Qaeda at this level is to entertain the broad network of organizations, to fund them to stabilize and leverage their support and to develop their reach. Over the years, al-Qaeda supported financially several entities, from Libya to the Philippines, from Indonesia to Somalia. Figures here range in millions of dollars.*
>
> *The second purpose of money at the super-structure level has been to pay for protection and asylum. Since 1991, al-Qaeda and Osama Bin Laden had to resettle in various countries after the opposition movement was banned from Saudi Arabia. It was the case in Sudan and Afghanistan for years.*[19]

Today's global terrorism requires money for much more than the cost of explosives and other instruments to facilitate terrorist attacks.[20] An expanding terror network must have enough funds to support recruitment, training camps and bases, housing and food, equipment, explosives, weapons, forged identity and travel documents, intelligence gathering, communications networks, bribery, as well as the day-to-day maintenance expenses of members

19 Ibid. 7.

20 Fletcher N. Baldwin Jr., 'The financing of terror in the age of the internet: wilful blindness, greed or a political statement?' (2004) 8(2) *Journal of Money Laundering Control* 127.

awaiting commands to launch operations.[21] In addition, funding is needed for propaganda purposes to include radio, print media and videos, to ensure continued support of existing members and to attract new members. Funding is also needed to maintain the families of the terrorists who are deployed as 'sleepers', and living undercover, who may be unable to support their dependents, as well as to compensate families of terrorists who are killed.

Brisard further estimates that al-Qaeda's financial needs in terms of infrastructure support account for as much as 90 per cent of total costs, whereas operational costs account for only 10 per cent,[22] thus highlighting why the sole focus of operational costs is inadequate. The total cost of maintaining the global Islamic terror network is estimated to be in the billions of dollars.[23] To sustain these operations, sophisticated multifaceted worldwide funding networks have been set in place over the past two decades.

Sources of Terrorist Funding: Overview

From a historic perspective, in its infancy, al-Qaeda is believed to have received financial support largely from bin Laden's personal fortune. Bin Laden's personal annual income is reported to have been approximately $1 million between 1970 and 1994.[24] In addition, al-Qaeda enjoyed contributions from its wide network of international sympathisers including governments and charitable organisations. As al-Qaeda became more established, the use of legitimate businesses operating as fronts, and dealing on financial markets, especially unregulated commodity markets and international trade, which converts cash into precious commodities such as diamonds and gold, were exploited. In addition, criminal activities such as extortion, smuggling, kidnapping, credit card fraud, identity theft, counterfeiting and the pirating of videos, compact discs, tapes and software continue to be used to obtain finance.

There are two main methods by which al-Qaeda is known to have raised funds for the purpose of terrorism, namely legal and illegal.[25]

21 Rachel Ehrenfeld, *Funding Evil Updated: How Terrorism is Financed and How to Stop It* (Bonus Books, 2004) 1.

22 Brisard, *Terrorism Financing* (n. 17). 7

23 Loretta Napoleoni, *Modern Jihad: Tracing the Dollars behind the Terror Networks* (Pluto Press, 2004).

24 National Commission on Terrorist Attacks in the United States, *Overview of the Enemy* (16 June 2004) 3. [Online]. Available at: http://www.9-11commission.gov.staff_statements/staff_statement15.pdf [accessed: 23 February 2010].

25 Peter A. Sproat, 'Counter-terrorist finance in the UK: A quantitative and qualitative commentary based on open-source materials' (2010) 13(4) *Journal of Money Laundering Control* 315.

Legal Sources

Legal sources of funding include sponsorship, charities, *zakat*,[26] as well as legitimate businesses operating as fronts.[27] Legal methods are often difficult to detect without specific intelligence, as the activities appear normal on the surface. Each of these key methods will be examined in turn.

CHARITIES

The use of charities for funding terrorism is also not a new concept.[28] The PLO and the IRA are both known to have used charities extensively for fund raising purposes. This is also the case with Islamist terrorist groups which according to the US State Department 2007 International Narcotics Control Strategy Report, unregulated charities have been a major source of financing to extremist and terrorist groups over the past 25 years.[29] Saudi charitable donations alone are estimated to amount to approximately $3 billion to $4 billion annually, of which 10–20 per cent is disseminated abroad.[30]

Some of the charities that have been supported by the Saudi al-Rajhi and bin Mahfouz banking families, have been identified in either a court of law or government reports as supporting al-Qaeda. These charities include the International Islamic Relief Organisation (IIRO), the Rabita Trust, which changed its name to Aid Organisation of the Ulema, the Benevolence International Foundation (BIF) also known as the Al-Bir Society, the SAAR network organisations, the Taibah International Aid Association, the Global Relief Foundation (GRF), the World Assembly of Muslim Youth (WAMY), the Islamic African Relief Charity, the Saudi High Commission, also known as the Saudi High Relief Commission or SRC, the Saudi Joint Relief Committee, Muwafaq or Blessed Relief Foundation, Al-Haramain Islamic Foundation, Mercy International Relief Organisation (Mercy) and the Muslim World League (MWL). Of these, the main charities that are directly involved in financing

26 See next section on *Zakat*.

27 Baldwin, 'The financing of terror in the age of the internet' (n.20).

28 Suzanne Fleury, 'Review of unfunding terror: the legal response to the financing of global terrorism' (2010) 7(1) *Journal of Homeland Security and Emergency Management* 67.

29 Christopher M. Blanchard and Alfred B. Prados, *Saudi Arabia: Terrorist Financing Issues*, CRS Report for Congress, Order Code RL32499, updated 14 September 2007. [Online]. Available at: http://www.fas.org/sgp/crs/terror/RL32499.pdf [accessed: 8 July 2011].

30 Jonathan M. Winer, Congressional testimony before the Committee on Senate Governmental Affairs, 31 July 2003. Mr. Winer, a former State Department official, is an independent consultant.

al-Qaeda are Al-Haramain Islamic Foundation, BIF, IIRO, MWL, Rabita Trust and WAMY.[31]

In addition, the confessions of former al-Qaeda representative in Southern Asia, Omar al Faruq, to the US authorities identify Al-Haramain as the key funding mechanism of all operations in Indonesia. Faruq further revealed that money was laundered through the foundation by donors from the Middle East and that the charity office was working under the control of a representative of Osama bin Laden.[32] However, although these examples demonstrate the involvement of some charities in the financing of terrorism, there is dispute as to whether all the elements within the charity are necessarily aware of its activities relating to terrorism.[33] Indeed there are numerous cases whereby charities have been overtaken by radical elements of Islam against the wishes of the original members through intimidation and violence.[34]

Moving forwards, it is necessary to look not only at methods to increase the transparency of charitable organisations in respect of their activities in general, but also their financial activities, which need to be monitored much more closely. What is clear, however, is the relationship between Islamic charities and *zakat*, without which Islamic charities would not be able to survive.[35] The Islamic concept of *zakat* is an obligatory almsgiving imposed on Muslims and charitable organisations are one of its key beneficiaries.[36] The next section will explore the concept of *zakat* in more detail, in particular its impact on Islamic society and on terrorist finance.

ZAKAT

Zakat is an obligatory almsgiving imposed on Muslims. The concept of *zakat* is important to understand not only for its significance within Islam, being one of the pillars of Islam, but also in the context of terrorist finance. The importance of *zakat* in Muslim society is highlighted in the sermon by Jamaal al-Din Zarabozo:

31 Blanchard and Prados, *Saudi Arabia* (n.29).

32 Brisard, *Terrorism Financing* (n.17).

33 Fleury, 'Review of unfunding terror' (n.28) 67.

34 Shima D. Keene, *A Trojan Horse for Terrorism: The Vulnerability and Abuse of Mosques by Militant Islam in the United Kingdom*, The Institute for Statecraft and Governance, Security Economics Programme Report, February 2010.

35 Moid U. Ahmad and Athar Mahmood, '*Zakat* fund: concept and perspective' (2009) 2(3) *International Journal of Monetary Economics and Finance* 197.

36 Russell Powell, 'Zakat: drawing insights for legal theory and economic policy from Islamic jurisprudence' (2009) 7(43) *University of Pittsburgh Tax Review*, Seattle University School of Law Research Paper no. 10–17. [Online]. Available at: http://ssrn.com/abstract=1351024 [accessed: 3 March 2010].

> *Zakat is one of the foundations of Islam. If the foundation is weak, then this weak foundation will have ramifications for other aspects of our lives. Today, how many Muslims in the world honestly, sincerely and properly pay zakat to purify their wealth and to help their Muslim brethren. Since we are missing lacking or very weak in that foundation, is it any surprise that so many Muslims are starving and in need today, so much Muslim wealth is wasted on luxury, so much Muslim wealth is spent on forbidden items and so little Muslim wealth is spent on jihad and sacrificing for the sake of Allah. The Messenger of Allah (peace be upon him) was ordered to fight the people until they made the shahada, established prayer and paid zakat. Let us make sure that we pay the zakat and fulfil all of the other pillars of Islam correctly and sincerely for Allah's sake, so that our Islam as a whole will be strong and Allah will be pleased with us.*[37]

Zakat is distributed to eight possible destinations known as *asnaf*,[38] which include the poor (*faqir*/*fuqara*), the needy (*miskeen*), the administrators of *zakat* (*amil*), those in debt (*gharimin*) and the cause of Allah (*fisabilliah*), which includes the building of mosques. It is important to note that Islamic banks apply *zakat* to every contract or transaction they handle amounting to 2.5 per cent.[39] *Zakat* is therefore a large source of income. The 6,000 members of the Saudi royal family alone, for example, are estimated to be worth $600 billion, making their *zakat* levy equivalent to a yearly $12 billion.[40]

Zakat can be donated in many forms. *Zakat* payments can be made to charities or directly to the needy themselves. Alternatively, *zakat* payments can be made through the government in Islamic countries such as Saudi Arabia, which collects a *zakat* tax. *Zakat* is calculated on capital and earnings from and on all proceeds, profits and gains from business, industry or personal work, and on property or monetary acquisitions of whatever type or description. These include commercial and financial transactions and dividends, livestock and crops.[41] In further detail, *zakat* is collected on gold, silver, land and property,

---

37 Jamaal al-Din Zarabozo, 'The Importance of Zakat'. Excerpted from The Friday Prayer (III) © IANA 1995. [Online]. Available at: http://www.islaam.com/Article.aspx?id=280 [accessed: 23 January 2010].

38 Guardia Di Finanza. 'The funding of international Islamic terrorism: strategic analysis profiles' 7. [Online]. Available at: http://www.gdf.it/Stampa/STUDI/2006fundingofinternationalislamicterrorism.pdf [accessed: 23 January 2010].

39 Ahmad and Mahmood, '*Zakat* fund' (n.35).

40 Guardia Di Finanza (n.43) 119. See also Sebastian R. Müller, 'Money War: Hawala and Its Use for Terrorism', University of Freiburg Institute for Economic Research, September 2004.

41 Ahmad and Mahmood, '*Zakat* fund' (n.35).

business stock, cash and bank, loans, company shares and mutual fund, Agricultural products, and farm stock including animals, poultry and fish.[42]

The magnitude of *zakat* is clear. Furthermore, following its audit trail is challenging particularly for voluntary donations, as anonymity is considered particularly pious and donors are concerned primarily with the act of almsgiving, which meets the religious requirement and purifies the intensions of the believer as opposed to how their money has been spent. Thus, charities and others receiving *zakat* in Saudi Arabia have traditionally had little accountability to their donors, including until recently the Saudi government.

Regulations relating to charitable institutions further add to the problem. In Saudi Arabia, *zakat* taxes are collected and controlled by the Directorate General of *Zakat* and Income Tax (DZIT) of the Saudi Ministry of Finance and National Economy.[43] DZIT donations usually take the form of bank transfers to more than 240 charities. Although the Directorate has strict instructions for organising, auditing and collecting *zakat* from all Saudis obligated to pay, it has had little guidance as to how these funds should be distributed.[44] Furthermore, there are no regulations regarding the oversight of these funds once they are received by the charities. As a result, charities in the Kingdom have been receiving, and continue to receive, billions of dollars from the government without any public accountability as to its destination.[45]

There is also evidence that *zakat* is abused by al-Qaeda to finance terrorism. According to Brisard, the al-Qaeda network extensively utilised the weakness of legislation to rely on funds diverted from *zakat* and other direct donations through Islamic banks. Furthermore, bin Laden had made regular calls for Muslims to donate through the *zakat* system to his organisation. In December 1998, during an interview with ABC News, bin Laden stated that:

> *Muslims and Muslim merchants, in particular, should give their zakat and their money in support of this state [Taliban regime]*[46] *which is*

42 Brisard, *Terrorism Financing* (n.17) 15.

43 Ministry of Finance, Saudi Arabia, 'A technical assessment of certain Saudi Arabia laws, regulations and institutions'. [Online]. Available at: http://www.mof.gov.sa/e_alzakah.html [accessed: 23 January 2010].

44 Samy Nathan Garas and Chris Pierce, 'Shari'a supervision of Islamic financial institutions' (2010) 18(4) *Journal of Financial Regulation and Compliance* 386.

45 Ministry of Finance, Saudi Arabia, 'A technical assessment of certain Saudi Arabia laws (n.43).

46 Referring to Afghanistan under the Taliban.

> *reminiscent of the state of Medina (Al-Munawwarah), where the followers of Islam embraced the Prophet of God.*[47]

Brisard believes that *zakat* is one of the most important sources of financial support for the al-Qaeda network. *Zakat* is the easiest and the most common way to raise donations in Saudi Arabia and the lack of regulatory oversight has resulted in the lack of transparency making attempts to follow any form of audit trail difficult. Through the abuse of this pillar of Islam and benefiting from the Saudi regulatory vacuum, al-Qaeda has been able to receive between $300 million and $500 million[48] over the last 10 years from wealthy businessmen and bankers, through a web of charities and companies acting as fronts, with the notable use of Islamic banking institutions.

Most of this financial backbone is still extant and able to support fundamentalist organisations. If addressing this issue appears to be a difficult task, it remains an essential way to stop the flow of money into the hands of terrorists. However, it should also be noted that the Saudi authorities have been working closely with the US in particular to rectify this situation, which is encouraging.

LEGITIMATE BUSINESSES

Many of al-Qaeda's operational cells have established legitimate businesses involved in a variety of sectors including construction, real estate, technology, finance and agriculture. Within Saudi Arabia, soft or non-existent regulation in terms of accounting rules and mandatory disclosures of company activities, have also provided an ideal environment for al-Qaeda to operate legitimate companies as fronts for the purpose of providing financial support to its terrorist activities.

Al-Qaeda's involvement with legitimate businesses can be divided into two broad categories. The first relates to the business network formed in Sudan between 1983 and 1996. The second relates to other al-Qaeda businesses across the globe used for offsetting losses made by some of the companies within the al-Qaeda conglomerate, as well as for money laundering purposes. This Sudanese business network included the protection provided by the Sudanese state itself, a factor that explains al-Qaeda's ability to remain an offensive organisation.

---

47 Brisard, *Terrorism Financing* (n.17) 14.
48 Ibid.

When bin Laden relocated to Sudan in 1991, his close relationship with the then controlling powerbase of Islamic leader Hasan al-Turabi, allowed bin Laden to set up several business ventures, invest in several large companies and banks, as well as undertake several civil infrastructure development projects. According to manuscripts from US court proceedings,[49] bin Laden established 30 companies ranging from high-tech labs engaged in generic research to civil engineering.[50] The 30 companies included Wadi al-Aqiq (holding company), Laden International (import-exports), Taba Investment (money exchange and currency trading), Al-Hiraj (construction),[51] Blessed Fruits (fruit picking and packaging), al-Qudurat Transportations (trucking), al-Themar al Mubaraka (farm produce processing and sales) and the International al-Ikhls Company (honey and sweets).

Bin Laden also owned the Saudi Binladin Group, a construction company originally part of his family Saudi conglomerate, which built roads and airport facilities in Sudan.[52] Bin Laden's Damazine farm, not only produced sesame, peanuts and white corn, but also acted as a base for providing training for Afghanistan graduates in weapons and explosives.[53]

Other business interests in Sudan included a bakery, a furniture company, a cattle breeding farm, goat skin processing, fishing boats and gum Arabic,[54] which was one of the most profitable businesses bin Laden acquired. Gum Arabic Company Limited, a firm which supplied 80 per cent[55] of the world demand for this product, gave bin Laden a virtual monopoly in the industry.[56] Bin Laden's International al-Ikhls Company in Sudan, produced honey and sweets at a factory in Kameen. The honey trade offered a double advantage in that it was not only a legal source of revenue, but also provided a useful cover for smuggling.[57] Illegal items such as drugs, arms, as well as gold, electronic equipment and cash, could be smuggled in honey containers thereby avoiding

49 *United States of America v Usama bin Laden et al.* (2001) 538 F.3d 71.

50 Napoleoni, *Modern Jihad* (n.23) 31.

51 Bin Laden funded the construction of the airport at New Sudan and the highway linking it to Khartoum. For the services of his construction company, Al-Hiraj was paid by the government in sesame seeds, which were then traded on the international market. Simon Reeve, *The New Jackals: Ramzi Yousef, Osama bin Laden and the Future of Terrorism* (Andre Deutsch, 1999) 178.

52 Brisard, *Terrorism Financing* (n.17).

53 Gunaratna, *Inside Al Qaeda* (n.1) 32.

54 Gum Arabic is produced from the sap of the acacia trees that grow in Sudan. It is used to make ink stick to newspapers, to prevent sediment forming in soft drinks and to create a protective shell around sweets and pills to keep them fresh.

55 Napoleoni, *Modern Jihad* (n.23) 161–2.

56 Reeve, *The New Jackals* ch. 9.

57 Napoleoni, *Modern Jihad* (n.23) 158–9.

detection as honey is not only messy to inspect, but also has a strong smell which conceals the smell of the smuggled items.[58]

Outside Sudan, real estate investments were scattered around the world to offset losses and maximise profits. The portfolio included real estate in London, Paris and the French Riviera; dairy businesses in Denmark; wood and paper industries in Norway; and a hospital equipment business in Sweden, the latter continuing to this day along with the real estate investments. According to Jacquard, bin Laden and his associates have also targeted the medical market in Egypt, Jordan and Iraq, which generates hundreds of millions of dollars in revenue, part of which is believed to fund his network of terrorist cells.[59]

In terms of financial investment, in 1998, through a contact at the Arab Banking Corporation, bin Laden is reported to have speculated on the French stock market in shares, including stocks from BNP and Société Générale, netting $20 million[60] profit. In addition, approximately $750,000[61] is believed to have been placed in short-term accounts in several financial markets on the Arabian Peninsula after the collapse of the Taliban regime. Elsewhere in Africa, bin Laden owned an ostrich farm and shrimp boats in Kenya. In the Middle East, bin Laden owned shares in the Al-Shamil Islamic Bank and large tracts of forest in Turkey; in Asia, agricultural holdings in Tajikistan; in Europe and the US, he owned holding companies, venture capital firms, banks and import-export companies.[62]

These businesses enabled bin Laden to offer safe haven and employment to al-Qaeda members, to provide bank accounts for several operatives, and to finance terrorist operations and facilities, training camps and arms buying. Most notably, this network was able to carry out legal financial transactions with Western banks and financial institutions with the guarantee of his prominent Saudi associates. The added benefit was that once the money had entered the Western financial system, the funds could move freely around the globe and accessed with ease.

58 Judith Miller and Jeff Gerth, 'Trade in honey is said to provide money and cover for bin Laden', *New York Times* (11 October 2001). [Online]. Available at: http://www.beekeeping.com/articles/us/honey_laden.htm [accessed: 20 October 2009].

59 Roland Jacquard, *In the Name of Osama bin Laden: Global Terrorism and the bin Laden Brotherhood* (Duke University Press, 2002) 110–11.

60 Ibid. 161–2.

61 Ehrenfeld, *Funding Evil Updated* (n.21) 161–2.

62 John Mintz, 'Bin Laden's finances are Moving target', *Washington Post* (28 August 1998).

Illegal Sources of Terrorist Funding

In addition to legal methods, al-Qaeda also relies on criminal means for financial support, especially when legitimate sources of funding are scarce. The key illegal sources of funding are examined in the next section.

CONFLICT DIAMONDS AND TANZANITE

Evidence of al-Qaeda's involvement in the diamond trade dates back to 1996. According to Nafeez Mosaddeq Ahmed, al-Qaeda's diamond trading operations began in 1996, but entered a 'third phase' in late 2000 when senior al-Qaeda leaders arrived in Liberia.[63] Mark Huband also reported that when $240 million of al-Qaeda's assets were frozen by the US government six weeks after the 1998 bombing of the US embassies in Kenya and Tanzania, bin Laden's then second-in-command, Ayman al-Zawahiri, wrote a letter instructing an al-Qaeda member to purchase diamonds.[64] Additionally, Belgian sources revealed that immediately prior to 9/11, bin Laden's associates converted $10 million[65] into precious stones as a safeguard against the possibility that Western governments would freeze accounts used by bin Laden's network.[66]

Soon after 9/11, it was discovered that al-Qaeda may in fact have bought up to $20m worth of Sierra Leonean diamonds through Antwerp-based dealers operating in Liberia.[67] Court transcripts from the 2001 trial of al-Qaeda operatives in the US reveal that the trade in rough diamonds and high value gemstones from Kenya and Tanzania had been an important part of al-Qaeda's financial structure.[68] These allegations have also been supported by the legal firm Motley Rice LLB, in South Carolina, leading the investigation on behalf of the 9/11 families' civil action against al-Qaeda's financiers.[69]

---

63 Nafeez Mosaddeq Ahmed, *The London Bombings: An Independent Inquiry* (Gerald Duckworth & Co. 2006) 244–57.

64 Ehrenfeld, *Funding Evil Updated* (n.21) 59.

65 Napoleoni, *Modern Jihad* (n.24) 182–3.

66 Mark Doyle, 'Sierra Leone rebels probe Al-Qaeda link' *BBC* (2 November 2001).

67 Mark Huband, 'Conflict diamonds spur code of practice', *Financial Times* (20 October 2002). [Online]. Available at: http://globalpolicy.igc.org/security/issues/diamond/2002/1030code.htm [accessed: 24 January 2010].

68 Global Witness, *For a Few Dollars More: How al-Qaeda Moved into the Diamond Trade* (Global Witness, April 2003).

69 Interview with Michael Elsner, Motley Rice, lead investigator and attorney, 25 October 2005, Motley Rice Office, South Carolina, USA. Elsner is a key member of the 9/11 and Anti-Terrorism Practice Group. He leads the investigatory team that is currently scouring the globe gathering liability evidence for the 9/11 families' civil action against al Qaeda's financiers and for 9/11 aviation litigation.

The motivation for al-Qaeda's use of diamonds is apparent. Diamonds can be easily hidden, they are difficult to trace and are exempt from traditional monetary and financial controls. In addition, diamonds retain their value,[70] which is particularly beneficial when operating in politically and economically unstable environments. Thus, there are four main reasons why al-Qaeda utilises diamonds. First, as a means of raising funds; second, in order to hide money targeted by financial sanctions; third, for money laundering purposes; and finally, to convert cash into a commodity that holds its value and is easily transportable.[71]

Until July 2001, al-Qaeda purchased diamonds from the Revolutionary United Front (RUF), the Liberian-backed rebels fighting for dominance in the West African nation of Sierra Leone, for less than the market price, and then resold them in Dubai, Mauritius and India for a profit.[72] The security was provided by the Liberian President Charles Taylor, who received $1million in cash in exchange for his consent to harbour al-Qaeda operatives in the summer of 2001. Taylor's involvement in the illegal diamond trade, weapons smuggling and terrorism was investigated by a specially appointed UN panel, which recommended that Taylor, together with his family and senior members of his government, be banned from international travel, a ban which was adopted by the Security Council in 2001.[73]

Al-Qaeda's contact with the RUF came through Ibrahim Bah, a Libyan-trained Senegalese, who had fought with Osama bin Laden in Afghanistan in the 1980s. He later returned to Africa where he became the key diamond dealer and weapon buyer not only for the RUF, but also for the Liberian President Charles Taylor, all the while maintaining his contacts with al-Qaeda. Diamonds bought by al-Qaeda were sold to the ASA Diam diamond trading company in Antwerp, Belgium, which was recommended to Bah in July 2000 by two al-Qaeda members, Samih Osailly and his cousin Aziz Nassour, a Lebanese diamond merchant. ASA Diam, which had been inactive for two years, agreed to manage al-Qaeda's gems and within six months had made $14 million in profits.[74]

Nassour had been previously implicated by the CIA for his involvement in the illegal trade of diamonds and emeralds on behalf of Hizbollah and was

70 Douglas Farah, 'Al-Qaeda cash tied to diamond trade', *Washington Post* (2 November 2001).
71 Global Witness, *For a Few Dollars More* (n.68) 6.
72 Ehrenfeld, *Funding Evil Updated* (n.21) 60.
73 Douglas Farah, 'African gems, al-Qaeda link established', *Washington Post* (29 December 2002).
74 Ibid.

banned from international travel by the UN.[75] Even though ASA Diam ceased reporting its sales of diamonds to the Antwerp Diamond Centre, Belgian investigators obtained records of the company's accounts and discovered deals worth millions of dollars. According to *The Times*, $20 million had been withdrawn from the accounts just prior to the 9/11 attacks, to fund the purchases of weapons,[76] further supporting earlier comments that Sierra Leonean diamonds may have been bought through Antwerp-based dealers operating in Liberia.[77]

Additionally, the trial of Wadih el Hage[78] provided some compelling evidence in relation to al-Qaeda's interest in precious stones. El Hage was a Lebanese naturalised US citizen, who for several years served as bin Laden's personal secretary. El Hage was arrested on 20 September 1998 and charged, convicted and sentenced to life in relation his involvement in the US Embassy bombings in Nairobi Kenya, and Dar-es-Salaam, Tanzania. Court testimonies reveal and confirm al-Qaeda's involvement in the diamond and tanzanite market based on El Hage's business cards, personal telephone directory, notebook, diary and testimony. The evidence presented not only confirmed al-Qaeda's links to the diamond industry, but also its involvement with tanzanite.[79] The diary also contained evidence of the gem being sold in London as well as the role played by the gemstone in money laundering and the financing of bin Laden's networks.[80]

Although it is difficult to quantify the level of abuse for terrorist finance purposes, what is clear from the evidence examined is that al-Qaeda cells in East Africa utilised the precious stones market as a means of both revenue and security for its cells in Kenya and Tanzania during times of financial difficulty. Despite the fact that the businesses are not believed to have been hugely profitable, the profits made through the trading of these stones were sufficient to make the cells financially self-sufficient.[81]

---

75 The Revised UN Travel Ban List, *The Perspective*, 31 December 2001. [Online]. Available at: www.theperspective.org/revisedtravelbanlist.html and www.hartford-hwp.com/archives/34/049.html [accessed: 23 January 2010].

76 Daniel McGrory, 'Al-Qaeda bought $20m diamonds to hide finances', *The Times* (30 December 2002).

77 Huband, 'Conflict Diamonds Spur Code of Practice'.

78 *Al Rajhi Banking and Investment Corporation v Wall Street Journal Europe*, SPRL [2003] EWHC 1776 (QB).

79 Douglas Farah, *Blood from Stones* (Broadway Books 2004) 63–5.

80 Glenn Simpson, 'Terrorist grid smuggled gems as early as '95, diary suggests', *Wall Street Journal* (New York, 17 January 2002).

81 Global Witness, *For a Few Dollars More* (n.68) 36.

KIDNAP AND RANSOM

For many years, hostage ransom payments have funded terrorist groups such as FARC.[82] There is also evidence of Islamic terrorist groups using hostage taking for both political and financial gain. One such example is the kidnapping of three Britons and one New Zealander working for Granger Telecom, a British company installing mobile communications systems in Chechnya. The engineers were kidnapped by Chechen Islamist rebels at the end of 1998. The rebels negotiated with Granger a ransom of $4 million. However, just before the transfer of money was to take place, the men were beheaded. According to Channel 4 Dispatches, investigation into the last hours of the hostages' lives revealed that bin Laden had paid $4 million[83] for the engineers to be executed.[84]

In this situation, clearly the involvement of al-Qaeda was not for financial gain, but for the purpose of propaganda. However, the use of 'kidnapping' is accepted and encouraged by al-Qaeda not only as a tool for achieving political goals, but as an effective method for obtaining finance. Al-Qaeda's goals and circumstances for kidnapping are detailed in the '*al-Qaeda Guide to kidnapping*'[85] written by Yassin Musharbash and made available on an al-Qaeda website by Abdul Aziz al-Muqrin, the former head of al-Qaeda in Saudi Arabia.[86] One of the five goals and circumstances listed in relation to kidnapping actively encourages this practice as a means of obtaining ransom money:

> 4. *Obtain ransom money – as, for example, our brothers in the Philippines, Chechnya and Algeria made happen and as our brothers in 'Mohammed's Army' in Kashmir did when they obtained $2 million*

---

82 Kidnap listing. [Online]. Available at: http://www.timripley.co.uk/terrorism/1999_2004.pdf.

83 BBC, *The Money Programme*, 21 November 2001.

84 Napoleoni, *Modern Jihad* (n.23) 169–70.

85 *Al-Qaeda's Goals and Circumstances for Kidnapping*. A kidnapping, described here as 'the arrest of one or more people from the opponents' side,' should serve the following purposes according to Muqrin:
1. Force the government or opponent to fulfil a specific set of demands.
2. Create a difficult situation for a government in its relations with the countries where the kidnapped persons come from.
3. Obtain important information from the hostages.
4. Obtain ransom money as, for example, our brothers in the Philippines, Chechnya and Algeria made happen and as our brothers in 'Mohammed's Army' in Kashmir did when they obtained $2 million in ransom. This money can then serve as financial support for an organization.
5. To draw attention to a specific concern – as occurred at the start of the Chechnya question or in Algeria, when our brothers hijacked a French plane.

86 Yassin Musharbash, *The Al-Qaida Guide to Kidnapping*. [Online]. Available at: http://service.spiegel.de/cache/international/0,1518,387888,00.html [accessed: 23 January 2010].

> *in ransom. This money can then serve as financial support for an organisation.*[87]

In May 2004, an essay was published in the tenth issue of al-Qaeda online magazine *Mu'askar al-Battar*, with the apparent goal of encouraging further hostage taking as well as attempting to add more professionalism to the criminal act of hostage taking. Since its publication, the document has been mirrored on countless websites used by Islamic extremists. *Spiegel Online*[88] has translated excerpts that provide a glimpse of the internal workings of al-Qaeda's kidnapping operations highlighting its use as a potentially profitable business. According to the document, al-Qaeda's kidnap strategy falls into two categories. The first is public kidnappings to be conducted for political/ propaganda purposes and the second is the kidnap of private individuals predominantly for financial gain.

As such, it is not surprising that numerous kidnappings have taken place in recent years involving al-Qaeda and its affiliates. The large majority have taken place in Iraq at the hand of the late al-Zarqawi, where more than 250 foreigners were abducted since the US-led invasion in 2003. Of the 250 abducted, at least 44 have been killed, 135 were released, 3 escaped, 6 were rescued and the fate of the others remain unknown.[89] The nationalities of those kidnapped include American, British, Lebanese, Jordanian, Egyptian, Turkish, Nepalese, South Korean, Pakistani, Italian, Bulgarian and French, demonstrating the indiscriminate nature of the individuals targeted.[90]

The motivation for the kidnappings for al-Qaeda has been both political and financial. Although Zarqawi accepted ransom payments for certain hostages considered to be 'non-strategic', the main motivation for the kidnappings seems to have been to seek maximum media impact.[91] However, the collection of ransom payments has also proved to be a lucrative business for al-Qaeda affiliates.

87 Ibid.

88 English language international edition of the German news source also includes in-depth special reports, blog and summaries of what the other German papers. [Online]. Available at: http://www.spiegel.de/international/ [accessed: 25 October 2009].

89 Daniel McGrory, 'How $45m secretly bought freedom of foreign hostages', *The Times* (22 May 2006). [Online]. Available at: http://www.timesonline.co.uk/article/0,,7374-2191229,00.html [accessed: 25 October 2009].

90 J.C. Brisard and Damien Martinez, *Zarqawi: The New Face of al-Qaeda* (Polity Press 2005) 142.

91 Ibid. 143.

According to Kuwait and Gulf Link Transport Co. Chief Executive Officer, Said Dashti, whose company paid $500,000 to secure the release of seven of their employees considered to be 'non-strategic' targets,[92] the kidnappers were:

> *... not trying to make a political statement, they were purely extortionists.*[93]

This statement was demonstrated by the fact that the group holding the seven truck drivers, which called itself 'The Holders of the Black Banners', had initially made political demands, namely the release of Iraqi detainees, but later dropped all demands and accepted a payment of $500,000. The company revealed that the kidnappers had originally demanded $6 million to $7 million in ransom.[94] Iraqi law enforcement sources have further revealed that approximately 30 people a day are abducted in Baghdad with most Iraqis taken being returned once their families had paid a ransom.[95] According to Iraqi counter-terrorism sources, despite denials by governments that ransom payments are paid, there is evidence that this is not the case:

> *Too often governments and their military keep secrets from each other, and certainly from us, and do what they want including paying out millions, no matter what their stated policy on ransoms.*[96]

The Japanese government, for example, strongly denied having offered a ransom for the release of Japanese hostage Shosei Koda despite a claim by a group of Islamic extremists that Japan had offered millions of dollars.[97] Similarly, the French government made similar denial statements when Florence Aubenas was freed in June 2005. A French government spokesman, Jean-François Cope said:

> *There was absolutely no demand for money. No ransom was paid.*[98]

92 One Egyptian, three Indians and three Kenyans.
93 Ravi Nessman, 'Seven foreign truckers freed in Iraq after ransom paid', *Associated Press* (2September2004).[Online].Availableat:http://www.helenair.com/articles/2004/09/02/national/a02090204_02.txt [accessed: 3 January 2010].
94 Ibid.
95 McGrory, 'How $45m secretly bought freedom of foreign hostages' (n.89).
96 Ibid.
97 'Japan denies having offered ransom to free Iraq hostage', *Asian Political News* (8 November 2004). [Online]. Available at: http://www.findarticles.com/p/articles/mi_m0WDQ/is_2004_Nov_8/ai_n6343630 [accessed: 3 January 2010].
98 McGrory, 'How $45m secretly bought freedom of foreign hostages' (n.89).

In Italy, on 30 January 2006, Gianfranco Fini, then Italian Foreign Minister, denied that Italy paid between $6 million and $10 million to free Giuliana Sgrena:

> *Italy did not pay any ransom to obtain the freedom of Giuliana Sgrena in Iraq or any other hostage. There is never a quid pro quo.*[99]

However, according to *The Times*, France, Italy and Germany sanctioned the payment of $45 million in deals to free nine hostages abducted in Iraq. All three governments have publicly denied paying any ransom money. But, according to the documents held by security officials in Baghdad, who have played a crucial role in the hostage negotiations, a sum of between $2.5 million and $10 million per person has been paid over the past 21 months. Among those said to have received cash ransoms was the gang responsible for seizing British hostages, including Kenneth Bigley, the murdered Liverpool engineer. The release of Rene Braunlich and Thomas Nitzschke, the two German engineers taken hostage on 24 January 2006 and released on 2 May 2006 for a reported $5 million payment, prompted senior Iraqi security officials to seek talks with leading Western diplomats in the capital on how to handle hostage release. When the men returned home, Alaa al-Hashimi, the Iraqi Ambassador to Germany, revealed that the German government had handed over a 'large amount' to free the engineers after 99 days in captivity. The kidnappers are understood to have asked for $10 million.[100]

Further examples of ransom payments include the $10 million payment by the French government for the release of the aforementioned Florence Aubenas, held for 157 days, and freed in June 2005 and a further $15 million for the release of Christian Chesnot and Georges Malbrunot, freed in December 2004. The Italian government is also believed to have paid $6 million for the release of Giuliana Segrena, taken in February 2005 and freed in March 2005 as well as a further $5 million for the release of Simona Pari and Simona Torretta, taken in September 2004 and freed 20 days later. In addition, the German government is believed to have paid $3 million to secure the release of Susanne Ostloff, taken on 25 November 2005, and freed three weeks later and an additional $5 million ransom for Rene Braunlich and Thomas Nitzschke, taken on 24 January 2006, and freed on 2 May 2006. Another example was the kidnapping of Ibrahim al-Maharmeh, a Jordanian businessman, kidnapped in Baghdad on

99 Ibid.
100 Ibid.

5 March 2005,[101] released after his family paid a ransom of US$100,000.[102] The Jordanian Foreign Ministry claimed that his captors had demanded a $250,000 ransom. His brother had also been abducted earlier and freed after the family paid a $50,000 ransom.[103]

There are also numerous cases of al-Qaeda and its affiliates taking and killing hostages for political and propaganda purposes. Examples include the kidnapping and murder of Daniel Pearl in February 2002 in Karachi, Pakistan. Pearl was investigating the case of Richard Reid, links between al-Qaeda and Pakistan's Inter-Services Intelligence (ISI), and the sum of $100,000 wired to 9/11 chief operative Mohammed Atta's account in the US by Ahmed Omar Saeed Sheikh, following instructions by Pakistani General Mahmoud Ahmad, the ISI director general at the time of the incident. In September 2004, two American engineers working in Iraq, Eugene Armstrong and Jack Hensley[104] and British engineer Ken Bigley, were kidnapped in the al-Mansour district of Baghdad, Iraq. The Americans were beheaded by Abu Musab al-Zarqawi in the same month, followed by Bigley's beheading in October. The violence continued in Iraq with the kidnap and murder of the next victim, Margaret Hassan, kidnapped in Baghdad on 19 October 2004 and killed four weeks later. In the same month, Shosei Koda, a Japanese citizen who was kidnapped and later beheaded in Iraq on 3 November 2004 while touring the country, also by al-Zarqawi.[105]

It is clear that kidnap is not only a profitable way for terrorists to raise finance, but also serves as a useful tool for political propaganda. The examples provided in this section alone amount to some $50 million paid to al-Qaeda affiliates for foreigners in Iraq between 2003 and 2005. The trend for the use of kidnap and ransom payments to finance acts of terrorism has also been seen in other regions such as Pakistan and Afghanistan. However, it is difficult to

101 'One Jordanian captured', *CBS News* (5 March 2005). [Online]. Available at: http://www.cbsnews.com/htdocs/america_at_war/postwar/hostages_1jordanianmarch.html [accessed: 3 January 2010].

102 'Jordanian kidnapped in Iraq was freed yesterday', *Gulf News* (3 August 2005). [Online]. Available at: http://archive.gulfnews.com/articles/05/03/08/155281.html [accessed: 3 January 2010].

103 'Update on hostages taken by insurgents', *Education in Peace in Iraq Centre*, 20 December 2005. [Online]. Available at: http://dev.epic-usa.org/index.cfm?page=weblog&subpage=display_blog&bid=48C7E7FC-5056-8861-6301EDCBC92FD038&d=20&m=12&y=2005 [accessed: 3 January 2010].

104 Adam Fresco, 'Briefing: al-Zarqawi's toll of atrocities', *BBC Online* (8 June 2006). [Online]. Available at: http://www.timesonline.co.uk/tol/news/world/iraq/article672808.ece [accessed: 3 January 2010].

105 Ibid.

determine the exact number of kidnappings and ransom monies paid for their release.

What is clear, however, is the success of hostage taking as a tool for obtaining finance for terrorist purposes.[106] The ability to raise significant amounts of money coupled with its added political value for terrorist organisations, makes kidnapping a likely modus operandi for al-Qaeda and its affiliates for the foreseeable future.[107]

FRAUD

According to Dennis Lormer, Chief of the Terrorist Financial Review Group in the FBI:

> *... there is virtually no financing method that has not at some level been exploited by terror groups. The ease with which these individuals (terrorists) can obtain false identification or assume the identity of someone else and then open bank accounts and obtain credit cards make these attractive ways to generate funds.*[108]

Credit-card information thefts are the latest in a wave of attacks by cyberspace criminals.[109] One FBI investigation revealed a network of mainly Middle Eastern computer hackers who have stolen thousands of credit card numbers from commercial Internet sites and used them to buy PCs, satellite dishes and stereos. The network's online hub is a website open to anyone where hackers freely exchange stolen card numbers and give advice on the finer points of computer crime.

Whilst the FBI is aware of the site, and has served search warrants on US-based Internet service providers for copies of the hackers' email addresses, the authorities have made no arrests so far. In addition, investigators have been

106 Judith Tinnes, 'Counting lives in a theater of terror: an analysis of media-oriented hostage takings in Iraq, Afghanistan, Pakistan and Saudi Arabia' (2010) 4(5) *Perspectives on Terrorism* 3. [Online]. Available at: http://terrorismanalysts.com/pt/index.php/pot/article/view/120/244 [accessed: 1 March 2009].

107 Everard Phillips, 'The Business of Kidnap for Ransom', in David Canter (ed.), *The Faces of Terrorism: Multidisciplinary Perspectives* (Wiley-Blackwell 2009) ch. 11.

108 Statement of Dennis Lormer, chief of the terrorist financial review group in the FBI before the Senate Judiciary Committee's subcommittee on Technology, Terrorism and Government information, 9 July 2002. [Online]. Available at: www.fbi.gov [accessed: 1 March 2009].

109 Travis C. Pratt, Kristy Holtfreter and Michael D. Reisig, 'Routine online activity and internet fraud targeting: extending the generality of routine activity theory' (2010) 47(3) *Journal of Research in Crime and Delinquency* 267.

slowed by the procedural difficulties of pressing charges against online thieves based abroad. The problem is further aggravated by the fact that e-criminals constantly change their Internet address to frustrate investigators.

Credit-card fraud is also increasingly used by terrorist organisations to finance their operations. Last summer, German police arrested 100 Islamic extremists from North Africa and the Middle East linked to an international network of credit card thieves. According to the FBI, two Algerians convicted of plotting to bomb Los Angeles International Airport in 1999, supported themselves through credit card fraud.

One case involved Middle Eastern graduate student Ali Al-Marri, detained in 2005 in Illinois after authorities discovered that his telephone calling card was used to dial the same number in the UAE used by 9/11 hijacker Mohamed Atta. Al-Marri was subsequently indicted on credit card fraud charges after investigators found hundreds of stolen card numbers on his home computer, according to a complaint filed in the US District Court in Manhattan.[110]

In terms of modus operandi, credit card and other personal information can be stolen through the use of a computer program known as a 'worm' or a 'Trojan horse', which is downloaded without the knowledge of the user whilst he or she is online on the Internet. Some of that information is then posted on a public website, under the search term 'cc fraud', where it is accessible to anyone. Such websites frequently contain a bulletin board where hackers exchange information, ideas and questions about the intricacies of hacking into commercial websites and using stolen credit card numbers.

One example is a visitor to the site from Jordan who posted a message in 2002 seeking help creating a false credit card and driver's licence. Another, from Oman, wanted advice on arranging the delivery of stolen merchandise to an untraceable drop spot. Another visitor, known as 'Nashu', posted an enquiry as to how his client in Spain, who was in possession of false identification, could pay money into his bank account. Although the site features a disclaimer that the contents are intended for 'educational purposes' only, the bulletin-board exchanges make clear that visitors' main purpose is to conduct fraudulent activity.[111]

110 US Department of Justice, 'Ali Al-Marri Indicted for Providing Material Support to Al-Qaeda', US DOJ.gov/opa Press Release (27 February 2009). [Online]. Available at: http://www.usdoj.gov/opa/pr/2009/February/09-ag-177.html [accessed: 9 July 2011].

111 Jack Dolan and Mike McIntire, 'Site shows pilfered credit card numbers', *Computer Crime Research Centre*. [Online]. Available at: http://www.crime-research.org/news/2002/11/Mess1902.htm [accessed: 1 February 2010].

There is also evidence of other methods being used to obtain information to allow criminals to carry out credit card fraud and identity theft. Investigations in the US and Europe have unveiled several credit card fraud and identity theft schemes, ranging from stealing luggage containing tourists' identity cards and personal information, to the manufacture of fake credit cards. These crimes are masterminded by members of criminal organisations which have infiltrated Western countries. In Chicago, a group of Algerians led by Youssef Hmimssa used cab drivers and waiters to commit 'skimming' fraud, whereby the credit card number is skimmed before being charged. Mourad Madrane, a Moroccan waiter, wore a pocket sized device on his belt that allowed him to swipe credit cards whilst carrying them from customers' tables to the cash registrar, thereby skimming the numbers.[112] Hmimssa then used them to make counterfeit credit cards.[113] According to the FBI, the 9/11 hijackers used similar techniques to support themselves.[114]

The use of credit card fraud by terrorists was also confirmed by Richard Rode, Deputy Assistant Director to the Office of Investigations, US Secret Service. Rode's testimony before the Senate Committee on Terrorism in February 1998 stated that several members of Middle Eastern terror groups had applied for and received as many as 40 credit cards each. He also added that this scheme was costing financial institutions in excess of $4.5 million annually.[115]

The link between fraud and terrorism is therefore clear, as is the level of technical sophistication used to commit these crimes. Fraud is without doubt profitable as well as being an established modus operandi by terrorist groups for obtaining funds. However, an equally if not more profitable method of raising illegal funding is the sale of counterfeit goods.

COUNTERFEIT GOODS

In recent years, there have been numerous reports establishing the link between counterfeiting and terrorist organisations, which use the sale of fake and unauthorised goods to raise funds, as well as for the purpose of money

112 'Waiter gets prison in credit card scheme', *Chicago Tribune* (1 September 2002).

113 Ann Mullen, 'Cell phony: Government's star witness says he's a scam artist, not a terrorist', *Metro Times* (16 April 2003). [Online]. Available at: http://www.metrotimes.com/editorial/story.asp?id=4801 [accessed: 1 February 2010].

114 *911 Digital Archive*, 'Hmimssa is charged in Detroit with having false identification documents and faces credit card fraud. charges in Chicago'. [Online]. Available at: http://www.911digitalarchive.org/crr/ documents/1000.pdf [accessed: 1 February 2010].

115 Napoleoni, *Modern Jihad* (n.23)170–71.

laundering. Furthermore, there is strong evidence to suggest that its use by terrorist groups is on the increase.[116] These allegations have been confirmed by Interpol, which has stated that the counterfeiting trade has been exploited by al-Qaeda and other terrorist groups.[117] According to Interpol officer John Newton:

> *... North African radical fundamentalist groups in Europe, al-Qaeda and Hezbollah all derive income from counterfeiting. This crime has the potential to become the preferred source of funding for terrorists.*[118]

Counterfeit goods used by terrorists are not restricted to products peddled by street merchants such as music CDs, sunglasses, T-shirts, cell phone covers, handbags and watches that bear well known and easily recognisable brand names. According to the International Anti-Counterfeiting Coalition, Inc. (IACC):[119]

> *Modern day counterfeiting operations are no longer limited to luxury goods and apparel related products. On a more sophisticated and organized level, counterfeiters and pirates are also trading on names and logos often associated with products like razor blades, shampoos, pharmaceuticals, foods, hand tools, auto parts, airline parts, light bulbs, film, skin lotions, laundry detergents, band-aids, insecticides, batteries, cigarettes and practically anything that bears a name that consumers recognize.*[120]

The attraction of counterfeiting to terrorist organisations stems mainly from its profitability as well as its relative anonymity. For example, the cost of a kilo of cocaine with a resell value of $94,000 is appropriately $47,000, amounting to a 100 per cent profit. In comparison, with the same outlay of $47,000, coupled with considerably less risk, a terrorist can acquire 1,500 pirated copies of

---

116 International Anti-Counterfeiting Coalition, *International/Global Intellectual Property Theft: Links to Terrorism and Terrorist Organisations* (White Paper, IACC, 2003) 3.

117 Carratu International, 'Rise in counterfeit market linked to terrorist funding'. Carratu International plc is a leading investigator of intellectual property abuse. [Online]. Available at: http://www.fraudaid.com/Scamspeak/conprods.htm [accessed: 14 October 2010].

118 Jon Ungoed-Thomas, 'Designer fakes are funding Al-Qaeda', *The Sunday Times* (20 March 2005). [Online]. Available at: http://www.timesonline.co.uk/article/0,,2087-1533025_2,00.html [accessed: 2 February 2010].

119 The International Anti-Counterfeiting Coalition (IACC) is a Washington, DC-based non-profit organisation devoted solely to combating product counterfeiting and piracy. It was formed in 1978 comprising of a cross-section of business and industry – from autos, apparel, luxury goods and pharmaceuticals to food, software and entertainment.

120 IACC (n.116).

Microsoft software, which can resell for a profit of 900 per cent.[121] In terms of the relative anonymity of the business, counterfeiting rings frequently operate as cash enterprises, leasing manufacturing equipment from third parties. The audit trail is virtually non-existent owing to poor record-keeping and as soon as there is any suspicion of detection, manufacturing locations can be switched, evidence destroyed and assets hidden very quickly.[122]

The proliferation of counterfeit pharmaceutical products is also a major concern with recent research highlighting that half the drugs currently obtained on the Internet were of dubious origin and that many were ineffective and some potentially dangerous. A study by the Spanish Consumers' Association in 2005 has shown that a quarter of 'e-pharmacies' sold medicines on the Internet illegally, and that many counterfeit medicines were repackaged products that had outlasted their original shelf life.[123]

However, the exact involvement between counterfeit pharmaceuticals and al-Qaeda is currently unknown. Historically, there is a large body of evidence indicating that terrorist organisations have been actively involved in large scale counterfeiting operations. In the 1990s, police in Northern Ireland seized thousands of counterfeit videos and audio cassettes, valued at over $2 million, produced by the IRA.[124] In addition, the IRA is also reported to have produced a counterfeit version of the livestock anti-parasite drug Ivomec in order to generate funds to acquire weapons.[125] The implication of counterfeit medicines for livestock is serious from a food security supply chain perspective as most meat purchased for human consumption is affected.

In terms of al-Qaeda and its affiliates, there have been several reports linking al-Qaeda to the trafficking of counterfeit goods. One example was in 2002 and involved the shipment of counterfeit products from Dubai to Copenhagen in Denmark, where Danish customs discovered a container with over one thousand crates full of counterfeit shampoos, creams, cologne and perfume ultimately bound for the UK. The intelligence services of Denmark, the UK and the US, together with the European Commission's Customs Coordination and

---

121 Ibid. 15.

122 Ibid.

123 Fraud Aid,'Rise in counterfeit market linked to terrorist funding', *Fraudaid.com* (23 February 2005). [Online]. Available at: http://www.fraudaid.com/Scamspeak/conprods.htm [accessed: 1 February 2010].

124 Global Options, *An Analysis of Terrorist Threats to America's Medicine Supply*, Reconnaissance International Report, 2003, sited in IACC (n.116) 15.

125 Ibid. 15.

Interpol, later confirmed that the sender of the counterfeit goods was a member of al-Qaeda.[126]

In the same year in France, three suspected members of the Salafist Group for Preaching and Combat, which has known links to al-Qaeda, were arrested for involvement in counterfeiting. On this occasion, 70 boxes of fake designer clothes were seized. In addition, the al-Qaeda training manual, confirms its support for the use of counterfeit products to obtain funds and as such, its use is likely to continue.

NARCOTICS

According to Ehrensfeld:

> *... the drug trade is also a triple-pronged weapon that helps terrorists to finance their activities, undermine targeted countries politically and economically, and creates crises in public health as well as to recruit new members by citing drug use as an example of Western social degeneracy and arguing that such corrupt societies must be destroyed.*[127]

Ehrensfeld describes drug money, not only as a tool to obtain funds, but suggests that it is the favoured method of *jihad*, as it also helps undermine targeted countries politically and economically, whilst creating public health crises. According to Ehrensfeld:

> *The al-Qaeda dependence on heroin began in the mid 1980s soon after Bin Laden established his organisation in Afghanistan, which is, was, and continues to be the world's major producer of heroin.*[128]

Afghanistan does indeed continue to be the world's biggest producer of heroin with its poppy economy estimated to equal half[129] of the country's legitimate GDP.[130] It is also true that the media has highlighted a few cases as evidence that al-Qaeda may be tapping into the opium economy in Afghanistan.

126 BBC, 'Al-Qa'idah Trading in Fake branded Goods', *BBC Monitoring* (11 September 2002).

127 Ehrenfeld, *Funding Evil Updated* (n.21) 3–4. Ibid.

128 Rachel Ehrenfeld, 'Terrorism's drug money' (Intelligence and Terrorism Information Centre, January 2004). [Online]. Available at: http://www.intelligence.org.il/eng/var/e_r/er_0104.htm [accessed: 3 February 2010].

129 Numerous estimates ranging from 50 per cent to 90 per cent exist.

130 Pierre-Arnaud Chouvy, 'Drugs and the financing of terrorism' (2004) 2 (20) *Terrorism Monitor*. [Online]. Available at: http://www.pa-chouvy.org/terrorism-monitor-afghanistan-drugs_financing_terrorism PRINT.html [accessed: 5 January 2010].

However, what is described as al-Qaeda 'dependence' on heroin is somewhat questionable, as al-Qaeda has numerous alternative sources of funding, contributing to the resilient nature of the organisation.

It is also relevant and necessary to make a distinction between al-Qaeda and the Taliban, especially as in recent years, there is increasing evidence that the two organisations do not necessarily see eye to eye. It is also worth noting that it was the Taliban who benefited from al-Qaeda's funding and not vice versa. This observation is supported by the 9/11 Commission which states that:

> *... prior to 9/11 the largest single al-Qaeda expense was support for the Taliban, estimated at about $20 million per year.*[131]

Moreover, knowledgeable observers agree that the drug trade at that time was the Taliban's second source of revenue, estimated at $80 million or $100 million in 1999. Outside Afghanistan, the Balkan route is believed to be used by al-Qaeda to traffic in drugs as well as to smuggle operatives into Europe, led by Muhammed al-Zawahiri, the brother of Ayman al-Zawahiri, Bin Laden's closest adviser.[132] Macedonia's Ministry of the Interior report in 2002 describes al-Qaeda's involvement with heroin trafficking, and other types of crime, in collaboration with local organised crime syndicates. There is also evidence of al-Qaeda's involvement with drug trafficking in the South American tri-border region at the intersection of Argentina, Brazil and Paraguay. According to Brazilian law enforcement, al-Qaeda's activities in the tri-border region include narcotics trafficking involving predominantly cocaine and heroin, as well as arms smuggling and counterfeiting.[133]

In terms of the role of drugs used by al-Qaeda to directly fund and facilitate terrorist operations, the Madrid bombings provide a noteworthy example. According to Spanish police, the means used to acquire the explosives, namely 210 kg of Goma-2, a type of dynamite,[134] was a 'direct-payment of narcotics'.[135] To elaborate, between 25 and 39 kg of hashish, together with a Toyota Corolla stolen from Madrid, were sold to finance the attacks. Although the quantity and value of the narcotics is minimal when compared to the overall drug economy discussed earlier in this section, this case nevertheless highlights the

131 Ibid.
132 Ehrenfeld, 'Terrorism's drug money' (n.128).
133 Ibid.
134 Steven Simon, *The Next Attack: The Globalisation of Jihad* (Hodder and Stoghton 2005) 13.
135 The Jamestown Foundation, 'The Madrid attacks: results of investigations two years later' (2006) 4(5) *Terrorism Monitor* 3.

willingness of al-Qaeda operatives to utilise whatever criminal means they have to plan and execute a terrorist attack, including the profits from the sale of narcotics.

EXPLOITATION OF FINANCIAL MARKETS AND INSIDER TRADING

Evidence of profits made from the financial markets was briefly touched upon under the section on 'legitimate businesses'. This section will go further to examine the illegal act of insider trading in relation to the 9/11 attacks. Many financial institutions as well as financial governing bodies, and government and law enforcement agencies, continue to deny that insider trading took place in relation to the 9/11 attacks.[136] However, there is undeniable evidence that suspicious activities did indeed take place. The facts are as follows.

In early September 2001, unusually high volume trade of five-year US Treasury note purchases were reported[137] according to the Security Exchange Commission (SEC).[138] These transactions included a single $5 billion trade.[139 140] The significance of the five-year Treasury note is that they are amongst the best investments in the event of a world crisis, especially involving the US. The notes are prized for their safety and their backing by the US government, and usually rally when investors flee riskier investments, such as stocks. During this time, suspicion of insider trading activities existed in many other countries leading to numerous other overseas investigations.[141] Countries carrying out investigations during this period included Belgium, France, Switzerland,

136 Marc Chesney, Remo Crameri and Loriano Mancini, 'Detecting informed trading activities in the options markets' (15 April 2010). [Online]. Available at: http://ssrn.com/abstract=1522157 [accessed: 5 January 2010].

137 *Chicago Sun-Times*, 'Probe of options trading link to attacks confirmed' (21 September 2001). [Online]. Available at: www.suntimes.com/terror/stories/cst-fin-trade21.html [accessed: 5 January 2010].

138 *911 Research*, 'Insider trading: pre-9/11 put options on companies hurt by attack indicates foreknowledge'. [Online]. Available at: http://911research.wtc7.net/sept11/stockputs.html#ref15 [accessed: 5 January 2010].

139 Charles Gasparino and Gregary Zuckerman, 'Treasury bonds enter purview of US ENQUIRY into attack gains', *Wall Street Journal* (2 October 2001).

140 9/11 timeline. [Online]. Available at: http://911research.wtc7.net/sept11/stockputs.html#ref15 [accessed: 5 January 2010].

141 Tom Bogdanowicz and Brooks Jackson, 'Probes into "suspicious" trading', *CNN* (24 September 2001). [Online]. Available at: http://cnnstudentnews.cnn.com/2001/WORLD/europe/09/24/gen.europe.shortselling/ [accessed: 4 February 2010].

Luxembourg, Monte Carlo, Cyprus, Italy, Japan and the UK.[142] In addition, Tokyo reported suspicious activity in the trading of futures contracts.[143]

The New York Stock Exchange (NYSE) also experienced unusually heavy trading in airline and related stocks during early September 2001.[144] The SEC investigated the trading of shares of some 38 companies in the days just before 9/11.[145] All 38 companies logically stood to be heavily affected by the attacks and included parent companies of major US airlines such as American, Continental, Delta, Northwest, Southwest, United, and US Airways, as well as cruise lines Carnival and Royal Caribbean, aircraft maker Boeing and defence contractor Lockheed Martin. The SEC also looked into suspicious short selling of numerous insurance company stocks, but, to date, no details of this investigation have been released. In addition, strong evidence of insider trading in Germany was reported at this time.[146] German Central Bank President, Ernst Welteke, reported that a study by his bank indicated that:

> *There are ever clearer signs that there were activities on international financial markets that must have been carried out with the necessary expert knowledge.*[147]

These suspicion transactions were not only in shares of heavily affected industries such as airlines and insurance companies, but also in gold and oil.[148] In addition, Welteke's researchers found almost irrefutable proof of insider trading.[149] Welteke also reported 'a fundamentally inexplicable rise' in oil

142 BBC, 'Bin Laden "share gains" probe', (18 September 2001). [Online]. Available at: http://news.bbc.co.uk/1/hi/ business/1548118.stm [accessed: 4 February 2010].

143 Fox News, 'EU Searches for suspicious trading', (22 September 2001). [Online]. Available at: http://www.foxnews.com/story/0,2933,34910,00.html [accessed: 4 February 2010].

144 Thomas Beaumert, 'Terrorism, News Flows and Stock Markets', in Harry Ward Richardson, Peter Gordon, James Elliott Moore (eds), *Global Business and the Terrorist Threat* (Edward Elgar Publishing Limited 2009) 119.

145 Gordon Marcy, 'SEC Probes Suspicious Trading' *Associated Press* (20 October 2001). See also 9/11 timeline. [Online]. Available at: http://911research.wtc7.net/sept11/stockputs.html#ref15 [accessed: 4 February 2010].

146 *Bloomerg News*, 'Germans probe pre-terrorism trading' (23 September 2001). [Online]. Available at: http://www.lossless-audio.com/usa/index0.php?page=2135678642.htm [accessed: 4 February 2010].

147 Philip Sherwell, 'Bin Laden rigged oil and gold prices – bank chief', *Daily Telegraph* (23 September 2001). [Online]. Available at: http://www.telegraph.co.uk/news/main.jhtml?xml=/news/2001/09/23/woil23.xml [accessed: 4 February 2010].

148 9/11–Insider Trading. [Online]. Available at: http://www.yirmeyahureview.com/archive/911/insider_trading.htm [accessed: 3 January 2010].

149 Carol Rosenberg, 'Father, friends paint different portrait of Atta', *Miami Herald* (24 September 2001).

prices[150] before the attacks and then a further rise of 13 per cent the day after the attacks. Gold prices[151] also increased non-stop for several days after the attacks. There was also a sharp increase in the short selling of the stocks of American and United Airlines on the NYSE prior to 9/11. A short sell is essentially a bet that a particular stock will drop in value. There was an increase of 40 per cent[152] of short selling over the previous month for these two airlines, compared to an 11 per cent[153] increase for other big airlines and 1 per cent for the exchange overall.[154] A significant profit was made as United Airlines stock dropped 43 per cent and American Airlines dropped 39 per cent[155] on the first day the market reopened after the 9/11 attacks.

Short selling of Munich Re, the world's largest reinsurer, was also later noted by German investigators. Inquiries into short selling of millions of Munich Re shares were also made in France days before the attacks. Munich Re stocks plummeted after the attacks, costing the company $2 billion.[156] Furthermore, there was suspicious trading activity involving re-insurers Swiss Reinsurance and AXA. There was also a short spike on Dutch airline KLM stock three to seven days before 9/11, reaching historically unprecedented levels.[157]

The Chicago Board Options Exchange also reported suspicious trading on Merrill Lynch and Morgan Stanley, two of the largest World Trade Centre (WTC) tenants between 6 September and 10 September 2001. From an average of 27 put option contracts in its shares bought on a daily basis in the first week of September, the figure increased to 2,157 for the three days before the attacks.[158] Merrill Lynch, also saw 12,215 put options bought between the 7 September

150 9/11 timeline. [Online]. Available at: http://911research.wtc7.net/sept11/stockputs.html#ref15 [accessed: 3 January 2010].

151 Sherwell, 'Bin Laden rigged oil and gold prices – bank chief' (n.147).

152 Laura Jacobs and Thomas Atkins, 'More unusual market activity reported before attacks', *Reuters* (20 September 2001).

153 'Complete 9/11 time-line'. [Online]. Available at: http://www.cooperativeresearch.org/timeline.jsp?timeline=complete_911_[accessed: 4 February 2010]. [Online]. Available at: timeline&before_9/11=insiderTrading [accessed: 3 January 2010].

154 Christian Berthelsen, 'Data shows heavy airline stock short selling', *San Francisco Chronicle* (22 September 2001).

155 Jacobs and Atkins, 'More Unusual Market Activity Reported before Attacks' (n.152).

156 *Dow Jones Business News*, 'The two big reinsurers say their attack losses will hot $3.2 billion' (20 September 2001).

157 Greg Farrell, 'More signs of odd stock trades found', *USA Today* (26 September 2001). [Online]. Available at: http://www.usatoday.com/money/general/2001-09-26-suspicious-trading.htm [accessed: 4 February 2010].

158 Chris Blackhurst, 'My story of terror insider dealers', *Independent* (14 October 2001). [Online]. Available at: http://news.independent.co.uk/business/news/article161862.ece [accessed: 4 February 2010].

and 10 September, when the previous days had seen averages of 252 contracts a day.[159]

A put option gives the buyer the right to sell the underlying security at a certain price on a certain date; the purchaser profits when the share price drops lower than the agreed sale price. In a short sale, an investor borrows stock from a broker and sells it, hoping to buy it back at a lower price. According to Dylan Ratigan of Bloomberg Business News, speaking on the trading on Morgan Stanley and other companies:

> *This would be one of the most extraordinary coincidences in the history of mankind if it was a coincidence.*[160]

French author Bernard Henri-Levy claims to know an anonymous manager at a bank in Dubai, who gave him astute and accurate tips on Arab banking. In 2002, the manager told Henri-Levy that:

> *We know a bank here that made a [put option] transaction between the 8th and 10th of September on certain Dow Jones blue-chip stocks for accounts linked to bin Laden. I know the name of a bank that, by shorting 8,000 shares of United Airlines on the 7th of September, then 1,200 shares of American Airlines on the morning of the 10th, allowed the attack to finance itself.*[161]

The manager refused to name the bank, but quoted bin Laden from a late September 2001 interview, stating that:

> *... al-Qaeda is full of young, modern, and educated people who are aware of the cracks inside the Western financial system, and know how to exploit them. These faults and weaknesses are like a sliding noose strangling the system.*[162]

Separately, the case of *US v Royer* provides an illustration as to how 'non-terrorists' can be seduced by the ability to make money through insider

159 Ibid.

160 *ABC News*, 'More attacks planned? Second wave of terrorist attacks feared' (20 September 2001). [Online]. Available at: http://www.cooperativeresearch.org/timeline.jsp?timeline=complete_911_timeline&before9/11=insiderTrading [accessed: 4 February 2010].

161 Levy, *Who Killed Daniel Pearl?* 312–13.

162 Ibid.

knowledge.[163] On the 10 September 2011, an investor, Amr Elgindy, ordered his broker to liquidate his children's $300,000[164] trust account fearing a sudden crash in the market. He also told his stockbroker that the Dow Jones average, then at 9,600, would fall to below 3,000. Elgindy was arrested in San Diego in May 2002, along with FBI agents Jeffrey Royer and Lynn Wingate, who, according to US government prosecutors, were using their FBI positions to obtain inside information on various corporations.

Royer admitted to providing Elgindy confidential details of federal investigations, including a probe of the 9/11 attacks,[165] although at the same time claiming that he did so to use Elgindy's knowledge to help develop evidence of criminal wrongdoing. However, following a 12-week jury trial in the US District Court for the Eastern District of New York in 2008, Royer was convicted by the jury of racketeering, securities fraud conspiracy, four substantive counts of securities fraud, conspiracy to obstruct justice in violation, obstruction of justice in violation and witness tampering and sentenced to a term of 72 months' imprisonment. Elgindy was also convicted of racketeering, five substantive counts of securities fraud and one count of conspiracy to commit violation of extortion and one substantive count of extortion, and two counts of wire fraud in violation and sentenced to a term of 135 months' imprisonment.[166]

Returning to the subject of unusual financial activities relating to 9/11, on 10 September 2001 suspicious trading on United Airlines stock occurred at the Pacific Exchange. The trading ratio on United Airlines was 25 times greater than normal at the Pacific Exchange.[167] Pacific Exchange officials later declined to state whether this abnormality was being investigated.[168] Some $2.5 million in put options on American Airlines and United Airlines were also reported as unclaimed.[169] Initially the SEC suspected that this was likely to be the result of the suspension in trading on the NYSE after the attacks. However, the money is

163 *United States v Royer* (2008) 549 F.3d 886.

164 Dean Calbreath, 'Once high-flying stock speculator Elgindy faces accusers this week', *San Diego Union Tribune* (16 June 2002). [Online]. Available at: http://www.signonsandiego.com/news/business/workplace/industry/20020618-9999_1b16elgindy.html [accessed: 4 February 2010].

165 'Ex-FBI agent admits giving out 9/11 data', *San Diego Tribune* (5 January 2005). [Online]. Available at: http://www.signonsandiego.com/uniontrib/20050105/news_1b5elgindy.html [accessed: 4 February 2010].

166 *United States v Royer* (n.163).

167 Christian Berthelsen, 'New scrutiny of airline options deals', *San Francisco Chronicle* (19 September 2006).

168 Ibid.

169 Christian Berthelsen and Scott Winokur, 'Suspicious profits sit uncollected', *San Francisco Chronicle* (29 September 2006).

unclaimed to this day and raises suspicions that the investors whose identities and nationalities have not been made public had advance knowledge of the attacks.

There was also an unusually large jump in purchases of put options on the stocks of UAL Corporation (UAL Corp.), the parent company of United Airlines, and AMR Corporation (AMR Corp.), the parent company of American Airlines, on major options exchanges in the US in the three business days before the attack. On one day, UAL Corp. put option purchases were 25 times greater than the year-to-date average. In the month before the attacks, short sales jumped by 40 per cent for UAL Corp. and 20 per cent for AMR Corp. Other financial professionals have told *The Chronicle* that an estimated $5 million to $10 million in all could have been made on the trades, including trading on other days and purchases of options on AMR Corp. It should be noted that two United Airlines and two American Airlines aircraft crashed in the attacks.

Meanwhile, at the Interdisciplinary Centre, a counter-terrorism think tank in Herzliya, Israel, a group headed by former Israeli intelligence officials issued a report on Osama bin Laden's finances claiming that insiders profited by nearly $16 million. According to the Centre, the money was made on 6, 7 and 10 September 2001 in transactions involving United Airlines, American Airlines, Morgan Stanley Dean Witter & Co. and Merrill Lynch & Co.

It is also interesting to note the sudden resignation of Deutsche Bank Executive Mayo Shattuck III, on 14 September 2001 as head of the Alex Brown unit of Deutsche Bank. Although there was no formal reason provided for the resignation by the bank, some elements of the financial community believe that the resignation was prompted by speculations of the role of Deutsche Bank in the pre-9/11 purchases of put options on the stock of companies most affected by 9/11.[170] Deutsche Bank is also one of the four banks most used by the bin Laden family.[171]

Against this body of evidence, the FSA, Britain's main financial regulator, cleared bin Laden and his associates of insider trading on 16 October 2001, claiming that after a thorough investigation, it had found no hard evidence of any such deals in London. It is therefore interesting that on 24 September 2001, Belgium's Financial Minister claimed that there were strong suspicions

170 Daniel Golden, James Bandler and Marcus Walker, 'Bin Laden Family could profit from a jump, in defense spending due to ties to U.S. bank', *Wall Street Journal* (27 September 2001).
171 *New York Times* 'Chief steps down at Alex Brown' (15 September 2001).

that British markets may have been used for 9/11-related insider trading in early September.[172] Additionally, neither the Chicago Board Options Exchange nor the SEC made any comment about their investigations into insider trading before 9/11.[173] Furthermore, on 22 July 2004, in a footnote contained in its Final Report, the 9/11 Commission dismissed allegations of insider trading in the days preceding 9/11. According to the Final Report, the put options of the parent companies of United Airlines and American Airlines were placed by a:

> *US-based institutional investor with no conceivable ties to al-Qaeda as part of a trading strategy that also included buying 115,000 shares of American on September 10. With respect to the highly suspicious trading on the parent company of American Airlines, the Commission stated that much of the trades were traced to a specific US-based options trading newsletter, faxed to its subscribers on Sunday, September 9, which recommended these trades.*

According to the 9/11 Commission:

> *The SEC and the FBI, aided by other agencies and the securities industry, devoted enormous resources to Allen Poteshman, a professor of finance investigating this issue, including securing the cooperation of many foreign governments. These investigators have found that the apparently suspicious consistently proved innocuous.*

It is also curious to note that spokesperson Paul Bresson announced on 19 September 2001 that the FBI had concluded that there was no insider trading in US securities markets by people with advance knowledge of the 9/11 attacks. According to Bresson, the vast majority of a pre-attack surge of trading in options that bet on a drop in the stock of AMR Corp. and UAL Corp. was conducted by investment hedge funds implementing bearish investment strategies or hedging a line position of common stock and was not linked to terrorism.

However, independent research would indicate otherwise a few months later. In March 2004, the University of Illinois published a paper demonstrating that the insider trading in options on United and American airline stocks

172 Complete 9/11 time-line (n.150).

173 David Plotz, 'What you think you know about Sept. 11 but don't', *Slate Magazine* (10 September 2003). [Online]. Available at: http://www.slate.com/id/2088092/ [accessed: 4 February 2010].

indicated that someone profited from foreknowledge of 9/11. Poteshman concluded that:

> *There is evidence of unusual option market activity in the days leading up to September 11 which is consistent with investors trading on advanced knowledge of the attacks.*[174]

What is difficult to determine is whether al-Qaeda had directly benefited from the profits made and, if so, to what extent this has contributed to the financing of terror. However, the case of insider dealing highlights and validates one key concern discussed in earlier chapters relating to the nature of the threat environment. The case on 9/11 related insider trading has highlighted the asymmetric environment previous discussed. The blurring of the 'enemy' is problematic as so many individuals, to include law enforcement, can be driven by personal greed and put aside interests in national security for personal gain. This is perhaps the reason why investigations into insider dealing proved to be inconclusive in that the authorities probably did not realise the complexity of the financial crime environment. This case has certainly opened up a can of worms, making the prospect of prosecution overwhelming as so many were guilty of financing terrorism under the broad definitions adopted by the Terrorism Act 2000 and by the FATF.

Conclusions

The chapter highlighted the importance of understanding the sources of funding used for terrorist attacks and explained why efforts to interdict the funding of terrorism should not focus purely on operational costs, but must ensure the inclusion of infrastructure support costs. In terms of the sources of terrorist funding, the distinction between legal and illegal methods was made, a key factor that distinguishes terrorist finance from other forms of financial and economic crime. The next question is how these funds are moved ultimately to the terrorist which enables a terrorist attack to take place. As such, the subsequent chapter will examine the mechanisms used by al-Qaeda to transfer funds and at the same time provide a vulnerability analysis to identify the extent of abuse by terrorist groups.

174 Allen M. Poteshman, *Unusual Option Market Activity and the Terrorist Attacks of September 11 2001*. 10 March 2004. [Online]. Available at: http://www.business.uiuc.edu/poteshma/WorkingPapers/UnusualOptionActivityAndTerroristAttacks10March2004.pdf [accessed: 4 February 2010].

4

Mechanisms of Illicit Funds Transfer

I'm gonna get rich patenting a better mousetrap.
Not me, I'm gonna get rich finding a bigger loophole.
Conversation overheard between two law-school students.[1]

Overview

The previous chapter examined the various sources of funding, both legal and illegal, used by al Qaeda and its affiliate organisations. In order for those funds to have utility to enable a terrorist attack to occur, the funds need to be transferred from its source to the beneficiary of the funds, in this case the terrorist, usually through a network of facilitators. Therefore, the identification of the mechanisms used to transfer these funds is essential, in order that appropriate disruption strategies can be adopted.

Terrorist funds are transferred through a variety of vehicles including formal banking system and informal value transfer systems, as well as through the physical transportation of cash and commodities.[2] Frequently, more than one system may be used dependent on a number of factors such as the geographical location of the origin of the funds, as well as its destination. A complex audit trail also gives the added benefit of partial anonymity, which is essential not only for terrorists, but for criminals wishing their activities, financial and otherwise, to remain surreptitious. The subject of the methods used to obtain that obscure financial audit trail will be discussed in depth in the

1 Jeffrey Robinson, *The Laundrymen* (Simon & Schuster UK Limited 1998) 76.
2 Fletcher N. Baldwin Jr., 'The financing of terror in the age of the internet: wilful blindness, greed or a political statement?' (2004) 8(2) *Journal of Money Laundering Control* 127.

subsequent chapter, prior to which it is necessary to develop an awareness of the key vehicles of funds transfer which may be utilised in that process.

The analysis will begin with the informal funds transfer system with a special focus on *hawala,* which has received much negative attention in relation to the transfer of terrorist funds since 9/11. The analysis will assess the degree to which this concern can be justified.

Informal Banking System – *Hawala* Case Study

Hawala is one of many informal money transfer systems in the world, collectively known as Informal Value Transfer Systems (IVTS). Other terminologies used include Alternative Remittance Services (ARS), Informal Funds Transfer (IFT), Informal Funds Transfer System (IFTS), as well as the underground, unregulated, quasi or parallel banking system.[3] In addition, terminologies such as *hundi, fei ch'ien,*[4] and *phoe kuan* are used, dependent on the geographic location and the ethnic group associated with the system. *Hawala* is a term that originated in India and is associated with 'trust', 'reference' or 'exchange'. The Arabic root h-w-l means to 'change' or 'transform'.[5] It is a trust-based system used to transfer funds across countries and continents.[6]

Hawala exponentially entered the lexicon of world leaders, the counter-terrorism community and media shortly after 9/11. In its fast developing 'war on terror', the Bush administration conducted a search not only for terrorists, but for a suitable accomplice in the world of finance. The accomplice they discovered was believed to be the *hawala* system, which was then presented as the main mechanism that terrorists used to transfer funds. The main reason for suspicion originated from the 9/11 Commission Report, which highlighted the use of *hawala* by al Qaeda. The report stated that:

> *Al Qaeda frequently moved money it raised by hawala, an informal and ancient trust-based system for transferring funds. In some ways,*

3 Nikos Passas, 'Informal value transfer systems and criminal organisations: a study into so-called underground banking networks' (1999). [Online]. Available at: http://usinfo.state.gov/eap/img/assets/4756/ivts.pdf [accessed: 20 November 2010].

4 Chinese equivalent of *hawala,* meaning 'flying money'.

5 Interpol, 'The hawala alternative remittance system and its role in money laundering' (Interpol General Secretariat, Lyon, January 2000). [Online]. Available at: http://www.interpol.int/public/financialcrime/moneylaundering/hawala/default.asp [accessed: 15 November 2010].

6 Thomas Viles, 'Hawala, hysteria and hegemony' (2008) 11(1) *Journal of Money Laundering Control* 25.

> *al Qaeda had no choice after its move to Afghanistan in 1996: first, the banking system there was antiquated and undependable; and second, formal banking was risky due to the scrutiny that al Qaeda received after the August 1998 East Africa Embassy bombings, including UN resolutions against it and the Taliban. Bin Laden relied on the established hawala networks operating in Pakistan, in Dubai, and throughout the Middle East to transfer funds efficiently. Hawaladars associated with al Qaeda may have used banks to move and store money, as did various al Qaeda fund-raisers and operatives outside Afghanistan, but there is little evidence that Bin Laden or core al Qaeda members used banks while in Afghanistan.*[7]

Despite the fact that the report clearly stipulates that al Qaeda's use of *hawala* in Afghanistan was not surprising owing to the lack of an effective formal banking sector, as well as specifying that al Qaeda 'may' have used banks outside Afghanistan, *hawala* has become almost synonymous with terrorist finance within the counter-terrorism community.[8] The lack of understanding of informal funds transfer systems by law enforcement and the judiciary in the UK has further impacted on *hawala's* negative image, not only in the context of terrorist finance, but in relation to broader money laundering offences.[9]

Part of the reason can be attributed to the use of the aforementioned associated terminologies such as 'underground', 'informal' and 'alternative'. Not only do these terminologies provide an undertone of criminality, which in itself may be perceived as being unfair, it is also misleading. For example, the term 'underground' banking is inaccurate as *hawala* is not underground in many parts of the world. Similarly 'alternative' banking is unsatisfactory in that it suggests the existence of other, mainstream or conventional remittance systems. Furthermore, even where an alternative system does exist, it may not be accessible to a vast majority of the population, making the informal systems the only viable option.

The use of the word 'informal' can also be problematic for two reasons. The first is that attempting to distinguish between informal and formal routes of money or value transfers is not always straightforward partly as the routes

7 9-11 Commission, *National Commission on Terrorist Attacks upon the United States*. 171 [Online]. Available at: http://www.9-11commission.gov/staff_statements/911_TerrFin_Ch1.pdf [accessed: 15 November 2010].

8 Viles, (n.6) 25.

9 *R v Ajit Arora & 1 Other* [2010] T2010/0358 (Croydon Crown Court). Observations as Expert Witness.

sometimes merge. Second, the term 'informal' is frequently used to describe financial systems which are not regulated. However, as *hawala* falls under the category of money transfer businesses (MSBs) in the UK, for example, which has been supervised by Her Majesty's Customs and Excise (HMRC) since June 2003,[10] one can argue that *hawala* is in fact 'regulated' by HMRC. As such, the use of the word 'informal' in this context is also not entirely appropriate.

In terms of its client base, *hawala* is used by a variety of individuals, organisations and governments for perfectly legitimate reasons. For example, expatriates and immigrants frequently use the service to send money back to their families and friends in their home countries. It is also used by legitimate companies, traders and government agencies conducting business in countries where inadequate formal financial systems exist as a result of political or economic instability.[11] In addition, in many developing countries, formal financial institutions frequently exist only in cities making informal systems the only available option for those individuals living in remote rural areas in those countries.

Even for those with access to other financial systems, *hawala* can serve as an attractive alternative for a number of legitimate reasons, including cost, speed, reliability and accessibility. The system operates 24 hours a day, seven days a week, and the service is quick, efficient,[12] and competitively priced. *Hawala* commission ranges from 0.25 to 1.25 per cent which is significantly lower than commissions charged by the formal banking sector.[13] The low cost is primarily due to low overheads and favourable exchange rates as well as integration with existing business activities.[14] Efficiency and speed plays an important part for many users with most transactions taking only one to two days as opposed to a week for the formal banking sector, not including other delaying factors such as bank and national holidays and weekends.[15] It is therefore no surprise that the *hawala* industry is popular and is worth some $200 billion a year.[16] Despite this, suspicion surrounding *hawala* exist, exacerbated by a number of myths, which need to be addressed.

---

10 M. Blackwell and D. Seddon, *Informal Remittances from the UK: Values, Flows and* Mechanisms (DFID report by the Overseas Development Group, Norwich, 2004).

11 FinCen, 'Informal Value Transfer Systems' (US Department of the Treasury Financial Crimes Enforcement Network Advisory Issue 33, FinCen Advisory, 2003) 2.

12 Jimmy Burns, Harbey Morris and Michael Peel, 'Assault on America terrorist funds', *Financial Times* (London, 24 September 2001).

13 L. Carroll, *Alternative Remittance Systems* (Interpol Secretariat, 1999, no. 20, 1999).

14 P.M. Jost and H.S. Sandhu, *The Hawala Alternative Remittance System and Its Role in Money Laundering* (Interpol General Secretariat, 2000).

15 Ibid.

16 UN Security Council Committee pursuant to Resolution 1267 (1999), 22 September 2002, 15.

PUTTING RIGHT THE MYTHS

One myth is that *hawala* is a paperless system which has no audit trail. The myth was brought about by official statements made by recognised authorities when little was yet known about the system by the West. One example is the misleading definition provided by the Australian National Crime Authority in 1991:

> *... an unofficial (or parallel) banking system ... , which enables funds to move from one country to another without production of a paper trail.*[17]

The definition is simply incorrect in that it is well documented that *hawaladars*[18] and other IVTS operators are known to keep ledgers and other forms of documentation. It is also common practice for *hawaladars* to maintain a separate book for each agent with whom they deal. Documentation usually includes *hawala* slips for each client containing a number or code, as well as customer identification documents and records.

Data collected includes the date of transaction, name and address of the sender and recipient, passport number or other identification number and the name of the counterpart dealer. In terms of accounting records, according to the World Bank:

> *... dealers maintain files with invoices and quotations, copies of receipts and transaction contracts and agreements. The accounts between the organisations are reconciled periodically and hawaladars maintain debit and credit columns in an accounting ledger book or computer.*[19]

In a later separate report, the World Bank confirmed that:

> *... access to financial records reveals that each transaction is carefully logged, and follows its own accounting procedures.*[20]

17 S. Keene, 'Hawala and related informal value transfer systems: an assessment in the context of organised crime and terrorist finance. Is there cause for concern?' (2007) *The Defence Academy Journal* 4.

18 A *hawaladar* is a *hawala* broker.

19 S.M. Maimbo, *The Money Exchange Dealers of Kabul: A Study of the Hawala System in Afghanistan* (Finance and Private Sector Unit, South Asia Region, World Bank, 2003).

20 Edwina A. Thompson, 'the nexus of drug trafficking and hawala in Afghanistan' (UNDC Report, *Afghanistan's Drug Industry: Structure, Functioning, Dynamics and Implications for Counter-Narcotics Policy*, 2006, chapter 6) 165.

The report also stated that transactions of an illegal nature such as drug trafficking were kept more discreetly although one *hawaladar* had confided that the drug-related financial transfer documents were kept on his son's computer at home as opposed to the business premises.[21]

Another myth is that 'Money never enters the formal banking system'.[22] On the contrary, *hawaladars*, especially those operating in an international environment will possess conventional bank accounts in which they deposit their clients' money, which they use to offset balances with their counterparts in other parts of the world.[23] One way in which to dispel these myths is to develop an understanding of the way in which the system operates.

HAWALA MECHANICS

The *hawala* system can be seen as consisting of two main components. The first is the sending and receiving of money referred to as the 'transfer' process, involving *hawala* dealers, also known as *hawaladars*. The second is the settlement process of the transactions which involve various intermediaries.[24] In terms of the transfer process, the sender contacts and provide funds to his agent with instructions to give funds to the intended recipient for which he receives an identifier, typically a code. The sender contacts the recipient with the identifier. At the same time, the Agent (Agent S) contacts the recipient's agent (Agent R) with instructions to pay the recipient. The recipient is then able to collect the funds from Agent, R., on provision of the identifier code for authenticity (see Figure 4.1).[25]

For the system to work effectively there must be pools of cash at both ends of the transaction. With every payment *a hawala* operator sends to his counterpart, an informal debt is created. If cash pools A and B were equal, settlement would consist of reciprocal payments covering each other's debts. However, as the relationship is likely to be asymmetric most of the time, alternative methods of settlement are necessary.[26] Many operators possess bank accounts in a central location to facilitate the consolidation of accounts thus reducing costs.

21 Ibid. 165.
22 UN General Assembly, (Special Session on the World Drug Problem, 8–10 June 1998).
23 Passas, *Informal value transfer systems and criminal organisations* (n.3).
24 N. Passas, *Informal Value Transfer Systems, Terrorism and Money Laundering* (Report to the National Institute of Justice, 2003).
25 Viles, 'Hawala, hysteria and hegemony' (n.6) 25.
26 These methods include cash payments, postal orders, checks, official drafts, bearer instruments or wire transfers and bank transfers.

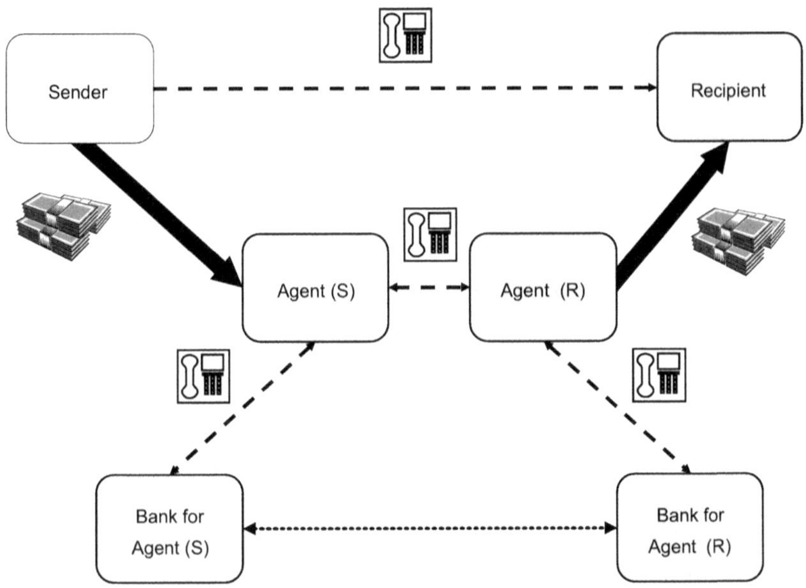

Figure 4.1 IVTS mechanism of funds transfer

The most popular centres for account consolidation include the key financial centres around the world such as Dubai,[27] New York, London, Hong Kong, Singapore and Switzerland.[28]

THREAT ASSESSMENT

Informal funds transfer systems such as *hawala* has generated significant concern over speculation of its use for criminal means especially since 9/11 as previously discussed. However, despite claims that the 9/11 hijackers utilised informal methods of transfer, in the large majority of cases, formal banking services including bank wire transfers and credit cards remitters were also utilised.[29] However, there is indeed evidence that *hawala* has been used by terrorists and criminals to purchase illegal arms, narcotics and other illegal

27 Interpol, 'The hawala alternative remittance system and its role in money laundering', Interpol General Secretariat (2003). [Online]. Available at: http://www.interpol.int/public/financialcrime/moneylaundering/hawala/default.asp [accessed: 15 November 2010].

28 Passas, *Informal Value Transfer Systems, Terrorism and Money Laundering* (n.24).

29 Shima D. Keene, *Al-Qaeda: Financing Terror* (Airey Neave Trust Report, 2005).

commodities, as well as to make corrupt payments, receive ransom demands and for money laundering purposes.[30]

In February 2000, the Asia Pacific Group (APG) collated 62 case studies relating to IVTS including the *hawala* system. The findings discovered a mix of legitimate and criminal funds, but confirmed that in most cases its use was legitimate. The findings also stated that in cases involving criminal proceeds, the large majority involved narcotic offences followed by people smuggling and revenue evasion. The report also confirmed the use of the 'formal' regulated financial sector alongside the 'informal' sector.[31] As such, *hawala* must not be singled out as a system that is vulnerable to abuse.[32]

REGULATION

The subject of *hawala* regulation has been a fiercely debated subject in recent years. The supporters of *hawala* regulation include the FATF mainly for the purpose of increasing transparency. However, critics argue that the cost of compliance for *hawaladars* is likely to prove to be too expensive, which in turn will force the system to go underground. This would then result in even less transparency as well as an increased risk of abuse by the adversary.[33]

In addition, the effectiveness of such regulation has also been questioned.[34] The regulatory requirements for the 'formal' financial sector in the UK, for example, has been criticised for being over-regulated. The sheer deluge of reporting requirements have led to a 'tick in the box' mentality where compliance procedures can be described as having become nothing more than an insurance scheme for financial institutions. A further concern relating to over regulation is that it may result in the focus away from financial crime to that of regulatory risk management. Against this background, it is not necessarily appropriate that the 'informal' sector is also forced down the same path.

30 Carroll, *Alternative Remittance Systems* (n.13).

31 M. Butler and R. Boyle, *Alternative Remittance Regulation Implementation Package: APG Typologies Working Group on Alternative Remittance and Underground Banking Systems* (Asia Pacific Group on Money Laundering, 2003).

32 Nikos Passas, 'Indicators of Hawala operations and criminal abuse' (2004) 8(2) *Journal of Money Laundering Control* 168.

33 Bruce Zagaris, 'Problems applying traditional anti-money laundering procedures to non-financial transactions, "parallel banking systems" and Islamic financial systems' (2007) 10(2) *Journal of Money Laundering Control* 157.

34 Fath El Rahman Abdalla El Sheikh, 'The underground banking systems and their impact on control of money laundering: with special reference to Islamic banking' (2002) 6(1) *Journal of Money Laundering Control* 42.

Although regulation should by no means be ruled out, it is important that it should be fit for purpose and not implemented for its own sake.

When contemplating possible regulation of *hawala*, it is important to note that any attempt to regulate the system cannot be achieved without understanding its inner workings. In addition, 'insider buy-in' is essential. What is meant by 'insider buy-in' is the consensus and input of the operators, users and intermediaries, which is necessary for regulation to be effective. It must also be remembered that Western models of regulation are not a guarantee for success and that prescribing regulation alone will not ensure compliance.[35]

This view was supported at the international conference on *hawala* held in April 2004, jointly hosted by the International Monetary Fund and the UAE.[36] The conference identified the challenges of implementing a regulatory framework for *hawala* and concluded that close consultations with *hawala* service providers were necessary to ensure the effectiveness of any new regulatory framework. As a follow up to the conference, discussions were held in selected countries in Europe, in the UAE and in the US between the private remittance sector and staff at the IMF. The UAE case is worthy of further elaboration, in order to highlight the challenges faced in attempting to regulate the informal 'banking' sector.

UAE CASE STUDY

Since 2002, when the UAE organised the first international conference on *hawala*, more than 260 traders have registered, and more than 100 applications are pending. In the UAE, *hawaladars*, are required to register with the Central Bank, keep records of the identities of their customers and alert authorities to any suspicious transactions. The Central Bank of the UAE did not want to outlaw *hawala* completely, as Saudi Arabia and Qatar had done, in recognition that such a ban would penalise the workers who relied on the system. According to Abdulrahim Mohamed al Awadi, Head of the Anti-money Laundering and Suspicious Cases Unit of the Central Bank, UAE:

> *The UAE is leading international efforts to regulate the informal sector. Hawala registration system is preventing money laundering*

35 Zagaris, 'Problems applying traditional anti-money laundering procedures to non-financial transactions, "parallel banking systems" and Islamic financial systems' (n.33).

36 C.S. Lee, M. Bokkerink and J. Smallwood, *Approaches to a Regulatory Framework for Formal and Informal Remittance Systems: Experience and Lessons* (International Monetary Fund Report, prepared by the Monetary and Financial Systems Department, 2005).

> *and terrorist financing, but still allowed workers to send money home cheaply.*[37]

However, in a report on money laundering released in March 2008, the US State Department noted that there had not been any reports of suspicious transactions by *hawaladars* in the UAE since the registration scheme started in 2002, bringing into question the overall effectiveness of registration.

Several reasons as to why the registration scheme in the UAE had been ineffective were highlighted in the report. First, no incentive to register has been offered to *hawaladars*. Second, there were no specific penalties for running an unregistered *hawala* business. Third, the difficulty of enforcement was acknowledged as being problematic. As such, it should be of no surprise to learn that there is evidence that many continue to trade without registering. In fact, the number of registered *hawalas* is believed to represent only a small percentage of *hawala* operations in the UAE, making its attempted regulation a mockery.

HAWALA: CONCLUSION

Informal transfer systems such as *hawala* have thrived typically in jurisdictions where the formal financial sector is either absent or weak.[38] The large majority serve legitimate needs and are frequently the only option available. If its use is to be discouraged, an alternative system must exist. Not only must this option exist, but it must also be an adequately attractive option to be able to become the preferred service. The solution is simply that of adopting competitive advantage in business. To achieve this aim, the service must be more economically viable compared to the existing system, as well as designed in a way as to be attractive to the community it intends to serve. It is encouraging that emerging technologies are beginning to allow alternatives such as M-Transfer services, which will be covered later in this chapter. However, it is unlikely that the change will happen overnight. Therefore, it is appropriate that efforts are made to increase the transparency of existing IVTS systems such as *hawala*.

Regulation is one possible option that was examined. It was noted that the Western model of regulation may not necessarily be appropriate. However, in

37 Gregor McClenaghan and Suleman Din, 'UAE: Hawala money transfers defy regulation efforts', *AML-CFT News* (28 August 2008) [Online]. Available at: http://aml-cft.blogspot.com/2008/08/uae-hawala-money-transfers-defy.html [accessed: 15 November 2010].

38 Passas, 'Indicators of Hawala operations and criminal abuse' (n.32) 168.

attempting to introduce any type of regulation, a thorough understanding of the inner workings of the system is required together with the support of those involved, coupled with a genuine understanding of local market conditions and customs. It must also be remembered that regulation is neither a guarantee for success and that prescribing regulation alone will not ensure compliance.

Looking ahead, an improved understanding of *hawala* and other similar systems should be encouraged through international cooperation. In addition, those involved in CTF and AML should develop a better understanding of the business model of informal systems in order that the appropriate mechanisms can be put in place to allow investigators to distinguish between legitimate and illegitimate operations. In conclusion, informal systems such as the *hawala* can be subject to abuse by terrorist and criminal funds. However, *hawala* and other IVTS networks are by no means the only or main vehicles for illicit funds transfers relating to organised crime and terrorism. The abuse of the formal banking system continues to be widespread, which is the next subject under the microscope.

Formal Banking System

The formal or regulated banking system plays an important role in the transfer of funds relating to both criminal and legitimate funding.[39] The large majority of financial services, including informal systems such as *hawala,* utilise the formal banking system, especially in relation to international transactions. In order that the mechanisms of fund transfers can be fully appreciated, it is important to develop an understanding of the formal banking system, without which the subject of adversary finances cannot be properly understood.

The formal banking sector can be divided broadly into commercial banking and investment banking. A commercial bank is an institution which accepts deposits and makes loans to businesses and consumers. Whilst commercial banks offer services to individuals, they are primarily concerned with receiving deposits and lending to businesses. The term 'commercial' is used to distinguish them from investment banks. Since the two types of banks no longer have to be separate companies, some have used the term 'commercial bank' to refer to banks which focus mainly on companies. Commercial banks have also been abused by terrorist and criminal organisations, and have served as a vehicle for money laundering as the next chapter will elaborate upon.

39 Peter A. Sproat, 'Counter-terrorist finance in the UK: A quantitative and qualitative commentary based on open-source materials' (2010) 13(4) *Journal of Money Laundering Control* 315.

INVESTMENT BANKS

The term 'investment bank' is generally applied to financial houses, which typically began trading as merchants and then expanded their role to financing the trading and commercial activities of others, especially in the international market place.[40] For many years, British financial houses were also known as merchant banks, reflecting their origins. Investment banks have retained their international presence and have a broad representation across the globe, particularly in the major financial centres, and have four main areas of activity.[41]

The first is corporate finance and advisory work, normally relating to new issues of securities for raising finance as well as other corporate services such as mergers and acquisitions. The second area of activity is Treasury dealing for corporate clients in various currencies, with financial engineering services to protect them from interest and exchange rate mechanisms. The third area of activity is investment management to include asset management, private banking for wealthy individuals and pension fund management. The fourth category of activity is securities trading and sales, which can be further divided into equities, fixed income and derivative products. This is an area of concern primarily as a result of the evidence relating to unusual trading activities associated with 9/11, discussed in the previous chapter.

In terms of economic crime, there is inadequate understanding of some of the financial instruments used, which can have a detrimental impact on financial investigations and prosecutions. Financial crime in this field can be challenging even to specialists such as forensic accountants and compliance officers. The attraction of the complexities of high finance to the criminal is clear, as the movement of illicit funding is best achieved when the financial audit trail is as complex as possible.

There is additional concern that financial markets are becoming sophisticated to the point where even financial experts are unaware of what lies behind the trades.[42] The increasing popularity of electronic trading methods such as

40 Lily Hua Fang, 'Investment bank reputation and the price and quality of underwriting services' (2005) 60(6) *Journal of Finance* 2729.

41 Katherine Tyler, 'UK bank-corporate relationships: large corporates' expectations of service' (1999) 17(4) *International Journal of Bank Marketing* 158.

42 Emilios Avgouleas and Stavros Degiannakis, 'Trade transparency and trading volume: the possible impact of the financial instruments markets directive on the trading volume of EU equity markets' (2009) 1(1) *International Journal of Financial Markets and Derivatives* 96.

high-frequency trading is a case in point.[43] High-frequency trading, referred to as HFT, is the execution of computerised trading strategies characterised by extremely short position-holding periods.[44] Quantitative investment computer programs are used to hold short-term positions in equities, options, futures, currencies, and all other financial instruments that possess electronic trading capability.[45] High-speed computers analyse market data, using algorithms to utilise trading opportunities that may open up for only a fraction of a second to several hours.[46]

High-frequency traders compete on the basis of speed with other high-frequency traders for very small, but consistent profits.[47] It is the accumulation of these multiples of small but consistent profits together with immediate realisation of these profits that make such forms of trading attractive. Furthermore, HFT is proving to be more profitable compared to traditional buy-and-hold strategies.[48] As a result, by the beginning of 2010, HFT accounted for over 70 per cent of equity trades taking place in the US, and is rapidly growing in popularity in Europe and Asia.

Aiming to capture just a fraction of a penny per share or currency unit on every trade, high-frequency traders move in and out of such short-term positions several times each day. Fractions of a penny accumulate quickly to produce significantly positive results at the end of every day.[49] In addition, HFT has become more popular recently owing to technological innovation, and growing awareness of its profitability.[50] However, one concern is that investment decisions are made based on mathematical models as opposed to fundamental analysis.[51] Traders not only do *not* carry out any form of analysis

43 Andrei Kirilenko, Mehrdad Samadi, Albert S. Kyle and Tugkan Tuzun, 'The Flash Crash: The Impact of High Frequency Trading on an Electronic Market' (2011). [Online]. Available at: http://www.q-group.org/pdf/Kyle-paper-Q-group_flash_crash_01182011_small.pdf [accessed: 12 March 2011].

44 Irene Aldridge, 'What is high frequency trading, after all?' *Huffington Post* (8 July 2010). [Online]. Available at: http://www.huffingtonpost.com/irene-aldridge/what-is-high-frequency-tr_b_639203.html [accessed: 1 October 2010].

45 Ellen Brown, 'Computerized front-running', *CounterPunch* (23 April 2010). [Online]. Available at: http://www.counterpunch.org/brown04232010.html [accessed: 15 November 2010].

46 Irene Aldridge, *High-Frequency Trading: A Practical Guide to Algorithmic Strategies and Trading Systems* (Wiley, 2009).

47 'Trade Worx / SEC letters', 21 April 2010. [Online]. Available at: http://sec.gov/comments/s7-02-10/s70210-129.pdf [accessed: 1 October 2010].

48 Aldridge, 'How Profitable Are High-Frequency Strategies?'

49 Aldridge, 'What is High Frequency Trading' (n.44).

50 Aldridge, 'How Profitable Are High-Frequency Strategies?' (n.48).

51 Fundamental analysis of a business involves the analysis of internal and external factor to determine its attractiveness from an investment perspective. Internal analysis will involve

in order to make their investment decisions, but are often not even aware of the business activity of the company behind the ticker.[52] This level of automation and focus on obtaining immediate profit at the expense of long-term security clearly raises concerns regarding the ability to manage investment risk as well issues relating to transparency in general.

From the point of view of possible criminal investigations, the situation begs the question as to whether the development of such mechanical trading mechanisms makes it possible to detect suspicious activities at all, yet alone report them to the relevant authorities. In a market where traders are considered to be well ahead of the regulators, the total dogmatic reliance on technology to manage risk has become an uncomfortable reality.

COMMERCIAL BANKS

All 'formal' money transfer activity must go through commercial banks. Investment banks, for example, utilise the services of commercial banks, and are therefore clients of commercial banks. Understanding the role of investment banks is important in the context of terrorist finance owing to the aforementioned evidence relating to insider trading. However, as the focus of this section is the transfer of funds from one location to another, which is the primary business of commercial banks, it is appropriate that attention should also be given to commercial banking operations.

Commercial banking can be divided into retail and wholesale operations. A retail bank offers banking services for individual customers, whereas a wholesale bank offers banking services for financial institutions. Retail banking is typical mass-market banking where individual customers use local branches of large commercial banks. Services offered include savings and checking accounts, mortgages, personal loans, debit cards and credit cards. In terms of

examination of the company's financial statements and its management. This is coupled with the analysis of external factors affecting the business such as competition, markets, and the economy. Fundamental analysis is performed on historical and present data, but with the goal of making financial forecasts.

52 Stock ticker is another expression for 'ticker' or 'ticker tape', the scrolling display on trading floors, at the bottom of a television or computer screen. The stock ticker shows the last sale price and volume of an equity trade. The trades printed on the stock ticker are updated continually throughout the trading day. The expression 'stock ticker' comes from 'ticker tape machine', which was a mechanical device invented in the 1870s which recorded, sent, and then printed (by punching holes) stock prices over telegraph wires. Stock ticker has now also come to mean an identifying letter symbol required for a security to trade on an exchange or through an over-the-counter system. [Online]. Available at: http://www.investorglossary.com/stockticker.htm [accessed: 15 November 2010].

the retail banking sector, the role of the FSA,[53] the UK regulatory body for the financial services industry, is to ensure that the financial institutions it overseas implement the recommendations provided by the FATF, as well as good practice in key areas such as the detection and reporting of suspicious financial transactions relating to money laundering and/or terrorist finance.[54] Areas of good practice under constant review include account opening procedures, proactive operational controls, the introduction and enhancement of automated transaction monitoring systems, training, and the implementation of effective Know Your Customer (KYC) procedures.[55]

One concern is that the guidelines provided by the FATF and the FSA represent only the minimum standard that all financial institutions should adopt, and that some are not even meeting these basic requirements. However, there are some that are truly committed to CTF and have invested and achieved standards, procedures and systems that are well above the required level. However, whether these higher standards have had any real impact on countering adversary finances is a separate matter, a subject that will be discussed further in Chapter 6.

Electronic Money

Another fast developing vehicle for transferring funds across the globe is electronic money. A number of electronic alternatives to cash, collectively known as electronic money,[56] have been introduced in recent years. Electronic money offers numerous benefits from a user perspective such as convenience, efficiency of transactions, lower transaction fees, and new business opportunities as a result of the expansion of economic activities on the Internet.[57] However,

53 The FSA is an independent non-governmental body, given statutory powers by the Financial Services and Markets Act 2000. It is a company limited by guarantee and financed by the financial services industry. Statutory objectives include maintaining confidence in the financial system; promoting public understanding of the financial system; securing the appropriate degree of protection for consumers; and the reduction of financial crime. [Online]. Available at: http://www.fsa.gov.uk/Pages/About/Who/index.shtml [accessed: 14 April 2010].

54 Jackie Johnson, 'Third round FATF mutual evaluations indicate declining compliance' (2008) 11(1) *Journal of Money Laundering Control* 47.

55 FSA, *1606 Money Laundering Statement* (FSA Report on the Prevention of Money Laundering, 15 July 2002 [Online]. Available at: http://www.fsa.gov.uk/pubs/other/ml_domestic_banking.pdf [accessed: 15 November 2010].

56 Electronic money is also known as e-currency, e-money, electronic cash, electronic currency, digital money, digital cash or digital currency.

57 Giorgio Merlonghi, 'Fighting financial crime in the age of electronic money: opportunities and limitations' (2010)13(3) *Journal of Money Laundering Control* 202.

there are also many potential issues of concern in terms of its macro-economic effects[58] as well as its use for the transfer of criminal funds.[59] Although the use of e-money has been relatively low-scale to date, the subject is worthy of consideration as an emerging concern.

ELECTRONIC CASH AND SMART CARDS

Electronic cash is also referred to as e-cash, digital cash and cyber-cash.[60] E-cash serves as a general term to describe any system which enables value storage and exchange to take place. The fact that it is 'electronic' means that the system does not use a physical medium, such as coins or paper documents.[61] The main disadvantage of electronic cash from a counter financial crime perspective is its similarity to traditional cash in that it cannot be easily traced.[62] In addition, electronic cash is potentially susceptible to forgery or double spending.[63]

The physical appearance of smart cards is very similar to that of a traditional credit card. The key difference is that the smart card contains a microprocessor and a storage unit, as well as an electronic microchip embedded in a small gold plate on the front of the card, as opposed to a conventional credit card or debit card, which has a magnetic strip on the back of the card. As such, smart cards are capable of storing at least 100 times more data than magnetic strip cards.[64] Smart cards also have an additional advantage for the user over debit and credit cards in that they can be used in an offline environment.[65]

Smart cards fall into two categories, the 'memory' smart card and the 'intelligent' smart card. The 'memory' smart card contains relatively less information and processing capabilities compared to its 'intelligent' sibling, and are typically used to record a monetary or unit value that the cardholder can spend. The 'intelligent' smart card on the other hand, has the additional

58 Exchange rate instabilities and shortage of money supplies could result in a situation whereby the total amount of electronic money could exceed to the total amount of real money available.

59 Merlonghi, 'Fighting financial crime in the age of electronic money' (n.57).

60 In 1995, CyberCash introduced the first commercial electronic wallet and which provided the foundation for the launch of CyberCoins in 1996. The new software package enabled consumers to download an empty electronic wallet and to then fill it with between $20 and $100 from their banks account before shopping on-line. Ref; www.cybercash.com.

61 Charles Wild, Stuart Weinstein and Neil MacEwan, *Internet Law* (Old Bailey Press, 2005) 124.

62 Merlonghi, 'Fighting financial crime in the age of electronic money' (n.57).

63 Wild et al. (n.61) 125.

64 Ibid.144.

65 Bank debit cards require that a good, reliable telecommunications infrastructure is in place as payments may only be made in an online environment. See also Wild et al. (n.61) 148.

feature of being able to add and process a wider variety of information components. They also have greater processing capabilities for programmed decision-making, necessary to meet multiple application requirements.[66]

Examples include the Octopus card in Hong Kong, which is a rechargeable smart card used in an electronic payment system. The system was originally launched in September 1997 as a fare collection system for the city's transport network, but has since evolved into an e-cash system for use in convenience stores, supermarkets, restaurants and parking garages. It has become one of the world's most successful electronic cash systems, with £13.4 million[67] Octopus cards in circulation with daily transactions of £9.4 million with a value totalling almost £5m.[68] The UK has adopted a similar smart card for use on the London Underground known as the Oyster card, which can also be used on London buses. Other cities have implemented similar electronic money systems including Singapore[69] and the Netherlands, which has also implemented an electronic money system known as Chipknip, based upon the same system in Hong Kong.

The main advantage of using a smart card over that of traditional cash is that cash is vulnerable to theft, whereas smart cards with identification pictures and/or passwords make them less susceptible to theft as their reusability value is substantially lower. In addition, smart cards provide an electronic record of purchases[70] and the ability to log transaction data which provide useful audit trail in financial investigations. However, despite positive aspects of the smart card including its audit trail, smart cards carry a number of security concerns. Some are concerned that smart cards may be getting too smart and storing too much personal data, making them attractive to criminals.

A case in point is the Malaysian smart card MyKad, which contains a wide range of information including the cardholder's national identification code, driver's licence and driving history, immigration details, health details, as well

66 Wild et al. (n.61) 144.

67 This is an impressive figure bearing in mind that seven million people live in Hong Kong.

68 Dan Ilett, 'Oyster and Octopus: a tale of two cities' contactless cards: does London aspire to Hong Kong's micropayments success?' Inside China: A Special Report (28 June 2006) Silicon.com [Online]. Available at: http://www.silicon.com/legacy/research/specialreports/china/0,3800011742,39159958,00.htm [accessed: 25 October 2010].

69 World Executive: Singapore City Guide [Online]. Available at: http://www.worldexecutive. com/locations/asia_pacific/singapore/singapore/transport.html [accessed: 25 October 2010].

70 This feature provides convenience to the business traveller and removes the anonymity of cash.

as electronic cash, bank account and credit card details.[71] This raises concerns in relation to possible identity theft, which in turn would allow further financial crimes to be committed. In the case of terrorist finance, revenue generated from such crimes may be used to fund acts of terrorism.

A further concern regarding the security of smart cards was highlighted by research conducted by Professor Bart Jacobs and his colleagues at Radboud University in Holland. The research published in 2008 revealed a weakness in the widely used Mifare Classic radio-frequency identification (RFID) chip which is used in building entry systems and is embedded in the Oyster card used on London's transport network.[72] Sensitive data stored on the Mifare Classic chip is protected by a unique number that acts as a key. When the chip, or a card bearing it, is placed near a reader it transmits and receives information based on its key. The security of the system depends on the key remaining secret. However, the flaw in the chip's design makes those keys easy to calculate and copy. According to Professor Jacobs:

> *Once we knew how the system worked and what the vulnerabilities were, it turned out to be very simple to actually clone cards, steal someone's identity and enter a building as someone else.*[73]

In an experiment, the Dutch researchers used an ordinary laptop to clone the smartcards, which gave them unlimited travel on the London Underground, to illustrate the security flaw. Despite claims by London Transport that the breach posed no threat to passengers and that the most anyone could gain from a rogue card is one day's travel, the associated security ramifications should not be ignored. Not only does the breach allow repeat offences where the card can be breached repeatedly on a daily basis to allow indefinite travel, there are also concerns relating to other similar cards[74] using comparable technology to conduct identity theft as well as access to thousands of government offices,

71 GMPC Project, 'Malaysia smart card'. [Online]. Available at: http://unpan1.un.org/intradoc/groups/public/documents/ Other/UNPAN022456.pdf [accessed: 8 July 2011].

72 The research paper was due to be published in March 2008. However, the release of the article was delayed after chip manufacturer NXP attempted to secure a court injunction against its publication. The paper was finally released on Monday at the European Symposium on Research in Computer Security (Esorics) 2008 security conference held in Malaga, Spain. See Peter Price, 'Oyster card hack details revealed' *BBC Online* (6 October 2008) [Online]. Available at: http://news.bbc.co.uk/1/hi/programmes/click_online/7655292. stm [accessed: 25 October 2010].

73 Price, 'Oyster card hack details revealed'.

74 Oyster cards feature the same Mifare chip used in security cards that provide access to thousands of secure locations. Security experts say the breach poses a threat to public safety and the cards should be replaced.

hospitals and schools. Furthermore, at the technical level, there are currently no known counter measures.

In addition, there are no measures to detect a breach. In response, the Dutch government is planning to replace all 120,000 smart cards used by their employees for access.[75] Therefore, it is advisable that other governments including the UK should consider further research and assessments in this field to determine the full extent of the vulnerability and to look for effective counter measures.

STORED-VALUE CARDS AND PREPAID CARDS

A stored-value card refers to the monetary value on a card and differs from prepaid cards where money is on deposit with the issuer similar to a debit card. One major difference between stored-value cards and prepaid debit cards is that prepaid debit cards are usually issued in the name of individual account holders, while stored-value cards are usually anonymous.[76]

The term 'stored-value' card means that the funds and/or data are physically stored on the card. With prepaid cards the data is maintained on computers affiliated with the card issuer. The value associated with the card can be accessed using a magnetic stripe embedded in the card, on which the card number is encoded; using RFID or by entering a code number, printed on the card, into a telephone or other numeric keypad. Typical applications of stored-value cards include transit system farecards and telephone prepaid calling cards. Typical applications of a prepaid card include payroll cards, incentive cards, gift cards and travel cards.[77]

Closed system prepaid cards have emerged and replaced the traditional merchant gift cards. The term 'closed system' implies that the cards are only accepted by a single merchant.[78] Purchasers typically purchase a card for a fixed amount and can only use the card at the merchant that issues the card.

75 'Hackers crack London tube Oyster card', *Darknet* (26 June 2008) [Online]. Available at: http://www.darknet.org.uk/2008/06/hackers-crack-london-tube-oyster-card/ [accessed: 25 October 2010].

76 Merlonghi, 'Fighting financial crime in the age of electronic money' (n.57).

77 Courtney J. Linn, 'Regulating the cross-border movement of prepaid cards' (2008) 11(2) *Journal of Money Laundering Control* 146.

78 Semi-closed system prepaid cards are similar to closed system prepaid cards. However, cardholders are permitted to redeem the cards at multiple merchants within a geographic area. These types of cards are issued by a third party, rather than the retailer who accepts the card. Examples include university cards and mall gift cards.

Generally, few if any laws govern these types of cards. In the US, for example, closed system prepaid cards are not subject to the PATRIOT Act, as the cards are anonymous and as a result, the identity of a customer is unknown. It is not surprising to note that closed system prepaid cards are increasingly becoming a way for Mexican drug cartels to smuggle money across the border.[79] It therefore follows that these cards can also be useful for other criminals including terrorists, who seek to utilise any loopholes in the law.[80] The existence of loopholes is common especially in relation to emerging technologies, where the full implications on the potential usage of that technology is not yet understand.

A more recent development is the use of mobile phones enabling smartcard holders to manage their prepaid card accounts. Advancements in mobile technologies have enabled the use of mobile phones to carry out a variety of functions in relation not only to prepaid cards, such as the ability to fill up their account and obtain a balance, but also to carry out a variety of funds transfers. Transactions utilising mobile telephones known as M-transfers have yet to reach mainstream consumers but are already active in many countries and are likely to become increasingly widespread.

M-Transfer

The lack of 'traditional' banking services in developing countries was identified earlier as one of the key reasons why informal funds transfer systems exist. In order for fund transfers to occur through the formal banking system, both the sender and the recipient must possess a bank account in order that funds can be transferred from the sender's account into the recipient's account. However, across the developing world, most individuals do not possess bank accounts.[81]

In South Africa, for example, there are 16 million people without bank accounts, out of an adult population of 47.7 million.[82] Several reasons exist. First, there is a general perception that banks impoverish and therefore a service that low-income families can ill afford. In addition, the lack of a permanent address

---

79 P.A. Johnstown, *Assessment: Prepaid Stored Value Cards*, National Drug Intelligence Center, 31 October 2006. [Online]. Available at: http://www.justice.gov/ndic/pubs11/20777/index.htm [accessed: 16 December 2009].

80 Merlonghi, 'Fighting financial crime in the age of electronic money' (n.57).

81 Indrani Medhi, S.N. Nagasena Gautama, Kentaro Toyama, 'A Comparison of Mobile Money-Transfer UIs for Non-Literate and Semi-Literate Users' (Proceedings of the 27th international conference on Human factors in computing systems, CHI '09 Boston, USA, 6 April 2009) .

82 Ivan Mortimer-Schutts, *The Transformational Potential of M-Transactions: Moving the Debate Forward* (The Policy Paper Series, no. 6, July 2007) 20.

can be problematic as banks are required to carry out customer due diligence as part of their account opening procedures, which involves proof of identification in the form of a permanent address. This is particularly problematic for those lifestyles which are nomadic. As a result, there is a reliance on cash, which is not only much less secure, but also problematic from an investigative perspective in that obtaining a financial audit trail is difficult.

In response, mobile phone technologies have been developed to offer financial services in markets where the costs of traditional retail banking have been too high, or where their distribution arrangements are inappropriate to serve low-income clients. In the space of a decade, mobile networks have become a significant part of the infrastructure in many developing countries and the integration of mobile telephone and banking services is beginning to make an appearance in many emerging and developing markets. Recent examples include Wizzit in South Africa, Globe in the Philippines and M-PESA in Kenya, which will be examined in turn.

CASE STUDY 1: M-PESA – KENYA

M-PESA is a new mobile payments system in Kenya, which was trialled in 2006 and launched in 2007.[83] At the core of M-PESA is a central float within which individual customer accounts are held, which is banked with the Commercial Bank of Africa.[84] The service comprises a simple registration process to set up a new account into which cash can uploaded (deposited) and downloaded (withdrawn) at a large number of Safaricom's re-seller airtime distribution agents.[85] Making a deposit is a similar process to topping up their airtime pre-pay balance in that the account identifier is the mobile phone number and the customer visits the very same place that they would go to buy airtime. There, the similarity ends as the M-PESA account is entirely separate to the pre-pay airtime credit system. Once registered, the customer can send funds to any other phone number, on any network. The receiver receives a text message

83 The pilot funding for M-PESA came from DFID, Vodafone and Safaricom.

84 The banking contract for the M-PESA float is between a newly created entity, Trust Co, formed by Vodafone. It is through the Trust Co and service level agreements with Safaricom that the account relationships are managed, and not between the bank and individual M-PESA customers. See Mortimer-Schutts, *The Transformational Potential of M-Transactions* (n.82) 14.

85 Pauline Vaughan, *Early Lessons from the Deployment of M-PESA, Vodafone's Own Mobile Transactions Service* (The Policy Paper Series, 'The Transformational Potential of M-Transactions-Moving the debate Forward', no. 6, July 2007).

that can be taken to a re-seller agent and 'cashed in', enabling person-to-person money transfer instantly over large distances.[86]

In addition, the M-PESA account balance may be used to buy goods and services including airtime credit for any other Safaricom pre-pay phone.[87] From a CTF and AML perspective, although the service offers a full transaction tracking and reporting system, numerous concerns currently exist. One is that its AML measures have not yet been developed, yet alone implemented.[88] A further concern is with reference to payments made to 'pay-as-you go' mobile phone accounts in that such accounts can be set up with virtually no due diligence and can be opened and closed with equal ease. 'Pay-as-you-go' mobile phones have proved to be popular with criminals for single use for 'voice' and there is clearly concern as to whether similar use may be adopted to carry out mobile funds transfers.

CASE STUDY 2: WIZZIT, SOUTH AFRICA

Wizzit is a virtual bank with no physical branches of its own. Mobile phone subscription customers can use their phone to make person-to-person payments, transfer money, purchase prepaid electricity, and buy airtime for a prepaid mobile phone. Holders of Wizzit bank accounts also receive a Maestro branded debit card that enables them to make purchases, obtain cash-back at retail outlets and withdraw money at any South African or Maestro labelled ATM anywhere in the world.[89] The only requirement is that a minimum deposit of between 50 and 100 Rand be kept in the account.[90] There are no minimum balance requirements or fixed monthly fee charge as a pay-as-you-go pricing model has been adopted. After the initial sign up charge of US$5.26, the only cost to the customer is the transaction charge which range from US$0.13 to US$0.66 per transaction, which is approximately 20 per cent less expensive compared to traditional banking charges on a like-for-like basis.

86 William Jack and Tavneet Suri, *Mobile Money: The Economics of M-PESA* (National Bureau of Economic Research Working Paper no. 16721, issued in January 2011).

87 Ignacio Mas, 'Designing Mobile Money Services Lessons from M-PESA' (2009) 4(2) *Innovations* 77.

88 Vaughan, *Early Lessons from the Deployment of M-PESA, Vodafone's Own Mobile Transactions Service* (n.85).

89 Medhi et al., 'A Comparison of Mobile Money-Transfer UIs for Non-Literate and Semi-Literate Users' (n.81) .

90 Groupe d'Economie Mondiale, *Transformational Potential of M-Transactions: Moving the Debate Forward* (The Policy Paper Series, no. 6, July 2007) 13.

To open a Wizzit bank account, a Wizzit agent is sent to the applicant's home or workplace. For most Wizzit customers, derogation from certain aspects of the AML and KYC requirements, the so-called Exemption 17, facilitates the opening of a bank account with relative ease. Exemption 17 states that AML and KYC requirements do not apply provided that the maximum balance of 25,000 rand and maximum transaction limits of 5,000 rand are not exceeded. In cases where these limits are exceeded the Wizzit account is suspended until the full AML and KYC compliant procedures are completed. It should be noted that fewer than 10 per cent of Wizzit's customers have ever exceeded the maximum thresholds set out in Exemption 17.[91] In other words, AML and CTF measures do not apply to over 90 per cent of customers. In addition, as the details of Exemption 17 are widely published, those wishing to avoid detection can do so with ease by ensuring that individual transactions limits are not exceeded.

From a consumer perspective, one of the main advantages is that the mobile transactional technology works on any handset, and SIM card, as well as across all the networks. In addition, the account can be used to send money in real time to any Wizzit account holder in South Africa, and overnight to any other bank account holder. This 'any-to-any' feature is seen as a significant advantage in giving Wizzit account the ability to transact with any mobile user regardless of the identity of their network operator or their bank. However, this advantage is clearly a concern in terms of its potential use for illicit funds transfers.

CASE STUDY 3: GLOBE TELECOM – PHILIPPINES

Globe Telecom's mobile financial transactions system known as G-Cash,[92] is the first mobile wallet service enabling cashless and card-less financial micro-transactions which delivers services with partners including banks, utility companies,16 retailers, governmental bodies and non-profit organisations. Globe also has G-Cash outlets at their retail units. As an indication of its size and reach Globe had 3,500 partners, including 27 international partners in 15 countries in 2006. In addition, customers are able to use Globe's retail units to deposit and withdraw cash.[93]

91 Ibid. 14.

92 The Globe Telecom formed a subsidiary G-Xchange Inc. (GXI) to manage G-Cash operations.

93 Groupe d'Economie Mondiale, *Transformational Potential of M-Transactions* (n.90) 15.

Registration for G-Cash services is a one-off process which involves the exchange of SMS[94] messages between Globe Telecom and its subsidiary Touch Mobile subscribers. To register, a subscriber is required to send an SMS to the telephone number 2882, with a self-nominated 4-digit PIN, mother's maiden name, first and last name, address and telephone number. These details are verified against the customer's ID when withdrawing cash. All transactions and remittances with G-Cash are SMS text driven. As with the other comparative M-transactions services, G-Cash users are able to load prepaid airtime credits on to their mobile phones and transfer both cash and airtime credits between customers of Globe Telecom and Touch Mobile. In addition, cash-in and cash-out services can be accessed through the partners on provision of a valid ID card and on completion of a form, also in SMS format, to comply with AML requirements.[95]

There are also set limits for money transfers. Current transaction limits are set at 10,000 Php, which equates to approximately US$200, per transaction. There are also daily limits amounting to 40,000 Php, approximately US$800, and monthly limit of 100,000 Php, which is the equivalent of US$2,000. The service is competitively priced compared to traditional banking systems with cash-in and cash-out transactions below 1,000Php charged at a flat 10.00Php and a one per cent charge for transactions above 1,000Php.[96] In order to comply with AML requirements, a number of measures have been put in place including transaction monitoring. Furthermore, SIM cards are checked for multiple registrations to the service by same phone number, the same name or the SIM card. In addition, continuous near-breaches of wallet limits are checked and noted. Although the service is preferable to cash, and G-Cash appears to be the most advanced out of the three M-Transfer systems examined in terms of AML/CFT procedures, numerous concerns remain.

M-TRANSACTIONS: CONCLUSIONS

All three case studies highlight the advantage of M-transactions over cash in that basic due diligence is carried out as part of its account opening procedures and an audit trail can be provided, if necessary. However, where financial service innovations are emerging outside of the traditional scope of responsibility of

94 Short Message Service (SMS) is the text communication service component of phone, web or mobile communication systems, using standardized communications protocols that allow the exchange of short text messages between fixed line or mobile phone devices.

95 Medhi et al., 'A Comparison of Mobile Money-Transfer UIs for Non-Literate and Semi-Literate Users' (n.81) .

96 Groupe d'Economie Mondiale, *Transformational Potential of M-Transactions* (n.90) 15.

financial market regulators, vulnerability exists. Loopholes such as Exemption 17 need to be identified and closed. Furthermore, there is a degree of urgency in its regulatory agenda, especially as the network structure emerging from the convergence between payments, retail banking and telecommunications will be difficult to alter once established. Hence it is all the more important that regulatory and institutional frameworks set the right incentives early on in the process of innovation, in order to capture the full benefits that may be generated through the development of m-banking and payment systems.

Conclusions

The chapter explored the key vehicles which can be abused by terrorists and criminals to transfer funds. It should also be noted that funds can be transferred through a variety of other means such as through the acquisition of assets, trade finance and third party entities. These mechanisms can not only be utilised by terrorists, but also by criminals who wish to keep their funding sources secret. The process is known as money laundering, which is the focus of the next chapter.

5

Money Laundering

> *The most efficient means of battling organized crime is to act against money laundering.*
>
> *Louis J. Freeh, Director of the FBI*[1]

Overview

Money laundering can be defined as:

> *... a process by which one conceals the existence, illegal source, or illegal application of income, and then disguises that income to make it appear legitimate.*[2]

The money laundering process utilises various vehicles and methods, many of which are also used by terrorist organisations to transfer funds.[3] Furthermore, where funding has been acquired though illegitimate means, such as narcotics trafficking or fraud, the predicate offence may be the same as those committed by Organised Crime Groups (OCGs). Some of the activities of OCGs and terrorist organisations, both in terms of how funds are acquired, as well as vehicles and methods used to transfer those funds, can be very similar. This has inevitably led to a lack of clarity in terms of the ability to differentiate between the two with some claiming the development of a so called 'nexus' between organised crime and terrorism. This paradigm has resulted in some confusion

---

1 Jeffrey Robinson, *The Laundrymen* (Simon & Schuster UK Limited 1998) 248.

2 US Senate, 'The Use of Offshore Banks and Companies' (Permanent Subcommittee on Investigations of the Committee of Governmental Affairs, Crime and Secrecy, 1983), 7, and see generally R.C.H. Alexander, *Insider Dealing and Money Laundering in the EU: Law and Regulation* (Ashgate 2007), Barry A.K. Rider, Kern Alexander, Lisa Linklater and Stuart Bazley (eds), *Market Abuse and Insider Dealing* (Tottel Publishing, 2009), ch. 7 and Barry Rider and Michael Ashe (eds) *Money Laundering Control* (Sweet and Maxwell, 1996).

3 Evan Bell, 'Concealing and disguising criminal property' (2009) 12(3) *Journal of Money Laundering Control* 268.

between money laundering and terrorist finance, which is problematic as it impacts directly upon the effectiveness of counter terrorist-finance (CTF) efforts made by both the private and public sectors.

The private sector plays a key role in the identification of suspicious funds relating to both terrorist finance and the proceeds of crime. However, the methods used for the identification of both categories are derived from anti-money laundering (AML) activity and not from terrorist finance. In essence, the private sector utilises existing AML detection methodology and technology to attempt to capture terrorist finance, which can be problematic.

In contrast to the silo structure of the public sector, the financial industry does not distinguish between terrorist finance and other types of financial crime. Although this lack of distinction has benefits, the downside is that AML technology is focused on identifying suspicious transactions that bear little resemblance to those sometimes used by terrorists.[4] Another concern is that the lack of differentiation has resulted in a one-size-fits-all approach. Unfortunately, there is no 'one-size-fits-all' approach to understanding and responding to the threat from money laundering and terrorist finance. Instead, in order to counter the problem of adversary finances, it is essential that the similarities and differences between terrorist organisations and OCGs are understood.

Similarities and Differences Between Terrorism and Organised Crime

One key difference between OCGs and terrorist organisations is in relation to their motivation and end goal. Many crimes are committed for financial gain and criminal organisations seek to maximise profit for money's sake and their motivation is to create as much personal wealth as possible.[5] In many ways, the drivers are similar to private sector organisations whose aim is also to maximise profit. The one key difference is that the latter attempts to achieve this through legitimate means, whereas OCGs will achieve this through any means available. The comparison is worthy of note as the countering of OCGs and OCG finance should focus on adopting business models for disruption.

---

4 David Chaikin, 'How effective are suspicious transaction reporting systems?' (2009) 12(3) *Journal of Money Laundering Control* 238.

5 Emmanouela Mylonaki, 'The manipulation of organised crime by terrorists: legal and factual perspectives' (2002) 2 *The International Criminal Law Review* 213.

The primary motivation for terrorism, however, is not financial. Instead, terrorist organisations aspire to ideological and political goals.[6] As a result, terrorists are able to generate income through their ability to raise money through donations from those who share their ideology and political ambitions. A significant portion of terrorist funding is derived from donors,[7] some of whom are fully aware of the intended purpose of their contributions, and others who are not.[8]

Given the choice, terrorists would ideally fund themselves through legitimate means. This is due to the fact that the planning and execution of terrorist activities is high risk. As such, it needs to remain covert in order to minimise disruption from the authorities to ensure that a successful terrorist attack can take place. As maintaining a low profile is high priority, the involvement in illegal activities may attract unwanted attention. In terms of disruption, even if the terrorist organisation and its activities are known to the authorities, there may be inadequate evidence to arrest or disrupt their activities based on terrorism charges alone. However, involvement in criminal activity enables arrests and subsequent criminal prosecutions to take place based on criminal activity. As such, it is in the interest of terrorists to appear as legitimate as possible at every level, for as long as possible.

Where legitimate sources of funding are unavailable, terrorist seek alternative sources by turning to criminal activity. As with criminal networks, terrorist organisations also derive funding from a variety of criminal activities ranging in scale and sophistication from low-level crime to involvement in serious organised crime.[9] Provided that the crime itself can be kept secret, the next hurdle that the terrorist has to overcome is to make the proceeds of his crime appear legitimate.

---

6 US Department of State, *Money Laundering and Terrorist Financing – A Global Threat*. [Online]. Available at: //www.state.gov/p/inl/rls/nrcrpt/2005/vol2/html/42380.htm [accessed: 29 December 2009].

7 Much of the money for the 9/11 attacks came from charities and wealthy individuals in the Middle East region, especially in Saudi Arabia. See 'Financing terrorism: looking in the wrong places', *The Economist* (20 October 2005) [Online]. Available at://economist.com/displaystory.cfm?story_ id=5053373 [accessed: 20 November 2009].

8 US Department of State, *Money Laundering and Terrorist Financing* (n.6).

9 FATF, *Global Money Laundering and Terrorist Financing Threat Assessment: A View of How and Why Criminals and Terrorists Abuse Finances, the Effect of This Abuse and the Steps To Mitigate These Threats* (FATF Report, July 2010) 8–9.

Here, terrorists and criminals such as drug dealers, share the same need. Both require their illegal sources of money to appear outwardly legitimate. In other words, the money needs to be laundered.

In terms of the relationship between money laundering and terrorist finance, many experts have referred to the source of the funds as a way to differentiate between the two.[10] The source is 'dirty' in money laundering whereas the source may be 'clean' or 'dirty' in the case of terrorist financing. Where the source is legitimate, 'clean' money can be described as been turned into 'dirty' money for use in terrorist attacks. This is a process some refer to as 'reverse' money laundering. However, this is a rather simplistic explanation as well as misleading, as in reality the movement of money is not reversed when the origin is clean. As such, it is necessary to develop an in-depth understanding of the money laundering process in order that a proper comparison can be made between terrorist finance and money laundering.

Money Laundering

Money laundering is not a new phenomenon. It is as old as the notion of property itself. The development of the concept of legal title to property simultaneously created the need to hide that property from third parties who sought to deprive the individual of their assets. The use of various methods and instruments to shield one's activities, especially one's economic activities from unwarranted third party scrutiny, has a long and legitimate history.[11]

Although the actual phrase 'money laundering' did not enter the judicial lexicon until the case of *US v $4,255, 625.39*, the origins of the contemporary money laundering problem can be traced to the US in the prohibition era.[12] This period marked the start of the transformation of organised crime into big business.

The illegal trade in alcohol created large fortunes for many gangsters, who required protection from the scrutiny of both the police and the Internal Revenue Service. To hide his money, Al Capone is said to have adopted a

10 Michelle Gallant, 'Promise and perils: the making of global money laundering, terrorist finance norms' (2010) 13(3) *Journal of Money Laundering Control* 175.

11 Barry A.K. Rider, 'Law: The War on Terror and Crime and the Offshore Centres: The 'New' Perspective?', in Donato Masciandaro (ed.), *Global Financial Crime: Terrorism, Money Laundering and Offshore Centres* (Ashgate Publishing 2004) ch. 2, 77.

12 *US v. $4,255,625.39* (1982) 551 FSupp 314.

simple system that involved the purchase of launderettes in order to mix his illegal bootlegging profits with his legal laundry profits. This anecdote is also said to reflect the linguistic origins of the term money laundering. However, Al Capone's fall for tax evasion caused money laundering techniques to become more sophisticated.[13]

In order to achieve the necessary level of sophistication, the financial audit trail needs to be complex. The journey is likely to utilise multiple transfer vehicles in multiple jurisdictions. However, criminals and terrorists are not alone in using money laundering techniques to disguise their audit trail. As Professor Barry Rider observed:

> *The process involved in laundering money, or other forms of wealth, are not necessarily abusive or an evil in themselves. Indeed, simply keeping wealth secret may not be objectionable in either a legal or moral sense. In certain circumstances it might well be prudent and beneficial.*[14]

It is this very mix of legitimate and illegitimate sources of funding that is laundered that Professor Rider highlights, which makes the role of countering money laundering both interesting and challenging. Criminals have always endeavoured to conceal the origin of illegally generated funds in order to erase all trace of their wrongdoings. Nevertheless, the forms and dimensions of this type of crime have evolved in recent years. Since the 1970s, the escalation of the drug market and globalisation of organised crime have led to a collective raised awareness with regard to the problem of money laundering.[15]

Where an individual or organisation wishes his or its financial activities to have minimum transparency, every attempt is likely to be made to make the financial audit trail as complex as possible.[16] The aim is to attempt to make financial investigations as difficult and lengthy as possible, causing the maximum headache for investigators. A further aim is that the financial evidence presented in court will prove to be too complex to be digested fully

---

13 Kristopher Jean Paul Hinterseer, 'Financial Secrecy and the Law: An Enquiry into the Legal Aspects of Money Laundering in a Political-Economic Context' (PhD Thesis, Institute of Advanced Legal Studies, University of London, 2001) 41. The thesis was substantially published in Kris Hinterseer, *Criminal Finance: The Political Economy of Money Laundering in a Comparative Legal Context* (Kluwer Law International 2002).

14 Barry Rider, 'The Price of Laundering Dirty Money' (Jesus College, University of Cambridge: Private Paper).

15 Jeffrey Simser, 'Money laundering and asset cloaking techniques' (2008) 11(1) *Journal of Money Laundering Control* 15.

16 Bell, 'Concealing and disguising criminal property' (n.3).

by the judicial system, and lead to the case being dismissed on the grounds of inadequate evidence, as the court struggles to tackle the complexities of the crime committed.[17] The complexity of the process of money laundering, which is utilised by criminals and terrorists alike, are frequently not adequately appreciated by the criminal justice system, as well as other government investigative bodies.[18] As Professor Barry Rider observed:

> *It must be appreciated that money laundering involves a series of stages and each stage will have its own characteristics. Those charged with the detection and investigation of such matters need to be alerted to the implication of a process which will have been carefully designed and structured with the objective of minimising exposure and, thus, the risk of interference. Sadly, legislators have often failed to appreciate the complexity of money laundering both in terms of its character and objectives. They have taken for granted a somewhat stylised model that rarely conforms to reality. Indeed, given the nature and expertise, not to mention resources, of those involved in this industry, there is every incentive for their services to be adapted to take full account of any new threat – including legislation. Their culture is one of evasion and adaptation.*[19]

In order to tackle terrorist and associated criminal finances, it is essential to develop an understanding of the broader money laundering environment, as well as to grasp why it occurs, who launders money and how it is achieved.

Who Launders Money?

Money is laundered for a wide variety of reasons. One reason for attempting to conceal money is if it is associated with criminal activity including terrorism. However, it is also possible that individuals or organisations may utilise money laundering techniques to hide money that has been derived from perfectly legitimate sources. For example, an individual may launder money in order to maximise his or her personal wealth to protect it from confiscation from the tax man, or a divorcing spouse.[20] Another example is where the individual

17 Kenneth Murray, 'The uses of irresistible inference; Protecting the system from criminal penetration through more effective prosecution of money laundering offences' (2011) 14(1) *Journal of Money Laundering Control* 7.

18 Simser, 'Money laundering and asset cloaking techniques' (n.15) 15.

19 Rider, 'The Price of Laundering Dirty Money' (n.14).

20 Simser, 'Money laundering and asset cloaking techniques', (n.15) 15.

may wish to neutralise the erosion of their assets by moving assets through a shell company into a less taxed jurisdiction. Corporations have also laundered money to avoid or evade taxes, to defraud their shareholders and to get around currency controls. For example, Italian designer Gucci allegedly laundered more than $11 million through shell companies, in order to avoid US taxes.[21]

Money laundering techniques have also been used to bribe potential clients. According to Jeffrey Robinson,[22] Gulf Oil moved $4 million through the Bahamas to bribe Korean and Bolivian politicians, whilst the Lockheed Corporation laundered $25.5 million through a Liechtenstein Trust,[23] using cash and bearer drafts to pay off Italian politicians. Lockheed also subscribed to the laundry facilities of US foreign exchange dealer Deak-Pereta, in order to bribe Japanese politicians. At Lockheed's request, Deakis reported to have laundered $8.3 million to help secure a large sale which emerged in the form of 15 untraceable payments to a Spanish priest in Hong Kong, who hand-carried the cash in flight bags and orange crates to Lockheed's customers in Tokyo.[24]

Governments have also been known to launder funds to finance 'black' operations. According to former FBI counter narcotics officer Jack Cole,[25] government money is used in undercover operations and disguised as illicit money in order that it can be used as bait to flush out illicit financial flows. Another example can be found during the Iran-Contra affair. The Iran-Contra affair was a political scandal in the US that came to light in November 1986 during the Reagan administration. President Ronald Reagan and other senior US officials secretly facilitated the sale of arms to Iran, the subject of an arms embargo, in the hope that the arms sales would secure the release of hostages and allow US intelligence agencies to fund the Nicaraguan Contras.[26]

21 Robinson, *The Laundrymen* (n.1) 24.

22 American-born author of 22 books on organised crime and money laundering.

23 Liechtenstein Trust is set up by a written agreement (Trust Deed) between the trustor (settlor) and trustee(s), or by a written Declaration of Trust by the trustor, matched by a written Acceptance of Trust by the trustee. The Trust Deed does not have to contain the names of beneficiaries. If the Trust Deed is deposited with the Registrar of Trusts, it will not be publicly available, and later instruments (for example, naming beneficiaries) will not have to be revealed. A registration fee of US$200 (at the time of writing) is payable on registration. [Online]. Available at://www.lawandtax-news.com/html/liechtenstein/jlilatolaw.html [accessed: 20 November 2009].

24 Robinson, *The Laundrymen* (n.1) 24.

25 Jack Cole, currently Board Chair of Law Enforcement against Prohibition. Presentation and meeting at the Twenty-Eighth International Symposium On Economic Crime, Jesus College, University of Cambridge, 5–12 September 2010.

26 The National Security Archive: The Iran-Contra Affair 20 Years On. [Online]. Available at://www.gwu.edu/~nsarchiv/NSAEBB/NSAEBB210/ [accessed: 29 September 2010].

The Iran-Contra affair had begun as an operation to improve US–Iranian relations. It was planned that Israel would ship weapons to a relatively moderate, politically influential group of Iranians, and then the US would resupply Israel and receive the Israeli payment. In return, the Iranian recipients had promised to do everything in their power to achieve the release of six US hostages, who were being held by the Lebanese Shia Islamist group Hezbollah, who in turn were unknowingly connected to the Army of the Guardians of the Islamic Revolution.[27] The plan deteriorated into an arms-for-hostages scheme, in which members of the executive branch sold weapons to Iran in exchange for the release of the American hostages.[28] Large modifications to the plan were devised by Lieutenant Colonel Oliver North of the National Security Council in late 1985, in which a portion of the proceeds from the weapon sales was diverted to fund anti-Sandinista and anti-Communist rebels, or Contras, in Nicaragua.[29] Whilst investigating the question of the arms-for-hostages deal, Attorney General Edwin Meese discovered that only $12 million of the $30 million the Iranians reportedly paid, had reached the government.

Lieutenant Colonel Oliver North of the National Security Council explained that the discrepancy had been caused by the fact that he had diverted funds from the arms sales to the Contras, with the full knowledge of National Security Adviser Admiral John Poindexter and the President.[30]

As this section has highlighted, money laundering techniques have been, and continue to be used by numerous individuals and organisations for a variety of reasons. Given the diversity of money launderers, an appreciation of the differing shades of money may be helpful. The financial flows associated with money laundering are almost entirely 'hot' in nature, where hot money refers to financial movements stimulated by adverse changes in economic, social and/ or political conditions.[31] However, within these 'hot' financial flows, differing shades of money exist, best described as white, grey, black or subterranean.

---

27 Tower Commission's Report. [Online]. Available at://www.presidency.ucsb.edu/PS157/assignment%20files%20 public/TOWER%20EXCERPTS.htm [accessed: 29 September 2010].

28 BBC, 'Reagan's mixed White House legacy' (6 June 2004). [Online]. Available at: //news.bbc.co.uk/1/hi/world/americas/213195.stm [accessed: 29 September 2010.

29 Gyeorgos C. Hatonn, *Chaparral Serendipity* (Phoenix Source Distributors 1993), 218.

30 Julie Wolf, 'The Iran-Contra Affair', *PBS* (8 May 2008). [Online]. Available at://www.pbs.org/wgbh/amex/reagan/peopleevents/pande08.html [accessed: 20 October 2010].

31 John Cuddington, 'Capital flight: estimates, issues and explanations' (1986) 58 *Princeton Studies in International Finance* 2.

Shades of Money

White money is also referred to as clean money and refers to 'ordinary' money that is obtained in small denominations through hard work and related bonuses, prudent investment or inheritance. The ultimate objective of the money launderer is to make money that falls into the other categories to appear 'white'. The direct opposite of clean money is dirty money, also referred to as 'black' money, which is obtained through criminal means.[32] Grey money is money that the owner wishes to disassociate himself or herself from, even though its origins may not have been illegal. One example, as previously mentioned is personal, where an individual may not wish his spouse, partner or relatives to be aware of his wealth for a variety of reasons. Another example is with respect to business competition where a business which is extremely profitable may wish to maintain a low profile to avoid attracting attention which may result in increased competition.

Another factor may be tax avoidance, which again is perfectly legal if obtained through a 'loophole' that the government has overlooked. A loophole will sometimes be closed by the government through changes in regulation once it has attracted enough attention. Therefore, it is in the interest of those individuals or an institution benefiting from a loophole to ensure that attention is not focused on the loophole by maintaining a low profile.

The final category of money is that obtained through the 'subterranean', otherwise referred to as the 'underground' economy. Various estimates for the underground economy exist, a task difficult to calculate owing to its clandestine nature. However, the figure is estimated to be in excess of $500 billion per annum for the US alone.[33] The subterranean economy can be described as being similar to the ancient bartering system, where a service is provided in return for another, with no actual exchange of money taking place.[34] Although this in itself is not illegal, there is loss of revenue from tax, as the 'income' is not reported. A further, and perhaps the real concern is that a substantial portion of the money may be illegal.

32 Simser, 'Money laundering and asset cloaking techniques' (n.15) 15.
33 Rider, 'Law: The War on Terror and Crime and the Offshore Centres' (n.11), 77.
34 For example, a gardener may offer gardening services to a hairdresser in return for a haircut.

Money Laundering Mechanism

Many forms of crime and misappropriation produce quantities of cash in relatively low denominations, which then needs to be consolidated into a form of wealth that can be more easily transported.[35] Contrary to popular belief, large amounts of cash cannot be transported in an attaché case. In reality, a million pounds, even in £50 denominations, will stack to a pile that is nearly 10 feet in height.[36] As a result, other methods of transfer are required. These methods are numerous and varied and are limited only by the ingenuity of the launderer.

The main objective of the money laundering process is to make the capital and assets that are illegally obtained seem as though they are derived from a legitimate source, and then insert them into economic circulation.[37] The basic money laundering model consists of three distinct stages, namely placement, layering and integration, as illustrated in Figure 5.1.

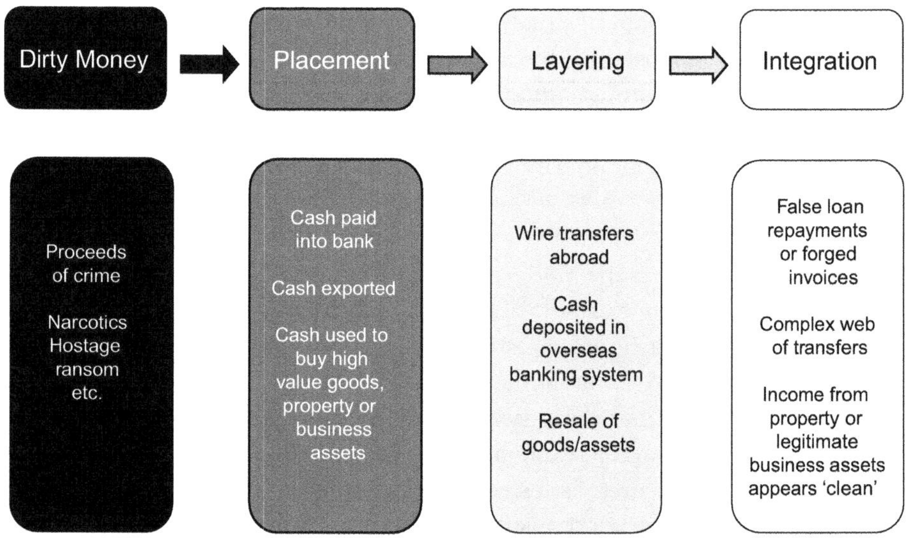

Figure 5.1 Basic money laundering model

35 Rider, 'Law: The War on Terror and Crime and the Offshore Centres' (n.11) 77. See also Barry A.K. Rider 'Pursuing Corruption: Civil Weapons: Old Law in New Battles' in *Legal Studies in the Global Era: Legal Issues Beyond Borders* (Japan Chuo University Press, 2010), 121–47 and Barry A.K. Rider, 'Corruption, the Sharp End of Governance' in Shazzeeda A. Ali (ed.), *Risky Business: Perspectives on Corporate Misconduct* (Caribbean Law Publishing Company 2011), 1–45.

36 Robinson, *The Laundrymen* (n.1)11.

37 Simser, 'Money laundering and asset cloaking techniques' (n.15) 15.

STAGE ONE: PLACEMENT

In this initial phase, cash is placed into circulation through a number of vehicles including financial institutions such as banks, as well as casinos, and Money Service Businesses (MSBs), both local and abroad. Examples include the *casas de cambio* operating on the US/Mexican border, global money transmitters such as Western Union and American Express, neighbourhood cheque-cashing businesses and Giro houses, which are wire-transfer businesses,[38] as well as informal systems such as *hawala*.[39]

STAGE TWO: LAYERING

In the layering phase, the disassociation of the funds from their illicit source takes place. The purpose of this stage is to make it more difficult to detect and uncover laundering activity. Layering is achieved through maximising inter-account transfers often through 'dummy' accounts set up for this purpose, passing through as many jurisdictions as possible, relying on secrecy laws and attorney-client privilege to obscure identity, and to deliberately create a complex web of financial transactions, whilst ensuring the attempted obliteration of any audit trail at every step of the process. Known layering methods include the conversion of cash into monetary instruments[40] and the sale of material assets bought with cash.[41]

STAGE THREE: INTEGRATION

The third and final stage is integration where the laundered funds are brought back into circulation in the form of clean and often taxable income.[42] This is dissimilar to layering, for in the integration process, detection and identification of laundered funds can only be provided through informants. There are numerous known methods such as property dealing, the use of front companies and false loans and invoicing. For example, the sale of property to integrate laundered money back into the economy is a common practice amongst criminals. Many criminal groups also use shell companies to buy property so

38 Robinson, *The Laundrymen* (n.1) 40.

39 See Chapter 4, Mechanisms of Illicit Funds Transfer.

40 Once the placement is successful within the financial system by way of a bank or financial institution, the proceeds can then be converted into monetary instruments. This involves the use of banker's drafts and money orders.

41 Assets that are bought through illicit funds can be resold locally or abroad and in such a case the assets become more difficult to trace and thus seize.

42 Simser, 'Money laundering and asset cloaking techniques' (n.15) 15.

that the proceeds from the sale would be considered legitimate. Furthermore, where front companies are incorporated in countries with corporate secrecy laws, the criminals are able to lend themselves their own laundered proceeds in an apparently legitimate transaction. The use of false invoices by import/export companies has also proven to be a very effective way for criminals to integrate illicit proceeds back into the economy. This involves the overvaluation of entry documents to justify the funds later deposited in domestic banks and/or the value of funds received from exports.

In addition, transactions used to obscure the source of the relevant funds will often be structured in such as manner as to render it almost impossible to obtain admissible evidence that would allow a court to establish the derivation of money.[43] Law enforcement agencies often refer to this process as layering, implying that with due diligence, the true facts may be uncovered through a progressive investigation. However, as Professor Rider observed:

> *While there have been cases where investigators have been able to peel off a series of layers to reveal what in fact took place, in the case of the more sophisticated structure, the concept of layering is too simplistic.*[44]

In reality, some money laundering operations are structured in a manner that resembles a mosaic or kaleidoscope, rather than a layer-cake. Transactions will not be progressive but parallel, establishing mutual obligations which can be married or crossed, often on a contingent basis, and which would not be substantiated to the satisfaction of a court applying conventional legal rules.[45] In attempting to understand money laundering, each piece of the mosaic or kaleidoscope must be understood individually in order that the pieces can then be placed back together to reveal the full picture. These individual pieces of mosaic translate into the various vehicles and mechanisms of the money laundering process.

In the same way that a medical doctor needs to understand the individual functions of the human anatomy in conjunction with the overall working of the human body in order to be able to properly diagnose and treat a patient, so must the financial investigator also understand both the individual elements as well as the bigger picture, which equates to the global financial environment. Having examined the broader elements of the financial crime environment, the

43 Bell, 'Concealing and disguising criminal property' (n.3) 268.
44 Rider, 'Law: The War on Terror and Crime and the Offshore Centres' (n.11) 79.
45 Ibid., 79.

next section will drill down in the detail of the key money laundering methods and instruments utilised by money launders.

Money Laundering Instruments

Numerous money laundering methods and instruments have been identified. However, both the 2008 and 2009 FATF[46] strategic surveillance exercises highlighted that a significant proportion of money laundering and terrorist finance activity involves cash. The report stated that:

> *Cash couriers and cash smuggling continue to be used, and cash placement is still an important activity for money launderers and terrorist financiers.*[47]

Cash clearly plays a key role throughout the money laundering process but is particularly relevant in the first stage of money laundering that of placement, and as such, the subject of cash serves as an appropriate starting point when examining the methods and instruments used to launder money.[48]

CASH

Many of the major sources of criminal proceeds, particularly narcotics trafficking, generate large amounts of cash. Other crimes such as identity fraud, access device fraud, and bank fraud can also generate large amounts of cash. For example, criminals engaged in access device fraud extract money from cash dispensers also known as ATMs[49] using stolen ATM card numbers and personal identification numbers (PINs). Other criminal activity which can generate large amounts of illicit cash include, but are not limited to, smuggling, corruption, bribery, extortion and illegal gambling.

46 The Financial Action Task Force (FATF) is an inter-governmental body whose purpose is the development and promotion of national and international policies to combat money laundering and terrorist financing. The FATF is therefore a 'policy-making body' that works to generate the necessary political will to bring about legislative and regulatory reforms in these areas. [Online]. Available at://www.fatf-gafi.org/pages/0,2987,en_32250379_32235720_1_1_1_1_1,00.html [accessed: 13 February 2011].

47 FATF, 'Global Money Laundering and Terrorist Financing Threat Assessment (n.9) 9.

48 Bell, 'Concealing and disguising criminal property' (n.3) 268.

49 An automated teller machine (ATM) is a computerised telecommunications device that provides the clients of a financial institution with access to financial transactions in a public space without the need for a cashier, human clerk or bank teller. ATMs are known by various other names including automatic banking machine and cash machine.

The source of terrorist funding can be derived from both illegitimate and legitimate sources where cash can either be generated or collected. For example, a number of terrorist groups engage in criminal activity such as narcotics trafficking, kidnapping and robbery or theft, to generate cash based income. Legitimate sources of funding such as charitable donations and the establishment of a legitimate business can also produce cash proceeds. In terms of expenditure, both pools of cash funds can then be used to pay directly for travel, training, the staging attacks and the acquisition of weapons or explosives.[50]

The placement of cash can be carried out through many processes. One example is currency smuggling, which involves the physical movement of currency and monetary instruments out of a country. The various methods of transport such as cash couriers do not leave a discernible audit trail, making investigations difficult.[51] Smurfing is another technique where cash is deposited at random quantities of less than the amount where reporting is required in that jurisdiction. For example, in the US, the threshold is $10,000, therefore random amounts of less than $10,000 will be deposited into variously named accounts including those held by relatives or friends at many different banks in order to minimise detection. It should be noted that due diligence rarely catches this activity.[52]

Bank complicity is another issue of concern and may also play a key role in the integration phase. This is when a financial institution, such as a bank, is owned or controlled by unscrupulous individuals suspected of conniving with drug dealers, other OCGs and terrorist organisations. The complete liberalisation of the financial sector without adequate checks also provides leeway for laundering. Money laundering using known foreign banks presents a difficult target for law enforcement, partly through the willing assistance of the foreign banks to money launderers, as well as other barriers including banking laws and regulations of other sovereign countries, which protect the identity and activities of criminals.

Currency exchanges and securities brokers also serve as vehicles of money laundering. In a number of transitional economies, the liberalisation of foreign exchange markets provides room for currency movements and as such, laundering schemes can benefit from such policies. Brokers can facilitate the process of money laundering through structuring large deposits of cash in

---

50 FATF, *Global Money Laundering and Terrorist Financing Threat Assessment* (n.9) 16.
51 FATF, *1996–1997 Report on Money Laundering Typologies*.
52 Bell, 'Concealing and disguising criminal property' (n.3) 268.

a way that disguises the original source of the funds. The blending of funds further disguises illegitimate funds. Financial camouflage is effective in that the best place to hide cash is with a lot of other cash. The alternative is to use the money from illicit activities to set up front companies. This enables the funds from illicit activities to be obscured in legal transactions.

Another method is to convert the cash into another form through the purchase of assets.[53] The purchase of assets with cash is a classic money laundering method. The major purpose is to change the form of the proceeds from conspicuous bulk cash to some equally valuable, but less conspicuous. Less bulky items such as diamonds, gold or even precious stamps and other collectibles are purchased domestically. The criterion is that they be of high value in relation to bulk, making them easy to smuggle physically, as well as relatively easy to reconvert into cash at the point of destination. High value assets such as property, vehicles and business assets can also be acquired, which can be sold during the layering phase.[54]

BANKS AND FINANCIAL INSTRUMENTS

Banks have the ability to legitimise illegitimate sources of funds by converting cash into reputable financial instruments such as T-bills, letters of credit, large denomination traveller's checks, real estate deeds or bank drafts. The conversion of cash into financial instruments was a reasonably easy method to launder money prior to 1990. However, current AML legislation and regulation has put in place various monitoring and discloser requirements, together with caps on currency transactions, which make this method more difficult for money laundering purposes.

Furthermore, owing to global pressures to comply with AML and CTF guidelines set up by the FATF, the days where a money launderer can walk into a bank with suitcases full of cash and deposit it in a bank, no longer exist in most jurisdictions. Nevertheless, the formal banking system continues to be heavily used in laundering money, especially during the later stages of the laundering process. Cash may enter the financial system through a weak link, namely a jurisdiction with high secrecy or low monitoring standards, or both, or alternatively through the sale of assets such as cars or property. However,

53 Petrus C. van Duyne, Melvin R.J. Soudijn, 'Hot money, hot stones and hot air: crime-money threat, real estate and real concern' (2009) 12(2) *Journal of Money Laundering Control* 173.

54 Bell, 'Concealing and disguising criminal property' (n.3) 268.

once money has entered the conventional banking system, it is then able to move through the usual channels with relative ease.

THE TAX HAVEN

Tax havens play a key role in money laundering.[55] To date, there is no agreed-upon definition of a tax haven or list of jurisdictions that should be considered tax havens.[56] However, numerous governmental, international and academic sources have identified a number of characteristics indicative of a tax haven. These include no or nominal taxes; the lack of effective exchange of tax information with foreign tax authorities; limited transparency in the operation of legislative, legal or administrative provisions; no requirement for a substantive local presence; and self-promotion as an offshore financial centre. A brief historical overview may be useful in understanding the development of tax havens.

In 1945, there were approximately 55 countries in the world. However, the appetite for independence has resulted in the growth of independent countries to almost 200 in 2010.[57] Independence often leads to a significant increase in operating costs, not all of which can be supported by inward cash flow. The initial borrowing from overseas banks only buys limited short-term success as credit lines soon become exhausted. In the meantime time, agricultural activity decreases as a shift to the cities occurs, driven by the perception of a better quality of life. As the country struggles to generate income, one ever present possibility is to operate as a tax haven, a conduit for tax evasion money, tax avoidance money or black market derived from crime.[58]

---

55 Robert Thomas Kudrle, 'Did blacklisting hurt the tax havens?' (2009) 12(1) *Journal of Money Laundering Control* 33.

56 Government Accountability Office, 'International Taxation: Large U.S. Corporations and Federal Contractors with Subsidiaries in Jurisdictions Listed as Tax Havens or Financial Privacy Jurisdictions' (GAO:GAO-09-157, 18 December 2008) [Online]. Available at://www.gao.gov/products/GAO-09-157 [accessed: 11 November 2010].

57 The best estimate is 195 comprising 192 members of the UN plus Vatican City and Kosovo. Taiwan is not included in the list, which is a subject of debate as to it whether, meets the requirements of independent country or state status. Taiwan was a member of the UN (and even the Security Council) until 1971, when mainland China replaced Taiwan in the organisation. Taiwan continues to press for full recognition by other countries, but China claims that Taiwan is simply a province of China. [Online]. Available at://geography.about.com/cs/countries/a/numbercountries.htm [accessed: 11 November 2010].

58 Jun Tang, Lishan Ai, 'Combating money laundering in transition countries: the inherent limitations and practical issues' (2010) 13(3) *Journal of Money Laundering Control* 215.

The oldest and best-known tax havens are the Cayman Islands, the Bahamas, Switzerland, Liechtenstein, the Netherlands, Antilles, Monaco, Macao, Hong Kong and Luxembourg, which have long served as refuges from death duties and high taxes. However, the above mentioned appetite for independence has resulted in the creation of many new havens. Examples include the New Hebrides, Andorra, the Caicos, Turk Island, the new nations of the Federated States of Micronesia and the Marshalls, as well as numerous other newly spawned nations in Africa, Asia and Europe. The sheer volume of these new tax havens will undoubtedly play an important role in money laundering as policing them for infractions is virtually impossible.[59]

BLACK MARKET

'Dirty' money can also be turned 'clean' through exchanging the original currency for another currency, such as US dollars or the euro. This can be achieved through the use of black markets utilising the black market rate, which runs in parallel to the country's official money rate. Through this mechanism, money can officially be sent back to the country in which the exchange was made. In countries with no exchange controls, money need not go through the black market. It can be changed at the official rate at any bank, without records. The system of using the parallel market involves two countries, but the risk is minimal provided that the person is not caught dealing with the black market money changer.

SHELL COMPANIES

The use of shell companies for money laundering purposes has already been mentioned earlier in the chapter. The term 'shell company' refers to non-publicly traded corporations, limited liability companies and trusts that typically have no physical presence other than a mailing address, and generate little to no independent economic value.[60] Shell companies are characterised by their lack of transparency, both in its formation and operation, which allows ownership and purpose to be disguised.[61] From a money laundering

---

59 Peter Schwarz, 'Money launderers and tax havens: two sides of the same coin?' (2010) *International Review of Law and Economics*. [Online]. Available at: http://www.sciencedirect.com/science [accessed: 12 January 2011].

60 FINCEN, 'U.S. Money Laundering Threat Assessment' (U.S. Money Laundering Threat Assessment Working Group, December 2005), 47. [Online]. Available at://www.fincen.gov/statutes_regs/guidance/pdf/Advisory OnShells_FINAL.pdf [accessed: 11 November 2010].

61 FINCEN, 'Potential Money Laundering Risks Related to Shell Companies' (Department of the Treasury Financial Crimes Enforcement Network, FIN-2006-G014, 9 November 2006). [Online].

perspective, the avoidance of the creation of any external record that could be used to initiate an audit or paper trail leading to subsequent stages or layers of the operation, is essential.[62] Its purpose is to confuse even the most dedicated and well-resourced investigators and to defeat any attempt to reconstruct a money trail. Shell companies assist in achieving this. The investigations are further complicated if the company in question is offshore.

OFFSHORE CENTRES

The terms 'offshore' and 'tax haven' have become almost interchangeable in the context of money laundering in that, from a UK perspective, all of the tax havens are 'offshore'. Offshore centres offer a number of practical advantages with respect to money laundering. First, it places the funds beyond the legal reach of the authorities in the jurisdiction where the profit was generated. Furthermore, even if the relevant laws were capable of application on an extra-territorial basis, involving another jurisdiction places significant practical barriers in the path of investigators in obtaining and securing evidence admissible in court.[63]

An additional concern is the ease and low cost of setting up and operating a personal offshore bank,[64] enabling the transfer of significant sums of money without detection, as inter-bank transfers are exempt from reporting requirements.[65] As a result, one-room operations in locations such as St Vincent, Anguilla, or the Cayman Islands have become popular. The bank can be 'owned' by a Cayman management service company, and the beneficiary owner need never be known to any investigator. Similarly, in Anguilla, no paid-up capital or reserves are required enabling banks to be set up with ease. Furthermore, Anguillan law states that a bank's licence and charter can be sold without government approval. However, changes in international banking laws and regulations post 9/11 have resulted in the setting up of offshore banks to be more expensive and cumbersome.[66]

Available at: http://www.fincen.gov/statutes_regs/guidance/pdf/AdvisoryOnShells_FINAL.pdf [accessed: 11 November 2010].

62 Rider, 'Law: The War on Terror and Crime and the Offshore Centres' (n.11) 77.

63 Ibid. 78.

64 Some bank haven countries even offer bank charters and licenses for as little as $60.00. See Panama Offshore Legal Services. [Online]. Available at: http://www.offshorelegal.org/offshore-banking/panama-offshore-banking/own-your-own-offshore-bank---get-an-offshore-banking-license.html [accessed: 12 July 2011].

65 For example, US federal law requires that any transfer of over $5,000 out of the US must be reported to the treasury. This, however, does not apply to inter-bank transfers.

66 Panama Offshore Legal Services (n.64).

BEARER BONDS

A bearer bond, also known as a coupon bond, is a debt security issued by a business entity, such as a corporation, or a government, and differs from the more common types of investment securities in that it is unregistered.[67] Bearer bonds are popular with investors keen to retain anonymity, and provide a superior alternative to cash for criminals wishing to launder money.[68] A further advantage for the launderer is the logistical practicality offered by bearer bonds. The logistical and associated security risks of transporting large amounts of cash can be eliminated through the use of these bonds in that a small piece of paper can represent a vast quantity of money.[69]

The City of London is the centre of the Eurobond market and a great attraction of the Euromarkets is the prevalence of 'bearer bonds' that conceal the identity of the owner. In comparison, it is interesting to note that the US Treasury stopped issuing bearer bonds in 1982 and the few that remain make up only 0.14 per cent of the market with only $5.2bn in paper certificates still outstanding.[70]

TAX-FREE MUNICIPAL BONDS

A municipal bond is a debt security issued by a state, municipality or county to finance its capital expenditures.[71] Potential issuers of municipal bonds include cities, counties, publicly owned airports and seaports, and any other governmental entity or group of governments below the state level, and are exempt from taxes. They are usually in bearer form and interest is paid by redeeming coupons. Municipal bonds are available only through brokerage houses and the broker keeps the name of the original purchaser, but intermediate sellers and buyers are not registered. These bonds may be purchased with cash through a third party, and the advantages of bearer bonds apply in terms of anonymity and its potential use as a vehicle for money laundering.

67 Investor Worlds. [Online]. Available at: http://www.investorwords.com/439/bearer_bond.html [accessed: 12 July 2011].

68 Bearer bonds are also negotiable bond where the coupons are attached to the bond, and each coupon represents a single interest payment. The holder submits a coupon, usually semi-annually, to the issuer or paying agent to receive payment.

69 Philip Thornton, 'Anonymous bearer bonds are the currency of choice for laundering', *Independent* (London, 6 September 2003).

70 Ibid.

71 [Online]. Available at: http://www.investopedia.com/terms/m/municipalbond.asp [accessed: 11 November 2010].

INSURANCE PRODUCTS

Insurance products are another illustration of covert investment where insurance agents are able to accept deposits in any amount, and no bank reports are necessary.[72] One example is the overseas 'Umbrella life policy' where an overseas insurance company[73] sells a life insurance policy in the form of an 'umbrella policy' which includes not only life insurance, but also investments. For example, a $300,000 policy may have $100,000 in full life insurance, and $200,000 in currencies, stocks, bonds, T-bills or other investments. However, the policy is classified as 'insurance', even though the 'insurance' component is only a part of the overall investment.

It is usually a single payment product, where the total cost for life is paid up at the time the policy is taken out. The cost may be $60,000 or more, depending on the makeup of the policy, for a $300,000 policy. The advantage of this type of policy to a 'normal' client is that when the insured passes away, his or her heirs receive the full value of the investments tax free, thus avoiding death duties.

From a money launderer's perspective, there are many ways in which insurance products can be used as a vehicle for money laundering.[74] First, the payment method of such an insurance policy can be numerous including payment to the insurance agent with cash. Unlike banks, the insurance agent does not have to report cash transactions over $10,000. The money launderer is then able to borrow up to 90 per cent of the value of his policy, and the money is sent to him wherever he desires, allowing easy anonymous access to his laundered criminal funds from around the globe.

Obstacles to Anti-Money Laundering

Numerous challenges currently exist in tackling money laundering. Two key challenges requiring attention are issues surrounding secrecy and gatekeepers, who are the first line of defence in terms of countering both terrorist finance and money laundering. As previously mentioned, certain jurisdictions are willing to offer banking and other facilities on the basis that secrecy will be assured. Although client confidentiality is attractive for many clients, there is

72 Haemala Thanasegaran and Bala Shanmugam, 'Exploitation of the insurance industry for money laundering: the Malaysian perspective' (2008) 11(2) *Journal of Money Laundering Control* 135.

73 Typically in Jersey, Switzerland, Hong Kong, or Australia.

74 Thanasegaran and Shanmugam, 'Exploitation of the insurance industry for money laundering' (n.72) 135.

clearly a downside from an AML perspective in that secrecy can be extremely obstructive to investigations and helpful to the criminal. In addition, there are some countries that have been prepared to facilitate the receipt of money, irrespective of its source.[75] As a result, jurisdictions that offer secrecy or in which the level of corruption is sufficient to ensure effective non-cooperation with foreign agencies, continue to be attractive to money launders.[76]

The second and related challenge is that of gatekeepers, who serve as the bridge between the criminal and the investigator. In order to effectively tackle money laundering, an understanding of the motivation of those involved in the process, including bankers, accountants, and lawyers is key. Although the large majority will aim to stay within the law, it must also be appreciated that the business of these individuals is not in counter-terrorism or to combat financial crime, but to make money. For many, the morality of their client is not on the top of their daily agenda. Staying within the right side of the law and meeting regulatory requirements may be a concern, as not meeting those requirements, and more importantly, getting caught, will lead to the disruption or even termination of their business activities, which is a situation to be avoided at all cost. However, as the conversation between the law students stated at the beginning of this chapter highlights, for many, the morality and end goal of the client, is not their *raison d'être*. Unless the client is a known terrorist or criminal, it must be remembered that the professions exists to provide the best possible service to its clients and to maximise their revenues in the process.[77]

It was only a decade ago that bankers would openly argue that the morality of their client was not their concern. Although it is doubtful that this attitude has fundamentally changed, it is recognised that it is no longer politically correct to openly admit this belief. In addition, education coupled with regulation has resulted in greater awareness of financial crime. It is important that this education and awareness must not only be continued, but expanded to the wider global community. Despite recriminations, what is clear is that the enemy is amongst us. No financial system is, or will be, free from abuse by terrorist and criminal organisations. Large financial centres such as London and New York, by virtue of their daily volume of money flows, continue to serve as major hubs for laundered funds and terrorist finance.[78] Consequently,

75 Adam Salifu, 'Can corruption and economic crime be controlled in developing economies: and if so, is the cost worth it?' (2008) 11(3) *Journal of Money Laundering Control* 273.
76 Rider, 'Law: The War on Terror and Crime and the Offshore Centres' (n.11) 78.
77 Ricardo Azevedo Araujo, 'Assessing the efficiency of the anti-money laundering regulation: an incentive-based approach' (2008) 11(1) *Journal of Money Laundering Control* 67.
78 Gallant, 'Promise and perils' (n.10) 175.

innovative 'carrot and stick' approaches must be developed and implemented, underpinned by effective monitoring and prosecutions, in order to persuade gatekeepers not to turn a blind eye to the problem of money laundering and terrorist finance, but instead become actively engaged in its prevention.

Anti-Money Laundering Legislation and Regulation

The UK has long recognised that third parties may be involved in facilitating the realisation of property which has been obtained unlawfully. Section 22(1) of the Theft Act 1968 states that:

> *A person handles stolen goods if (otherwise in the course of stealing) knowing or believing them to be stolen goods he dishonestly receives the goods, or dishonestly undertakes or assists in their retention, removal, disposal or realisation, by or for the benefit of another person, or if he arranges to do so.*[79]

This provision, while being very wide-ranging in its effects, relates solely to goods which are or which represent the proceeds of stolen goods and did not cover the drugs issue which was tackled in later legislation, namely, Section 27 (1) of the Misuse of Drugs Act 1971, which permitted the court to:

> *... order anything shown to the satisfaction of the court to relate to the offence, to be forfeited and either destroyed or dealt with in such other manner as the court may order.*

This legislation allowed the forfeiture of property, whether money, drugs, weapons or vehicles found in the possession of the convicted person and used in the continuance of offences under the Misuse of Drugs Act 1971. However, in 1980, the House of Lords made an historic ruling, which restricted the scope of section 27 of the Misuse of Drugs Act 1971. In the case of *R v Cuthbertson*,[80] an appeal was allowed against the forfeiture of £750,000 and was significant in that it exposed the limitations in the existing legislation regarding forfeiture. This led to the setting up of the Hodgson Committee with the brief of inquiring into ways of filling the vacuum created in the law by this decision. The Committees findings, along with the deliberations of the Home Affairs Select Committee

79 Section 22 'Handling stolen goods'. See Lexus Nexus Electronic Library.
80 [1981] AC 470, [1980] 2 All ER 401.

which followed, led to the passing of the Drug Trafficking Offences Act 1986 (DTOA).

This was the first statute to categorise money laundering as a criminal offence and therefore notable in the chronology and evolution of laws to fight the money launderer. Subsequently, this has now been extended to new laws, which cover laundering of the proceeds of all crime while various other related provisions have been added.

The International Perspective

Twenty-five years ago, few countries, if any, had laws that made money laundering a criminal offence. However, the emergence of international consensus about not only the need to control money laundering, but also the use of criminal law as the primary legal mechanism thorough which this objective is to be accomplished, has made the lack of such laws the exception, rather than the norm. The drive behind the implementation of such laws was driven by the challenges posed by the exponential growth of organised crime and the narcotics trade since the 1980s, the realisation that money laundering can compromise the stability of financial markets by creating and contributing to financial crises, as well as the problems associated with investigating and prosecuting such activities.

In recognition that money laundering in many cases has an international dimension, the FATF on Money Laundering was established by the G-7 Summit, held in Paris in 1989.[81]As an inter-governmental body, its purpose is to develop and promote policies, both at national and international levels, to combat money laundering and terrorist financing. The Task Force is therefore a 'policy-making body' which works to generate the necessary political will to bring about national legislative and regulatory reforms in these areas. The FATF established a series of Recommendations in 1990,[82] revised in 1996 and in 2003, to provide updated guidelines to serve as the basic framework for AML efforts.

81 Recognising the threat posed to the banking system and to financial institutions, the G-7 heads of state or government and president of the European Commission convened the Task Force from the G-7 member states, the European Commission and eight other countries.

82 In April 1990, the FATF issued a report containing a set of Forty Recommendations, which provide a comprehensive plan of action needed to fight against money laundering.

In 2001, the development of standards in the fight against terrorist financing[83] was added to its mission.[84] The FATF currently comprises 34 member jurisdictions and 2 regional organisations,[85] representing most major financial centres in all parts of the globe. In terms of jurisdictions that are not participating, the FATF began the Non-Cooperative Countries and Territories (NCCTs) exercise in 1998.[86] Forty-seven jurisdictions were referred to the NCCTs process and were reviewed in two rounds[87] and a total of 23 jurisdictions[88] were identified as NCCTs.[89]

Although NCCTs may only represent a small percentage compared to those who are compliant with FATF recommendations, it must be remembered that these jurisdictions serve as the weak link where criminal finances may enter the financial system. Furthermore, once money has entered the financial system, it can travel with ease with little risk of detection. Therefore it is essential that all the weak links are strengthened in order to prevent abuse of the financial system that allows money laundering to occur.

CHALLENGES TO ANTI-MONEY LAUNDERING LEGISLATION AND REGULATION

Money laundering is essentially a political issue with legal and economic ramifications. As such, the laws and regulations that attempt to mitigate money laundering inevitably become forged within the crucible of the political process. As Hinterseer observes:

> *Since politics is about power and the struggle to obtain, extend, and wield influence, government legislation bears the imprint of the conflict, negotiation, and compromise that characterises the policy formulation and legislative processes. One of the legal ramifications of this idea is that once drafted and translated into legislation, the negotiated and*

83 In October 2001 the FATF issued the Eight Special Recommendations to deal with the issue of terrorist financing. The continued evolution of money laundering techniques led the FATF to revise the FATF standards comprehensively in June 2003. In October 2004 the FATF published a Ninth Special Recommendations, further strengthening the agreed international standards for combating money laundering and terrorist financing – the 40+9 Recommendations.

84 FATF, 'About the FATF' [Online]. Available at://www.fatf-gafi.org [accessed: 28 October 2010].

85 Ibid.

86 FATF, 'Annual Review of Non-Cooperative Countries and Territories 2006–2007' (FATF Eighth NCCT Review, 12 October 2007) [Online]. Available at: http://www.fatf-gafi.org/ [accessed: 28 October 2010].

87 31 in 2001 and 16 in 20012.

88 15 in 2000 and 8 in 2001.

89 FATF, 'Annual Review of Non-Cooperative Countries and Territories 2006–2007' (n.86).

> *compromised policy becomes part of the corpus of the law. The effect of this is that the new legislation will either ameliorate or exacerbate the inherent ambiguities, contradictions, and loopholes that exist within the law, and which money launderers exploit to escape legal sanction.*[90]

A further challenge in terms of combating money laundering is society's perception with regard to morality, where the question of 'legality' comes into play. In criminal law, there is a relationship between what society believes to be immoral and the criminalisation of that activity. It follows therefore, that the activity of laundering money is illegal because it is considered to be immoral. However, even if an act is 'illegal', it does not necessarily follow that society also believe it to be immoral. This is significant, as it impacts the effectiveness of the law in practice.

If an act that is 'criminal' in the eyes of the law of that jurisdiction is considered *not* to be immoral by society, the law is reduced to a mere obstacle that needs to be overcome. In other words, the existence of that law criminalising that act will not adequately deter an individual from committing that act on moral grounds. Provided that enough safety measures are built in and the risk of getting caught is minimised, the criminal act will take place regardless of the law that may exist.

The subject of narcotics is a case in point and is central to the debate on money laundering as the concept originated from the laundering of the proceeds of crime associated with the narcotic trade.[91] Many argue that societal attitudes need to change before counter narcotics can be effective. In addition, there has been an over-emphasis to combat the supply side, which is seen by law enforcement and policy makers as the main solution. As a result, the drug trade is often depicted as a set of problems created by producer countries such as Colombia and Afghanistan.

However, the 'criminal' entrepreneurs within these countries are merely responding to the market demand that exists within the developed economies. Instead, the subject should be considered from a demand, as well as a supply side perspective. As the basic laws of supply and demand dictate, a change in demand has a direct impact on supply in relation to the price of the goods or services. The economic model of price determination states that if demand

90 Hinterseer, *Criminal Finance* (n.13) 55.

91 Salifu, 'Can corruption and economic crime be controlled in developing economies' (n.75), 273.

decreases and supply remains unchanged, the price will decrease. It follows that if demand reduces dramatically, it will no longer be economically viable for the supplier to continue supplying the goods or services. If the quantity of supply cannot be suppressed adequately artificially,[92] the most logical alternative is to attempt to lower demand so that supply automatically falls.

From the 'demand side' perspective, the criminalisation of narcotics is a hotly debated subject with many arguing in favour of legalisation. The continued use of illegal substances demonstrates that 'society' does not necessarily consider the recreational use of illegal substances to be morally objectionable. The global consumption of illicit substances has remained stable[93] with between 155 and 250 million people[94] [95] reported as using such substances, of which between 16 and 38 million were identified as 'problem' drug users in 2008.[96] Furthermore, an overall increase in cocaine use has been observed in Europe in the last decade.[97] In the UK, cocaine has been a problem drug for some time. Since 2000, there has been a large increase in reported episodes of non-fatal hospital admissions for cocaine poisoning in England as well as an upward trend of cocaine related deaths since 2004.[98] In addition, opium production increased from 445 metric tonnes in 1995 to 657 metric tonnes in 2009,[99] further illustrating the continuing demand for narcotics.

Equally, the impact of the narcotics industry on society and its economy is a double-edged sword, making the countering of the narcotics industry somewhat complex. The negative aspects of narcotics, such as its impact on the user's health, the cost to society and the economy, as well as its association with serious organised crime, is well known and understood. At the same time, the irony is that the narcotics trade has proved to be positive from a country's economic perspective in certain circumstances. This is the reason why governments have perhaps not been as committed as they can be in attempting to eradicate the drugs trade.[100] For example, in Columbia, cocaine has created wealth and employment, as well as provided vital capital for economic

92 By 'artificial', the use of external force such as confiscation is implied, which is external to normal competitive market behaviour.
93 UN World Drug Report 2010, 126. [Online]. Available at: http://www.unodc.org/documents/wdr/WDR_2010/World _Drug_Report_2010_lo-res.pdf [accessed: 11 November 2010].
94 Representing 3.5% to 5.7% of the population aged 15–64.
95 UN World Drug Report 2010 (n.93) 123.
96 Representing between 10–15% of estimated drug users.
97 UN World Drug Report 2010 (n.93) 177.
98 Ibid. 178.
99 Ibid. 137.
100 Salifu, 'Can corruption and economic crime be controlled in developing economies' (n.75) 273.

growth.[101] According to Salomon Kalmanovitz, an economist at Colombia's central bank:

> *Cocaine stopped the balance of payments from collapsing, which would have pushed us into the spiral of hyper-devaluation and hyper-inflation that shook most of the rest of the continent, for which the 1980s were a lost decade.*[102]

In the case of Columbia, the cocaine trade has provided subsistence for thousands of peasant farmers who would otherwise be forced into poverty. Furthermore, in countries where the rule of law is weak and government bureaucracy lacks transparency and accountability, the operation of the economy is often characterised by bribery and corruption, leading to economic growth that is invariably sub-optimal. In these situations, the taxes and other resources collected by the state from the general population are often simply used to supplement the bank accounts of those in power instead of being used to devise and implement sustainable development strategies. In the absence of social welfare programmes, the underground economy often provides social safety by providing employment, which in some cases may make the difference between subsistence and destitution. Furthermore, the informal economic activity may itself prove to be an engine for economic growth.

As a result, it is not surprising that in less developed economies, where economic opportunities upon which to base economic growth are limited, that governments may either overlook, or even choose to promote informal economic activity, which may help to facilitate economic development.[103] This is particularly the case with respect to the financial services industry, especially in countries where natural resources are lacking.[104] It is against this background, that the importance of the negative impacts of money laundering activity should be understood.[105] This must then be emphasised in order to discourage those who facilitate money laundering activity to instead become actively engaged in its prevention.

---

101 Simon Strong, *White Wash: Pablo Escobar and the Cocaine Wars* (Pan Books 1995) 185. Strong continues, 'So crucial to the economy did the money become during the 1980's that in moments when the cocaine supply was interrupted, or when it was simply feared that it would be because of government repression, the price of the black-market dollar leaped. After the murder of the minister of justice, Rodrigo Lara Bonilla, it soared 50 per cent.'

102 Ibid. 184.

103 Hinterseer, *Criminal Finance* (n.13) 105.

104 Examples include the Bahamas and Cayman Islands.

105 Salifu 'Can corruption and economic crime be controlled in developing economies' (n.75) 273.

Negative Impact of Money Laundering

There is evidence that money laundering and terrorist financing activities can undermine the integrity and stability of financial institutions and systems, discourage foreign investment, and distort international capital flows.[106] In addition, it can encourage criminal activity to the point that it overshadows legitimate activity.

Somalia is a case in point, where a significant proportion of ransom payments from maritime piracy enter the Somali economy via payment for services. The ransom payments are also laundered through the purchase of consumer durables, such as high-end vehicles and real estate to such an extent that piracy proceeds have contributed to a real estate bubble in piracy havens such as Eyl.[107] Although this has created hubs of economic activity around piracy centres, the lack of investment in infrastructure and public services, coupled with deteriorating law and order, continues to affect the business climate.

The piracy fuelled business has overshadowed the non-crime economy and there is also the danger that ransom payments are creating new and better equipped warlords with potentially adverse consequences for political reconciliation in Somalia. Not only is there concern that whatever economic activity there is, that it is essentially criminal in that it is linked to piracy, but that the level of economic activity is unsustainable. In addition, investors, both domestic and international, are discouraged due to the poor security climate.[108] The potential consequence is that if economic activity, both piracy and non-piracy related decreases significantly, that this will lead to further destabilisation of the region.

A further concern is in relation to the global nature of the problem. As elaborated in earlier chapters, globalisation has resulted in an increasingly interconnected world, where the challenges presented by such illegal activities cannot be contained within a single nation. As problems in one country can quickly spread to other countries in the region or to other parts of the world, the concern becomes truly global. Money launderers exploit differences between

106 Norman Mugarura, 'The effect of corruption factor in harnessing global anti-money laundering regimes' (2010) 13(3) *Journal of Money Laundering Control* 272.

107 Anecdotal evidence suggests that property prices rose sharply between 2007 and 2008. See Raymond Gilpin, *Counting the Costs of Somali* Piracy (Center for Sustainable Economies, US Institute of Peace Report, 22 June 2009).

108 Ibid.

national AML laws and systems, and are especially attracted to jurisdictions with weak or ineffective controls where they can move their funds more easily.[109]

Therefore, it is in the interest of the global financial community that strong AML/CTF regimes are implemented not only in their own jurisdictions but elsewhere around the globe.[110] At the same time, in order to counter the problem of money laundering, it is essential to understand not only how, but why money laundering occurs. This is relevant as certain pre-requisites exist for an individual to engage in the activity of money laundering as the subsequent section will highlight.

To Launder or not to Launder?

The question as to why money laundering occurs, when subjected to economic analysis reveals insights that are both interesting and important. In Hinterseer's adaptation of Indigo Walter's model of capital flight, an analytic framework to examine the variables that are relevant to an individual's decision to engage in money laundering activity is examined. The model assists in highlighting the factors that shape how a money laundering operation is structured, executed, and wound-up. Six assumptions underpin the model, which will be examined in turn.

1. Individuals are risk averse: they seek maximum financial return at minimal financial risk.

This is a standard economic assumption that may not be entirely appropriate in the context of money laundering. As Hinterseer argues:

> *... maximum return at minimum risk is not what motivates those who engage in money laundering, which instead is maximum protection at minimal risk regardless of the return. Criminal entrepreneurs who participate in the narcotics trade, for example, are, according to police*

109 Mugarura 'The effect of corruption factor in harnessing global anti-money laundering regimes' (n.106) 272.

110 IMF, 'The fight against money laundering and the financing of terrorism fact sheet', 10 September 2010. [Online]. Available at: http://www.imf.org/external/np/exr/facts/aml.htm [accessed: 10 November 2009].

> *statistics, often willing to pay in commission up to 25 per cent of the gross sum they have to be laundered.*[111]

However, it may also be argued that those who engage in money laundering activity are not necessarily risk adverse. As Hinterseer elaborates:

> *... the idea is that when an individual examines various money laundering strategies, one factor they will take into account is return. After all, there is no point in laundering money if most of the money is paid out to cover the costs associated with creating and implementing a money laundering strategy.*[112]

In other words, those who launder money can be considered as being 'risk averse' in that the process still needs to be economically beneficial, even at the extra cost of services needed to manage the associated risks. To describe it another way, a lower percentage of profits is better than a higher percentage of nothing as a result of insufficient security measures resulting in the confiscation of the funds.

2. Individuals are rational, but not necessarily moral: although individuals may be economically risk averse, individuals are not necessarily legally risk averse because they may be willing to trade-off greater financial returns against greater legal risks that are associated with the pursuit of illegal activity.

The 'rationality' of individuals is another standard economic assumption that is often heavily criticised. Some argue that the conduct of individuals, especially in a criminal context, may be viewed as irrational as is the case when political factors come into play. In the context of money laundering, this assumption would be inappropriate without the added provision that the individual may not be moral. It can be argued that a rational individual will rarely intentionally violate the law because of the potential penalties. However, the concept that an individual may be rational, but not moral, aims to incorporate the notion that the risks associated with breaking the law may be seen as acceptable dependent on the rewards at stake. In other words, the law may be seen merely as an obstacle to be overcome rather than a set of rules that should be followed.[113]

111 Hinterseer *Criminal Finance* (n.13) 24.

112 Ibid. 24.

113 Christopher Stanley, 'Speculations on the Conflict of Discourses: Finance, Crime and Regulation' (1996) 4(3) *Journal of Financial Regulation and Compliance.*

3. Penalties imposed by the law are quantifiable in the form of money: individuals assess the costs associated with prison terms, other legal penalties, and social sanction in financial terms.

What the assumption implies is that the individual confronts an incentive framework that is quantifiable in order that the relationship between risk and return can be assessed in monetary terms.

4. Money laundering services and instruments are assumed to have value: as objects with value, demand for these services and instruments will exist, which means that they can be bought and sold.

The purpose of this assumption is to ensure that the inputs associated with the money laundering process can be reduced to monetary terms and be interpreted as a risk minimising cost to enable money laundering to occur. This assumption is supported by Professor Rider who observed that:

> *It must be remembered that the laundering of money is a cost, and both the launder and his principals will only wish to expend what is necessary and prudent to ensure the relevant funds remain beyond the reach of law enforcement agencies or others interested in locating them.*[114]

5. Demand for money laundering services is a negative function of price: the higher the cost to structure, execute, and wind-up a money laundering operation, the lower the demand for such services.

As such, money laundering instruments and services may be traded like any other set of goods and services so that a higher price is associated with less demand.

6. Portfolio allocations that demand the use of greater quantities of money laundering services will force individuals into riskier asset allocations: investment strategies involving money laundering may preclude the use of certain risk hedging strategies.[115]

This assumption highlights the possibility that the various investment methods and techniques that could be used to hedge risk and financial loss may not

114 Rider 'Law: The War on Terror and Crime and the Offshore Centres' (n.11) 78.
115 Hinterseer *Criminal Finance* (n.13) 108–109.

be an option as a result of the clandestine nature of the funds. However, as Hinterseer observes:

> *This may or may not be the case depending on the particular facts of the situation. The idea, however, is that, ceterus parabis, the larger the money laundering operation, the harder it is to hide.*[116]

The six assumptions suggest that an individual who has money to be laundered, confront a trade-off between three variables, namely risk, return, and secrecy. Based on the relative demand for each factor, a personalised set of preference functions is then developed that reflect the individual's choices based upon available financial resources as well as various other variables and constraints confronting that individual. In other words, an individual will balance the perceived benefits and costs associated with trading-off the three variables against each other.

The idea that greater returns are associated with greater risks is standard in economic theory. However, the standard theory relates to financial and economic risks as opposed to legal risks. In other words, an individual who invests in relatively higher risk economic activity will expect to earn a greater financial return to compensate for the additional risk, whilst issues relating to legal risk are subsumed in the decisions concerning the secrecy variable.[117] In other words, the economic benefit of laundering must outweigh the costs, and AML measures must take these factors into consideration to be effective.

Conclusions

Money laundering is a phenomenon that cannot be eliminated. In addition, it facilitates a wide range of unlawful activity that takes place in the underground economy, which has developed as a natural adjunct to the legal economy. As such, money laundering can be seen as the interface of these two economies which allows the underground to grow by enabling resources to flow between the two sectors. However, the challenge is that the mechanisms used by criminals to facilitate money laundering flows, including banking, legal and accounting tools, are also used by businesses in the legal economy for legitimate commercial purposes such as hedging risk and the reduction of

116 Ibid. 108–109.
117 Ibid. 114–15.

tax liability. The result is a murky mixture of financial flows consisting of the various shades of money.

As a process, money laundering therefore rests on a legal-illegal dichotomy. What determines whether these tools are used for legal or illegal purposes depends on the intention with which they are used. Furthermore, recent advances in technology, coupled with trade liberalisation, have led to the integration of foreign markets. This in turn has led to increased competition and liquidity resulting in a single borderless global money marketplace. Although the advantages from a commercial perspective are clear, the new financial environment brings numerous challenges to those who attempt to counter the problem. It is only when these challenges are fully appreciated that the task of intervention can take place effectively.

6

Key Methods of Intervention

> *Money underpins all terrorist activity. The disruption of terrorist financing is a key element of the government's overall fight against terrorism. It requires government, law enforcement agencies, and the financial and charitable sectors to work closely together and the measures outlined in the strategy will ensure a partnership approach to the new and increasing challenges we face.*
>
> *Home Office Minister, Tony McNulty*[1]

Overview

Following the 9/11 attacks in 2001, the first financial strike by the US in the so-called 'global war on terror' came in the form of Executive Order 13224,[2] which targeted the financial assets of organisations and individuals linked to terrorism, including al-Qaeda. Executive Order 13224 was followed by numerous initiatives by the US, UK and various international bodies creating many new organisations with the aim of attacking terrorist financial networks. These multilateral initiatives led to the designation of 315 entities and seizures amounting to $200 million[3] in monetary and other assets in over 1,400 accounts worldwide, as well as the arrests of over 4,000 suspects,[4] including many senior

1 HM Treasury, *The Launch of Anti-Money Laundering and Counter-Terrorist Finance Strategy* (HM Treasury, The Financial Challenge to Crime and Terrorism Report, issue 10, 8 March 2007) [Online]. Available at: www.hm-treasury.gov.uk/documents/financial_services/money/fin_money_index.cfm [accessed: 14 April 2010].

2 Executive Order 13224 [Online]. Available at: http://www.treas.gov/offices/eotffc/ofac/sanctions/t11ter.pdf [accessed: 14 April 2010].

3 Global Enforcement Regimes, 'Transnational Organised Crime' (International Terrorism and ML TNI Crime and Globalisation seminar, Amsterdam 28–29 April 2005) 20 [Online]. Available at: http:/www.tni.org/crime-docs/enforce.pdf#search=%22terrorist%20 finance%20%20%22UK%20treasury%22%20filetype%3 Apdf%22 [accessed: 14 April 2010].

4 Ibid.

al-Qaeda operatives, making the countering of terrorist finance one of the most active dimensions in the global war on terror.

Within the UK, a counter-terrorist finance (CTF) programme was established with the aim to disrupt the support networks that make terrorism possible. The framework of CTF measures also provided a mechanism to publicly identify suspected individuals and groups engaged in or linked to terrorism, and prevent them both from raising or transferring funds. Since 2001, there have been £400,000 of cash seizures under the Anti-Terrorism, Crime and Security Act 2001; £110,000 of forfeited funds; £475,000 of funds seized under the Proceeds of Crime Act 2002; and £382,000 subject to Treasury asset-freezes all in relation to terrorist cases, excluding the £78 million that was frozen until 2002 as part of UK action against the Taliban.[5] However, it is also worth noting that when looking closely at those frozen assets, most of them have now been unfrozen.[6]

The events of 9/11 have also led to increased international cooperation.[7] Over 100 countries have offered increased intelligence support leading to intensified counter-terrorist operations being undertaken by more than 200 intelligence and security services worldwide.[8] In addition, at the Asia-Pacific Economic Cooperation Forum (APEC) Summit in Shanghai, China, in October 2001, APEC leaders issued a statement on counter-terrorism in which they strongly condemned the 9/11 attacks and pledged to improve counter-terrorism cooperation through a number of means.

These have included putting in place appropriate financial measures to prevent the flow of funds to terrorists, including work on combating financial crimes through the APEC Finance Ministers Working Group on Fighting Financial Crime, as well as more involvement in related international standard setting regimes. These initiatives have led to agreements to undertake early and constructive consultation prior to designating terrorist assets, exchanging information on national legal criteria required to freeze terrorist funds and updating global assessments of frozen terrorists' funds.

---

5 UK Treasury Statement on Terrorist Finance 19 July 2005.

6 P.A. Sproat, 'Counter-terrorist finance in the UK: A quantitative and qualitative commentary based on open-source materials' (2010) *Journal of Money Laundering Control*, 13(4) 315.

7 R.E. Bell, 'The confiscation, forfeiture and disruption of terrorist finances' (2003) *Journal of Money Laundering Control* 7(2) 105.

8 Dean C. Alexander and Yonah Alexander, *Terrorism and Business* (Transnational Publishers 2002) 184.

However, in terms of the actual impact on terrorist activities, it seems that little, if any real progress has been made.[9] The 'Patterns of Global Terrorism' Report, which the US State Department was mandated to produce, was dropped, officially on grounds of poor methodology. Furthermore, a briefing given by the State Department on Capitol Hill and leaked to the press, confirmed that terrorism had risen sharply since 9/11. Terrorist incidents worldwide tripled in 2004 from 203 to 655. Even excluding Iraq, the figure doubled; terrorist attacks there having increased nine fold to 198 'significant' attacks.[10]

These facts raise the question as to why the so-called 'war on terror' along with other 'wars' such as the 'war on drugs' continues to be ineffective. Furthermore, as counter finance strategies play such a key role as part of the overall counter-terrorism effort, the reality in terms of its ineffectiveness to date must be accepted, together with the reasons as to why this is the case. Furthermore, a willingness to embrace new ideas both strategically and tactically is necessary.

As previous chapters have highlighted, the existing multilateral effort is based on the notion that terrorists will exploit the weakest links in the global financial system. Attempts have been made, and continue to be made, to strengthen those weak links, and there is no doubt that certain aspects of the global financial environment have become more hostile to terrorist financiers and money launderers in recent years. In an effort to keep pace with the constantly mutating nature of terrorist finance and financial crime in general, international regulators continue to introduce new regulations which have been described as a 'regulatory tsunami'.[11] However, despite the deluge of new legislation and regulation designed to tackle the threat, the reality is not very promising.[12]

At the root of the problem is the insufficient understanding of terrorist finance and other related financial crime. This has resulted in an over simplistic understanding of the subject which leads to an unsophisticated approach in tackling the problem at all levels. The reality is that those tasked with the detection and interdiction of terrorist funds are frequently inadequately

9 El-Fatih A. Abdel Salam, 'War on terror: fantasy and fiction behind the mythology of terrorist financing' (2009) 17(1) *Intellectual Discourse*. [Online]. Available at: http://www.iium.edu.my/intdiscourse/index.php/islam/article/viewArticle/4 [accessed: 5 April 2010].

10 Global Enforcement Regimes (n.3).

11 J. Loden, 'The Need for an Ideological Response to Islamic Extremism' (MSc Diss., Cranfield University, DCMT, 2005).

12 Peter A. Sproat, 'Counter-terrorist finance in the UK' 315.

equipped with the necessary knowledge and tools to collect and present evidence that will result in a successful conviction. Unless the right questions are asked, and the search taken into the right places by talking to the right people, the CTF effort will remain no more than the pursuit of a self-fulfilling prophecy. An appropriate starting point in examining existing efforts to date in the UK is to examine its CTF strategy.

UK Counter-Terrorist Finance Strategy

The UK's CTF strategy is part of the overall counter-terrorism strategy known as CONTEST.[13] The first CONTEST strategy was announced in 2003 with its purpose to counter the threat from international terrorism. In 2009, the revised strategy known as CONTEST 2 was published. CONTEST 2 builds upon the original strategy, taking into account the evolution of the threat, reflecting the lessons learned since 2003.[14] Delivery of the strategy continues to be organised around the four work streams that of 'Pursue' to stop terrorist attacks, 'Prevent' to stop people becoming terrorists or supporting violent extremism, 'Protect' to strengthen protection against terrorist attack and 'Prepare' to mitigate the impact of a terrorist attack where an attack cannot be stopped.[15]

From a CTF perspective, CONTEST 2 places renewed emphasis on the importance of understanding and tackling terrorist finance. The revised strategy focuses on the prevention of money being raised and used for attack planning in the UK and against UK interests, the disruption of the funding of al-Qaeda and its affiliates and associates by targeting donors, facilitators and the terrorist financial infrastructure, and the development of understanding in relation to the funding of radicalisation and disrupting the movement of funds into this country for that purpose.[16] CONEST 2 is encouraging in that it demonstrates the political support in tackling the complex issues relating to terrorist finance, and has served as an important vehicle to kick start a number of key inter-governmental initiatives relating to terrorist finance. These initiatives are not only furthering the understanding of the subject, but better enabling operational effectiveness in utilising financial intelligence tools to tackle counter-terrorism. However, despite this renewed commitment, numerous challenges continue to

13 Audrey Kurth Cronin, 'The evolution of counterterrorism: will tactics trump strategy?' (2010) 86(4) *International Affairs* 837.

14 Home Office, 'CONTEST Strategy 2' (UK Strategy for Countering International Terrorism, 24 March 2009) 8.

15 Ibid. 13.

16 Ibid. 77.

exist that undermine the effectiveness of CONTEST 2's strategic objectives in relation to the interdiction of terrorist funds.

Financial Disruption Strategies

The Pursue work stream of CONTEST aims to reduce the terrorist threat to UK and UK interests overseas through the detection and investigation of terrorist networks and the disruption of their activities.[17] The intelligence agencies, together with law enforcement, the Ministry of Defence, the Foreign and Commonwealth Office and other 'Pursue' stakeholders, continue to enhance the UK's capability to disrupt terrorist operations through a number of disruption strategies. From a CTF perspective, the disruption strategies adopted either directly or indirectly impact upon the funding of terrorism.

In terms of direct methods of the disruption of terrorist funding, the seizure of funds, financial sanctions, asset-freezing or other means of denying the source of money, such as the disruption of a courier or disruption of target communications affecting the transfer of funds, may be adopted.[18] Indirect methods include the detention of a target or associates, the prevention of travel and the conducting of disruptive interviews to persuade an individual of influence to cease activity that funds terrorism.

Continuing on the theme of influence, fracturing relationships between key players and their networks have historically proved to be successful. In addition, the introduction of the Home Office Warnings Index (HOWI) further supports the disruption activities described.[19]

Smart Sanctions

Existing CTF measures which target specific individuals and organisations responsible or associated with the funding of terrorism can be described as falling under the category of smart sanctions. The origin of smart/targeted

17 Cronin, 'The evolution of counterterrorism' (n.13) 837.

18 Bell, 'The confiscation, forfeiture and disruption of terrorist finances' (n.7) 105.

19 HOWI is a database containing a watch list of persons who are of interest to the core border agencies. A passenger's document is swiped and the machine readable zone containing the biographic data and passport details are searched against the system records. [Online]. Available at: http://www.publications.parliament.uk/pa/cm200506/cmselect/cmhaff/775/775awe62.htm [accessed: 11 January 2011].

sanctions predates the events of 9/11. Nevertheless, a brief background may be helpful in understanding the concept which led to its development. Prior to the existence of 'smart' sanctions, the use of 'standard' economic sanctions against 'enemy states' including those who supported terrorism, was commonplace. However, traditional economic sanctions have long been recognised as being ineffective.[20] In addition, they possess a highly undesirable side effect in the form of an indiscriminate impact on a country, which can entail severe negative humanitarian consequences for the civilian population.[21]

This side effect is particularly of concern in the context of terrorism. Islamic terrorism frequently utilises the suffering of innocent civilian populations in two ways. First, through emphasis of the 'victim hood' of those people, either the victims themselves or those who empathise with those individuals who are radicalised so that they can be recruited into the terrorist organisations. Second, such examples of unjust treatment are used to attract funding, which in turn is used for the purpose of financing terrorism. This is of particular importance, as the origin of much of the donor funding is derived through appealing to the charitable nature of wealthy individuals who may or may not be aware of the ultimate purpose of their financial donations.

In terms of traditional sanctions, the UN recognised in 2000 that:

> *... sanctions remain a blunt instrument, which hurt large numbers of people who are not their primary targets.*[22]

And furthermore:

> *When robust and comprehensive economic sanctions are directed against authoritarian regimes, a different problem is encountered. Then, tragically, it is usually the people who suffer, not the political elites whose behaviour triggered the sanctions in the first place.*[23]

---

20 Daniel W. Drezner, 'Sanctions sometimes smart: targeted sanctions in theory and practice' (2011) 13(1) *International Studies Review* 96.

21 Peter L. Fitzgerald, 'Smarter Smart Sanctions' (2007) 26 *International Studies Review* 37.

22 UN, 'Secretary-General Reviews Lessons Learned During 'Sanctions Decade'' (Press Release SG/SM/7360, 17 April 2000). [Online]. Available at: http://www.un.org/News/Press/docs/2000/20000417.sgsm7360.doc.html [accessed: 17 November 2010].

23 Ibid.

In response, the Swiss government initiated a series of conferences known as the Interlaken Process,[24] where representatives from the UN, government and the private sector held a dialogue aimed at identifying methods of applying financial sanctions in a more targeted and efficient manner.[25] The technical and judicial principles to improve the application of financial sanctions were developed at two seminars held on March 1998, and again in March 1999 in Interlaken. The results of the Interlaken Process, which were published in the form of a manual in 2001, significantly advanced the collective understanding of the feasibility of targeted financial sanctions.[26]

To elaborate further, the focus of Interlaken I, the first meeting, was on the specific technical requirements of financial sanctions and identified a number of preconditions necessary for targeted sanctions to be effective. These included the need for clear target identification and the ability to identify and control financial flows. The need to extend the analysis to include a wide variety of financial assets including property was also identified. Participants also noted that speed and discretion in determining targets and the specific sanctions were critical to success.[27]

The second Interlaken meeting not only further developed recommendations on the technical aspects of targeting, but addressed issues arising from differences in implementation of financial sanctions among states. For example, the lack of legal authority necessary to implement the requirements of Security Council resolutions in some jurisdictions was highlighted. It was further noted that even among those with such capacity, great variation existed in terms of implementation and enforcement, which undercut the overall effectiveness of UN sanctions. In response, a model law was developed that would enable states to implement UN-authorised targeted financial sanctions quickly, fully and consistently. In addition, standardised texts or building blocks of language were developed that the Security Council could use in drafting sanctions resolutions to promote more uniform implementation across member states.

---

24 The Interlaken Process website provides the findings and discussions of the process, including the published outcomes of Interlaken I and II. [Online]. Available at: www.smartsanctions.ch [accessed: 1 January 2011].

25 State Secretariat for Economic Affairs SECO website http://www.seco.admin.ch/themen/00513/00620/00639/00641/index.html?lang=en.

26 Targeted Sanctions Project, 'Summary of the Interlaken Process' (Watson Institute for International Studies, Brown University, Interactive Sanctions Digest) 1. [Online]. Available at: http://www.watsoninstitute.org/tfs/CD/ISD_Summary_of_Interlaken_Process.pdf [accessed: 17 February 2010].

27 Ibid.

Overall, the Interlaken seminars concluded that targeted financial sanctions were technically feasible, but that concrete measures at a national and international level were necessary for the instrument to be developed more fully and made effective.[28] Following the Interlaken Process, Germany and Sweden organised a series of further seminars on targeted sanctions. The Bonn-Berlin Process focused on travel and air traffic related sanctions as well as on arms embargoes. The Stockholm Process dealt with the practical feasibility of implementing and monitoring targeted sanctions.[29]

Twelve years on since the first Interlaken meeting, the so-called 'smart' or targeted sanctions have been developed to target individuals, companies and organisations, or restrict trade with key commodities. Examples include financial sanctions such as the freezing of funds and other financial assets, the ban on transactions, and investment restrictions, as well as trade restrictions on particular goods such as arms, diamonds, oil, lumber or services.[30] In addition, other disruption measures such as travel restrictions, diplomatic constraints, cultural and sports restrictions and air traffic restrictions were also added.[31] The most significant of these measures in relation to the disruption of terrorist funds is considered to be asset-freezing.

Asset Freeze

An asset freeze is considered for use to prevent terrorist acts by preventing funds, economic resources or financial services from being used or diverted for terrorist purposes. An asset freeze can be applied to groups as well as individuals. In terms of legislation relating to asset-freezing, the primary aim of Part II of the ATCSA 2001 is to prevent terrorists from accessing their money.[32] It permits HM Treasury to freeze the assets of overseas governments or residents who have taken, or are likely to take, action to the detriment of the UK's economy or action constituting a threat to the life or property of a national or resident of the UK.[33]

---

28 Targeted Sanctions Project (n.26).

29 State Secretariat for Economic Affairs (n.25).

30 Michael Bothe, 'Security Council's targeted sanctions against presumed terrorists: the need to comply with human rights standards' (2008) 6(3) *Journal of International Criminal Justice* 541.

31 State Secretariat for Economic Affairs (n.25).

32 H. Barnett, *Constitutional and Administrative Law* (Cavendish, 2004) 695.

33 This provision repealed the Emergency Laws (Re-enactments and Repeals) Act 1964, which provided for the freezing of the UK assets of foreign governments and certain foreign individuals in such time of emergency, s.2. The 1964 Act also allowed for the asset freezing to cases where action constitutes a threat to life or property in the UK.

HM Treasury is permitted to make a freezing order if two statutory requirements are met. First, they must reasonably believe that action threatening the UK's economy or the life or property of UK nationals or residents has taken place, or is likely to take place.[34] Secondly, the persons involved in the action must be resident outside the UK or be an overseas government.[35] The freezing order prevents all persons in the UK from making funds available to, or for the benefit of, a person or persons specified in the order.[36]

HM Treasury is also required to keep the freezing order under review and to determine whether it should continually be enforced over a period of two years.[37] Once the UK had adopted and implemented UN Resolution 1373, HM Treasury froze the assets of individuals and organisations who were suspected of financing terrorism.[38] The government published a list of 77 organisations and 48 individuals whose accounts have been frozen following 9/11.[39] The list included individuals and organisations listed under Presidential Executive Order 13,223, the US list of the 22 most wanted terrorists; the list of UK proscribed terrorist organisations and individuals and organisations also listed by the US in November 2001.[40]

However, the ability of HM Treasury to freeze the assets of suspected terrorists has been criticised and these powers have been declared as inappropriate use of emergency legislation.[41] It has also been argued that these powers are the result of the:

> *... headlong rush to drive the Anti-terrorism Crime and Security Act through Parliament with little or no time to consider whether a more*

34 The Act provides that HM Treasury is not required to prove actual detriment to freeze the assets of a suspected terrorist, but that a threat is sufficient. There is no condition that there should be a suspicion of criminal activity, nor a condition that any criminal activity exists. See Current Law Statutes 2001, vol.2, 12–13.

35 Terrorism Act 2000 s.4(1)(a) and (b).

36 Terrorism Act 2000 s.5.

37 Terrorism Act 2000 ss.7 and 9.

38 O. Elagab, 'Control of terrorist funds and the banking system' (2006) 21(1) *Journal of International Banking Law and Regulation* 38.

39 Terrorism Act 2000 Sch.1 Pt II. A complete list of individuals and organisations that have had their assets frozen is available from the Bank of England website at www.bankofengland.co.uk.

40 See Home Office website for proscribed terrorist list at: www.homeoffice.gov.uk. See also the Terrorism Act 2000 (Proscribed Organisations) (Amendment) Order 2005 (SI 2005/2892). For a more detailed assessment of this procedure and discussion of the human rights implications see B. Dickson, 'Law versus terrorism: can law win?' (2005) 1 *European Human Rights Law Review* 11.

41 Hansard, HL col.357 (28 November 2001).

appropriate and effective system for forfeiture of terrorist cash could be devised.[42] [43]

These provisions do, however, allow the government to counter the risks of assets being used to finance terror. The importance of freezing assets cannot be underestimated as it remains an important weapon to counter-terrorist finances.[44]

Prior to 9/11, HM Treasury froze £90 million of terrorist assets, which is attributed towards the fall of the Taliban in Afghanistan in 2002.[45] After this initial success, HM Treasury has only been able to freeze a further £10 million.[46] It has been suggested that this success can be measured in the actual amount of money frozen. However, it is also recognised that although the headline figure thus generated is doubtless politically satisfying to some, it cannot be taken as a reliable measure of effectiveness.

In the UK, the Treasury is also responsible for the implementation and administration of international financial sanctions and has ownership of the domestic asset-freezing regime. The Treasury's Asset-Freezing Unit (AFU) is responsible for designating persons who will be subject to asset-freezes under the Terrorism Order 2006, but is advised by the intelligence agencies and/or police, who submit Statements of Case setting out the reasons why a person should be subjected to a freeze. Proposals for asset-freezing are kept under review by the Asset-Freezing Working Group (AFWG), which is chaired by the Treasury and meets every month. Once Treasury Ministers have agreed to proceed with an asset freeze, the AFWG notifies the banks, who are then obliged to freeze any financial facilities named individuals may be using. The individual will also receive a letter from the Treasury informing them that they will not be able to access their funds, together with an explanation for the action taken.[47]

42 P. Binning, 'In safe hands? Striking the balance between privacy and security, anti-terrorist finance measures' (2002) 6 *European Human Rights Law Review* 737.

43 J. Johnson, '11th September, 2001: will it make a difference to the global anti-money laundering movement?' (2002) 6(1) *Journal of Money Laundering Control* 10.

44 Cabinet Office, *The UK and the Campaign against International Terrorism* (Progress Report. Cabinet Office, London, 2002) 26.

45 This was a UN-led initiative. The UN Security Resolutions were implemented by the Terrorism (UN Measures) Order 2001 (Amendment) Regulations 2004 (SI 2004/2309) and the Taleban and Al-Qa-ida (UN Measures) Order 2002 (SI 2002/111). Binning noted that 'the UK has frozen the assets of over 100 organisations and over 200 individuals'.

46 HM Treasury, *Combating the Financing of Terrorism* (a report on UK action) 27.

47 The AFU also issues licences for individuals to draw modest funds to cover living costs. Appeals against AF can be made to the High Court.

In addition, EU listing is considered when it is judged that an EU-wide asset freeze would reinforce a domestic asset freeze/proscription. Two terrorist freezing lists currently exist in the EU. The first[48] relates to al-Qaeda and the Taliban, and the second to the EU's 'autonomous' measures list containing groups not related to al-Qaeda and the Taliban that fall under the EU's agreed definition of terrorism.[49] Groups can be proposed for EU listing by member states and non-EU countries, normally in writing to the Presidency with an 'open' Statement of Reason (SoR) that can be released to the individual/entity if listing is agreed.

The existing list is reviewed by the Common Position 931 Working Group, which takes decision on consensus. The same group also considers new listing proposals. When a proposal for listing is put forward, member states may place a reserve on it, either because they feel there is insufficient evidence or sometimes for political reasons. Appeals are made to the Court of First Instance, which may grant a right to take the appeal to the European Court of Justice. To de-list a group, a written request must be made to the Council Secretariat and the Presidency. Member states must then follow the same procedure as for listing.

As a member of the UN, the UK along with other member states is required to freeze the assets of persons who are associated with terrorism. Obligations under resolution 1373 had been implemented by the Treasury by a number of

48 Flows from the UN designation, therefore added automatically to the EU's common position on measures against terrorist organisations. Since the UN deals with all groups linked to AQ and the Taleban, these are not discussed within the EU, but asset freezing is automatic.

49 Article 1: Terrorist offences reads as follows. Each EU member state has to take measures to ensure that terrorist offences: 'include intentional acts, by their nature and context, which may be seriously damaging to a country or to an international organisation, as defined under national law, where committed with the aim of:
(i) seriously intimidating a population, or
(ii) unduly compelling a government or international organisation to perform or to abstain from performing any act, or
(iii) destabilising or destroying the fundamental political, constitutional, economic or social structures of a country or international organisation' and Article 1.e (Art 3.f in the Commission draft) now reads, where the above would result in:
'causing extensive damage to a Government or public facility, a transport system, an infrastructure facility, including an information system, a fixed platform located on a continental shelf, a public place or private property likely to put in danger human lives or produce considerable economic loss'.
The inclusion of 'a fixed platform located on a continental shelf' is new and could embrace the occupation of the 'Brent Spa' oil platform by Greenpeace. See Eugenia Dumitriu, 'The EU's definition of terrorism: The Council frame-work decision on combating terrorism' (2004) 10(5) *German Law Journal Special Edition*. [Online]. Available at: http://www.germanlawjournal.com/pdfs/Vol05No05/PDF_Vol_05_No_05_585-602_special_issue_Dumitriu.pdf [accessed: 20 January 2011].

Orders in Council made under section 1 of the UN Act 1946 (the 'UN Act').[50] However, the UK legislation that allowed the Treasury to freeze the assets of those suspected of involvement in terrorism was quashed by the UK Supreme Court on 27 January 2010.[51] The Supreme Court held that the 2006 Order was *ultra vires* the UN Act and on 4 February 2010 made an order quashing the 2006 Order. The Supreme Court did not rule upon the lawfulness of the 2001 Order or the 2009 Order but, both Orders were liable to be quashed on the same grounds as the 2006 Order.

Following the Supreme Court's decision, emergency legislation was rushed through Parliament in the form of the Terrorist Asset-Freezing (Temporary Provisions) Act 2010, effectively preserving the lawfulness of the steps taken under the quashed orders. The Temporary Provisions Act provided that the UN Terrorism Orders were deemed to have been validly made under the UN Act and for directions made imposing asset-freezes to have effect, for the period from Royal Assent (10 February 2010) until 31 December 2010.[52] The Act therefore maintained terrorist asset-freezing restrictions which had been quashed by the Supreme Court ruling or which were vulnerable to being quashed as a consequence of that ruling.

This permitted adequate time for the passage of primary legislation which would remedy the breaches of fundamental law which rendered the Orders '*ultra vires*' or outside the lawful power of the executive. As such, the Terrorist Asset-Freezing etc. Bill was introduced on 16 July 2010,[53] which received Royal Assent on 16 December 2010 to become the Terrorist Asset-Freezing etc. Act 2010. The purpose of the Bill and subsequent Act was to

50 Under section 1 of the UN Act, there is a power to make an Order in Council to give effect to any decision of the UN Security Council where such provision appears 'necessary or expedient for enabling those measures to be effectively applied'. The Orders made under section 1 of the UN Act to give effect to obligations under resolution 1373 were the Terrorism (UN Measures) Order 2001 (the '2001 Order'), the Terrorism (UN Measures) Order 2006 (the '2006 Order') and the Terrorism (UN Measures) Order 2009 (the '2009 Order'). In these Notes, those Orders are referred to collectively as the 'UN Terrorism Orders'. The 2006 Order replaced and revoked the 2001 Order save that directions designating persons under article 4 of the 2001 Order which remained in force on the date the 2006 Order came into force continued to apply and the provisions of the 2001 Order continued to apply to such directions. Similarly, the 2009 Order replaced and revoked the 2006 Order save that directions under article 4 of the 2006 Order, which remained in force on the date the 2009 Order came into force, continued to apply and the provisions of the previous Orders continued to apply to such directions.

51 *HM Treasury v Ahmed* [2010] All ER (D) 40.

52 Parliament, 'Terrorist Asset-Freezing etc. Bill [HL] 2010-11'. [Online]. Available at: http://services.parliament.uk/bills/2010-11/terroristassetfreezingetchl.html [accessed: 12 July 2011].

53 HM Treasury, 'The Terrorist Asset-Freezing etc. Bill' 16 July 2010. [Online]. Available at: http://www.hm-treasury.gov.uk/fin_sanctions_terrorist_assetfreezingbill.htm [accessed: 12 July 2011].

> *... put the UK's asset-freezing regime under UN Resolution 1371 (2001) on a secure legislative footing.*[54]

However, the case of *A v HM Treasury*,[55] together with *R (on the application of Youssef) v HM Treasury*[56] and *HM Treasury v Al-Ghabra*,[57] brought to the fore issues in relation to counter-terrorism legislation and the various asset-freezing schemes that have been implemented in recent years.[58] It is also worth noting that orders in the present case are currently[59] applied to 33 individuals and account for £151,000 of a total of around £375,000 terrorist asset-freezing.[60]

THE TERRORIST ASSET-FREEZING ETC. BILL

The Terrorist Asset-Freezing etc. Bill represented the coalition government's[61] response to the Supreme Court's decision in *HM Treasury v Ahmed*[62] concerning the lawfulness of measures enabling the Treasury to freeze the assets of a person whom it has reasonable grounds for suspecting is, or may be a person who facilitates the commission of acts of terrorism.

The case was the first appeal to have been heard in the Supreme Court which held that the use of the Order in Council procedure, whereby the measure is simply laid before Parliament, without any opportunity for scrutiny or debate, was outside the powers which had been granted to the executive under section 1 of the UN Act 1946. The Supreme Court also described in strong terms the impact on the individual of such measures as 'drastic', 'oppressive' and having the effect that 'designated persons are effectively prisoners of the state'.[63]

However, the response to the Bill was not entirely positive. A *Joint Report by Liberty and Justice* criticised the Bill as continuing to fail to respect fundamental rights and freedoms and the due process of law. The Joint Report proposed a number of amendments to address this situation, the most important of which

54 Treasury Commercial Secretary Lord Sassoon.
55 *A v HM Treasury* [2010] UKSC 2, [2010] 4 All ER 745, [2010] 2 WLR 378, [2010] All ER (D) 179.
56 *R (on the application of M) v HM Treasury and other actions* [2008] UKHL 26.
57 *Al-Ghabra v HM Treasury* [2010] 4 All ER 829.
58 *A v HM Treasury; R (on the application of Youssef) v HM Treasury, HM Treasury v Al-Ghabra* [2010] UKSC 2, See also Ben Middleton, 'Freezing terrorist assets,' *Journal of Criminal Law* (2010) 74(3) 209.
59 As at January 2011.
60 Hansard, HC Deb, 8 February 2010, vol. 505, col. 657.
61 UK Coalition government formed in May 2010 comprising Conservatives and Liberal Democrats.
62 [2010] UKSC 2.
63 Ibid.

was to take the decision on whether to designate an individual as being subject to asset-freezing orders away from the executive, and place it in the hands of the courts. The report argued that the current proposal, whereby the Treasury would still take the decision to freeze assets but would give a right of appeal to the High Court, was flawed in that it places the onus on the individual to challenge the punishment meted out to him without charge or trial, rather than requiring that a case be proved against him.

The *Joint Report* also highlighted concerns regarding secret evidence used in court, pointing to the unhappy precedent of the control orders regime when it comes to the effectiveness and legality of trials held behind closed doors in which the individual concerned has limited ability to challenge the evidence against him.[64] The criticism was made that previously, it was only in totalitarian states, where an individual or entity could be stripped of their assets in such a manner. Recent terrorism legislation now permits individuals to be deprived of everything they own without charge and on mere suspicion. The *Joint Committee on Human Rights Report*[65] also made several recommendations for further improvements to the Bill from a human rights perspective.

The first was with reference to the use of secret evidence. Recommendations were made to ensure that its use was fair by making clear that the government must provide sufficient information about the allegations against an individual to enable them to give effective instructions to the special advocate who represents their interests[66] A further comment was made that the use of secret evidence should never be allowed to cause unfairness to people who are made the subject of what was referred to as 'draconian' measures.

A second recommendation called for the clarification that asset-freezes can only be imposed where the relevant facts about involvement in terrorism have been proved 'on the balance of probabilities'. Furthermore, a more detailed justification for enabling the government, rather than the courts, to impose final asset-freezes was recommended together with a requirement for providing for the independent reviewer of the terrorist asset-freezing regime to be appointed by and report directly to Parliament, as opposed to the government.

64 BBC, 'Peers back Terrorist Asset Freezing Bill' *BBC* (27 July 2010). [Online]. Available at: http: // news.bbc.co.uk/democracylive/hi/house_of_lords/newsid_8856000/8856247.stm [accessed: 30 July 2010].

65 *Joint Committee on Human Rights Report: Terrorist Asset-Freezing etc. Bill* (Preliminary Report). [Online]. Available at: http://www.parliament.uk/business/committees/committees-a-z/joint-select/human-rights-committee/news/third-report/ [accessed: 30 July 2010].

66 Ibid. para 37–39.

TERRORIST ASSET-FREEZING ETC. ACT 2010

The Terrorist Asset-Freezing etc. Act 2010 received Royal Assent on 16 December 2010.[67] As a result, the Terrorist Asset-Freezing (Temporary Provisions) Act 2010 was repealed and amendments were made to the Counter-Terrorism Act 2008.[68] The legislation consists of two parts. The purpose of Part 1 of the Act is to give effect in the UK to resolution 1373 (2001)[69] adopted by the UN Security Council on 28 September 2001 ('resolution 1373') relating to terrorism and resolution 1452 (2002)[70] adopted on 20 December 2002 ('resolution 1452') relating to humanitarian exemptions. It also provides for enforcement of Regulation (EC) 2580/2001 on specific measures directed at certain persons and entities with a view to combating terrorism ('the EC Regulation').[71]

The purpose of Part 2 of the Act is to make amendments to Schedule 7 to the Counter-Terrorism Act 2008. Schedule 7 provides the Treasury with powers by directions to impose financial restrictions in relation to persons connected with a country (a 'country of concern') in response to money laundering, terrorist financing or the development or production of nuclear, radiological, biological or chemical weapons that poses a risk to the national interests of the UK, or where the FATF has advised that measures should be taken in relation to the country because of the risk of terrorist financing or money laundering activities. Furthermore, amendments to Schedule 7 included powers to clarify the persons to whom a direction may be given, to broaden the definition of persons in relation to whom restrictions may be applied, and to introduce a prohibition on circumventing the requirements of a direction. As the Act has

67 Terrorist Asset-Freezing etc. Act 2010. [Online]. Available at: http://www.legislation.gov.uk/ukpga/2010/38/notes/division/1 [accessed: 15 April 2011].

68 SI 2001/3365, SI 2003/1297, SI 2005/1525, SI 2006/2657, SI 2009/1747, SI 2009/1911, SI 2009/1912 revoked; SI 1998/3132, SI 2007/2157, SI 2007/3298, SI 2009/209, SI 2001/3801, SI 2002/111, SI 2005/3389, SI 2007/2157, SI 2007/3298, SI 2009/209 amended; SR 1980/346 amended. Source: lexisnexis.com.

69 Resolution 1373 includes a requirement that Member States of the United Nations must (a) prevent the financing of terrorist acts, including the freezing of funds and economic resources of persons who commit or attempt to commit terrorist acts or participate in or facilitate such acts, and (b) prohibit their nationals and those within their territories from making funds, financial services or economic resources available to such persons.

70 Resolution 1452 introduces exemptions to prohibitions on making funds, financial assets or economic resources available to permit payments necessary to meet basic humanitarian needs (such as payments for foodstuffs, rent or mortgage, medicines and medical treatment, taxes, insurance premiums, public utility charges and legal fees and expenses) and payments necessary to meet extraordinary expenses.

71 On 18 March 2010, the government published a public consultation with regard to the content of Part 1 of the Act. A draft Bill and draft Explanatory Notes were annexed to the consultation. This consultation closed on 18 June 2010 and the government's (2) response to the consultation replies was published on 15 July 2010. Part 1 of this Act is broadly based on the consultation draft.

only recently come into force, public opinion and response is unavailable at the time of this writing. However, it is highly probable that the concerns and criticisms expressed in the aforementioned *Joint Report* in relation to the Terrorist Asset-Freezing etc. Bill remain.

The focus of this chapter so far has been on the government's efforts to disrupt the funding of terrorists through asset-freezing and other measures. However, much of the funds seized would not be brought to the attention without the assistance of the financial sector. In recognition of the importance of the role financial institutions play in relation to the countering financial crime, regulations and enforcement measures have been put in place to ensure compliance.

Financial Sector Regulation

The UK has a long history of imposing reporting requirements on financial and credit institutions.[72] The first reporting requirements were contained in the Drug Trafficking Offences Act 1986, which was amended by the Criminal Justice Act 1993 (CJA 1993). The CJA 1993 was described as a crucial step, as it amended the legislation in relation to the reporting requirements.

It also gave effect to the European Directive on Money Laundering[73] and introduced the concept of mandatory reporting, whereby a person who knows or suspects that another person is engaged in drug money laundering is under a legal obligation to report the knowledge or suspicious transaction.[74] The requirements on mandatory reporting have been consolidated by the Proceeds of Crime Act 2002 (POCA 2002) and the Money Laundering Regulations 2003.[75] Furthermore, Schedule 2 Pt III to the ATCSA 2001 makes it an offence of failure to disclose knowledge or suspicion that another person has committed an offence under ss.15–18 of the TA 2000, which covers acts of terrorism. Binning described this offence as almost identical to the offence of failing to disclose information under POCA 2002.[76]

72 Ricardo Azevedo Araujo, 'Assessing the efficiency of the anti-money laundering regulation: an incentive-based approach' (2008) 11(1) *Journal of Money Laundering Control* 67.

73 R. Stokes and A. Arora, 'The duty to report under the money laundering legislation within the UK' 3 (2004) *Journal of Business Law* 332.

74 Ibid.

75 M. Isaacs, 'Money laundering dilemmas for banks' (2004) 19(8) *Journal of International Banking Law and Regulation* 284.

76 POCA 2002 ss.330-332. For a more detailed discussion of some of the problems caused by the reporting requirements under the Proceeds of Crime Act 2002 see generally N. Ryder and A.H. Baker,

In terms of ensuring compliance, the FSA is an independent non-governmental body, given statutory powers by the Financial Services and Markets Act 2000 to regulate the financial services industry in the UK. As such, the FSA has a wide range of rule-making, investigatory and enforcement powers. The regulations and guidelines are wide ranging and are detailed in the FSA *Handbook* and applicable not simply to the treatment of criminal funds, but provides guidance on matters relating to governance in general. For example, the *Handbook* specifies that a firm should segregate the duties of individuals and departments in such a way as to reduce opportunities for financial crime or contravention of requirements and standards under the regulatory system. As part of this requirement, it is recommended that the duties of front-office and back-office staff should be segregated so as to prevent a single individual initiating, processing and controlling transactions.[77]

The importance of the segregation of powers was highlighted by the collapse of Barings Bank[78] in 1995 after one of the bank's employees, Nick Leeson,[79] lost £827 million speculating primarily on futures contracts. Leeson had hidden the losses in an obscure account called Error Account 88888 which, upon discovery, led to the bank's collapse and its subsequent sale to the Dutch banking and insurance group ING for £1.[80] The predominant reason why the situation was allowed to occur was due to the fact that Nick Leeson had responsibility for both front and back-office functions, which enabled him to abuse his position to keep the losses unreported for a significant period of time. Following the incident, the Board of Banking Supervision of the Bank of England launched an investigation led by Britain's Chancellor of the Exchequer immediate after the event. The findings were published in a report released on 18 July 1995 and highlighted the management failures of Barings Bank. Lord Bruce of Donington, in the House of Lords' debate on the report observed that:

> *Barings' collapse was due to the unauthorised and ultimately catastrophic activities of, it appears, one individual (Leeson) that*

'The legal profession sighs a relief: Bowman and Fels an appropriate response to P v P?' (2005) 39(3) *The Law Teacher* 388 and E. Powles, 'All that glisters is no gold: laundering the UK money laundering regime' (2006) 65(1) *Cambridge Law Journal* 40.

77 FSA Handbook: SYSC 3.2. [Online]. Available at: http://fsahandbook.info/FSA/html/focus-on-FCRMAML/SYSC/3/2 [accessed: 26 June 2010].

78 James Reason, *UK's Oldest Investment Bank (1762 to 1995: Managing the Risks of Organizational Accidents* (Ashgate 1997) 29.

79 Nicholas 'Nick' Leeson is a former derivatives broker whose fraudulent, unauthorised speculative trading caused the collapse of Barings Bank, for which he pleaded guilty to fraud and was sentenced to six and a half years in prison.

80 BBC, 'How Leeson broke the bank', *BBC News Online* (22 June 1999). [Online]. Available at: http://news.bbc.co.uk/1/hi/business/375259.stm [accessed: 3 January 2010].

> *went undetected as a consequence of a failure of management and other internal controls of the most basic kind. The words I venture to emphasise to your Lordships are these: as a consequence of a failure of management and other internal controls of the most basic kind.*[81]

Although Leeson' case is one that related to fraud, it is not difficult to see that if instead he had intended to carry out other financial crimes, such as the funding of terrorism or money laundering, that the lack of appropriate internal controls would have enabled him to carry out these other financial crimes with relative ease.

Against the background of the Leeson disaster, as well a general tightening of requirements in relation to financial crime, existing regulations require financial institutions to put in place various systems and controls. For example, a firm must take reasonable care to establish and maintain effective systems and controls for compliance with applicable requirements and standards under the regulatory system, and for countering the risk that the firm might be used to further financial crime. Furthermore, a firm must ensure that these systems and controls enable it to identify, assess, monitor and manage money laundering risk; and are comprehensive and proportionate to the nature, scale and complexity of its activities.[82] In addition, it is a requirement to carry out regular assessments of the adequacy of these systems and controls to ensure that it continues to comply with SYSC 326A R.[83]

In terms of the identification of its money laundering risk and in establishing the nature of these systems and controls, the FSA recommends that a firm should consider a range of factors, including its customer, product and activity profiles; its distribution channels; the complexity and volume of its transactions; its processes and systems; as well as its operating environment.[84] It further recommends that the systems and controls include the appropriate training for its employees in relation to money laundering and that procedures are in place to ensure delivery of relevant information to its governing body and senior management. Furthermore, measures must be place to ensure that money laundering risk is taken into account in its day-to-day operation,

81 Testimony of Lord Bruce of Donington: Lords Hansard text for 21 Jul 1995, 250 [Online]. Available at: http://www.parliament.the-stationery-office.co.uk/pa/ld199495/ldhansrd/vo950721/text/50721-14.htm [accessed: 3 January 2010].

82 FSA Handbook (n.77) SYSC 3.2.6A.

83 Ibid. SYSC 3.2.6C.

84 Ibid. SYSC 3.2.6F.

including in relation to the development of new products; the taking-on of new customers; and changes in its business profile.[85]

There is also a requirement to appoint a money laundering reporting officer (MLRO), with responsibility for oversight of its compliance with the FSA's rules on systems and controls against money laundering; and ensure that its MLRO has a level of authority and independence within the firm and access to resources and information sufficient to enable that individual to carry out that responsibility.[86] In addition to the appointment of a MLRO, the setting up of a separate compliance function is recommended.[87] Furthermore, the regulation stipulates that a compliance function should be staffed by an appropriate number of competent staff who are sufficiently independent to perform their duties objectively and that it should be adequately resourced and should have unrestricted access to the firm's relevant records as well as ultimate recourse to its governing body.[88] The regulations also remind firms of their separate obligations to comply with relevant legal requirements, including the TA 2000, POCA 2002 and the Money Laundering Regulations.

Due Diligence: KYC Requirements

The 'Know Your Customer' (KYC) requirement is essentially the due diligence procedures which should be carried out as part of the initial client acceptance procedures.[89] These include the verification of identity through the presentation of ID documentation usually in the form of a passport, together with utility bills to verify address. Other risk factors to be taken into consideration include the geographical location of the client in terms of whether it is categorised as a high-risk country, in addition to whether the client is registered as a PEP.[90] KYC is frequently also referred to as Business Entity Profiling. A business entity can be an individual account holder or a corporation. The profiling is based on a decision as to whether that 'business entity' is high or low risk, which is determined predominantly by checking which country they are operating from, as well as their transactional history. Further basic due diligence procedures

85 Ibid. SYSC 3.2.6G.

86 The role of the MLRO within a firm is to act as the focal point for all activity within the firm relating to AML. SYSC 3.2.6J 01/03/2006 http://fsahandbook.info/FSA/html/focus-on-FCRMAML/SYSC/3/2.

87 FSA Handbook (n.77) SYSC 3.2.7.

88 Ibid.

89 Kim-Kwang Raymond Choo, 'PEPs risks and mitigation' (2008) 11(4) *Journal of Money Laundering Control* 371.

90 Politically Exposed Person.

are also carried out ensuring that they do not hold a criminal record or on a sanctions list such as HM Treasury Consolidated List of Financial Targets in the UK.

In the case of private banks, KYC requirements are more stringent compared to other retail financial services owing to the perception of higher risk posed as a result of the higher value status of its client base. Additional requirements include due diligence on account holders and underlying beneficial owners, including the establishment of the origin of wealth and source of funds deposited. FSA guidelines stipulate that a key consideration in determining possible suspicion is whether there is clear justification for clients conducting business in a certain way.[91] An important starting point is the purpose and reasons for opening an account. On deciding whether an account should be opened or otherwise, additional factors such as the anticipated account activity, estimated net worth, clients' business and business structures, must be taken into consideration.[92]

Account opening is of crucial importance as the balance of power still lies with the banks to determine whether the client relationship can be safely undertaken.[93] In order to carry out the necessary risk assessment, the FSA Guidance Notes state that relationship managers should record visits to clients' businesses or homes and gather information including changes in client profiles, expectations of product usage, volumes and turnover going forward, together with any international dimension to the client's activities and the risk status of the jurisdictions involved.[94] Once the account has been set up, all that the bank can do is to have the relevant mechanisms in place to monitor the financial activities of that client.

Transaction Monitoring

It is a requirement in the UK that all financial institutions have a system to monitor financial transactions and to report any suspicious activity to the FIU

91 FSA, *Review of Private Banks' Anti-Money Laundering Systems and Controls* (FSA Review, London, July 2007, 16). [Online]. Available at: http://www.fsa.gov.uk/pubs/other/money_laundering/systems.pdf [accessed: 12 April 2010].

92 Ibid.

93 Antoinette Verhage, 'Supply and demand: anti-money laundering by the compliance industry' (2010) 12(4) *Journal of Money Laundering Control* 371.

94 FSA, *Review of Private Banks' Anti-Money Laundering Systems and Controls* (n.91).

in the form of a suspicious activity report (SAR).[95] As a result, most key financial institutions in the UK have invested in advanced monitoring and analytical software such as AML Sentinel, which involves a proactive automated decision-making process allowing the detection and assessment of unusual transactions, which, upon further investigation, can lead to an active response such as the creation and the reporting of suspicious transactions.[96]

The 'intelligent data warehouse' allows individual customer profiles and transaction details to be stored, enabling the financial investigator to apply behavioural models to detect unusual financial behaviour. Factors examined include who they transact with, when and how often they transact, as well as which products they use to transact. In addition, the 'Security Blanket' produces a risk management process enabling additional external factors to be added in the calculation of a 'risk scoring', which in turn leads to an alert generation that can be further interrogated by a financial investigator.[97]

The first stage of the risk-based financial monitoring process begins with financial profiling. Financial profiling takes into consideration factors such as age, profession, known income and expenditure. Other factors such as peer group analysis are used to set parameters indicating normal activity. Financial transactions are then monitored using the rules derived from the financial profiles. Any transactions that fall outside these 'normal' parameters flag up an alert which is subsequently investigated by one of the bank's specialist financial investigators. To elaborate further, transaction monitoring can be divided into automated and manual monitoring. The systems use either 'profiling' or 'rules-based' methods of monitoring financial transactions. Both techniques were designed to identify unusual transactions to produce alerts, which were then investigated manually to determine whether they should be reported to SOCA[98] as suspicious (see Figure 6.1).

95 Trifin J. Roule and Jeremy Kinsell, 'Legislative and bureaucratic impediments to suspicious transaction reporting regimes' (2002) 6(2) *Journal of Money Laundering Control* 151.

96 Matthew H. Fleming, 'Issues in measuring the efficacy of a suspicious activity reports (SARs) regime' (2007) 70 *Amicus Curiae* 9.

97 Michael Levi and John Burrows 'Measuring the impact of fraud in the UK: a conceptual and empirical journey' (2008) 48(3) *British Journal of Criminology* 293.

98 SOCA was the UK FIU until its closure and incorporation into the NSA in June 2011.

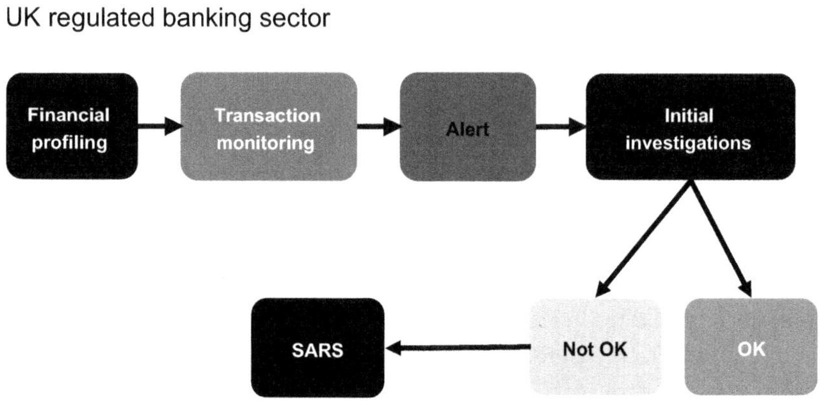

Figure 6.1 Suspicious activity reporting process

Profiling methodologies use statistical techniques to compare recent patterns of transaction activity in terms of volume and value to historic patterns of activity for the same transaction type. In addition, a 'peer group' analysis is applied to determine whether recent activity was 'unusual'.[99] On the other hand, 'rules-based' monitoring methods involve determining whether transactions with particular characteristics[100] exceeded certain absolute thresholds or were within certain fixed ranges,[101] or whether the transactions met relative measures.[102] While these 'relative measures' or 'relational rules' are a form of profiling, they are based on simple arithmetic comparisons, as opposed to the statistical profiling techniques utilised in profiling.[103]

From a CTF risk perspective, numerous concerns exist. First, the customer type needs to be intelligence led. Although intelligence sharing has improved in recent years, it is still far from adequate.[104] In addition, as the financial institutions rely heavily on sanctions lists for due diligence purposes, these lists need to be up to date. Unfortunately, a general complaint from the financial sector is that these lists are often out of date and contain too little information to

99 In other words, over a defined threshold or standard deviation from the norm. See FSA: Review of private banks' (n.91) 24.
100 Such as customer, product, jurisdiction.
101 Such as volume, value and frequency.
102 For example, large volume in comparison to recent account or peer group activity.
103 FSA, *Review of Private Banks' Anti-Money Laundering Systems and Controls* (n.91).
104 Jackie Johnson, 'Third round FATF mutual evaluations indicate declining compliance' (2008) 11(1) *Journal of Money Laundering Control* 47.

be of real use. As such, the more diligent institutions are turning to commercial intelligence companies for the necessary information, at extra cost, resulting in a certain level of resentment for understandable reasons.[105]

The account relationship may also be problematic in that an allegation that proves to be false can lead to litigation at both individual and organisational levels. This is problematic not only for the financial sector, but also for those involved in other professions such as the legal and accountancy professions, as false reporting may not only lead to litigation, but also result in that individual being struck off and unable to practice. It is not surprising therefore, that suspicious activity is frequently not flagged up until more than ample evidence is collected to ensure that the reasons for suspicion can be fully justified.

However, this cautious approach, however understandable, is problematic as it prevents a proactive approach needed as part of the 'Prevent' strand of the overall counter-terrorism effort. The main usefulness of SARs are to provide an early warning system, which it clearly fails to do as it exposes those who produce the reports to a high level of risk, whilst at the same time not providing any protection for at least attempting to contribute to the counter finance effort.[106] As such, the 'two sticks and no carrot' approach, referring to a situation whereby one is punished for not reporting by the authorities, but equally punished for reporting by the accused party, whilst at the same time not being rewarded for any efforts made, appears rather harsh. This is particularly the case bearing in mind the cost incurred by the financial sector to ensure compliance.

The Cost of Compliance

The financial expenditures made by financial institutions in order to comply with both AML and CTF requirements have been considerable, especially in the aftermath of 9/11. One example is a process known as 'remediation', whereby financial institutions are required to conduct a check of all existing customers in their databases to verify personal information, as well as to check names against sanctions lists. According to KPMG,[107] such a process can cost a large multinational bank between £20m and £30m. Although there is increasing emphasis on this process in the US, in the UK, the regulators downgraded

105 Fleming, 'Issues in measuring the efficacy of a SARs regime' (n.96).
106 Roule and Kinsell (n.95) 151.
107 KPMG is a global accountancy firm.

the requirement to a recommendation on grounds of cost after several retail banks had undergone the process.[108] However, by the time the process was downgraded, the large majority of banks had already carried out their remediation process and, as the process was originally a one-off requirement; the downgrade in many ways was meaningless. Furthermore, the downgrade has not impacted on expenditure to meet ongoing regulatory requirements in the field of AML and CTF.

The monitoring of all financial transactions and the requirement to provide SARs to SOCA requires considerable ongoing expenditure in terms of the maintenance of sophisticated databases and analysis software, as well as personnel. The total cost to financial institutions of complying with CTF regulations is difficult to determine, partly because many institutions tackle the issue in tandem with money laundering, although the British Banking Association (BBA) estimates that banks in Britain spend approximately £250m each year to comply with regulations on money laundering and terrorist finance combined.[109] However, the huge investment in countering the threat does not necessarily equate to effective prevention. Many argue that this has resulted in the over-regulation of the financial sector leading to a climate where financial institutions are more concerned with regulatory risk management as opposed to tackling the risks associated with financial crime.

The debate of over-regulation set aside, much of the financial sector's expenditure is on monitoring transactions for the purpose of detecting suspicious activity. The cost would not be such a bitter pill to swallow, if it was not for the fact that the SARs produced for the purpose of detecting terrorist finances were so questionable.

Suspicious Activity Reports (SARs)

Whenever criminals come into contact with the financial system, they can generate vital clues that can lead to their disruption and apprehension.[110]

108 'Financing terrorism – Looking in the wrong places', *The Economist* (20 October 2005). [Online]. Available at: http://economist.com/displaystory.cfm?story_id=5053373 [accessed: 12 March 2010].

109 There is evidence to support the claims made by the British Bankers Association, see Fleming (n.95) 18. KPMG, however, estimated that the costs to business on an annual basis are nearer £60 million. 'The lost trail efforts to combat the financing of terrorism are costly and ineffective', *The Economist* (London, 22 October 2005) 13.

110 Fleming, 'Issues in measuring the efficacy of a suspicious activity reports (SARs) regime' (n.96).

To maximise the impact of this financial intelligence, the UK's AML and CTF measures require financial institutions to know their customers, keep proper records and report suspicious activity.[111] Furthermore, an individual or organisation who suspects that an offence has been committed under the TA 2000 is legally required to complete a SAR.

SARs can provide an essential pool of financial intelligence and place the private sector in the forefront of the fight against terrorism. SARs, also known as 'disclosures', contribute intelligence to existing law enforcement operations, identify the proceeds of crime, and initiate investigation into previously unknown criminal activities. Unusual or suspicious activities can also be identified not only through the monitoring of transactions, but also through monitoring customer contacts, such as meetings, discussions and in-country visits, as well as third party information such as newspapers, the Internet as well as vendor databases.[112] Knowledge of the client's environment in terms of an understanding of the political situation in their home country may further contribute to its analysis.[113]

In the aftermath of the 9/11 attacks, attempts to clamp down on terrorist finance initially resulted in a veritable flood of data on customer transactions deemed to be suspicious. In the US, from inception of the SAR requirement in April 1996 through to June 2003, a total of 1,126,488 SARs were filed, with the volume of filings increasing from 52,069 during 1996 to 273,823 in 2002.[114] According to Dillon of KPMG, the total number of SARs filed in the US more than tripled between 2001 and 2004, surpassing 685,000 in 2004, reflecting the impact of the 9/11 attacks on SARs.[115] However, when examining the actual number of SARs filed each quarter, as opposed to looking at the cumulative figures to date, the increase in volume in the immediate aftermath of the attacks represents an 'emotional' response by the financial institutions.

---

111 Roule and Kinsell, 'Legislative and bureaucratic impediments to suspicious transaction reporting regimes' (n.95) 151.

112 Until April 2006, this role was undertaken by NCIS and handed over SOCA, which in turn faced closure in June 2011 to be incorporated into the newly formed National Crime Agency. Review of the SARs Regime (London: SOCA, 2006, 5. For a detailed commentary on what amounts to suspicion in such instances see The Law Society, *The Guide to the Professional Conduct of Solicitors 1999* (London: The Law Society, 1999), Annexe 3B. Blank SAR forms can be downloaded from the home page of the SOCA at www.soca.gov.uk.

113 FSA, *Review of Private Banks' Anti-Money Laundering Systems and Controls* (n.91) 25.

114 International Narcotics Control Strategy Report – 2003 (Bureau for International Narcotics and Law Enforcement Affairs, March 2004). [Online]. Available at: http://www.state.gov/p/inl/rls/nrcrpt/2003/vol2/html/29910.htm [accessed: 23 January 2010].

115 'Financing terrorism', *The Economist* (n.108).

Furthermore, of the 69 financial institutions, including five foreign banks licensed to conduct business in the US; three banks filed 155 of the 290 SARs.[116] Although the response is understandable in that these banks had provided a service to at least one of the 19 hijackers and needed to be seen to be contributing towards the 'financial war on terror', the over-cautious approach by these banks have a negative impact on detecting possible genuine suspicious activity for several reasons. First, volume does not necessarily equate to quality. The deluge of poor-quality data simply adds to the workload of law enforcement agencies without increasing the possibility of detecting something that is worthwhile. In other words, it simply wastes police time.

It is also relevant to note that the over provision of data is a popular method used by unscrupulous financial institutions to hide genuinely suspicious transactions. By appearing to comply with relevant regulations, the institutions file numerous SARs on transactions which are unlikely to be criminal in nature. The effect is to put investigators off the scent, allowing genuinely suspicious transactions to go unnoticed.

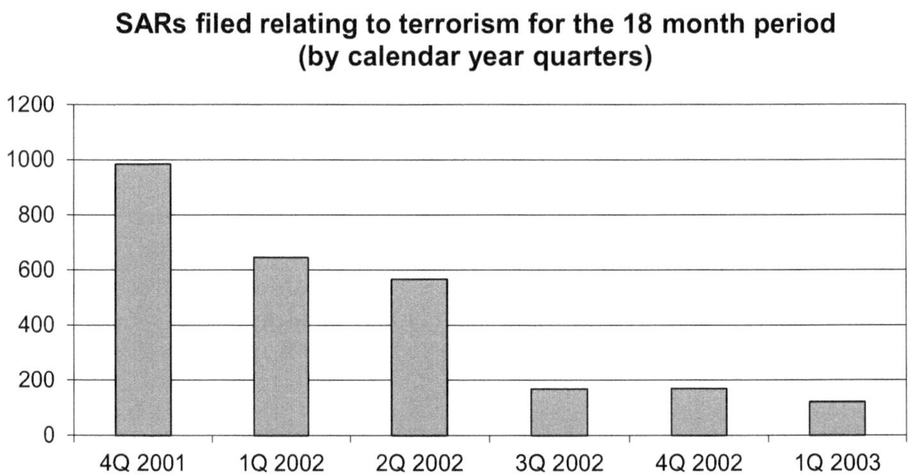

Figure 6.2 SARs related to terrorism in 2001 and 2002

116 This represented 53.4 percent of the terrorism related SARs filed during the period 1 October 2002 and 31 March 2003. See International Narcotics Control Strategy Report (n.114).

A review carried out by FINCEN[117] in the US in 2003[118] into SARs submitted in the US further identified several interesting trends. For example, the number of SARs submitted by financial institutions reporting suspected terrorism or terrorist financing began to decline steadily after the initial increase following 9/11, as can be seen in Figure 6.2, further supporting the view of an emotional response. FINCEN also reported that 290 SARs were filed between 1 October 2002 and 31 March 2003 referencing terrorism.[119] A third of the SARs reported[120] were based on matches of names on the Office of Foreign Asset Control's (OFAC) list of Specially Designated Nationals and Blocked Persons, the USA PATRIOT Act's Section 314(a) Information Requests from law enforcement, or names gleaned from media reports, as well as subpoenas issued by law enforcement.[121]

However, the large majority, representing the remaining two-thirds of all SARs were filed based on other grounds. FINCEN reported that some of the additional submission appeared to have been based on proactive initiatives by institutions. However, other explanations are also possible. There is a general recognition that financial institutions have become more aware of possible indicators of financial activity and transactions by suspected terrorists and terrorist organisations. The result is that they are no longer solely dependent on official lists. The reason for this proactive behaviour is twofold. First, some of the financial institutions are clearly committed to the prevention of terrorism and are keen to do everything in their power to prevent the financing of terrorism. The second relates to the aforementioned inadequacy of the official lists and for regulatory risk management purposes.

To elaborate further, the main criticism has and continues to be that the lists provided by official sources are more often than not, outdated. As such, institutions are forced to seek proactive measures to comply with various legal and regulatory requirements by turning elsewhere for information that may provide indications as to whether an individual or organisation may be involved in terrorism.[122] These alternative sources include private financial intelligence companies involved in the provision of terrorist related financial intelligence, as well as public sources such as the media.

117 The US Department of the Treasury established the Financial Crimes Enforcement Network in 1990 to provide a government-wide multi-source financial intelligence and analysis network. See FINCEN website accessed 8 January 2011 http://www.fincen.gov/about_fincen/wwd/.

118 International Narcotics Control Strategy Report 2003 (n.114).

119 Alleged suspicious activity amounts ranged up to $193 million.

120 More specifically 84 SARs representing 29 percent of terrorist related SARs filed.

121 International Narcotics Control Strategy Report 2003 (n.114).

122 Roule and Kinsell, 'Legislative and bureaucratic impediments to suspicious transaction reporting regimes' (n.95).

Another concern is that the increase in the volume of reporting did not necessarily represent an increase in threat from terrorist finance. Although the criteria used by the financial institutions to file the reports appear sensible, the sudden increase in SARs in the first quarter of the attacks, followed by three continual declines and the subsequent stabilisation at the mid 100 levels, indicate that the aforementioned accusation of an emotional response by the financial sector can indeed be justified. The situation in the UK was not dissimilar.

In the UK, approximately 250,000 SARs were filed in 2005, three-fifths of which originated from banks. This again represents a considerable increase compared to 13,000 reported in 2000 and 31, 251 reported in 2001.[123] However, the BBA estimates that only 3 to 4 per cent of the SARs filed in Britain involve terrorist financing.[124] Although this is only a small percentage, some have suggested that these reports have contributed to the fight against terrorist finance and terrorism in the UK in general.[125] At the same time, there are many practitioners who dispute this. However, whether the cost of expenditure to date by the private sector can be justified, has been, and continues to be a heavily debated topic.[126] It seems appropriate therefore, to assess the effectiveness of the SARs regime to date.

EFFECTIVENESS OF THE SARS REGIME

The cost of compliance to the financial institutions would in many ways be more tolerable if investment could be directly translated into effectiveness. However, the effectiveness of the existing suspicious activity reporting regime has been questioned in a number of areas. The UKFIU, for example, states that it is neutral as to whether increases or decreases in SARs are positive or negative.[127] In other words, one cannot take comfort in the fact that the volume of reporting has increased. Furthermore, there is evidence that some suspicious activities go unreported.

123 BBA, 'One Year On from September 11 – why banks are key to leading the attack on terrorist finance' (30 August 2002). [Online]. Available at: http://www.bba.org.uk/bba/jsp/polopoly.jsp?d=222&a=683 [accessed: 27 January 2010].

124 'Financing terrorism', *The Economist* (n.108).

125 David Chaikin, 'How effective are suspicious transaction reporting systems?' (2009) 12(3) *Journal of Money Laundering Control* 238.

126 Araujo, 'Assessing the efficiency of the anti-money laundering regulation: an incentive-based approach' (n.72).

127 SOCA, The SARs Regime Annual Report 2009, 14.

In addition, it can be argued that although the number of SARs may have increased, the volume of reports does not necessarily reflect the quality of the reports produced, especially in relation to terrorist finance. In fact, the deluge of SARs, giving the impression of compliance to the relevant authorities, has been known to be used to mask genuinely suspicious transactions.[128]

A number of studies have also questioned the effectiveness of the SARs regime.[129] A 2003 study by KPMG identified a number of deficiencies with the reporting requirements.[130] The report made a series of recommendations aimed at improving the monitoring of law enforcement outcomes and the provision of training.[131] The Lander Review noted that since the publication of the KPMG Report:

> *... progress has been made ... but the concerns that led to the commission of the KPMG review have remained.*[132]

Fleming also noted that, despite an improvement in the SAR regime following the KPMG review, SARs were still under-used by law enforcement agencies in the UK.[133] Fleming criticised the regime because law enforcement bodies continue to have poor management information on how SARs are utilised.[134] A Cabinet Office Report also criticised the SARs regime claiming that:

> *... no records are kept of the quality of disclosures in the United Kingdom or the extent to which they have assisted law enforcement in prosecuting either money laundering or predicate offences.*[135]

Lord Carlile, in his annual report on the operation of the TA 2000, also commented that:

128 Araujo, 'Assessing the efficiency of the anti-money laundering regulation: an incentive-based approach' (n.72).
129 M.H. Fleming, *UK Law Enforcement Agency Use and Management of SARs: Towards Determining the Value of the Regime* (London: Home Office, 2005).
130 KPMG, *Money Laundering: Review of the Reporting System* (London, 2003), 14 at para.2.3.1.
131 Ibid.
132 SOCA, *Review of the SARs Regime* (SOCA, 2006) 5.
133 Fleming, *UK Law Enforcement Agency Use and Management of* SARs (n.129).
134 Ibid.
135 Cabinet Office, *The UK and the Campaign against International Terrorism – Progress Report* (Cabinet Office, London, 2002) 24.

> *... there are concerns in the business sector about difficulties of compliance and the serious consequences that may flow from this.*[136]

It has also been argued that the reporting requirements under the ATCSA 2001 are difficult to understand and that they are simply not working. Furthermore, some commentators have argued that the reporting requirements should be abandoned and those resources should be redirected elsewhere to combat terrorist finances.[137] Others have taken the view that the only feasible application for the data is for post event analysis to trace networks that sustain terrorist movements.[138] As true as this may be, as the purpose of SARs is to act as a pre-event warning, this view further supports the opinion that the current SARs regime needs to be improved.

A further concern from a CTF perspective is that SARs may be more helpful in the detection of suspicious financial activity for non-terrorist related crimes. Within the UK, the Asset Recovery Working Group, in conjunction with the UKFIU matches the names of individuals with outstanding confiscations held on the Joint Asset Recovery Database (JARD) against ELMER. This has led to the identification of over 500 SARs which were received after the date of the confiscation order and therefore of potential value.[139] Similarly a matching exercise on data on organised crime groups from the Association of Chief Police Officers in Scotland (ACPOS) successfully identified over nine hundred relevant reports and demonstrated the potential value of SARs for an ACPOS Organised Crime Mapping Project.[140]

However, the potential of the utility of SARs is far from being reached.[141] This view was supported by a report published by the House of Lords Select Committee on the EU in July 2009 on its findings from its inquiry into money laundering and the financing of terrorism. The Committee's remit was to examine international cooperation to counter money laundering and the financing of terrorism. The government, including the UKFIU, was scrutinised as part of the inquiry and a certain number of the Committee's recommendations

136 Home Office, *Report on the Operation in 2004 of the Terrorism Act 2000.* (Home Office, London, 2004) 19–20. For similar criticisms of the SARs regime see J. Wadsley, 'Banks in a bind: the implications of the money laundering legislation' (2001) 16(5) *Journal of International Banking Law* 125 and R. Jones, 'Money laundering: some changes in prospect' (2004) 25 *Company Lawyer* 323.

137 'The lost trail-efforts to combat the financing of terrorism are costly and ineffective', *The Economist* (London, 22 October 2005).

138 Ibid.

139 SOCA, *The SARs Regime Annual Report 2009* (n.127) 21.

140 Ibid.

141 Chaikin, 'How effective are suspicious transaction reporting systems?' (n.125) 238.

were directed at the SARs regime. Recommendations included suggestions for potential improvement, including the burden on the private sector and providing more feedback to industry.[142]

In response, SOCA's Annual Plan for 2009/10 set out an objective of the reformed SARs regime of allowing greater value to be extracted from SARs data by law enforcement end users. The plan stated its objective[143] as attempting to increase the contribution of SARs to the prevention and detection of money laundering and terrorist financing, and increasing their contribution to asset recovery activity; and increasing the contribution of SARs to reducing the harm of crime and terrorism.[144]

This was to be achieved by focusing on four aims, namely through ensuring that the appropriate SARs were submitted by the full range of reporting sectors, the maximisation of the use of information provided by reporters to understand, prevent and detect crime and terrorism and recover criminal assets, the enhancement of the technical capabilities and experience of reporters and end users, as well as the improvement of the governance and transparency of the regime. The report also made four recommendations.

The first was to intensify the dialogue with the private sector including increased levels of case by case feedback, second, to conduct a cost/benefit analysis of the SARs regime, third, that consideration should be given to amending the POCA 2002 to include a *de minimis* exclusion; and finally that the Information Commissioner should review and report on the operation and use of the ELMER database.[145]

Working in reverse order, the Commissioner completed his review in 2010 and reported his findings to the Committee in January 2011. The Committee expressed its concerns that access, either directly or indirectly, to the ELMER database[146] remained 'too wide'. The Commissioner's review also noted doubts about the justification of reporting transactions with very low levels of suspicion, and maintained the overall view that the reporting of suspicious activity in ELMER was disproportionate, and that if too much information was collated on low levels of suspicion, that the process would be devalued as a

142 SOCA, *SARs Regime Annual Report 2009* (n.127) 8.
143 To be achieved within three years.
144 SOCA, *SARs Regime Annual Report 2009* (n.127) 33.
145 Ibid. 32.
146 The ELMER database holds detailed personal records involving over 1.5 million suspicious activities.

result.[147] Furthermore, the Information Commissioner's report is believed to justify the Committee's view that the ELMER database is not fully compliant with the Data Protection and the Human Rights Act.[148]

With reference to the possible amendment to POCA 2002 in relation to the inclusion of a *de minimis* exclusion, although the general *de minimis* limit for those businesses with less than €15,000 VAT-exclusive turnover per annum was suggested in the consultation,[149] no affirmative action has since been taken. It was also noted that the response to the suggestion was mixed, with Banks and accountants generally in favour of the existing approach.[150]

In terms of the cost/benefit analysis of the SARs regime, HM Treasury's report published in June 2011 entitled 'Review of the Money Laundering Regulations 2007: June 2011 the Government response' did provide some analysis into the matter. The Government's assessment was that overall, the Regulations were effective and proportionate at an aggregate level, but that the risk to the UK from money laundering and terrorist financing 'remained significant'. The report also recognised the regulatory burdens on businesses and highlighted several existing inadequacies especially in relation to regulatory guidance, which some stakeholders found to be 'too lengthy, and at times unhelpfully vague'.[151] However, any meaningful analysis of the cost/benefit of the SARs has yet to be produced.

Finally, the need to intensify the dialogue with the private sector including increased levels of case by case feedback has become somewhat of an on-going mantra. However, given the current economic climate, even given the best intent, it is unlikely that any effective dialogue can be developed in the near future given the resources in both the private and public sectors. Furthermore, there are numerous issues which currently act as bottleneck to successful public/private sector collaboration, which will be examined in more depth in the proceeding chapter.

147 'Concerns remain over data protection at SOCA' 21 January 2011 [Online] Available at http://www.wired-gov.net/wg/wg-news1.nsf/0/A58DC446249263C08025781F002BB9EB?OpenDocument [accessed: 26 May 2012]

148 Parliament House of Lords European Union Committee, 'Money laundering: data protection for suspicious activity reports report 6th report of session 2010-11', House of Lords papers 82 2010-11, TSO (The Stationery Office) [Online] Available at http://www.tsoshop.co.uk/bookstore.asp?Action= Book&ProductId=9780108472992 [accessed: 26 May 2012]

149 HM Treasury, 'Government publishes consultation on changes to Money Laundering Regulations 2007' 7 June 2011, [Online] Available at http://www.hm-treasury.gov.uk/press_55_11.htm [accessed: 26 May 2012]

150 Review of the Money Laundering Regulations 2007: June 2011, the Government response [Online] Available at http://www.hm-treasury.gov.uk/d/consult_money_launder_regs2007_gov_response.pdf [accessed: 26 May 2012]

151 Ibid., p7

Conclusions

Various powers now exist to counter the financing of terrorism. For example, the UK's terrorist asset-freezing powers publicly identify suspected individuals and groups linked to terrorism. These powers also freeze any existing assets and disable terrorists' ability to raise or move further funds. As such, recent legislation relating to terrorism finance that has permitted the implementation of these powers were examined.

The Asset Freezing Unit[152] was by up by HM Treasury to increase the expertise and operational focus that the government is able to bring to bear in this area, enabling the UK to be more effective and proactive in freezing assets of suspected terrorists and facilitators. By the end of September 2008, a total of 252 separate accounts used by suspected terrorists and containing over £670,000 were frozen in the UK through the Treasury's AFU.[153] The TA 2000 created specific terrorist finance offences and there have been five convictions since 2006 including the radical preacher Omar Brooks,[154] who was convicted of raising money to support terrorism in Iraq.[155]

The detection of potential suspicious activities is carried out by the intelligence agencies as well as the financial institutions. The financial institutions are obliged to monitor and report any suspicious transactions in the form of SARs for further investigation by FIUs of that country. It is therefore critical that the financial institutions have sufficient information on the nature of the threat to enable them to adopt a risk-based approach to their implementation of money laundering and terrorist finance requirements. Unfortunately, this is something that they presently do not have.

It is also necessary to be realistic about expectations by understanding the limitations of such measures. The government claims that it is leading the international community's attempt to prevent and detect the financing of terrorism. HM Treasury declared that CTF measures introduced since 2001 have prevented some terrorist attacks,[156] and the UK legislative response towards the

152 Set up in October 2007.

153 Home Office, CONTEST Strategy 2 (n.14) 77.

154 AKA Abu Izadeem, born Trevor Brooks. See Dominic Casciani, 'Radical preacher released early', BBC (6 May 2009). [Online]. Available at: http://news.bbc.co.uk/1/hi/uk/8035827.stm [accessed: 14 February 2011].

155 Home Office, CONTEST Strategy 2 (n.14) 77.

156 HM Treasury, Pre-budget Report 2005.

prevention of terrorist finances has been described as vigorous.[157] Furthermore, the IMF has concluded that the UK has a strong legislative regime to prevent terrorist finances, but also warned that there was room for improvement.[158]

However, Binning took the view, that whether the measures will be effective is somewhat debatable.[159] After all, neither the TA 2000 nor the ATCSA 2001 was able to prevent the terrorist attacks in London on July 7, 2005. Irrespective of any representations that the UK legislative response towards the prevention of terrorist financing is working, their overall effectiveness must be questioned. What makes it impossible for laws to prevent such atrocities is that many of the terrorist cells are self-financing, and are thus beyond the scope of any specific domestic or international legislation.[160] It can be argued that the fight against terrorist finance in the UK requires more than just legislation.[161]

Numerous concerns have been highlighted in this chapter not simply in relation to the SARs regime but in relation to the disruption of terrorist finances in general. Some of the challenges have already been touched upon, but need to be elaborated further. Chapter 7 devotes its attention to understanding the key challenges that need to addressed, which in turn will form the basis of the conclusion and recommendations in the final chapter.

157 HM Treasury, *Combating the financing of terrorism – A report on UK, October 2002*, 27 [Online]. Available at: http://www.hm-treasury.gov.uk/Documents/International_Issues/terrorist_financing/int_terrorfinance_combatfinance.cfmp [accessed: 20 October 2009].

158 International Monetary Fund, UK: Financial System Stability Assessment including Reports on the Observance of Standards and Codes on the following topics: Banking Supervision, Insurance Supervision, Securities Regulation, Payment Systems, Monetary and Financial Transparency, Securities Settlement Systems, and Anti-Money Laundering and Countering Terrorist Financing (Washington: International Monetary Fund, 2003) 99.

159 P. Binning, 'In safe hands? Striking the balance between privacy and security-anti-terrorist finance measures' (2002) 6 *European Human Rights Law Review* 737. See also J. Johnson, '11th September, 2001: will it make a difference to the global anti-money laundering movement?' (2002) 6(1) *Journal of Money Laundering Control* 10.

160 Joynt, 'The bombers' money trail', *BBC* (London, 18 July 2005) See also J. Patrick, 'Tricks of the terrorist finance trade' (London 18 July 2005).

161 In February 2006, Gordon Brown announced that the government was to publish a consultation paper aimed protecting terrorists from abusing wire transfers and charities; secondly, to encourage greater co-operation between HM Treasury and the financial services sector so that they can prevent the use of financial networks to advance terrorism; thirdly, the creation of new multilateral arrangements to strengthen the pre-emptive asset freezing regime under Pt II of the ATCSA 2001. See Chancellor of the Exchequer speeches 11/06, HM Treasury, 13 February 2006, 'Securing our Future'. [Online]. Available at: www.hm-treasury.gov.uk [accessed: 20 January 2011].

7

Addressing Key Challenges

... I have seen the enemy and he is us

Walter Crawford Kelly (Jr)[1]

Overview

The previous chapter examined a number of ways in which the interdiction of terrorist funds and associated criminal property can occur. In addition, the numerous improvements made in tackling adversary finances, both in terms of legislation and regulation to date has been highlighted. At the same time, the effectiveness of these efforts has also been questioned. Although it is important to recognise the achievements made to date, especially since 9/11, it is necessary to embrace the unpalatable truth, that these efforts have not had a huge impact upon terrorist and related criminal funding. As such, the situation requires a fundamental rethink in the way the threat is countered.

It is also clear that a better understanding of the subject of financial crime is necessary throughout the stakeholder community. According to Nick Kochan, author of a recent book on financial crime,[2] the British government has failed to invest in sufficiently skilled law enforcement personnel or regulators to police its large financial sector.[3] In addition, there is a need to move away from individualistic to a network centric understanding and approach where individual nodes of that broader network are familiar with the 'bigger picture'. More specifically, what Kochan is referring to is the need to understand the challenge not only in terms of one's own specific area of responsibly, but also

1 Jeffrey Robinson, *The Sink: How Banks, Lawyers and Accountants finance Terrorism and Crime and why the Government can't stop them* (Robinson 2004) 325.

2 Nick Kochan, *The Washing Machine: Money, Crime and Terror in the Offshore System* (Duckworth 2006).

3 J. Loden, 'The Need for an Ideological Response to Islamic Extremism' (MSc Diss., Cranfield University, DCMT, 2005).

as part of the overall network of activity relating to terrorist finance and related enterprise crime.

It is important of course to perform one's own specific duties to the best of one's abilities, whether as an intelligence analyst, law enforcement investigator, prosecutor, judge or compliance officer. However, this individualistic approach alone is no longer adequate in attempting to tackle the threat.

The term 'interdisciplinary' and the need to break down 'silos' have entered the popular vocabulary of the counter-terrorism community in recent years. This is undoubtedly a positive move. However, often the problem is that many are uncertain as to how to make this a reality. The emergence of cross governmental agencies is promising and has undoubtedly moved understanding in the right direction in addition to breaking down organisational cultures that alienate each of the silos from each other. However, the understanding needs to go even deeper and the complexity of interdisciplinary relationships need to be better appreciated. A network of potential threat finance specialists already exists to some extent, but the network is disjointed. To unify this group begins with the acknowledgement of the various sectors of the counter terrorist finance (CTF) community. There is also a further need to understand the challenges that each face to see whether a support network infrastructure can be set up of mutual benefit. To that end, some of the key challenges facing both the private sector and public sectors will be examined.

The challenges covered include those affecting the financial sector, the government and law enforcement community, as well as the judiciary. Efforts in the financial sector will be explored first, examining a number of specific problems that need to be addressed, namely account opening procedures and financial profiling methodologies. Next, some issues that affect both the private and public sectors will be explored under the headings of private/public sector collaboration, data deluge and the measurement of success. This will be followed by the key challenges affecting the judiciary, to include the use of intercept material, secret evidence and the use of financial experts as expert witnesses, as well as legislative challenges posed by the existence of human rights legislation, which periodically challenge the legality of counter-terrorism legislation. Finally, a discussion on the international dimension that allows the challenges to be viewed from a global perspective will conclude the chapter.

Account Opening Procedures

The previous chapter elaborated on the existing regulatory requirements, focusing on the need for financial institutions to carry out due diligence in the form of Know Your Customer (KYC) procedures, prior to accepting an individual or organisation as a client. It should be further noted that the requirement applies not only to banks prior to the opening of a bank account, but extends to other sectors to include estate agents, as well as legal and accountancy firms, which also play a key role in the prevention of terrorist and other criminal finance.[4]

The documentation typically required for this purpose falls into one of two categories. The first is in relation to the individual, who is the potential client, where formal documentation is required in the form of a photo ID to prove that he or she is the individual he or she claims to be. This requirement is satisfied on production of a passport or a driving licence which is in date and contains a recent photograph of the individual. The second requirement is in relation to proof of address, which can be satisfied on presentation of an original, as opposed to a photocopy of a household utility bill. An original utility bill such as telephone, water, gas or electricity in the holder's name, must be produced.[5] Once the member of staff examining the documentation is satisfied, a photocopy can then be taken to be kept as proof that the correct account opening procedures were followed.[6]

The requirements in themselves are straight forward. However, two specific challenges exist which can be described in terms of an internal threat and an external threat. To begin with the latter, the presentation of forgeries by criminals is problematic. Furthermore, the increasing sophistication of the forgeries presented exacerbates the problem.

In addition, globalisation has resulted in the need for staff to serve non-UK citizens with foreign passports more frequently. As the forgers are located throughout the world, not only does the member of staff examining the

4 Antoinette Verhage, 'Supply and demand: anti-money laundering by the compliance industry' (2010) 12(4) *Journal of Money Laundering Control* 371.
5 If the individual is not the utility account holder, for example is a tenant or the account is held in the name of a partner or spouse, the utility bill will still be acceptable provided that it is accompanied by the letter from the utility account holder confirming that the address resides at that address with an explanation of the relationship.
6 David Chaikin, 'How effective are suspicious transaction reporting systems?' (2009) 12(3) *Journal of Money Laundering Control* 238.

documentation need to be familiar with what a genuine passport looks like from each of those countries, he or she also needs to be familiar with as many of the known 'fake' passports, so that they are able to distinguish between a genuine and a forged passport or driving licence.

An additional problem is in keeping up with the developing technologies of modern passports. Many countries now issue e-passports which contain biometric features in an attempt to counter fraud. All passports issued in the UK are now 'biometric'[7] where the chip inside the passport contains biometric data as well as information printed on the personal details page of the passport, which can then be read electronically to identify the passport-holder.[8] Furthermore, these technologies are continuously updated in order to attempt to keep pace with emerging security threats.

For example, the latest new design for the British passport was revealed by the Home Office in October 2010.[9] The improvements included a change in the location of the RFID chip,[10] making it less visible and better physically protected where an attempt to tamper with the chip will not only be more difficult, but also more noticeable. In addition, the personal details page was moved from the rear of the passport to the second page, with a new laminate transparent coating containing a number of holograms for added security. However, the addition of such 'Hi-tech' biometric passports used by Britain and other countries does not guarantee security.[11]

There is evidence that many have been hacked by computer experts, throwing into doubt fundamental parts of the UK's £415m scheme to load passports with information such as fingerprints, facial scans and iris patterns.[12]

7 Biometric details are those which are unique to the individual such as fingerprint, the iris and facial features.

8 UK Direct Government website, 'What are biometric passports?' [Online]. Available at: http://www.direct.gov.uk/en/TravelAndTransport/Passports/Applicationinformation/DG_174159 [accessed: 12 April 2010].

9 From October 2010, anyone issued a passport will receive a revamped version with enhanced security features that protect against fraud.

10 Radio-frequency identification (RFID) is a technology that uses communication through the use of radio waves to transfer data between a reader and an electronic tag attached to an object for the purpose of identification and tracking.

11 Ben Schouten and Bart Jacobs, 'Biometrics and their use in e-passports' (2009) 27(3) *Image and Vision Computing, Special Issue on Multimodal Biometrics* – Multimodal Biometrics Special Issue 305.

12 Bobbie Johnson, 'Hackers crack new biometric passports', *e Guardian* (7 August 2006). [Online]. Available at: http://www.guardian.co.uk/technology/2006/aug/07/hacking.security [accessed: 10 January 2011].

According to Lukas Grunwald, a consultant with a German security company,[13] a method for cloning the information stored in the new passports had been discovered whereby data can be transferred onto blank chips, which could then be implanted into fake passports, a flaw which undermines the entire project.[14] Despite these challenges, most experts feel that the use of technology to counter such crimes is of benefit. However, there is a more fundamental threat that also needs to be addressed, that of tackling the threat from within.

The insider threat is an unpalatable reality.[15] The task of checking documents is usually carried out by employees who are relatively unskilled and low paid. This is problematic for several reasons. First, the 'unskilled' factor may contribute to their inability to identify complex forgeries. Second, the high turnover, which is characteristic of these types of employees, usually results in the fact that the provision of training to attempt to arm them with the necessary skills is not always possible as they may not be around long enough to participate in various in-house training programmes.[16] Another concern which has been expressed by experts is that low pay may lead to a lack of motivation as well as susceptibility to bribery compared to their more qualified and better remunerated counterparts, who are likely to hold more permanent positions.

This lack of motivation coupled with the knowledge that they may not be employed for a long duration of time may encourage those individuals to take the risk of bribery. This could be in the form of either actively participating in criminal activity or simply by turning a blind eye to forged documents in the knowledge that by the time that the documents have been identified as fraudulent, they will probably no longer be working for that organisation. Furthermore, the audit trail may be made deliberately vague so that any future investigation will prove that the available evidence, or rather the lack of it, is inconclusive to the extent that the organisation is unlikely to be able to take the necessary action against its former employee or contractor.

A further concern is that the task of checking documentation for KYC purposes is sometimes carried out by front line sales staff, whose main motivation is to reach their sales targets. In addition, their salaries or promotion

13 Speaking at the Defcon security conference in Las Vegas, 2006.
14 Johnson, 'Hackers crack new biometric passports' (n.12).
15 Matt Bishop, Sophie Engle, Sean Peisert, Sean Whalen and Carrie Gates, 'Case Studies of an Insider Framework' (HICSS, 42nd Hawaii International Conference on System Sciences, 2009) 1–10.
16 This is also a concern with similar staff working in call centres which have been identified as been abused by criminals to conduct ID theft.

may be linked directly to sales generated, making risks associated with potential financial crime of even less interest. Furthermore, in the event that the KYC procedures were not carried out adequately and the organisation is discovered to have allowed money laundering or the financing of terrorism to take place, it is interesting to note that it is usually the compliance officer or the MLRO, who will be blamed, and perhaps more importantly, risk prosecution by the FSA leading to a significant personal fine. It is not surprising therefore that the checks carried out by non financial crime/compliance staff have often been unsatisfactory. There is clearly a conflict of interest here that needs to be addressed and the attendance of in-house courses on AML and CTF alone do little to make these individuals take the subject of financial crime seriously. Managers, as well as senior members of organisations need to be aware of these issues and ensure that mechanisms are put in place whereby these risks can be minimised.

Financial Profiling

Once the various hurdles of KYC and account opening procedures have been overcome and the account is opened, which in turn enables the account holder to conduct financial activity, the second tier of defence kicks in. This is the monitoring of active accounts in order that any suspicious financial activity can be identified and reported to the relevant authorities.[17] However, many involved in the monitoring of financial transactions claim that financial profiling for the purpose of detecting terrorist finance, simply does not work. One of the issues is the methodology used by the private sector to detect possible terrorist funding.

According to Graham Dillon[18] of KPMG, AML detection technology is focused on identifying suspicious transactions that bear little resemblance to those typically used by terrorists.[19] Another major challenge facing financial institutions relating to terrorist finance is that financial transactions by terrorists appear normal on the surface and are virtually impossible to detect without the help of specific intelligence.[20] For example, a close examination

17 Trifin J. Roule and Jeremy Kinsell, 'Legislative and bureaucratic impediments to suspicious transaction reporting regimes' (2002) 6(2) *Journal of Money Laundering Control* 151.

18 Director, KMPG Forensic.

19 'Financing terrorism: looking in the wrong places', *The Economist* (20 October 2005). [Online]. Available at: http://economist.com/displaystory.cfm?story_id=5053373 [accessed: 20 September 2009].

20 Non-financial intelligence.

of the bank records of the 9/11 hijackers revealed no suspicious patterns.[21] It is also worth noting that the formal banking system was heavily used by the 9/11 hijackers for transferring money. Although the monitoring systems in place today have become more sophisticated compared to the pre-9/11 era, the case of the 9/11 hijackers demonstrates that it is unlikely that the financial transactions made by the hijackers would have been detected as suspicious, even with the sophisticated financial monitoring technology available today. This is predominantly due to the fact that terrorist profiling essentially does not work in isolation. For effective detection to take place, these systems need to be used in conjunction with reliable intelligence. This is where private public sector cooperation becomes essential.

It is also interesting to note that the SARs relating to terrorist finance continue to use profiles matching the modus operandi of the 9/11 hijackers. The financial activities under observation included wire transfers predominantly to and from Middle Eastern countries; frequent use of domestic and foreign ATMs, large currency transactions, as well as payments to flight schools.[22] SARs were also filed based on one or more of the following criteria which the financial institution believed might be associated with terrorist activity such as even dollar deposits followed by like-amount wire transfers, frequent domestic and international ATM activity, no known source of income, and the use of the Internet to move funds to and from high risk countries and geographic locations, frequent address changes, occupation 'student' primarily in flight schools, purchases of military items or technology, and media reports on suspected or arrested terrorists or groups.

Although some of the criteria appear sensible, one has to question the validity of some of the selection criteria, which can only be described as being 'reactive' in nature. Given that it is unlikely that the exact modus operandi will be used to carry out another attack in the immediate future,[23] it may be advisable for financial institutions to take a more proactive approach when choosing their criteria for the selection of suspicious financial activities.[24] At the same time, obtaining such insight is problematic for the private sector

21 Shima D. Keene, *Financing 9/11* (Airey Neave Report, October 2005).

22 US Department of State, *International Narcotics Control Strategy Report 2003*, Bureau for International Narcotics and Law Enforcement Affairs, March 2004. [Online]. Available at: http://www.state.gov/p/inl/rls/nrcrpt/2003/vol2/html/29910.htm [accessed: 20 September 2009].

23 Some may argue the case for a copycat attack; however, the likelihood of al-Qaeda carrying out an identical attack with the identical preparations seem unlikely.

24 Jackie Johnson, 'Third round FATF mutual evaluations indicate declining compliance' (2008) 11(1) *Journal of Money Laundering Control* 47.

as much of the information needed is not publicly available. Such intelligence can only be obtained through sources in law enforcement and the intelligence communities. Even where relationships exist between the two sectors, there are a number of factors that prevent an adequate level of collaboration.

Public/Private Sector Collaboration

The relationship between the public sector and the private sector has long been recognised as being of paramount importance in countering the finances of terrorists and criminals alike. However, many challenges have existed and continue to exist in terms of adequate information sharing. Initial criticism came predominantly from the financial institutions. Banks highlighted the need for better information sharing between the private and public sectors and criticised the quality of the intelligence they were receiving. For example, the financial monitoring department of one major bank was provided with a threat report that warned that the person of interest was last seen taking photographs of a particular building that could be a potential target of a terrorist attack. Due to 'security clearance' issues, the bank was not provided with a name or any other information relating to the individual, which would allow the bank to identify whether he was a customer. The case illustrates a complete lack of understanding by the public sector as to what type of 'intelligence' the private sector requires, which is of concern.

Bridging the 'security clearance' issue continues to be a challenge. Initial exchange programmes between the financial sector and law enforcement for example, proved not to be particularly helpful and demoralising for both parties involved. The main criticism has been that individuals from the private sector seconded into the public sector were almost always not allowed to participate in full and were left with little to do. There is also the additional difficulty of cultural differences leading to mistrust of the private sector, coupled with a lack of understanding as to what intelligence the private sector can provide, which continues to cause the partnership to fail.

However, in recent years, initiatives such as the Vetted Group has contributed to achieving a better information sharing environment without endangering issues of national security.[25] Recent recommendations by SOCA in their 2008 SARs Annual Report stated that more use would be made of Vetted Group

25 The Vetted Group comprises representatives of the reporting sectors and law enforcement. Its aim is to discuss sensitive casework and reporting issues.

members and other trusted partners to quality assure information products.[26] The Vetted Group has also been engaged in a number of SARs-related projects. This has included members carrying out a thematic review looking at the best practice of the accountancy sector in relation to the submission of consent SARs and identifying the quality of reporting in relation to Politically Exposed Persons (PEPs) and corruption.[27]

In October 2008, the UKFIU commissioned KPMG, through the Vetted Group, to carry out a survey to research effective means of communication with small and medium-sized businesses (SMBs). Effective communication with these 'hard to reach' businesses is essential in order to highlight the risks posed by money laundering and organised crime. The resultant research has highlighted a number of issues which have been incorporated into the UKFIU's outreach strategy, and is assisting in raising awareness of the AML Regime.[28] However, it is disappointing that despite these positive steps that the work of the Vetted Group appears to have slowed down considerably resulting in very limited output since early 2010.[29]

It is clear that the importance of the relationship between the public and private sector needs to be strongly emphasised in order that it can be further developed. In addition, much of the contact between the two sectors continues to be reactive in nature as contact is usually initiated by individual enquiries led by law enforcement investigations. From a law enforcement perspective, this is a useful relationship as banks are then able to provide the authorities with the necessary financial intelligence to be used in prosecutions. However, there is clearly further scope for the private sector to play a far more proactive role in countering terrorism and organised crime, provided they can be sufficiently motivated and rewarded.[30]

Measuring Success

The one factor that both the private sector and the public sector have in common is the need to be able to justify their own existence through the

26 SOCA, *The SARs Regime Annual Report 2009*, 19.
27 Ibid. 20.
28 Ibid. 19.
29 Interview with Vetted Group Member Bob Upton, former Head of AML Monitoring, Lloyds, 11 July 2011.
30 Ricardo Azevedo Araujo, 'Assessing the efficiency of the anti-money laundering regulation: an incentive-based approach' (2008) 11(1) *Journal of Money Laundering Control* 67.

ability to illustrate their own effectiveness. The ability to measure success is often fundamental at a number of levels. At an individual level, recognition of success can lead to career development accompanied by financial benefits such as a higher pay grade or bonus, as well as an increase in status. Such recognition also affects departments and entire organisations in that it is likely to impact its future budget, which in turn will affect its operational capability in terms of available resources. Recognition of success and consequent reward, financial or otherwise, will also lead to increase in morale and motivation which is essential, both at individual and organisational levels.

On the other hand, the inability to demonstrate success may endanger the organisation's future existence. However, the problem with counter-terrorism, as well as security in general, is that its purpose is to 'prevent' a criminal activity from occurring. Success in business for example, may be measured through the simple calculation of profit. However, this clearly cannot be applied to counter-terrorism. As the late Professor Paul Wilkinson observed:

> *Fighting terrorism is like being a goalkeeper. You can make a hundred brilliant saves but the only shot that people remember is the one that gets past you.*[31]

From a private sector perspective, departments responsible for CTF activity become a cost centre. From a business point of view, its purpose is preventative in that the *raison d'être* of the department is to ensure that they comply with various legal and regulatory requirements. This is viewed as a necessity predominantly to avoid cost in terms of a financial penalty such as a fine, or loss of income owing to forced suspension of front office activities, or reduced business as a result of damage to its reputation. However, psychologically, being a cost centre has negative connotations in terms of cooperation from front office staff whose interest is to maximise profit. Their relationship inevitably becomes one of tolerance as opposed to a willingness to engage.[32] Compliance officers in particular, are very much seen by front office personnel as 'internal policemen', and are often regarded as people to avoid as they are commonly associated with additional, unnecessary and burdensome work, which will detract from their 'real' work, that of making money. If, on the other hand, legal and compliance departments are able to contribute more positively to business, they may be viewed as a member of the team as opposed to the

31 Paul Wilkinson, *Global Economic Impact*. [Online]. Available at: http://www.icfaiuniversitypress.org/books/TerrorismGlobalEconomic-ovw.asp [accessed: 20 September 2009].

32 Discussions with front-office staff at Barclays Capital, 10–12 March 2010.

enemy, leading to a more constructive relationship. However, this will require a shift in corporate attitudes which, as with any major organisational change project, must be initiated, implemented and supported on an on-going basis, by the highest levels of that organisation.

From a public sector perspective, there are a number of ways to measure success in terms of countering the financing of terrorism. However, these must be viewed with caution. For example, a reward structure can be put in place in recognition of asset seizures. This may provide an incentive for individual officers and departments to confiscate more assets, which can then be translated into a quantifiable factor in the measurement of success. However, the confiscation of assets which may be quantifiable is meaningless unless the figure can be expressed as a ratio or percentage of the overall quantity of criminal assets. After all, a number is simply a number unless it can be put into context, which can only be done as a measure relative to another number.

To elaborate, in cases where more criminal assets are confiscated but the overall number of criminal assets also increases, this is clearly not a good situation. However, if the number of seizures fall, but the number of overall criminal assets fall even lower, this is a good result, as it demonstrates that a higher percentage of criminal assets are being confiscated. However, as the overall figure of criminal assets is unlikely to be known, a partial equation is statistically meaningless.

The use of statistical analysis in such situations is also dangerous for other reasons. For example, the basis of success in operations in Iraq and Afghanistan by the US were often measured in terms of body count of the enemy. Unfortunately, for every combatant killed, a 'martyr' is created, and consequently, several more militants emerge. In other words, it is quite possible that the extra body count, which may be considered to be a positive factor from the US's perspective, has made the situation far worse than before the individual was eliminated.

Furthermore, the morality behind the approach in both examples is also somewhat questionable. Is it necessarily right that public servants should financially benefit either at an individual or organisation level for carrying out their public duty? Would such incentives lead to corruption? It is not the purpose of this publication to further evaluate these concerns. Nevertheless, these are questions that need to be taken into consideration when assessing the overall CTF effort.

Data Deluge

It was only a couple of decades ago that the lack of information and data was seen as being problematic and great efforts were made to attempt to acquire more information.[33] However, the situation has now reversed. The information revolution brought about by advancements in technologies coupled with globalisation, has resulted in excessive data where methods to restrict the data flow has now become a key area of focus.[34] Data deluge is an issue that is affecting the entire globe and is beginning to transform businesses, governments and science, as well as everyday life. According to *The Economist* magazine, mankind created 150 exabytes[35] of data in 2005. In 2010, this figure increased to 1,200 exabytes.[36] Merely keeping up with this flood is challenge enough, yet alone the need to further analyse the data in order to detect patterns, as well as to extract useful information, which becomes harder still.

Against this background, the challenge of those tasked with the identification of possible terrorist funds is vast. To put this challenge into perspective, the bank accounts of more than 5,000 suspected terrorists are being monitored by Britain's biggest financial institutions.[37] This figure is the Security Services' highest estimate yet for the number of British-based individuals suspected of involvement in plotting terrorist attacks. According to senior banking sources, 200 current accounts have recently been frozen as part of the fight against the financing of 'Islamic' terrorism.[38] According to HSBC, in excess of 5,000 UK accounts had been 'flagged up' and monitored as part of evidence-gathering against suspects. In addition, given that each of these individuals will be part of a network, it is essential that activities of the wider network are also monitored. As such, the actual number of financial transactions that need to be monitored on a daily basis is phenomenal.

33 T. Hey and A. Trefethen, 'The Data Deluge: An e-Science Perspective' in F. Berman, G. Fox and T. Hey (eds), *Grid Computing: Making the Global Infrastructure a Reality* (John Wiley & Sons 2003) ch. 36.

34 Gordon Bell, Tony Hey and Alex Szalay, 'Beyond the Data Deluge' (2009) 323 (5919) *Computer Science* 1297.

35 Billion gigabytes.

36 'The data deluge, businesses, governments and society are only starting to tap its vast potential', *The Economist* (25 Feb 2010). [Online]. Available at: http://www.economist.com/node/15579717 [accessed: 10 January 2011].

37 Mark Townsend, 'Bank deals of 5,000 terror suspects tracked', *Observer* (10 September 2006). [Online]. Available at: http://www.guardian.co.uk/terrorism/story/0,,1869045,00.html [accessed: 7 June 2011].

38 Ibid.

A further problem relates to the identification of individuals through their names. The concept of 'name matching' may initially appear fairly straight forward. To use an example of an English name, if the bank account of 'John Smith' is to be identified and monitored, the first step would be to ensure that the correct John Smith has been identified. This could be achieved through first identifying all the John Smiths. Second, additional information such as a mobile telephone number or address could be added to the selection criteria. By eliminating all the John Smiths who do not live at that address, or own that telephone number, the refined search should result in one result, John Smith, the person of interest. However, attempting to use similar tactics to Arabic names is more difficult.

A fundamental problem is that the 'structure' of Arabic names is different compared to their Western equivalent, and the translation into Romanised form can result in several versions of the same name. This further adds to the problem of data deluge as monitoring technologies struggle to identify the individual in question, yet alone his financial transactions. If John Smith had an alias, it is most likely that it is deliberate. With Arab names, even if an individual has several aliases, it is quite possible that in some cases, they are simply translations of the same name, therefore cannot immediate be assumed as being suspicious.

In attempting to identify what is suspicious, one needs to identify what is 'normal' so that a process of elimination can then be applied to be left with what is not normal, therefore suspicious. However, this cannot be achieved if that standard of 'normality' is based upon Western standards when dealing with non-Western issues. As such, a deeper understanding of the cultural differences and its practical application need to be considered.

Cultural Considerations

The lack of understanding of cultural differences and practices has affected, and continues to affect, the efficacy of CTF measures. Two examples will be used to demonstrate the problem. The first example is the language barrier with specific reference to the aforementioned understanding, or rather, the lack of understanding of Arabic names. In countries such as Iraq and Afghanistan, the name also serves as an address. In the Arab world, a name follows a strict pattern through the paternal line. Arabic is a Semitic language which uses a trilateral root system where the unwritten vowels add to the confusion to non-Arabic speakers.

The naming convention of an Arabic name consists of five main components. The first is the first name, which is a personal name given shortly after birth as is the case in the West. Examples include Muhhamad, Ibrahim and Ahmed. The title, which usually describes some admirable quality of the person, or what the person aspires to, is also frequently imbedded into the name and has religious connotations. For example al Hajj refers to the one who has gone on a pilgrimage to Mecca (Sunni) and al Rashid means the rightly guarded.

An additional component is the *Siffa* which describes the occupation of the individual. Examples include al-Haddad, the ironsmith, Jawahirji, the goldsmith, al-Mohandas,[39] the engineer and an-Najar, the carpenter.[40] A *Siffa* can also be geographical or based on the physical features or characteristics of the individual. Examples include al-Suri, the Syrian and al-Misri, the Egyptian, al-Asla, the bald, al-Ashqar, the blond, al-'Amma, the blind, and al-Taweel, the tall. An Arabic name is also able to reveal lineage, geography, political connections, the language spoken, tribal affiliation, ethnicity, religion and occupation, as well as physical characteristics of the individual. If a name is taken literally and translated into a Romanised English format, this will frequently result in confusion. However, if the names are interpreted correctly, it can be used to learn more about the individual compared to a Western name.

However, this requires the willingness to understand different cultures. One problem in countering the finances of terrorists has been the application of Western standards to non-Western countries in general. Measures that work in Western cultures may not necessarily be appropriate in others. For example, many countries in the Middle East and Africa, in particular the economically less developed countries are cash dependent for a variety of reasons. Furthermore, very few people possess bank accounts in developing countries. In such situations, the monitoring of the movement of funds through bank accounts is meaningless. Also, in countries such as Afghanistan, money is not the only currency. In many of the bazaars bartering takes place to buy goods and services paid for using a number of different currencies as well as goods such as agricultural products, an animal such as a goat, hashish or opium. In such situations, a broader understanding of the workings of the local economy coupled with cultural understanding is necessary in order that the most appropriate counter strategies can be applied.

39 UAE: First Name or Title? [Online]. Available at: http://www.executiveplanet.com/index.php?title =United_Arab_Emirates_First_Name_or_Title%3F [accessed: 11 January 2011].

40 Thomas Patrick Hughes, *A Dictionary of Islam: Being a Cyclopaedia of the Doctrines, Rites, Ceremonies, and Customs, Together With the Technical and Theological Terms, of the Muhammadan Religion* (Asian Educational Services, New Delhi India, London 1885) 152.

Organisational Structures and Attitudes

Another element of culture relates not to cultures in the anthropological context, but relating to organisational structures and attitudes. In terms of organisational structure, despite the emergence of cross governmental agencies, the criticism of silo working continues to be problematic. It is no longer appropriate that the various elements of the counter-terrorism community operate in their own individual comfort zones. As challenging as it may be, the battle against terrorism and organised crime must be fought on a level playing field. Secondly, there is a further problem within individual silos in terms of organisational attitude. Kenneth Murray, Head of Forensic Accounting at the Scottish Crime and Drug Enforcement Agency (SCDEA) argues that:

> *... the full potential of POCA 2002 in the fight against Organised Crime is now capable of being realised through pro-active money laundering investigation but that this may require the forging of new attitudes in both Law Enforcement and the Prosecution authorities.*[41]

Although Murray is speaking in relation to narcotics money laundering, the same equally applies to terrorist finance and the wider economic crime environment, where prosecutors and law enforcement need to wean themselves away from the attitude that financial complexity is something to be feared. Some legal minds dislike numbers, and there is an excessive sensitivity to the expected limitations of juries to understand financially based cases. This can at times lead to an almost palpable attitude of defeatism arising whenever cases involving a degree of financial complexity are discussed. The main issue rests not with the complexity of the financial evidence, but the way in which it is presented, where expert witnesses play a key role.

Financial Expertise: The Use of Expert Witnesses

An expert witness is a witness, who by virtue of education, training, skill, or experience, is believed to have expertise and specialised knowledge in a particular subject, sufficient that others may officially and legally rely upon his or her specialised opinion. In cases relating to the financing of terrorism or related financial crimes, such as money laundering, the financial audit trail is frequently complex. A further challenge is that as international high

41 Kenneth Murray, 'Dismantling organised crime groups through enforcement of the POCA money laundering offences' (2010) 13(1) *Journal of Money Laundering Control* 7.

finance is complex by nature, specialised knowledge is essential in determining whether the transactions are genuinely suspicious. This is crucial as there is a tendency for non-experts to view any audit trail that is vaguely complex as being suspicious. The role of the financial expert witness in court is to be able to digest and present the evidence in a way that enables the court to understand what the relevant evidence is. By placing this evidence in the relevant context, the court is then able to assess its significance for itself.[42]

However, the fundamental question is whether expert witnesses should be used purely to express his or her expert opinion, or be allowed to go further to provide and interpret the evidence to prove the heart of the matter. The cautionary argument presented by some prosecutors in relation to proving criminality using the evidence of complex audit trails, is that particular care needs to be taken with the handling of circumstantial evidence, and that the use of audit trails in particular might present a particular problem.[43] This problem centres on the issue of whether expert financial evidence can be used to provide opinion on the 'ultimate issue' of a case.

In the case of *R v Gokal*,[44] it was established that it is permissible for a financial expert to express his opinion as evidence that an arrangement of transactions of great complexity were such as to demonstrate dishonest collusion. However, there is a critical distinction between use of expert witnesses to obtain their expert opinion and the use of expert evidence to prove the heart of the issue. It could be argued that the primary role of financial experts is not simply to express an opinion, but to present evidence in a way that a jury is able to draw an inference. This view is supported by Murray:

> *It may be that the circumstances of how that evidence is used and presented may constitutes what amounts to an opinion, but the primary focus for the forensic accountant is to establish what the facts are in relation to a series of financial events and by shining a forensic light on these in order to provide the jury with a proper understanding of what has occurred.*[45]

42 Ibid.

43 Jonathan Fisher QC 'Criminal property – prove it.' *Money Laundering Bulletin April 2006* (Informa UK Limited; www.informafinance.com).

44 [1999] 97 04132S2.

45 Murray, 'Dismantling organised crime groups through enforcement of the POCA money laundering offences' (N41) 7.

If the expert is successful in presenting the facts in a case, the evidence should speak for themselves, and the more compelling the evidence, the more irresistible the relevant inference. There is a prevailing presumption amongst legal circles that the expert witness is there primarily to present an opinion rather than be the embodiment of a means of presenting complex evidence. However, the role of the financial expert is the presentation of evidence that otherwise would not be available to the court. The submission of the expert report constitutes the evidence, but the provision of the report alone is simply inadequate.

The subject of expertise is particularly of concern in the context of secret evidence in court, as experts necessary to interpret the evidence may not be permitted access. The subject of secret evidence has been highlighted as problematic for several reasons, which will be elaborated upon shortly. The subject is important in the context of terrorist finance as much of the relevant financial intelligence is obtained through covert means. The information is useful in obtaining an understanding of terrorist finance and may be used to disrupt operations abroad. However, back on UK soil, the use of covertly acquired evidence such as intercept material is problematic.

Intercept Material

The interception of private communications including phone calls, emails, text messages and post, is a long-established intelligence and evidence-gathering technique. In the context of terrorist finance, as fund transfers can be made through mobile means, such as the Internet or mobile phone, and furthermore, the intent to send or confirm the sending and receiving of funds can be achieved through email, SMS text massages or voice communication, intercept evidence plays a key role in the identification of proactive evidence-gathering.

However, the UK has barred the use of intercepted communications as evidence in legal proceedings since 1984,[46] and is the only common law country

46 Although the statutory bar has only been in place since the Interception of Communications Act 1984, for many years before that the British government maintained an informal ban on its use. This informal ban dates from at least the beginning of the twentieth century. For further details see Justice's report *Intercept Evidence: Lifting the Ban* (October 2006) and the report of the Chilcot *Review of Intercept as Evidence* (January 2008).

to do so.[47] The statutory bar on using intercept material in court is currently contained in the Regulation of Investigatory Powers Act 2000, which states that:

> *... no evidence shall be adduced, question asked, assertion or disclosure made or other thing done in, for the purposes of or in connection with any legal proceedings which (in any manner) ... discloses, in circumstances from which its origin [from an interception warrant or an unlawful interception] may be inferred, any of the contents of an intercepted communication or any related communications data.*[48]

Section 17(1)(b) goes further to stipulate that any evidence that would even 'tend to suggest' that an interception warrant has been applied for, or issued, or is about to be issued would not be allowable. However, the Act also states exceptions to the rule allowing the use of intercept material in certain circumstances. Examples include interception made with the knowledge of one party without the need for a warrant,[49] where it was made overseas,[50] and where the communication is to or from a prison.[51] In such cases, the evidence is admissible in criminal proceedings in the usual manner. Similarly, there is no bar to the use of evidence from surveillance that does not involve direct interception of private communication. In other words, a recording of a phone call made from a phone tap[52] would be inadmissible,[53] whereas a recording of the same phone call from a listening device in the same room would be admissible.[54]

Other exceptions also exist. For example, the use of intercept material is allowable in some of the civil proceedings involving closed evidence and

47 The status of intercept evidence in the Republic of Ireland is the same as that in the UK prior to 1984. There is no statutory bar but neither is it used by prosecutors.

48 Section 17(1) (a).

49 Section 48(4).

50 Section 4(1).

51 Section 4(4).

52 Prior to the introduction of digital phone lines telephone lines were analogue and interceptions were made by directly tapping into the wire carrying the call. The advent of digital telephony has led to the development of different interception methods.

53 *Justice Report*, 'Secret Evidence' June 2009, 155. [Online]. Available at: http://www.justice.org.uk/images/pdfs/Secret%20Evidence%20-%20June%202009%20-%20website%20version.pdf [accessed: 13 October 2010].

54 Part II of the 2000 Act governs directed and intrusive surveillance other than interceptions. For examples of admissible evidence from bugs see *R v Allsop and others* [2005] EWCA Crim 703; *R v E* [2004] EWCA Crim 1243; and *R v Smart and Beard* [2002] EWCA Crim 772 (DAT recordings of a suspect speaking into a telephone was not an 'interception' within the meaning of s1(1) of the 1985 Act). See also *Justice Report*, 'Secret Evidence' (n.53) 155.

special advocates.[55] The Regulation of Investigatory Powers Act also allows for disclosure of intercept material to a prosecutor in criminal proceedings[56] for the purpose only of prevention of a miscarriage of justice. If, for example, intercept material, such a telephone call, demonstrated that a key prosecution witness was lying, a recording of the call could then be disclosed privately to the prosecutor to ensure that either the prosecution was dropped or, at least, that the witness's evidence was withdrawn, and any part of the prosecution case that relied on it was supported by alternative evidence. This places enormous trust in the diligence of those responsible for interceptions to bring relevant material to the attention of prosecutors. However, recent research carried out by Justice indicate that there is serious doubt as to whether this is the case.[57]

Intelligence versus Evidence

The situation is exacerbated by the fact that much of the so-called 'secret' evidence is not 'evidence' but 'intelligence'. Evidence is the product of a criminal investigation involving police detectives interviewing witnesses, gathering forensic material and following leads. Intelligence, on the other hand, is the product of the security and intelligence services who, despite their expertise in intelligence, some claim have no background in evidence-gathering and for whom the prosecution of suspected terrorists is much less of a priority compared to the disruption of their activities.

One argument put forward against the use of intelligence in court is the reliability of that material in that it may contain second or third-hand hearsay, information from unidentified informants, information received from foreign intelligence liaisons, data-mining and intercepted communications. There is an additional concern that there may be the use of hypotheses, predictions and speculations of the intelligence services themselves. As such, much of the 'intelligence' would and should be inadmissible in court. However, many point out that this is not a criticism of the intelligence services, but that it is a criticism of the use of intelligence as evidence.[58]

The concerns highlighted demonstrate the lack of understanding of how intelligence is collected and analysed and verified against other intelligence

55 Section 18(1), as amended by section 9 of the Prevention of Terrorism Act 2005 and section 69 of the Counter-Terrorism Act 2008.

56 Section 18(7)(a).

57 *Justice Report* (n.53) 156.

58 Ibid. 217–18.

to determine its validity. However, these procedures in themselves need to remain secret, which again makes it difficult for those outside the intelligence community to determine its quality and as such, their suspicions are understandable. There is also credibility in the comment that intelligence is used mainly for disruption purposes. However, as prosecutions play a key role in the disruption of those involved in terrorist finance and others involved in the broader criminal financial network, efforts must be made by the intelligence services to be able to produce open-source material that may be used in court.

It has long been recognised that there is an over-classification of sensitive material within the intelligence community. The inclusion of a single piece of intelligence that is classified as 'Top Secret', for example, will make the classification of that entire document also 'Top Secret'. There are many good reasons for this practice. However, as the wider distribution of intelligence is so vital, the intelligence services need to find ways to allow more of their intelligence to be unclassified.

Furthermore, the use of foreign intelligence in particular, has been heavily criticised. In February 2009, the UN Special Rapporteur on human rights and counter-terrorism criticised the use of foreign intelligence as evidence:

> *... sanctions against a person should not be based on foreign intelligence, unless the affected party can effectively challenge the credibility, accuracy and reliability of the information and there are credible grounds to believe that the information is accurate and reliable.*[59]

However, this concern relates not simply to foreign intelligence but to secret evidence in general.

59 Martin Scheinin, Special Rapporteur on the promotion and protection of human rights and fundamental freedoms while countering terrorism (A/HRC/10/3, 4 February 2009), para 74. See also para 29: 'information gathered for 'strategic intelligence' ... must not be used in court proceedings when there is no judicial supervision attached to measures directed at named individuals. The Special Rapporteur has noted with concern that in different courts, the line between such strategic intelligence and probative evidence has become blurred to the advantage of different forms of 'national security imperatives' Judicial approval for a special investigative technique must be given in order to make permissible the use of the fruits of the technique as evidence in court.

Secret Evidence

It is a basic principle of a fair hearing that a person must know the evidence against him, which forms the basis of British justice. However, many believe that this core principle has been undermined by the use of secret evidence. Furthermore, the use of secret evidence has grown dramatically in UK courts in the past 10 years. Its application has also grown in that secret evidence can now be used in a wide range of cases including deportations hearings, control orders proceedings, parole board cases, asset-freezing applications, pre-charge detention hearings in terrorism cases, employment tribunals and even planning tribunals.

The result is that defendants in some criminal cases are now being convicted on the basis of evidence that has never been made public. Evidence from anonymous witnesses has also been used in hundreds of criminal trials. Since the introduction of the use of secret evidence in 1997, almost 100 special advocates, who are prohibited from communicating with those they represent, have been appointed.[60]

The case of *Kadi v Council of the EU and the Commission*[61] highlights the problem of the use of secret evidence used in asset-freezing proceedings.[62] The defendants, Mr Kadi and the Al Barakaat International Foundation, had been named as terrorist financiers in Annex I of the EU regulation. However, the defendants had had no knowledge as to the reasons why they had been listed, or the evidence supporting those reasons.

The main complaint by the defendants was based on the fact that they had not been given the opportunity to contest the findings and that their right to be heard had been violated.[63] The Court concluded that these rights 'were patently not respected'[64] in the defendant's case.[65]

60 *Justice Report* (n.53) 5.

61 *Kadi v Council of the EU and the Commission* [2008] c-415/05P 3 CMLR41. See also *Justice Report* (n.53) 106.

62 The case concerned various international measures aimed at terrorist financing after 9/11. In particular, both UN Security Council Resolution 1390 (2002) and EU Council Regulation 881/2002 directed the assets of Al Qaeda and associated groups to be frozen.

63 *A and others v HM Treasury* [2008] EWCA Civ 1187, para 348.

64 *Kadi v Council of the EU and the Commission* [2008] c-415/05P 3 CMLR41, para 334.

65 Ibid. para 348.

Similarly, in *A, K, M, Q and G*,[66] the bank accounts and assets of the defendants had been frozen after being named by the Treasury under two Orders in Council: the Al-Qaida and Taliban (UN Measures) Order 2006 and the Terrorism (UN Measures) Order 2006.[67] As with the case of *Kadi*, the use of secret evidence meant that they had no information concerning the reasons why they had been listed. The decision to use closed source evidence in asset-freezing cases had been agreed by the Treasury, on the advice of law enforcement agencies, where there are strong operational reasons to impose a freeze, but insufficient open-source evidence available.[68]

Mr Justice Collins in the High Court initially upheld the defendants' appeals, quashing the orders on the grounds that, among other things, they afforded the defendants no opportunity to make 'meaningful representations'.[69] However, the High Court's ruling was reversed by the Court of Appeal which although it accepted the Orders' lack of procedural safeguards, considered that this was not sufficient to make them unlawful.[70] Lord Justice Sedley expressed his disapproval in a dissenting judgment, describing the asset-freezing scheme as:

> *... markedly deficient in the opportunity which it gives, or which is provided by other means, to ensure that a freezing order cannot be made or confirmed without a fair hearing.*[71]

In the case of *Kadi*, the court's decision which favoured the defendant was based on the fact that the Council neither communicated to the defendants the evidence used against them to justify the restrictive measures imposed on them, nor afforded them the right to be informed of that evidence within a reasonable period after those measures were enacted, and that the defendants were not in a position to make their point of view in that respect known to advantage. Therefore, their rights of defence, in particular the right to be heard,

66 *A, K, M, Q and G v HM Treasury* [2008] EWHC 869.
67 *A and others v HM Treasury* [2008] EWCA Civ 1187.
68 Written ministerial statement of Ed Balls MP, Hansard, 10 Oct 2006: cols 11–12WS.
69 *A, K, M, Q and G v HM Treasury* [2008] EWHC 869 (Admin), see para 14: 'there was no means whereby G could mount an effective challenge to his listing since he did not know nor was there any procedure whereby he could be informed of what material had led the Committee to list him. It is known that he was listed following information given against him by the government. Thus, without the support of the government, his chances of achieving delisting are infinitesimal'; and para 16: 'It is I think obvious that this procedure does not begin to achieve fairness for the person who is listed. Governments may have their own reasons to want to ensure that he remains on the list and there is no procedure which enables him to know the case he has to meet so that he can make meaningful representations.'
70 *A, K, M, Q and G v HM Treasury* [2008] EWHC 869 (Admin) para 60.
71 Ibid, para 140.

had not been respected. Among other things, the Court noted the judgment of the European Court of Human Rights (ECHR) that there were:

> *... techniques which accommodate, on the one hand, legitimate security concerns about the nature and sources of information taken into account in the adoption of the act concerned and, on the other, the need to accord the individual a sufficient measure of procedural justice.*[72]

The case of Kadi highlights how the use of secret evidence can be counter-productive in that the decision to freeze and confiscate terrorist assets can be overruled by a court of law on the grounds of human rights. This brings another dimension in terms of challenges faced by cases relating to terrorist finance, that of human rights legislation.

Human Rights Legislation

Any commentary on the freezing of suspected terrorist assets must briefly consider its legality under the ECHR. Article 1 of the First Protocol of the ECHR provides that every person is entitled to the peaceful enjoyment of his possessions, except in the public interests and subject to the principles of international law.

Two decisions of the European Court of First Instance (CFI) offer some guidance as to whether Pt II of the Anti-Terrorism, Crime and Security Act (ATCSA) 2001 breaches the ECHR.[73] As previously stated, all members of the UN are required to freeze the funds and other resources of suspected or known terrorist organisations.[74] These resolutions were given legal effect within the EU in 2002, and it imposed a series of specific measures against individuals and organisations which are associated with al-Qaeda, Osama bin Laden and the Taliban.[75] In the cases of Yusef and Kadi,[76] the applicants in this instance requested that Council Regulation (881/20), which implemented UN Resolution 1373, be annulled.

---

72 *Kadi v Council of the EU and the Commission* [2008] c-415/05P 3 CMLR41, para 344.

73 *Ahmed Ali Yusuf and Al Barakaat International Foundation v Commission* [2005] T-306/01 and *Yassin Adbullah Kadi v Council and Commission* [2005] T-315/01 For a more detailed discussion of these cases see C. Tomuschat, see judgment of the Court of First Instance of 21 September 2005, nyr. [2006] 2 C.M.L.R. 537 at 537-551.

74 UN SC Res 1373, 56th Sess., 4385th Mtg. Art.1(a).

75 Council Resolution 881/2002.

76 UN SC Res 1373 (n.74).

The claim failed on several grounds. First, the CFI ruled that the European Council is competent to freeze the funds of individuals in connection with the fight against international terrorism. Secondly, that the EU is bound to follow any obligations from the Charter of the UN, in the same way as member states of the UN are. Thirdly, the freezing of the applicant's funds did not infringe the fundamental rights and the applicants had not been arbitrarily deprived of their right to property. The CFI justified this part of the decision as the freezing of the funds amounts to a fundamental aspect of the UN's legitimate fight against international terrorism. Furthermore, unlike the confiscation of the proceeds of crime, the freezing of funds is precautionary and only a temporary measure.

Therefore, the CFI held that it does not affect the very substance of the right of a person under Art.1 of the First Protocol of the ECHR. Pt II of the ATCSA 2001 does not breach Art.1 of the First Protocol of the ECHR, as yet however, these provisions have not yet been challenged in the UK courts. Nevertheless, the legality of terrorism related cases will undoubtedly continue to be challenged under ECHR.

The International Dimension

Owing to the effects of globalisation and the nature adversary finances, which tend to be international in nature in the context of international terrorism, an understanding of the challenges of the UK alone is inadequate. Instead, the subject must be understood in its full global context, as weaknesses outside the UK also impact the effectiveness of the UK CTF regime. Furthermore, legislatively, as a member of the EU, the UK is subject to EU legislation, therefore a brief analysis of EU legislation and its challenges are also appropriate.

EUROPEAN UNION (EU)

In terms of EU legislation, the first Money Laundering Directive of 1991 required the imposition of an obligation on financial institutions to establish customers' identity and report any suspicion of money laundering. It was based on the 40 recommendations of the FATF on money laundering, of which the EU is a member. The second Directive of 2001 extended the number of crimes to which the provisions applied and widened the range of professions, who had to observe it to include lawyers, auditors, accountants, notaries, casinos and estate agents. It also provided for the establishment of financial intelligence units in each member state to which suspicious transactions reports (STRs)[77] were to be made.

The third Directive was adopted by the Council on 20 September 2005 and extended the provisions to any financial transaction, which might be linked to terrorist activities. Further provisions of the third Directive included identity checks on customers opening accounts so that accounts could not be held anonymously; as well as the regulation of cross border movement of transactions exceeding €15,000, stricter checks on PEPs, and penalties for failure to report suspicious transactions to national financial intelligence units.[78] However, the third Directive has faced much opposition and criticism. The banking and financial institutions felt that the disclosure requirements imposed were far too heavy a burden on the financial community. Of particular concern were provisions on PEPs and the obligation, in relation to transactions made by companies, to identify large shareholders. These concerns were put forward as amendments, but were rejected by the European Parliament. The European Banking Industry Committee also had serious reservations about the third Directive, in particular that the concept of 'beneficial owner'[79] was too specific and that the definition of PEPs stood in contradiction to the risk-based financial approach, in that it included everyone, not just those posing a genuine risk.

The Federation of European Banks (FEB), whilst welcoming the new directive as a positive step, also regretted the limited application of the risk-based approach. The FEB considered that the banks' lack of access to reliable information would not enable them to identify the beneficial owners properly. In addition, the European lawyers association, the Council of the Bars and Law Societies of Europe (CCBE), also argued that the reporting provisions of the second Directive threatened the independence of lawyers and therefore the fundamental right to legal advice and representation.[80] As a result, in a letter to the Commission on 8 February 2005, the Presidents of the European Bars called for a halt to the proposed third Directive, a plea that was ultimately unsuccessful.

77 Also known as SARs.

78 EU, 'Adoption of anti-Money Laundering Directive will strike a blow against crime and terrorism', EU Press Releases, Brussels, 7 June 2005. [Online]. Available at: http://europa.eu/rapid/pressReleasesAction.do?reference=IP/05/682&format=HTML&aged=0&language=EN&guiLanguage=en [accessed: 20 February 2011].

79 Shareholders to be identified in the case of corporate transactions.

80 Council of Bars and Law Societies of Europe (CCBE), *Money Laundering: Recent Developments in Europe: The Third Money Laundering Third Directive*. [Online]. Available at: http://www.ccbe.org/doc/En/speech_tyre_money_laundering_iba_180906.pdf [accessed: 20 February 2010].

Another issue surrounding the third Directive is with regard to its implementation, which many consider was carried out in haste. The second Money Laundering Directive was only adopted in 2001 and was due to be transposed into national law by June 2003. However, by this date, only around half the member states had done so.[81] In those member states where the second Directive has been implemented, the level and therefore the burden of reporting varied considerably. Additionally, a commitment within the second Directive not to legislate further until an evaluation had been carried out has not been respected. In the light of the serious concerns over the second Directive, proposals for a third Directive were seen by many as premature and inappropriate. This opinion was clearly shared by the CCBE:

> *... discussions on a third directive were concluded at an alarming pace without regard to the concerns raised by the CCBE (on the legality of the second directive).*[82]

Finally, the overall effectiveness of the third Money Laundering Directive in general has come into question. Even leaving aside the points made above, there is still a question as to what extent this legislation is actually effective in combating money laundering and terrorist finance. Is it fulfilling its function or does it simply put irksome and money-wasting obstacles in the way of financial transactions carried out by businesses and consumers? Many argue that, without further study, the answer to this question remains unknown.

FINANCIAL ACTION TASK FORCE (FATF)

The FATF has had a significant impact on CTF efforts worldwide in that only those seen to have successfully adopted its recommendations are regarded as being committed to the fight against CTF. The eight special recommendations are particularly significant and draw upon the content of the '40 Recommendations', but were much more closely concerned with terrorist funding.

The seven parts of the new guidelines include the criminalisation of terrorist funding and connected money laundering, followed by the seizing and confiscating of terrorist assets. However, the FATF has been criticised for giving relatively little thought to implementation, with decisions being left up

81 EuroActiv, 'Money laundering', 17 March 2006. [Online]. Available at: http://www.euractiv.com/en/financial-services/money-laundering/article-139944 [accessed: 20 January 2010].

82 Ibid.

to individual member states without sufficient guidance or support from the FATF. In addition, it has yet to develop interpretations based on the experience of member states and is effectively still at the data gathering stage.[83] As the FATF is essentially a monitoring and coordinating multilateral organisation, its means are limited to cope with its new mandate. So far 151 countries have committed to implementing the 40+8 recommendations. However, the IMF and the World Bank claim the countries' actions on the CTF recommendations lag behind efforts to fight money laundering.[84]

Part of the challenge is a lack of teeth. The FATF contends that its main source of leverage is a blacklist of countries that have failed to adopt or implement adequate laws. The blacklist contained 15 countries in 2000, including the Cayman Islands and Lebanon. The latest blacklisted produced on the 18 February 2010 contains seven countries, namely Iran, Angola, Ecuador, Ethiopia, Pakistan, the Democratic Republic of Korea and Turkmenistan.[85] The FATF at the same time also produced a grey list consisting of 20 countries, Antigua and Barbuda, Azerbaijan, Bolivia, Greece, Indonesia, Kenya, Morocco, Myanmar, Nepal, Nigeria, Paraguay, Qatar, Sri Lanka, Sudan, Syria, Trinidad and Tobago, Thailand, Turkey, Ukraine, Yemen.[86] However, many experts do not believe that the countries identified are the only trouble spots. Indeed, sceptics question how some countries including Russia[87] have managed to avoid the list of shame.

Most problematic of all may be the countries that do not even pretend to follow the FATF process. Between 2000 and 2006, the FATF systematically examined jurisdictions identified as 'non-cooperative countries and territories' (NCCTs). During this process, 23 jurisdictions were listed owing to a lack of an effective AML/CFT system. According to the FATF, all of the 23 jurisdictions that had been identified as NCCTs in 2000 and 2001, had made significant progress, and the last country was removed from the list in October 2006. As such, as of October 2006, there are no Non-Cooperative Countries and Territories in the context of the NCCT initiative.[88] However, this does not mean

83 Valpy FitzGerald, *Global Financial Information, Compliance Incentives and Conflict Funding* (Working Paper no. 96, QEH Working Paper Series – QEHWPS96).

84 *The Economist*, 'Financing terrorism: looking in the wrong places', (20 October 2005).

85 FATF Blacklist as at 18 February 2011. [Online]. Available at: http://www.acfsnet.org/index.php?option=com_content&view=article&id=143&Itemid=169 [accessed: 12 July 2011].

86 FATF Grey List as at 18 February 2011. [Online]. Available at: http://www.acfsnet.org/index.php?option=com_content&view=article&id=142&Itemid=168 [accessed: 12 July 2011].

87 Russia joined the FATF as an observer organisation to the FATF in 2003.

88 FATF, *About the Non-Cooperative Countries and Territories (NCCT) Initiative*. [Online]. Available at: http://www.fatf-gafi.org/document/51/0,3746,en_32250379_32236992_33916403_1_1_1_1,00.html [accessed: 12 July 2011].

that all jurisdictions are now fully compliant. It is worth noting that the FATF has not reviewed any new jurisdictions since 2001 in the framework of the NCCT initiative. Furthermore countries such as Libya, Vietnam and Venezuela remain outside the organisation, as are some of the African countries, which is of particular concern.

UNITED NATIONS (UN)

The UN has pioneered the response to combat terrorist finance and in 1999, adopted the International Convention for the Suppression of the Financing of Terrorism.[89] This Convention contained a series of measures aimed at counteracting the movement of funds suspected of terrorist purposes and served as a precedent for UN Security Council Resolution 1373. Resolution 1373 has been described as 'the most important international instrument as regards terrorism and finance'.[90] In particular, the obligation on member states to freeze assets is absolute, and compels collective application.[91]

The Resolution imposes four obligations on members of the UN.[92] First, it specifically requires states to thwart and control the financing of terrorism.[93] Secondly, it criminalises the collection of terrorist funds in states territory.[94] Thirdly, it freezes funds, financial assets and economic resources of people who commit or try to commit acts of terrorism.[95] Finally, it prevents any nationals from within their territories providing funds, financial assets and economic resources to people who seek to commit acts of terrorism.[96]

UNSCR 1373 is implemented in the UK by the Terrorism (UN Measures) Order 2001, which came into force on 10 October 2001. To monitor enforcement of these measures, the Security Council created the Counter-Terrorism Committee (CTC), whose primary function has been to strengthen the counter-terrorism capacity of UN member states. The CTC has served as a 'switchboard', helping to facilitate the provision of technical assistance to countries needing

89 It must be noted, however, that the Convention is 'restricted to terrorist acts with an international element'.
90 Editorial, 'Terrorism and international finance: recent developments from the perspective of international law' (2002) 4(1) *Journal of International Banking Law* 9.
91 A. Kruse, 'Financial and economic sanctions: from a perspective of international law and human rights' (2005) 12(3) *Journal of Financial Crime* 218.
92 Cabinet Office, *The UK and the Campaign against International Terrorism Progress Report* (London, 2002) 24.
93 S.C. Res, 1373, U.N. SCOR, 56th Sess., 4385th Mtg. Art.1(a).
94 Ibid. Art.1(b).
95 Ibid. Art.1(c).
96 Ibid. Art.1(5).

such help to implement counter-terrorism mandates. It has also attempted to coordinate the counter-terrorism efforts of a wide range of international, regional, and sub-regional organisations within and beyond the UN system. It has been argued that Resolution 1373 forms the basis of the international effort to CTF. Myers noted that the resolution:

> *... presents a powerful tool to leverage cooperation by all states on financing issues, information sharing, police action, criminal prosecution, asset forfeiture, and border control.*[97]

However, Myers also noted that:

> *... while it contains strong language, the resolution still has grey areas, such as its failure to define the term terrorist.*[98]

Resolution 1373 has also been criticised as it provides the individuals and organisations who have been accused of supporting terrorism with no opportunity within the UN to challenge the listing by the UN CTC.[99] A further criticism is that UN Resolution 1373 will actually have a limited impact on the extensive number of sources available to terrorists and their continued ability to raise monies.[100] Despite such criticisms, Resolution 1373 has influenced a number of jurisdictions to tackle terrorist finances.[101]

Notwithstanding the high level of support for the UN stance on terrorist financing, the implementation of UN Resolution 1373 is not universal. For instance, the response of Saudi Arabia is debatable,[102] because it has been argued by several studies that it provides an unprecedented source of funding to al-Qaeda. As seen in Chapter 3, it has been argued that al-Qaeda has been

97 J.M. Myers, 'Disrupting terrorist networks: the new US and international regime for halting terrorist finance' (2003) 34 *Law & Policy International Business* 17.

98 These powers already existed under previous US legislation, 'yet the new sanctions also significantly expanded on existing ones'. See B. Zagaris, 'The merging of the anti-money laundering and counter-terrorism financial enforcement regimes after September 11, 2001' (2004) 22 *Berkley Journal International Law* 123.

99 B Zagaris, 'The merging of the anti-money laundering and counter-terrorism financial enforcement regimes after September 11, 2001' (2004) 22 *Berkley Journal International Law* 123.

100 M. Levitt, 'Stemming the follow of terrorist financing: practical and conceptual challenges' (2003) 27(1) *The Fletcher Forum of World Affairs* 63.

101 For an analysis of other jurisdictions see A. Chukwuemerie, 'International legal war on the financing of terrorism: a comparison of Nigerian, UK, US and Canadian laws' (2006) 9(1) *Journal of Money Laundering Control* 71.

102 *UN, Terrorism Financing Roots and trends of Saudi terrorism financing: Report prepared for the President of the Security Council*. UN, New York, 2002; and D. Srour, S. Fischer and L.L.P Mandell, 'Money laundering, terrorism financing and financial networks' (2003) 1367 PLI/Corp 411.

able to misuse companies and charitable contributions made via Zakat to fund their terrorist activities.[103] It has been estimated that terrorists have been able to gain approximately $300 million to $500 million of such funds over a 10-year period in Saudi Arabia alone.[104]

Raphaeli argued that Saudi Arabia is 'unquestionably the largest cash source of cash to al-Qaeda and other terrorist organisations'.[105] As a result of Resolution 1373:

> *... we are left with a patchwork of domestic, bilateral, and regional efforts that at best work in parallel but not complimentary fashion, and at worst work at cross-purposes.*[106]

It might be that the conduct giving rise to the funds is regarded as a criminal offence in the country concerned, while the same conduct would not be regarded as even improper elsewhere, and certainly not in the country where the money comes to nest.[107]

To date, the UN counter-terrorism programme has had a mixed record of accomplishment.[108] In the first four years after the opening of the Convention on terrorist bombings, only 28 states had ratified the agreement. After September 2001, an additional 122 states ratified the convention, bringing the total to 150

103 M.M. Metwally, 'Economic consequences of applying Islamic principles in Muslim societies' (1997) 24 (7/8/9) *Journal of International Social Economics* 941.

104 Jean-Charles Brisard, *Terrorism Financing: Roots and Trends of Saudi Terrorism Financing* (Report prepared for the President of the Security Council, United Nations 19 December 2002, New York). Despite the allegations made in this report the 9/11 Commission concluded that there was no direct evidence that Saudi Arabia was involved in the funding of the attacks. See 9/11 Commission, above fn.18 and *Congressional Research Service, Saudi Arabia: Terrorist Financing Issues* (Washington: Congressional Research Service, 2005) 5. Furthermore, these allegations have been refuted by Saudi Arabia. See Royal Embassy of the Kingdom of Saudi Arabia, Press Release, 'Response to CFR Report', 17 October 2002 and Royal Embassy of the Kingdom of Saudi Arabia, Press Release, 'Saudi Arabia blasts CFR task force report', 15 June 2004.

105 G. MacMull, 'Removing the charitable veil: an examination of US policy to combat terrorist funding charities post 9/11' (2004) 10 *New England Journal of International & Comparative Law* 121.

106 M. Levitt, 'Stemming the follow of terrorist financing: practical and conceptual challenges' (2003) 27(1) *The Fletcher Forum of World Affairs* 6.

107 Barry A.K. Rider, 'Law: The War on Terror and Crime and the Offshore Centres: The "New" Perspective?' in Donato Masciandaro (ed), *Global Financial Crime: Terrorism, Money Laundering and Offshore Centres* (Ashgate Publishing, 2004) ch. 2, 75–6.

108 David Cortright, 'A Critical Evaluation of the UN Counter-Terrorism Program: Accomplishments and Challenges' Fourth Freedom Forum, Paper presented at: Global Enforcement Regimes Transnational Organized Crime, International Terrorism and Money Laundering Transnational Institute (TNI) Amsterdam, 28–29 April 2005. [Online]. Available at: http://www.tni.org/crime-docs/cortright.pdf [accessed: 12 January 2010].

in 2006.[109] In the first two years of the Convention on terrorist financing, only five states ratified the agreement, but since September 2001, 148 additional nations[110] have ratified it.

These results show that the UN, and especially the CTC, has been very successful in mobilising the international community, in most regions of the world, to create a legal foundation for institutionalising the battle against terrorism. Evaluating whether states are actually implementing these two Conventions and complying with the requirements of Resolution 1373 is a difficult challenge. There are no agreed criteria for evaluating implementation capabilities, or determining what additional steps a state should take to achieve compliance. The CTC has not yet attempted such an effort, but in 2003 one of its staff experts conducted an informal analysis to gain an overall picture of international compliance.

The findings were that approximately 30 countries were considered to have achieved a considerable degree of compliance with Resolution 1373, whilst approximately 60 states were judged by the expert to be in transition, moving gradually into compliance.[111] In addition, the largest group of approximately 70 states were categorised as willing but unable to comply. These were countries that generally supported CTC efforts but faced a range of difficulties that prevented full compliance including civil conflict, extreme poverty and social hardship. A final group of approximately 20 states were described as inactive. These were countries that were materially able to comply but for a variety of reasons had chosen not to do so.[112]

The legal expert performing the informal analysis of member state compliance also evaluated the performance of regional organisations. It was reported that the overall coordination among regional organisations had improved, but some regions had continued to lag behind and as a general rule, the more economically developed regions had higher levels of counter-terrorism capability than less developed regions. In Europe, the Americas and

109 Ibrahim A. Gambari, UN Under-Secretary-General for Political Affairs Commonwealth Ministers Reference Book 2006 'A multilateral response to terrorism'. [Online]. Available at: http://www.un.org/terrorism/docs/gambari_med-final.pdf [accessed: 12 January 2010].

110 UN A/60/825, General Assembly, 27 April 2006, Sixtieth session, Agenda items 46 and 120 'Uniting against terrorism: recommendations for a global counter-terrorism strategy', Report of the Secretary-General. [Online]. Available at: http://www.un.org/unitingagainstterrorism/chap3.htm and http://www.un.org/unitingagainstterrorism/sg-terrorism-2may06.pdf [accessed: 12 January 2010].

111 Cortright 'A Critical Evaluation of the UN Counter-Terrorism Program' (n.108) 7.

112 Ibid. 7.

the Asia Pacific region, counter-terrorism coverage was extensive, as reflected by ratification of international agreements and the development of a considerable organisational infrastructure. Other regions were less well covered and were described by the expert as a 'legal no-man's land.' These regions, including West Asia and parts of Africa, lacked the organisational infrastructure to fully address UN counter-terrorism mandates.[113]

THE UNITED STATES

The fight against terrorist finance is largely dependent upon a highly coordinated and effective level of international cooperation. In an attempt to tackle the global threat of terrorist finance, the US Government ensured that the USA PATRIOT Act 2001 included a series of extraterritorial provisions which will require foreign banks to comply with the provisions of this controversial piece of legislation.[114] However, this policy is seriously flawed as its success is solely dependent upon the support of other nations, which cannot always be guaranteed. Myers took the view that the US cannot:

> *... reach foreign financial institutions and block terrorist accounts. Local governments must be persuaded to do that. Allies are important in the physical struggle against terrorism.*[115]

Others have also commented that although the international response to terrorist finance has been heavily influenced by the US, that it must be led by the UN, which is seen as being in the best position to lead the international coalition against terrorism.[116]

Nevertheless, the impact of US legislation on the rest of the world has been considerable. For example, the PATRIOT Act has had a significant impact on the level and depth of compliance required not only for those operating in the US, but any institution or intermediary that deals with the US or transacts its

113 Ibid. 8.

114 See USA PATRIOT Act 2001 ss.311, 312 and 313. For a more detailed commentary on these provisions see E. Preston, 'The USA PATRIOT Act: new adventures in American extraterritorially' (2002) 10(2) *Journal of Financial Crime* 105.

115 Myers, 'Disrupting terrorist networks: the new US and international regime for halting terrorist finance' 17.

116 Art.1 para.1 of the Convention, the UN (1999). Hardister has criticised the impact of this international Convention because it has no international enforcement mechanisms and it only applies to signatories. See A.D. Hardister, 'Can we buy peace on earth?: The price of freezing terrorist assets in a post-September 11 world' (2003) 28 (624) *North Carolina Journal of International Law and Commercial Regulation* 605.

business in US currency. Consequently, it is likely that the US requirements will become the international norm, regardless of strategies and initiatives adopted in the UK and elsewhere.[117] In addition, the extent of the US. Government's change of attitude since 9/11 on such mattrs as financial privacy and the 'legitimacy' of offshore 'tax efficient' activities has been profound. As Professor Rider observes:

> ... *While, in many areas of the legal system, we are used to legislation being little more than a reaction to an event, such as a scandal that has outraged public sentiment, the magnitude of the impact of our lives of some laws now being enacted in the wake of the attack on the USA has perhaps not been appreciated.*[118]

Furthermore, existing US legislation coupled with measures to follow, is highly likely to have a serious impact on those jurisdictions that have been regarded, appropriately or otherwise, as 'non-cooperative'. There is indeed a possibility that their financial institutions may well find themselves practically excluded from the international markets. The potential consequence of this is alarming. As Professor Rider observes:

> ... *when many Western and socially responsible governments, including the UK government, are addressing problems of social exclusion resulting, in part, from a lack of access to banking and related services, it seems strange that we should be contemplating the de facto exclusion of whole continents. Of course, the issues are complex and the appropriateness of particular initiatives differs from country to country and society to society. What is clear, however, is that there is a very real danger we will do far greater long term and systemic damage to our financial and corporate world than Osama bin Laden would have dreamed possible.*[119]

The message is that although it is understandable that jurisdictions such as the US may wish to protect themselves from the dangers of terrorism by strengthening domestic measures, and as a consequence refuse to work with countries that are not natural allies, the global nature of finance is such that it is no longer possible to ignore the global consequences of such actions.

117 Rider, 'The War on Terror and Crime and the Offshore Centres (n.107) 73.
118 Ibid.
119 Ibid. 73.

Conclusions

Prior to the events of 9/11, the international community's attempts to legislate against financial crime were directed towards the prevention of fraud, money laundering and the illegal drugs trade.[120] [121] [122] As a result, regulatory and law enforcement bodies were not focused on tackling terrorist funding.[123] [124] 9/11 set in motion a new and inventive legislative approach towards attacking the sources of terrorist funding and assets.[125] McCulloch and Pickering noted that after 9/11 'measures targeted at the financing of terrorism gained great momentum',[126] and Navias commented that as a result of the terrorist attacks 'financial warfare emerged as a major instrument of anti-terrorist strategic operations'.[127] Therefore, the terrorist attacks of 9/11 had an instantaneous effect,[128] which changed the international communities' policy towards the prevention and detection of terrorist funding.[129] [130]

As true as this may be, this chapter addressed a number of challenges which unless they are overcome adequately, will continue to obstruct efforts to interdict the financing of terrorism and related enterprise crime. The proceeding final chapter will provide an overall conclusion together with

120 W. Allen, 'The war against terrorism financing' (2003) 6(4) *Journal of Money Laundering Control* 306.

121 H. Ping, 'The new weapon for combating money laundering in the EU' (2004) 8(2) *Journal of Money Laundering Control* 116.

122 J. Fisher, 'Recent development in the fight against money laundering' (2002) 17(3) *Journal of International Banking Law* 67.

123 P. Binning, 'In safe hands? Striking the balance between privacy and security: anti-terrorist finance measures' (2002) 6 *European Human Rights Law Review* 737.

124 J. Johnson, '11th September, 2001: will it make a difference to the global anti-money laundering movement?' (2002) 6(1) *Journal of Money Laundering Control* 10.

125 J. Winer and T. Roule, 'Fighting terrorist finance' (2002) 44(3) *Survival* 89.

126 J. McCulloch and S. Pickering, 'Suppressing the financing of terrorism: proliferating state crime, eroding censure and extending neo-colonialism' (2005) 45 *British Journal of Criminology* 470.

127 M.S. Navias, 'Financial warfare as a response to international terrorism' (2002) 73(1) *The Political Quarterly* 61.

128 Editorial, 'Terrorism and international finance: recent developments from the perspective of international law' (2002) 4(1) *Journal of International Banking Law* 9. Akindemowo remarked: 'The horror and condemnation provoked by the 9/11 attacks widely expressed, a new determination to address, and counter, the evils of global terrorism emerged.' See O.E. Akindemowo, 'The pervasive influence of anti-terrorist financing policy: post 9/11 non-bank electronic money issuance' (2004) 19(8) *Journal of International Banking Law and Regulation* 289.

129 N.S. Jamwal, 'Hawala: the invisible financing system of terrorism' (2000) 26(2) *Strategic Analysis* 181. Passas took the view that: 'the main problem is that [US] law enforcement did not focus very much on these types of transaction, network and ethnic group involved before 9/11.' See N. Passas, 'Law enforcement challenges in hawala-related investigations' (2004) 12(2) *Journal of Financial Crime* 112.

130 Nicholas Ryder, 'A false sense of security? An analysis of legislative approaches towards the prevention of terrorist finance in the US and the UK' (2007) *Journal of Business Law* 821.

recommendations for the way forwards, in order that adversary finances can be dealt with more effectively in the future.

8

Conclusions and the Way Forwards

> *... we can create what some will call a modern 'Bletchley Park' with forensic accounting of such intricacy and sophistication in tracking finance and connections that it can achieve, for our generation, the same results as code breaking at the original Bletchley Park did sixty years ago.*[1]
>
> *Gordon Brown*

Eliminating an organisation's economic base is the key to its destruction. The effective targeting of the financial streams of terrorist organisations will lead to the destruction of its economic base, directly impacting not only its capability, but its ability to survive. The potential power of unleashing the full understanding of global financial networks cannot be more heavily emphasised. The subject of finance should not be treated as a standalone subject, but instead as knowledge that is capable of supporting existing efforts to counter both terrorism and organised crime. Furthermore, financial network analysis may be used to support and further develop existing and ongoing work to validate existing hypotheses where intelligence can be weak and, as such, should be considered as an integral part of any criminal investigation.

The potential impact of effectively tackling adversary finance was highlighted by Gordon Brown during his speech given to Chatham House on 10 October 2006, where he described a future vision capable of creating what could one day be referred to as the 'Bletchley Park' of the twenty-first century. However, at this moment in time, that vision is a distant dream as the community fails to even begin to ask the right questions, look in the right places or consult the right people to obtain the necessary knowledge.

---

1 HM Treasury, 'Meeting the terrorist challenge'. [Online]. Available at: http://www.hm-treasury.gov.uk/press_72_06.htm [accessed: 12 January 2011].

On a positive note, the importance of tackling adversary finances has been recognised and there is political will to embrace the challenge. The problem is the lack of leadership to enable that commitment to flourish. However, the UK's commitment to countering adversary finances has been reflected in the existence of legislation and regulation to combat financial crime including terrorist finance and money laundering. In terms of the legislative environment, UK terrorism legislation is well established pre-dating 9/11, owing to the existence of Irish terrorism.

In addition, since 9/11, much of the legislation has been updated with further new legislation introduced to tackle the threat from Islamic terrorism and the financing of terrorism, as well as the broader finances of OCGs. Examples include the Terrorism Act 2000, the Anti-Terrorism, Crime and Security Act 2001, the Proceeds of Crime Act 2002 and the more recent Asset-Freezing Act of 2010. In addition, the counter-terrorist finance regime is further supported by regulations relating to money laundering as well as various orders in Council, which implement UN Security Council Resolutions. Yet despite the existence of relevant legislation and regulation to combat adversary finances, the current environment continues to favour the terrorist. This in itself has brought into question the extent of the efficacy of the legal and regulatory system within the UK, in tackling terrorist funding and associated criminal property.

The lack of success in tackling adversary finances to date can be explained partly by the numerous challenges that exist that act as a barrier to existing efforts. For example, the legality of convictions obtained under terrorism legislation is, and will undoubtedly continue to be, challenged by other conflicting legislation such as ECHR. Much of the key 'evidence' is derived from intelligence sources. However, the use of secret evidence has come under heavy criticism and the use of intercept material is inadmissible in court. In addition, the judiciary face a number of internal challenges which need to be addressed. The lack of familiarity with the basic concepts of terrorist finance, criminal finance and finance in general is of concern. Unless the level of understanding of the subject can be improved throughout the judicial system, there is concern as to whether justice can be achieved in the courtroom. This also raises questions as to whether existing investigation and detection methods, coupled with the way in which the evidence is presented in court is adequate.

Furthermore, the tendency to shy away from material involving financial complexity, as well as the inadequate use of expert witnesses, has been noted. The situation equally applies to information technology, which is a further concern as the cyber environment becomes increasingly relevant in the context not only to terrorist finance, but financial crime in general. Instead, complexity should be considered more of a challenge than a problem and be embraced. Given the right tool kit in terms of skill sets and attitudes, the challenge can then become an opportunity. The fact is that delineation of complex audit trails provides a powerful means of dismantling adversary organisations.

In the case of money laundering for example, such schemes are designed to provide false stories for documented money transfers. By mapping out the scheme and exposing the differences between the true reasons for the money transfers and the presented reasons, the criminality of purpose is laid bare. Furthermore, the complicity of the various participants can be revealed through the same process as a result of the ways in which they are shown to have participated, which will indicate compelling evidence regarding their knowledge of the money's criminality. The essential tenets of a set of successful convictions can thus begin to take shape.[2]

The necessity to educate the judiciary to include barristers, judges as well as the jury has already been highlighted. However the need for education also extends to law enforcement who leads investigations on terrorist finance. The disruption of adversary enterprises requires skills and resources, not always easily identified within traditional policing agencies. Furthermore, the type of intelligence that is required for effective disruption is rarely available in police agencies. Consequently, there is a tendency to outsource specialist expertise outside the traditional law enforcement environment. This is problematic for several reasons.

First, owing to the high cost of employing external experts, specialists are only brought in at a certain point of the investigation for a limited period time. As such, the expertise is brought in on a 'demand-led' basis, which further contributes to the reactive approach that fails to recognise the importance of financial intelligence as a proactive intelligence tool. Furthermore, the use of external experts may lead to profound issues relating to accountability.[3] Instead, expertise must be fully integrated, and not used simply to perform an advisory function.

2 Kenneth Murray, 'Dismantling organised crime groups through enforcement of the POCA money laundering offences' (2010) 13(1) *Journal of Money Laundering Control* 7.

3 Barry A.K. Rider 'Law: The War on Terror and Crime and the Offshore Centres: The "New" Perspective?' in Donato Masciandaro (ed.), *Global Financial Crime: Terrorism, Money Laundering and Offshore Centres* (Ashgate Publishing, 2004) ch. 2, 92.

The lack of in-house financial expertise also continues to undermine CTF efforts at every level. In terms of financial expertise, some have recognised the discipline of forensic accountancy as playing a key role and encourage its further use. Law enforcement agencies such as the Scottish Crime and Drug Enforcement Agency (SCDEA) have incorporated a forensic accountancy function as part of its overall law enforcement operations. This is clearly a very promising step. However, that resource is not only extremely limited but confined to tackling money laundering. In addition, the use of forensic accounting in isolation also has its limitations.

In terms of regulation, the method used to detect potentially suspicious financial activity is essentially flawed in that it is based on traditional anti-money laundering detection techniques, which is distinct from terrorist finance. As such, the existing 'one-size-fits-all' approach is inadequate in tackling terrorist finance. Financial profiling is only effective when supported by relevant intelligence. This intelligence is lacking owing to a number of challenges including security clearances and the lack of trust, as well as organisational barriers that exist between the private and public sectors. In addition, the financial sector is regulated to the point where some consider the industry to be suffering from over-regulation. The consequence is that the deluge of reporting requirements leads to a 'tick in the box' mentality, where the countering of adversary finances becomes an exercise concerned purely with regulatory risk management as opposed to its intended purpose, that of proactively dealing with the underlying problem of financial crime.

Furthermore, despite the huge cost of compliance borne by the financial sector, the results have been disappointing. The quality of the output in terms of suspicious activity reports remains highly questionable and as such, has little practical application in countering terrorist finance. This in turn makes the ongoing cost of compliance a particularly bitter pill to swallow. The financial sector's role as the unpaid policeman also continues to cause much resentment especially against the backdrop of the continuing economic downturn, which has led to the public hatred of financial institutions. As financial institutions' role as the first line of defence against financial crime is so important, this raises the question as to whether too much 'stick' is appropriate.

A further barrier to existing counter-finance efforts relates to organisational structure. Human beings are essentially tribal in nature. Therefore, it is natural that groups are formed on the basis of a number of factors including personal background, profession, race, common interest and so forth. These inevitably become individual institutions in themselves which become so insular that actively engaging outside the comfort of one's own cocooned silo becomes a real challenge, irrespective of whether there is a common goal. However, it is also equally curious to note that these restrictions appear to be far less problematic for adversary organisations. Of course, they have the added advantage that they are not confined by legislative or regulatory restrictions. However, it is the fluidity of the network structure which characterises both terrorist and criminal organisations that makes them more adaptable and resilient.

In attempting to counter such an adversary, the criticism of silo working becomes even more pertinent. The existence of Chinese walls is a double-edged sword in that it not only protects but denies vital access and knowledge to those who require it. It is no longer appropriate that the various elements of the counter-terrorism community operate in their own individual comfort zones. As challenging as it may be, the battle against terrorism and organised crime must be fought on a level playing field, if there is to be any chance of success.

Despite recognition of this weakness and attempts to address this issue through the creation of cross governmental agencies, fusion centres and other forums which encourage stakeholders to work more closely together, the impact to date has been somewhat limited. The existing asymmetry has developed partly due to the external circumstances described earlier. However, as in any battle, the threat must be countered by attempting to mirror the capabilities of that threat. This, we are not doing, and must do, to avoid defeat. To correct the situation involves not only an understanding of the opponent, but a simultaneous look at the self to assess the asymmetry and to see how it can be corrected to one's own advantage.

In a game of chess, the pieces on the chess board each have a distinct function dependent on their own individual capability and restrictions in terms of movement which in turn determine their tactical role. The disadvantage of one piece is compensated by the strength of another. It is this networked approach that brings strength to the whole. The situation can be applied to CTF where a chess piece represents an institution, whether in the private or public sector, within the CTF community. Furthermore, the chess pieces not only represent stakeholders limited to domestic players, but include international players. It is the existing inability to engage adequately with all the players in the team, which further impacts upon the asymmetry that is giving the adversary the advantage.

It must be remembered that it does not matter how well one group is performing in the context of the overall counter-terrorism effort. That situation is clearly positive for that particular organisation, but the existing challenge is such that no single organisation can tackle the threat alone. Here an analogy of a musical band may be appropriate. It does not matter how brilliant each musician may be, if he or she does not take notice of the other musical instruments in the band. Currently, each of the stakeholders in the counter-terrorism community can be seen as musicians in such a band, playing simultaneously, but the tune being played by each musician is in a different key, as well as frequently from an entirely different score.

A number of specific problems also exist that undermine existing CTF efforts. The individual challenges highlighted may only apply to certain elements of the stakeholder community. However, it is key that these challenges are understood in a collective environment as the interconnected nature of the problem is such that a failure in one segment ultimately affects the entire counter threat finance effort.

The appreciation of the subject of terrorist finance in terms of knowledge and understanding remains poor. The understanding of the subject has undoubtedly improved since 9/11, but remains inadequate at all levels. The knowledge gaps vary from very limited knowledge where real knowledge is substituted by myths, to an overspecialisation on specific areas of expertise and the failure to understand the subject in its broader context. The knowledge gaps frequently result in unfounded suspicion. In addition, many are quick to opt for a simplistic understanding of the financing of terrorism. Many view counter threat finance activity as a task of 'following the money' and fail to acknowledge its greater potential. This approach is of concern as it can undermine the overall counter-terrorism effort.

In addition, much of the existing analysis is based on a simplistic adoption of finance with an over-emphasis on 'money' and an inadequate focus on the broader economic implications, which needs to be addressed. Existing knowledge gaps are caused partially by the lack of expertise in global finance which restricts the scope of investigations, limiting the ability to exploit available financial intelligence, and ultimately impacts the analysis provided. The focus and energy spent on tracking the numerous low-hanging fruit which are easy targets whilst neglecting upstream financiers who direct their actions is a case in point.

Furthermore, there is an over-emphasis on disruption, where the goals are so focused that they frequently fail to acknowledge the damage that action might be causing in the wider context, which in turn exacerbates the underlying problem. For example, the pursuit of *hawaladars* is an easy target both in the UK as well as abroad. However, the broader economic consequence of such actions must be appreciated. The disruption of a single *hawaladar*, especially if the action is not justified, will do more to promote terrorism than to prevent it.

This is particularly the case when kinetic action is taken. Even when the action is non-kinetic, but nevertheless disruptive, the disruption often applies not only to the individuals targeted, but to the whole community they serve. Such action is the equivalent to all the banks including ATMs being closed down indefinitely. Clearly such disruption in the West would be met with total outcry. Why then is it that this type of action is somehow acceptable when conducted on foreign soil? In such situations the collateral damage, albeit in purely economic terms, in unacceptable. It is actions like these that enrage the local population to the extent that they decide to take up arms against the perpetrators. As such, any parallel activity to attempt to win the 'hearts and minds' of these people are lost.

A further problem is the inability to tackle the real source of the problem by focusing investigations within the comfort zone in terms of technical understanding, political pressure and jurisdictional challenges. This leads to an approach that can only be described as a self-certifying prophecy. This is particularly relevant in the international context as terrorist finance and related organised crime is international in nature. An appreciation of local market conditions and the global economic network needs to be better understood as the direct application of Western practices are more often than not, inappropriate in other cultures and will prove to be counter-productive.

In terms of strategic direction, the overall strategy relating to the countering of terrorist finance as articulated in CONTEST2 has not been put into practice effectively. The gap between strategy and the implementation of that strategy can be explained in part by the existing tactical approach adopted by all levels of the CTF community. Furthermore, inadequate in-house expertise is exacerbated by data deluge, and data paucity leads to a reactive 'fire-fighting' approach. As such, the move towards the adoption of an appropriate strategy underpinned by effective tactics is essential.

There are two main 'health' warnings that also need to be addressed. The first is with respect to the 'approach' of countering adversary finances although this equally applies to tackling crime including terrorism in general. It is always possible to make further incremental improvements in an attempt to keep pace with the ever mutating threat from terrorism and related enterprise crime. However, the never ending pursuit of catch up with the terrorist or criminal is no longer adequate. As Professor Rider observed:

> *Of course, in truth, thinking criminals have always sought to place themselves beyond the reach of the law, and it is not just a matter of having a faster horse!*[4]

The second 'health warning' is with respect to both the legislative and regulatory environment pertaining to terrorist funds and associated criminal property. Here, the potential cost of Western regulation in its global context must be considered. The high level of legal and regulatory risks may persuade Western financial institutions simply to deny access to the 'Western' banking and financial system to those in these other countries considered to be too high risk. It must be remembered that the costs for those operating under these new laws in satisfying the extended and expanded due diligence requirements are likely to be extremely expensive. Indeed, even where access is available, it may well be at a cost beyond the reach of many individuals and institutions within the more vulnerable developing economies. As such, the highly vulnerable states may well find themselves effectively deprived of the advantages and services of those more developed and stable countries that are able to espouse the sort of measures found in legislation such as the PATRIOT Act. The inevitable consequence is that such acts will lead to the development of two separate worlds which is precisely something that should be avoided.[5] The question then becomes what can be done to turn this situation around?

The real problem is that the traditional approach that of incremental improvements is no longer sufficient in the asymmetric security environment of the twenty-first century. Instead, it is essential that counter-finance methods that are more sophisticated and holistic be developed and implemented to tackle the existing asymmetric financial and economic environment which currently favours the terrorist, insurgent and associated criminal organisations. Despite achievements made both in terms of knowledge and understanding in relation to terrorist finance, as well as their practical application with respect

4 Rider, 'Law: The War on Terror and Crime and the Offshore Centres' (n.3) 64.
5 Ibid. 92–3.

to legislation and the formulation of appropriate strategic direction, the impact on terrorism and related organised crime has been minimal.

It must be remembered that financial networks are not concrete, static targets but are instead fluid in nature. It is therefore inappropriate to adopt strategies that are applicable to hard targets associated with traditional warfare. The challenge is to ensure that finance reach its intended target, but is denied to the enemy. Financial networks can be best conceptualised as controlling a flow of resource. Traditional measures adopted in economic warfare, such as sanctions, aim to turn economic 'rivers' into arid wastelands resulting in widespread collateral damage. Strategies must be adopted to ensure that the financial river-flow is redirected to enable droughts to be created in the appropriate locations, starving its intended victims, whilst ensuring continued safe supply to the rest.

The countering of the financing of terrorism is essentially about the ability to develop and utilise financial intelligence effectively. Financial intelligence is a multi-faceted weapon that can be used in a number of ways. For example, it is a weapon of influence which may be deployed as part of psychological operations. As such, the use of finance as a tool for influence should be further explored. For example, the coercion framework of tipping adversaries' cost-benefit decisions to one's own advantage should be further examined. Financial intelligence holds special utility in that it is easily controlled to actionable outcomes designed to influence target behaviour, the target being any individual or organisation in the financial logistical supply chain. Influence is reliant on the successful manipulation of incentives and disincentives. This involves shaping the spectrum of options that are available to groups through tailored and focused activities aimed at specific pressure points.

These are precisely the tactics that corporations adopt to obtain competitive advantage over their competition. As there are many similarities between 'organised' criminal and terrorist enterprises, as earlier chapters have discussed, it is appropriate that existing 'business' models be adopted and adapted in the fight against organised crime and terrorism.

It must also be remembered that the stakeholders of countering adversary finances consist not only those directly involved in the fight against terrorism and organised crime, namely the intelligence agencies, law enforcement and the judiciary, but also all those affected by it. The wider network includes financial institutions, insurance companies, global corporations, law firms and various government departments, as well as the general public. What is needed is a new discipline that brings together the skills in financial intelligence analysis, forensic accounting and police investigation methods, coupled with an interdisciplinary understanding of economics, accounting, psychology, information technology, risk management and the law. This new discipline has been coined by the author as 'forensic finance.' The use of the term 'forensic' is appropriate in that financial intelligence is also a forensic tool, which provided it is collected and presented appropriately, may be effective in securing convictions in a court of law.

Forensic finance adopts a more sophisticated inter-multidisciplinary approach, not simply through the amalgamation of different subject expertise, but also by attempting to bridge the various gaps in terms of knowledge as well as change in the fundamental attitude of these organisations. The weaknesses of current methods and systems need to be addressed, which can only be achieved through the comprehensive understanding of a variety of interrelated subjects. As long as this situation is allowed to continue, the existing asymmetric environment will favour the terrorist/criminal.

Forensic finance has the potential to become a 'hyper-strategic' weapon owing to the fact that 'financial war' is easily manipulated and allows for concealed actions, as well as having the capacity to be highly destructive. Furthermore, financial warfare is likely to be an increasing form of conflict as a result of its position which lies at the intersection of powerful long-term trends in technology, networks, information and finance. The precise targeting feature of financial warfare, relative to conventional economic warfare, marks a significant change in the nature of conflict.

It has long been recognised that the fight against the interdiction of adversary funds cannot be fought in isolation by any single organisation. The new subject, that of forensic finance, aims to serve as an instrument to bridge existing knowledge gaps through the amalgamation of the existing knowledge base in addition to bringing new knowledge to the subject in an attempt to further unite stakeholders. This in turn aims to provide new thinking and direction, both strategically and tactically, in order that the counter-terrorism community is then better equipped to deal with the day-to-day task of countering not only terrorist finance, but terrorism and related organised crime as a whole. This publication aims to serve as an introduction to the discipline of forensic finance and the new counter threat finance strategies that will emerge from the adaptation of the discipline.

What this new strategy will require, however, is a very different approach, particularly by law enforcement, where the skills of tax investigation and financial intelligence officers will be placed at a premium. Furthermore, achieving such a strategy will undoubtedly require the restructuring of organisations, forces and doctrines, and perhaps most importantly, a restructuring of the 'mindset' in order to address the changing nature of the threats that are most likely to challenge those powers in the asymmetric security environment of the twenty-first century.[6]

6 Albert A. Nofi, *Recent Trends in Thinking about Warfare*, CRM D0014875.A1/Final September 2006, Defense Technical Information Center.

Bibliography

9/11 Commission Report. [Online]. Available at: http://www.9-11commission.gov/report/911Report.pdf [accessed: 20 January 2011].

9-11 Commission, *National Commission on Terrorist Attacks upon the United States.* [Online]. Available at: http://www.9-11commission.gov/staff_statements/911_ TerrFin_Ch1.pdf [accessed: 15 November 2010].

Ahmad, M.U. and Mahmood, A., 'Zakat fund: concept and perspective' (2009) 2(3) *International Journal of Monetary Economics and Finance* 197.

Ahmed, N.M., *The London Bombings: An Independent Inquiry* (Gerald Duckworth & Co. 2006).

Akindemowo, O.E., 'The pervasive influence of anti-terrorist financing policy: post 9/11 non bank electronic money issuance' (2004) 19(8) *Journal of International Banking Law and Regulation* 289.

Aldridge, I., *High-Frequency Trading: A Practical Guide to Algorithmic Strategies and Trading Systems* (Wiley 2009).

Alexander, D.C. and Alexander, Y., *Terrorism and Business* (Transnational Publishers 2002).

Alexander, K., 'Extraterritorial US banking regulation and international terrorism: the Patriot Act and the international response' (2002) 3(4) *Journal of International Banking Regulation* 307.

Alexander, R.C.H., *Insider Dealing and Money Laundering in the EU: Law and Regulation* (Ashgate 2007).

Alix, E.K., *Ransom Kidnapping in America, 1874–1974: The Creation of a Capital Crime* (University Press 1978).

Allen, W., 'The war against terrorism financing' (2003) 6(4) *Journal of Money Laundering Control* 306.

Aninat, E., Hardy, D. and Johnson, R.B., 'Combating money laundering and the financing of terrorism' (2002) 39(3) *Finance and Development* 44.

Araujo, R.A., 'Assessing the efficiency of the anti-money laundering regulation: an incentive-based approach' (2008) 11(1) *Journal of Money Laundering Control* 67.

Asams, J., *The Financing of Terror* (Simon & Schuster 1986).

Avgouleas, E. and Degiannakis, S., 'Trade transparency and trading volume: the possible impact of the financial instruments markets directive on the trading volume of EU equity markets' (2009) 1(1) *International Journal of Financial Markets and Derivatives* 96.

Bailey, F. and Moar, M., 'The Vertex Project: children creating and populating 3D virtual worlds' (2001) 20(1) *International Journal of Art and Design Education* 20.

Baldwin, F.N. Jr., 'The rule of law, human rights and proportionality as components of the war against terrorism: is the US judiciary in self-imposed exile?' (2004) 7(3) *Journal of Money Laundering Control* 218.

—— 'The financing of terror in the age of the internet: wilful blindness, greed or a political statement?' (2004) 8(2) *Journal of Money Laundering Control* 127.

Barnett, H., *Constitutional and Administrative Law* (Cavendish 2004).

Basel Committee on Banking Supervision, International Organization of Securities Commissions and International Association of Insurance Supervisors, *Initiatives by the BCBS, IAIS and IOSCO to combat money laundering and the financing of terrorism* (June 2003).

Battula, B.P., Rani, K., Prasad, S. and Sudha, T., 'Techniques in computer forensics: a recovery perspective' (2009) 3(2) *International Journal of Security* 27.

Baumann, C.E., *The Diplomatic Kidnappings: A Revolutionary Tactic of Urban Terrorism* (Martinus Nijhoff 1973).

Baumann, C.E., *The Diplomatic Kidnappings: An Overview* (International Terrorism: Proceedings of an Intensive Panel at the 15th Annual Convention of the International Studies Association. Milwaukee, WI, U.S.A.: Institute of World Affairs, University of Wisconsin, 1974).

Beaty, J. and Gwynne, S.C., *The Outlaw Bank: A Wide Ride into the Secret Heart of BCCI* (Random House 1993).

Beaumert, T., 'Terrorism, News Flows and Stock Markets' in Harry Ward Richardson, Peter Gordon and James Elliott Moore (eds), *Global Business and the Terrorist Threat* (Edward Elgar 2009).

Bell, R.E., 'The prosecution of computer crime' (2002) 9(4) *Journal of Financial Crime* 308.

—— 'The confiscation, forfeiture and disruption of terrorist finances' (2003) 7(2) *Journal of Money Laundering Control* 105.

—— 'Concealing and disguising criminal property' (2009) 12(3) *Journal of Money Laundering Control* 268.

Bell, G., Hey, T. and Szalay, A., 'Beyond the data deluge' (2009) 323(5919) *Computer Science* 1297.

Bellman, K. and Landauer, C., 'Playing in the MUD: virtual worlds are real places (2000) 14(1) *Applied Artificial Intelligence* 93.

Benjamin, D. and Steven, S., *The Age of Sacred Terror* (Random House 2002).

Bergen, P.L., *Holy War: Inside the Secret World of Osama bin Laden* (Phoenix 2002).

Berkowitz, L., *The Concept of Aggressive Drive: Advances in Experimental Social Psychology* (Academic Press 1965).

Biersteker, T.J. and Eckert, S.E. (eds), *Countering the Financing of Terrorism* (Routledge 2008).

Binning, P., 'In safe hands? Striking the balance between privacy and security, anti-terrorist finance measures' (2002) 6 *European Human Rights Law Review* 737.

Birrell, D., 'Relative deprivation as a factor in conflict in Northern Ireland' (1972) 20 *Socio-political Review* 317.

Blackwell, M. and Seddon, D., *Informal Remittances from the UK: Values, Flows and Mechanisms* (DFID report by the Overseas Development Group, Norwich, 2004).

Blanchard, C.M. and Prados, A.B., *Saudi Arabia: Terrorist Financing Issues* (CRS Report for Congress, Order Code RL32499, updated 14 September 2007). [Online]. Available at: http://www.fas.org/sgp/crs/terror/RL32499.pdf [accessed: 8 July 2011].

Bolz, F. Jr., Dunois, K.J. and Schilz, D.P., *The Counterterrorism Handbook: Tactics, Procedures and Techniques* (CRC Press 2005).

Borgia, G., *Human Aggression as a Biological Adaptation: The Evolution of Human Social Behaviour* (Elsevier 1980).

Bothe, M., 'Security Council's targeted sanctions against presumed terrorists: the need to comply with human rights standards' (2008) 6(3) *Journal of International Criminal Justice* 541.

Brisard, J.C. and Martinez, D., *Zarqawi: The New Face of al-Qaeda* (Polity Press 2005).

Brisard J-C, *Terrorism Financing: Roots and Trends of Saudi Terrorism Financing* (Report prepared for the President of the Security Council, United Nations 19 December 2002, New York).

Broadhurst, R., 'Developments in the global law enforcement of cyber-crime' (2006) 29(3) *Policing: An International Journal of Police Strategies & Management* 408.

Brown, D., Dalton, J. and Hoyle, H., 'Spatial forecast methods for terrorist events in urban environments' (2004) 3073 *Intelligence and Security Informatics*.

Brungsa, A. and Jamieson, R., 'Identification of Legal Issues for Computer Forensics' (2010) 3(2) *Journal of Digital Forensic Practice* 140.

Bureau for International Narcotics and Law Enforcement Affairs, *International Narcotics Control Strategy Report – 2003* (Bureau for International Narcotics and Law Enforcement Affairs, March 2004).

Burgess, R.G., *The Unstructured Interview as Conversation: Field Research: A Sourcebook and Field Manual* (Routledge 1982).

Burke, J., *Al-Qaeda: Casting a Shadow of Terror* (Tauris & Co 2003).
Butler, M. and Boyle, R., *Alternative Remittance Regulation Implementation Package: APG Typologies Working Group on Alternative Remittance and Underground Banking Systems* (Asia Pacific Group on Money Laundering, 2003).
Cabinet Office, *The UK and the Campaign against International Terrorism – Progress Report* (Cabinet Office, London, 2002).
—— *The UK and the Campaign against International Terrorism* (Progress Report, London, 2002).
—— *The UK and the Campaign against International Terrorism Progress Report* (London, 2002).
Campbell, G., *Blood Diamonds* (Westview Press 2002).
Çapin, T.K., *Avatars in Networked Virtual Environments* (Wiley 1999).
Capotorto, G., 'How Terrorists Look at Kidnappings' in B.M. Jenkins (ed.), *Terrorism and Personal Protection* (Butterworth 1985).
Capra, Fritjof, 'September 11: True Security – We cannot fight terrorism effectively without understanding its roots' *Resurgence* 211. [Online]. Available at: http://www.resurgence.org/resurgence/issues/capra211.htm [accessed: 17 October 2009].
Carroll, L., *Alternative Remittance Systems* (Interpol Secretariat, no. 20, 1999).
Cartwright, R., *The Globalization of Business* (Palgrave Macmillan 2004).
Cassidy, W.L., *Political Kidnapping: an Introductory Overview* (Sycamore Island Books 1978).
Castronova, E., 'The price of bodies: a hedonic pricing model of avatar attributes in a synthetic world' (2004) 57(2) Kyklos 173.
Chaikin, D., 'How effective are suspicious transaction reporting systems?' (2009) 12(3) *Journal of Money Laundering Control* 238.
Chami, R., Cosimano, T.F. and Gapen, M.T., *Beware of Emigrants Bearing Gifts: Optimal Fiscal and Monetary Policy in the Presence of Remittances* (International Monetary Funds Working Paper, 2006).
Chen, H., Chung, W., Qin, J., Reid, E., Sageman, M. and Weimann, G., 'Uncovering the dark Web: a case study of jihad on the Web' (2008) 59(8) *Journal of the American Society for Information Science and Technology* 1347.
Chopra, V.D., *Global Challenges of Terrorism* (Gyan Publishing House 2002).
Chouvy, P.A., 'Drugs and the financing of terrorism' (2004) 2(20) *Terrorism Monitor*.[Online].Availableat:http://www.pa-chouvy.org/terrorism-monitor-afghanistan-drugs_financing_terrorism PRINT.html.
Christia, F. and Semple, M., 'Flipping the Taliban: how to win in Afghanistan' (2009) 88 *Journal of Foreign Affairs* 34.
Chu, Y.K., 'International triad movements: the threat of Chinese organised crime' (1996) Conflict Studies 291.

Chu, Y.K., *The Triads as Business* (Routledge 2006).

Chu, Yiu Kong, *International Triad Movements: The Threat of Chinese Organised Crime* (Conflict Studies 291, Research Institute for the Study of Conflict and Terrorism, 1996).

Chukwuemerie, A., 'International legal war on the financing of terrorism: a comparison of Nigerian, UK, US and Canadian laws' (2006) 9(1) *Journal of Money Laundering Control* 71.

Ciluffo, F., *Russian Organised Crime: Global Organised Crime Project* (The Centre for Strategic and International Studies, 1997).

Clutterbuck, R.L., *Kidnap and Ransom: The Response* (Faber & Faber 1978).

Cohen, L.E. and Land, K.C., 'Age structure and crime: symmetry versus asymmetry and the projection of crime rates through the 1990's' (1987) 52 *American Sociological Review* 170.

College of International and Security Studies, *The Financing of Terrorism* (Program on Terrorism and Security Studies, 2004).

Collins, E., *Killing Rage* (Granta Books 1997).

Comer, M.J., *Corporate Fraud* (Gower Publishing 1998).

Coogan, T.M., *The IRA* (Harper Collins 1995).

Cooley, J.K., *Unholy Wars: Afghanistan, America and International Terrorism* (Pluto Press 2000).

Cooper, H.H.A., 'The terrorist and the victim' (1978) 1(2) *Victimology: An International Journal* 229.

Copeland, T., 'Is the "new terrorism" really new? An analysis of the new paradigm for terrorism' (2001) 21(2) *Journal of Conflict Studies*. [Online]. Available at: http://www.peacestudiesjournal.org.uk/dl/Feb%2006%20SPENCER%20version%202.pdf [accessed: 12 January 2010].

Corbin, J., *Al-Qaeda: In Search of the Terror Network that Threatens the World* (Thunder's Mouth Press/Nation Books 2002).

Cordes, B., Jenkins, B.M. and Kellen, K., *A Conceptual Framework for Analyzing Terrorist Groups* (RAND Corporation, June 1985).

Corrado, R.R., 'A critique of the mental disorder perspective of political terrorism' (1981) 4 *International Journal of Law and Psychiatry* 293.

Corrigan, M., *A Month in Money Laundering* (Deloitte and Touche LLP, June 2004).

Costigans, S.S. and Gold, D. (eds), *Terronomics* (Ashgate 2007).

Crenshaw, M., 'The causes of political terrorism' (1981) 13(4) *Comparative Politics* 379.

—— *The Psychology of Political Terrorism. Political Psychology: Contemporary Problems and Issues* (Jossey-Bass 1983).

—— *Origins of Terrorism: Questions to Be Answered, Research to Be Done* (Woodrow Wilson Centre 1990).

—— *How Terrorists Think: What Psychology Can Contribute to Understanding Terrorism* (Praeger 1992).

—— 'The psychology of terrorism: an agenda for the 21st century' (2000) 21(2) *Political Psychology* 405.

Creveld, M. van, *The Rise and Decline of the State* (Cambridge University Press 1999).

Cronin, A.K., 'The evolution of counterterrorism: will tactics trump strategy?' (2010) 86(4) *International Affairs* 837.

Cuddington, J., 'Capital flight: estimates, issues and explanations' (1986) 58 *Princeton Studies in International Finance* 2.

Daily Telegraph, 'What's a website, asks judge at internet trial' (London, 18 May 2007).

Daly, M. and Wilson, M., *Evolutionary Psychology of Male Violence* (Routledge 1994).

Damphousse, K., *The Internet: a Terrorist Medium of the 21st Century* (Sage Publications 1998).

DeRosa, M., *Data Mining and Data Analysis for Counterterrorism* (CSIS Press 2004).

Diamond, D.W., 'Financial intermediation and delegated monitoring' (1984) 51 *Review of Economic Studies* 393.

Dicken, P., *Global Shift: Reshaping the Global Economic Map in the 21st Century* (Sage Publications 2003).

Dozier, R.W., *Why We Hate* (McGraw-Hill 2002).

Drainville, A.C., *Contesting Globalisation* (Routledge 2003).

Drake, C.J.M., 'The role of ideology in terrorists target selections' (1998) 10(2) *Terrorism and Political Violence* 53.

Drezner, D.W., 'Sanctions sometimes smart: targeted sanctions in theory and practice' (2011) 13(1) *International Studies Review* 96.

Durham, W.H., 'Resource competition and human aggression' (1976) 51 *The Quarterly Review of Biology* 385.

Duyne, P.C. van and Soudijn, M.R.J., 'Hot money, hot stones and hot air: crime-money threat, real estate and real concern' (2009) 12(2) *Journal of Money Laundering Control* 173.

Ehrenfeld, R., *Funding Evil Updated: How Terrorism Is Financed and How to Stop It* (Bonus Books 2004).

Elagab, O., 'Control of terrorist funds and the banking system' (2006) 21(1) *Journal of International Banking Law and Regulation* 38.

Ellis, B., 'Countering complexity: an analytical framework to guide counter-terrorism policy-making' (2003) 6(1) *Journal of Military and Strategic Studies* 42.

Ellsberg, D., *The Theory and Practice of Blackmail* (Rand Corporation, 1968).
Emerson, S., *American Jihad: The Terrorist Living amongst Us* (Simon & Schuster 2002).
Erikson, E.H., *Identity, Youth and Crisis* (Faber & Faber 1968).
European Banking Industry Committee (EBIC), *EBIC Comments on the Proposal for a New EU Directive on Money Laundering* (EBIC, September 2004).
Evans, Jonathan. Article about threats to UK. [Online]. Available at: https://www.mi5.gov.uk/output/director-general.html [accessed: 15 October 2009]
Evans, M., 'From Kadesh to Kandahar: military theory and the future of war' (2003) 16(3) *Naval War College Review* 132.
Everett, C., 'Who is responsible for policing the Internet?' (2009) 9(5) *Computer Fraud & Security* 5.
Faist, T., *The Volume and Dynamics of International Migration and Transnational Social Spaces* (Oxford University Press 2000).
Fang, L.H., 'Investment bank reputation and the price and quality of underwriting services' (2005) 60(6) *Journal of Finance* 2729.
Farah, D., *Blood from Stones* (Broadway Books 2004).
Ferracuti, F., *A Sociopsychiatric Interpretation of Terrorism* (Sage Publications 1982).
Financial Action Task Force, *Report on Money Laundering Typologies* (FATF, 1999).
—— *Basic Facts about Money Laundering* (FATF, June 2003).
—— *Report on Money Laundering and Terrorist Financing Typologies 2003–3004* (FATF, 2004).
—— *The Financial War on Terrorism: A Guide by the Financial Action Task Force* (France, OECD, 2004).
—— *Money Laundering and Terrorist Finance Typologies 2004–2005*. [Online]. Available at: http://www.fatf-gafi.org/dataoecd/16/8/35003256.pdf#search=%22FATF%20%22Money%20Laundering%20typologies%22%22 [accessed: 15 October 2009].
—— *Annual Review of Non-Cooperative Countries and Territories 2006–2007* (FATF, Eighth NCCT Review, 12 October 2007).
—— *Global Money Laundering & Terrorist Financing Threat Assessment: A view of how and why criminals and terrorists abuse finances, the effect of this abuse and the steps to mitigate these threats* (FATF Report, July 2010).
—— *About the Non-Cooperative Countries and Territories (NCCT) Initiative*. [Online]. Available at: http://www.fatf-gafi.org/document/51/0,3746,en_32250379_32236992_33916403_1_1_1_1,00.html [accessed: 12 July 2011].
FinCen, 'Informal Value Transfer Systems' (US Department of the Treasury Financial Crimes Enforcement Network Advisory Issue 33, FinCen Advisory, 2003).
—— *US Money Laundering Threat Assessment* (US Money Laundering Threat Assessment Working Group, December 2005).

—— *Potential Money Laundering Risks Related to Shell Companies* (Department of the Treasury, Financial Crimes Enforcement Network, FIN-2006-G014, 9 November 2006).

Fink, A., *Conducting Literature Reviews* (Sage Publications 1998).

Fisher, J., 'Recent development in the fight against money laundering' (2002) 17(3) *Journal of International Banking Law* 67.

Fitzgerald, P.L., 'Smarter Smart Sanctions' (2007) 26 *International Law Review* 37.

FitzGerald, V., *Global Financial Information, Compliance Incentives and Conflict Funding* (Working Paper no. 96, QEH Working Paper Series – QEHWPS96).

Fleming, M.H., *UK Law Enforcement Agency Use and Management of SARs: Towards Determining the Value of the Regime* (Home Office, 2005).

—— 'Issues in measuring the efficacy of a Suspicious Activity Reports (SARs) regime' (2007) 70 *Amicus Curiae* 9.

Fleury, S., 'Review of unfunding terror: the legal response to the financing of global terrorism' (2010) 7(1) *Journal of Homeland Security and Emergency Management* 67.

Flint, C. and Radil, S.M., 'Terrorism and counter-terrorism: situating al-Qaeda and the global war on terror within geopolitical trends and structures' (2009) 50 *Eurasian Geography and Economics* 150.

Ford, P.J., 'Paralysis lost: impacts of virtual worlds on those with paralysis' (2001) 27(4) *Social Theory and Practice* 661.

Forest, J.J.F. (ed.), *The Making of a Terrorist: Recruitment, Training and Root Causes* (Praeger Security International 2006).

Frost, R.M., 'Nuclear and radiological terrorism' (2005) 45 *Adelphi Paper* no. 378.

FSA, *Review of Private Banks' Anti-Money Laundering Systems and Controls* (FSA Review July, 2007).

Gallant, M., 'Promise and perils: the making of global money laundering, terrorist finance norms' (2010) 13(1) *Journal of Money Laundering Control* 175.

Garas, S.N. and Pierce, C., 'Shari'a supervision of Islamic financial institutions' (2010) 18(4) *Journal of Financial Regulation and Compliance* 386.

Ghosh, T.K., Prelas, M.A., Viswanath, D.S. and Loyalka, S.K., *Science and Technology of Terrorism and Counterterrorism* (Marcel Dekker 2002).

Gibb, Frances, 'Judge halts terror trial to ask: what's a website?' *The Times* (London, 18 May 2007).

Gilligan, G., 'Going underground: the not so new way to bank' (2001) 9(2) *Journal of Financial Crime* 105.

Gilligan, J., *Violence: Reflections on Our Deadliest Epidemic* (Jessica Kingsley 2000).

Gilpin, R., *Counting the Costs of Somali Piracy* (Center for Sustainable Economies, US Institute of Peace Report, 22 June 2009).

Giustozzi, A. (ed.), *Decoding the New Taliban: Insights from the Afghan Field* (Columbia University Press 2009).

Global Enforcement Regimes, *Transnational Organised Crime* (International Terrorism and ML TNI Crime and Globalisation seminar, Amsterdam 28–9 April 2005). [Online]. Available at: http://www.tni.org/crime-docs/enforce.pdf#search=%22terrorist%20finance%20%20%22UK%20treasury%22%20filetype%3 Apdf%22 [accessed: 14 April 2010].

Global Witness, *For a Few Dollars More: How al-Qaeda Moved into the Diamond Trade* (Global Witness, April 2003).

Godfrey, C., Eaton, G., McDougall, C. and Culyer, A., *The Economic and Social Costs of Class A Drugs Use in England and Wales, 2000*. (The Home Office Research, Development and Statistics Directorate, July 2002).

Gould, Harold A. and Spinney, Franklin C., '4GW is Here!' *Center for South Asian Studies Newsletter* (University of Virginia 2001). [Online]. Available at: www.virginia.edu/soasia/newsletter/Fall01/warfare. html [accessed: 10 October 2009] and http://www.smallwarsjournal.com/documents/4gw.htm [accessed: 10 October 2009].

Government Accountability Office, *International Taxation: Large U.S. Corporations and Federal Contractors with Subsidiaries in Jurisdictions Listed as Tax Havens or Financial Privacy Jurisdictions* (GAO: GAO-09-157, 18 December 2008).

Grabosky, P.N. and Smith, R.G., *Crime in the Digital Age: Controlling Telecommunications and Cyberspace Illegalities* (Transaction 1998).

Gray, D.H., 'The importance of the Internet to the post-modern terrorist and its role as a form of safe haven' (2009) 25(3) *European Journal of Scientific Research* 396.

Gray, J., *Al Qaeda and What It Means to Be Modern* (Faber & Faber 2003).

Greenberg, M R, *Update on the Global Campaign against Terrorist Financing* (Council on Foreign Relations, 2004).

Groupe d'Economie Mondiale, *The Transformational Potential of M-Transactions-Moving the debate forward* (The Policy Paper Series, no. 6, July 2007).

Guardia Di Finanza, *The Funding of International Islamic Terrorism: Strategic Analysis Profiles*. [Online]. Available at: http://www.gdf.it/Stampa/STUDI/2006fundingofinternationalislamicterrorism.pdf [accessed: 23 January 2010].

Gunaratna, R., *Inside Al Qaeda: Global Network of Terror* (Hurst & Co. 2003).

Hall, W.M., *Stray Voltage: War in the Information Age* (Naval Institute Press 2003).

Hammes, T.X., '4GW: our enemies play to their strengths' (2004) *Armed Forces Journal* 40.

—— *The Sling and the Stone: On War in the 21st Century* (Zenith Press 2004).

—— 'Insurgency: modern warfare evolves into a fourth generation' *Strategic Forum* 2 14 Jan 2005. [Online]. Available at: http://www.ndu.edu/inss/strforum/SF214/SF214.pdf.

Hardister, A.D., 'Can we buy peace on earth? The price of freezing terrorist assets in a post-September 11 world' (2003) 28 (624) *North Carolina Journal of International Law and Commercial Regulation* 605.

Harris, N., *Thinking the Unthinkable: The Immigration Myth Exposed* (I.B. Tauris & Co. 2002).

Hassel, C., 'Terror: the crime of the privileged: an examination and prognosis' (1977) 1(1) *Terrorism* 1.

Hatonn, G.C., *Chaparral Serendipity* (Phoenix Source Distributors 1993).

Haynal, A., Molnar, M. and Pumege, G. de, *Fanaticism: A Historical and Psychoanalytical Study* (Schocken Books 1983).

Hayter, W., 'The politics of kidnapping' (1971) 14(4) *Interplay* 25.

Held, D., McGrew, A., Goldblatt, D. and Perraton, J., *Global Transformations: Politics, Economics and Culture* (Polity Press 2000).

Henderson, H., *Global Terrorism: The Complete Reference Guide* (Checkmark Books 2001).

Herman, M., *Intelligence: Power in Peace and War* (Cambridge University Press 1996).

—— *Intelligence Services in the Information Age* (Frank Cass 2002).

Heskin, K., 'The psychology of terrorism in Northern Ireland' (1984) 15 *Irish Journal of Psychology* 269.

Hey, T. and Trefethen, A., 'The Data Deluge: An e-Science Perspective' in F. Berman, G. Fox and T. Hey (eds), *Grid Computing: Making the Global Infrastructure a Reality* (John Wiley & Sons 2003).

Hillis, K., *Digital Sensations: Space, Identity and Embodiment in Virtual Reality* (University of Minnesota Press 1999).

Hinterseer, K., *Criminal Finance: The Political Economy of Money Laundering in a Comparative Legal Context* (Kluwer Law International 2002).

HM Treasury, *Informal Consultation on the Third EC Money Laundering Directive* (HM Treasury, May 2004).

—— *The Launch of Anti-Money Laundering and Counter-Terrorist Finance Strategy* (HM Treasury, The Financial Challenge to Crime and Terrorism Report, Issue 10, March 2007).

Hoffer, E., *The True Believer* (Harper and Row 1961).

Hoffman, B., *Al Qaeda, Trends in Terrorism, the Future Potentialities: An Assessment* (The Rand Corporation, Washington DC, 8 May 2003).

Hollin, C.R., *Psychology and Crime: An Introduction to Criminological Psychology* (Routledge 1998).

Home Office, *Consultation Paper on a Code of Practice for Voluntary Retention of Communications Data* (London, March 2003).

—— *One Step Ahead: A 21st Century Strategy to Defeat Organised Crime* (London, March 2004).
—— *Report on the Operation in 2004 of the Terrorism Act 2000* (London, 2004).
—— *Policing in the 21st Century: Reconnecting Police and the People* (2009). [Online]. Availableat:http://www.homeoffice.gov.uk/publications/consultations/policing-21st-century/[accessed: 25 August 2010].
—— *CONTEST Strategy 2* (UK Strategy for Countering International Terrorism, 24 March 2009).
—— *The Technical and Cost Issues Associated with Interception of Communication at Certain Communications Service Providers*. [Online]. Available at: http://www. home office.gov.uk/ oicd/techcost.pdf [accessed: 2 February 2010].
—— *Report on Policing in the 21st Century: Reconnecting Police and the People Table One: New Roles for Key Individuals and Organisations* (Home Office, 26 July 2010).
Homer-Dixon, T.F., Boutwell, J.H. and Rathjens, G.W., 'Environmental change and violent conflict' (1993) 268 *Scientific American* 38.
Horgan, J. and Taylor, M., 'Playing the "Green Card": financing the Provisional IRA: Part 1' (1999) 11(2) *Terrorism and Political Violence* 1.
House of Commons. *Report on the Official Account of the Bombings in London on 7 July 2005* (The Stationery Office, 11 May 2006).
Howard, R.D. and Sawyer, R.L., *Terrorism and Counterterrorism: Understanding the New Security Environment* (McGraw-Hill 2004).
Hubbard, D., 'Extortion threats: the possibility of analysis' (1975) 1 *Assets Protection* 17.
—— 'Terrorism and protest' (1978) 2 *Legal Medical Quarterly* 188.
Hudson, R., *The Sociology and Psychology of Terrorism: Who Becomes a Terrorist and Why?* (The Federal Research Division, Library of Congress, September 1999).
Hudson-Smith, A., *30 Days in Active Worlds: Community, Design and Terrorism in a Virtual World. The Social Life of Avatars: Presence and Interaction in Shared Virtual Environments* (Springer 2002).
Hughes, T.P., *A Dictionary of Islam: Being a Cyclopaedia of the Doctrines, Rites, Ceremonies and Customs, Together With the Technical and Theological Terms, of the Muhammadan Religion* (Asian Educational Services 1885).
Hunton, P., 'The stages of cybercrime investigations: bridging the gap between technology examination and law enforcement investigation' (2011) 27(1) *Computer Law & Security Review* 61.
Hussey, J. and Hussey, R., *Business Research* (Macmillan Press 1997).
IMF, *The Fight against Money Laundering and the Financing of Terrorism Fact Sheet* (IMF, 10 September 2010).

International Anti-Counterfeiting Coalition, *International/Global Intellectual Property Theft: Links to Terrorism and Terrorist Organisations* (White Paper, IACC, 2003).

Interpol, *The Hawala Alternative Remittance System and Its Role in Money Laundering* (Interpol General Secretariat, Lyon, January 2000).

—— *The Hawala Alternative Remittance System and Its Role in Money Laundering* (Interpol General Secretariat, 2003).

Ireye, A., *Global Community: The Role of Intentional Organisations in the Making of the Contemporary World* (University of California Press 2002).

Isaacs, M., 'Money laundering dilemmas for banks' (2004) 19(8) *Journal of International Banking Law and Regulation* 284.

Jack, W. and Suri, T., *Mobile Money: The Economics of M-PESA* (National Bureau of Economic Research Working Paper no. 16721, issued in January 2011).

Jacquard, R., *In the Name of Osama bin Laden: Global Terrorism and the bin Laden Brotherhood* (Duke University Press 2002).

Jamwal, N.S., 'Hawala: the invisible financing system of terrorism' (2000) 26(2) *Strategic Analysis* 181.

Jararatna, N., *Understanding and Evaluating Methodologies* (NIMSAD 1999).

Jenkins, B.M., *Terrorism and Kidnapping* (Rand Corporation, 1974).

Jenkins, M., 'Foreword' in Ian Lesser, *Countering the New Terrorism* (RAND Corporation, 1999).

Johnson, J., 'In pursuit of dirty money: identifying weaknesses in the global financial system' (2001) 5(2) *Journal of Money Laundering Control* 126.

—— '11th September, 2001: will it make a difference to the global anti-money laundering movement?' (2002) 6(1) *Journal of Money Laundering Control* 10.

—— 'Third round FATF mutual evaluations indicate declining compliance' (2008) 11(1) *Journal of Money Laundering Control* 47.

Johnson, T.H. and Mason, M.C., 'Understanding the Taliban and insurgency in Afghanistan' (2007) 51(1) *Orbis* 71.

Joint Committee on Human Rights Report, *Terrorist Asset-Freezing etc. Bill* (Preliminary Report). [Online]. Available at: http://www.parliament.uk/business/committees/committees-a-z/joint-select/human-rights-committee/news/third-report/ [accessed: 30 July 2010].

Jost, P.M. and Sandhu, H.S., *The Hawala Alternative Remittance System and Its Role in Money Laundering* (Interpol General Secretariat, 2000).

Junger-Tas, J., *Delinquent Behaviour among Young People in the Western World* (Kugler 1994).

Justice Report, *Secret Evidence* (Justice Org, June 2009).

Kaldor, M., *New and Old Wars: Organised Violence in a Global Era* (Polity Press 1999).

Kaplan, A., *The Psychodynamics of Terrorism* (Pergamon 1981).
Keene, S.D., *Al-Qaeda: Financing Terror* (Airey Neave Trust Report, 2005).
—— 'Hawala and related informal value transfer systems: an assessment in the context of organised crime and terrorist finance. Is there cause for concern?' (2007) *The Defence Academy Journal* 4.
—— *A Trojan Horse for Terrorism: The Vulnerability and Abuse of Mosques by Militant Islam in the United Kingdom* (The Institute for Statecraft and Governance, Security Economics Programme, February 2010).
—— 'Terrorism and the Internet: a double edged sword' (2011) 14(4) of the *Journal of Money Laundering Control.*
Kelly, R.E., 'From the "global war on terror" to containment: an opinion brief' (2008) 2(4) *Perspectives on Terrorism.* [Online]. Available at: http://www.terrorismanalysts.com/pt/index.php/pot/article/view/34/html [accessed: 2 February 2010].
Kersten, A., 'Financing of terrorism: a predicate offence to money laundering' (2002) 4(2) *European Journal of Law Reform* 299.
Kizza, J.M., 'Computer crime investigations: computer forensics' (2010) 978 *Computer Science* 263.
Knapp, M.G., 'The concept and practice of jihad in Islam' (2003) 33 *Parameters US Army War College Quarterly* 45.
Kochan, N., *The Washing Machine: Money, Crime and Terror in the Offshore System* (Duckworth 2006).
Kometer, M., *The New Terrorism: The Nature of the War on Terrorism* (US Air University Press 2004).
Konrad, K., *Terrorists: What Are They Like? How Some Terrorists Describe Their World and Their Actions* (RAND, N-1300-SL Santa Monica, CA, 1979).
—— *On Terrorists and Terrorism* (RAND, N-1942-RC Santa Monica, CA, 1982).
Kontorovich, E., 'An empirical examination of universal jurisdiction for piracy' (2010) 104 *American Journal of International Law* 9.
KPMG, *Money Laundering: Review of the Reporting System* (London, 2003).
Kruse, A., 'Financial and economic sanctions: from a perspective of international law and human rights' (2005) 12(3) *Journal of Financial Crime* 218.
Kruse, H., 'The Islamic doctrine of international treaties' (1954) *Islamic Quarterly* 152.
Kudrle, R.T., 'Did blacklisting hurt the tax havens?' (2009) 12(1) *Journal of Money Laundering Control* 33.
Kuhn, T.S., *The Structure of Scientific Revolutions* (University of Chicago Press 1962).
Kushner, D., 'My avatar, my self' (2004) 107(3) *Technology Review* 50.

Kwang, K. and Choo, R., 'PEPs risks and mitigation' (2008) 11(4) *Journal of Money Laundering Control* 371.

Kwok, M.L. and Paterson, R.E., 'Political kidnapping: 1968–1973' (1974) 6 *Journal of Contemporary Revolutions* 75.

Laqueur, W., *Terrorism* (Weidenfeld and Nicolson 1977).

—— *The New Terrorism: Fanaticism and the Arms of Mass Destruction* (Oxford University Press 1999).

Lasch, C., *The Culture of Narcissism* (W.W. Norton 1979).

Lastowka, F.G. and Hunter, D., 'The laws of the virtual worlds' (2004) 92(1) *California Law Review* 3.

Lee, C.S., Bokkerink, M. and Smallwood, J., *Approaches to a Regulatory Framework for Formal and Informal Remittance Systems: Experience and Lessons* (International Monetary Fund Report, prepared by the Monetary and Financial Systems Department, 2005).

Lee, D.R., 'Free riding and paid riding in the fight against terrorism' (1988) 78(2) *American Economic Review* 22.

Lehr, P., 'Somali piracy: the next iteration' (2009) 3(4) *Perspectives on Terrorism* 26.

Levi, M. and Burrows, J., 'Measuring the impact of fraud in the UK: a conceptual and empirical journey' (2008) 48(3) *British Journal of Criminology* 293.

Levi, M. and Gillmore, W., 'Terrorist finance, money laundering and the rise and rise of mututal evaluation: a new paradigm for crime control?' (2002) 4(2) *European Journal of Law Reform* 337.

Levitt, M., 'Stemming the flow of terrorist financing: practical and conceptual challenges' (2003) 27(1) *The Fletcher Forum of World Affairs* 59.

Levy, B.H., *Who Killed Daniel Pearl?* (Duckworth 2004).

Lewis, B., *The Political Language of Islam* (University of Chicago Press 1988).

—— *Assassins: A Radical Sect in Islam* (Weidenfeld and Nicolson 2001).

Lim, Y.F., *Cyberspace Law: Commentaries and Materials* (Oxford University Press 2002).

Lind, W.S., Nightengale, K., Schmitt, K.J., Sutton, J.W. and Wilson, G.I., 'The changing face of war: into the fourth generation' (1989) *Marine Corps Gazette* 22.

Linn, C.J., 'Regulating the cross-border movement of prepaid cards' (2008) 11(2) *Journal of Money Laundering Control* 146.

Longstaff, P.H., *Security, Resilience and Communication in Unpredictable Environments Such as Terrorism, Natural Disasters and Complex Technology* (Harvard University, 2005).

Lutz, J.M. and Lutz, B.J., *Global Terrorism* (Routledge 2004).

Lyons, H.A. and Harbinson, H.J., 'A comparison of political and non-political murderers in Northern Ireland, 1974–1984' (1986) 26 *Medicine, Science and Law* 193.

MacMull, G., 'Removing the charitable veil: an examination of US policy to combat terrorist funding charities post 9/11' (2004) 10 *New England Journal of International & Comparative Law* 121.

Maimbo, S.M., *The Money Exchange Dealers of Kabul: A Study of the Hawala System in Afghanistan* (Finance and Private Sector Unit, South Asia Region, World Bank, 2003).

Makarento, T., 'Crime, terror and the central Asian drug trade' (2002) 6 *Harvard Asia Quarterly*.

Manningham-Buller, E., Terrorist threat to UK – MI5 chief's full speech, *Times Online* November 10, 2006. [Online]. Available at: http://www.timesonline.co.uk/tol/news/uk/article632872.ece [accessed: 20 October 2009].

Margolin, J., *Psychological Perspectives in Terrorism* (Jay Jay Press 1977).

Marsden, P., *The Taliban War, Religion and the New Order in Afghanistan* (Oxford University Press 2002).

Marshall, E., 'Kidnapping epidemic: a form of political terrorism' (1974) 170 *New Republic* 15.

Mas, I., 'Designing mobile money services lessons from M-PESA' (2009) 4(2) *Innovations* 77.

Masciandaro, D. (ed.), *Global Financial Crime: Terrorism, Money Laundering and Offshore Centres* (Ashgate 2004).

McCauley, C., *Social Psychology of Terrorist Groups* (Frank Cass 1987).

McCulloch, J. and Pickering, S., 'Suppressing the financing of terrorism: proliferating state crime, eroding censure and extending neo-colonialism' (2005) 45 *British Journal of Criminology* 470.

McDermott, T., *Perfect Soldiers* (Harper Collins 2005).

Means, J., 'Political kidnapping and terrorism' (1970) 255 *North American Review* 16.

Merari, A., *The Readiness to Kill and Die: Suicidal Terrorism in the Middle East* (Cambridge University Press 1990).

Merlonghi, G., 'Fighting financial crime in the age of electronic money: opportunities and limitations' (2010) 13 (3) *Journal of Money Laundering Control* 202.

Metwally, M.M., 'Economic consequences of applying Islamic principles in Muslim societies' (1997) 24 (7/8/9) *Journal of International Social Economics* 941.

Middleton, B., 'Freezing Terrorist Assets, A v HM Treasury; R (on the application of Youssef) v HM Treasury, HM Treasury v Al-Ghabra [2010] UKSC 2' *Journal of Criminal Law* (2010) 74(3) *Journal of Criminal Law* 209.

Millbank, D., *International and Transnational Terrorism: Diagnosis and Prognosis* (CIA, 1976).

Ministry of Finance, Saudi Arabia, *A Technical Assessment of Certain Saudi Arabia Laws, Regulations and Institutions*. [Online]. Available at: http://www.mof.gov.sa/e_alzakah.html [accessed: 23 January 2010].

Moore, T., Clayton, R. and Anderson, R., 'The economics of online crime' (2009) 23(3) *Journal of Economic Perspectives* 3.

Moorehead, C., *Fortune's Hostages: A Study of Kidnapping in the World Today* (Hamilton 1980).

Morgan, M.J., 'Origins of the new terrorism' (2004) *Parameters US Army War College Quarterly* 30.

Mortimer-Schutts, I., *The Transformational Potential of M-Transactions: Moving the Debate Forward* (The Policy Paper Series, no. 6, July 2007).

Muenz, R., *Towards a European Migration Policy. Challenges and Opportunities for the EU and Its Member States* (Hamburg Institute for International Economics, 2004).

—— *Dimensions and Impacts of Demographic Aging: The Case of Europe and Its Public Pension System* (Hamburg Institute for International Economics, 2005).

Mugarura, N., 'The effect of corruption factor in harnessing global anti-money laundering regimes' (2010) 13(3) *Journal of Money Laundering Control* 272.

Murray, K., 'Dismantling organised crime groups through enforcement of the POCA money laundering offences' (2010) 13 *Journal of Money Laundering Control* 7.

—— 'The uses of irresistible inference: protecting the system from criminal penetration through more effective prosecution of money laundering offences' (2011) 14 *Journal of Money Laundering Control* 7.

Myers, J.M., 'Disrupting terrorist networks: the new US and international regime for halting terrorist finance' (2003) 34 *Law & Policy International Business* 17.

Mylonaki, E., 'The manipulation of organised crime by terrorists: legal and factual perspectives' (2002) 2 *The International Criminal Law Review* 213.

Nakamura, L., *Cybertypes: Race, Ethnicity and Identity on the Internet* (Routledge 2002).

Napoleoni, L., *Modern Jihad: Tracing the Dollars behind the Terror Networks* (Pluto Press 2004).

National Commission on Terrorism, *Countering the Changing Threat of International Terrorism: Report on the National Commission on Terrorism* (Washington, GPO, 2000).

National Commission on Terrorist Attacks upon the United States, *9/11 Commission Report: Final Report of the National Commission on Terrorist Attacks upon the United States* (Official Government Edition 2004).

—— *Overview of the Enemy*, (16 June 2004) 3. [Online]. Available at: http://www.9-11commission.gov.staff_statements/staff_statement15.pdf[accessed:23February 2010].

National Criminal Intelligence Service, *UK Threat Assessment: The Threat from Serious Organised Crime* (NCIS 2003).

National White Collar Crime Centre and the Federal Bureau of Investigation, *IC3 2004 Internet fraud: Crime Report* (FBI, 2004).

Navias, M.S., *Finance Warfare as a Response to International Terrorism* (The Political Publishing Co. 2002).

Navias, 'Financial warfare as a response to international terrorism' (2002) 73(1) *The Political Quarterly* 61.

Nawaz, S, McKinnon, R. and Webb, R., *The War on South Asia's Hawala Networks: Fighting Financial Crime or Undermining Financial Services for the Poor?* (Institute for Development Policy Management, Manchester University, 2002).

Nelson, B. and Bates, A., *Global Anti-Money Laundering Survey 2004: How Banks Are Facing up to the Challenge* (KPMG, 2004).

Nofi, Albert A., *Recent Trends in Thinking about Warfare*, CRM D0014875.A1/ Final. (Defense Technical Information Center, September 2006). [Online]. Available at: www.dtic.mil [accessed: 10 December 2009].

Norton, J.J., *Banks: Fraud and Crime* (Lloyd's of London Press and the Centre for Commercial Law Studies and the Chartered Institute of Bankers 1994).

Ohmae, K., *The Mind of the Strategist* (McGraw-Hill 1982).

Ondrejka, C., 'Escaping the gilded cage: user created content and building the metaverse' (2004) 49(1) *New York Law School Law Review* 81.

Ormerod, D., *Criminal Law: Cases and Materials* (Oxford University Press 2009).

Orozno, M., *Worker Remittances: The Human Face of Globalization* (Working Paper commissioned by the Multilateral Investment Fund of the Inter-American Development Bank, October 2002).

Orr, Deborah, 'Manningham-Buller was right about the Iraq war' *Guardian* (London, 22 July 2010).

Partnership Africa Canada, *The Failure of Good Intensions: Fraud, Theft and Murder in the Brazilian Diamond Industry* (Diamonds and Human Security Project May 2005).

Passas, N., *Informal value transfer systems and criminal organisations: a study into so-called underground banking networks* (1999). [Online]. Available at: http:// usinfo.state.gov/eap/img/ assets/4756/ivts.pdf [accessed: 20 November 2010].

—— 'Hawala and other informal value transfer systems: how to regulate them?' (2003) 5(2) *Risk Management* 49.

—— *Informal Value Transfer Systems, Terrorism and Money Laundering* (A Report to the National Institute of Justice, 2003).

—— 'Indicators of Hawala operations and criminal abuse' (2004) 8(2) *Journal of Money Laundering Control* 168.

—— 'Law enforcement challenges in hawala-related investigations' (2004) 12(2) *Journal of Financial Crime* 112.

Pearlstein, R.M., *The Mind of the Political Terrorist* (Scholarly Resources 1991).

Pearson, G. and Hobbs, D., *Middle Market Drug Distribution* (Home Office Research, Development and Statistics Directorate, November 2001).

Peterson, R.E., 'Political kidnapping: a new risk in international business' (1978) 8 *Interfaces* 46.

Philippsohn, S., 'The dangers of new technology: laundering on the Internet' (2001) 5(1) *Journal of Money Laundering Control* 87.

Phillips, E., 'The Business of Kidnap for Ransom' in David Canter (ed.), *The Faces of Terrorism: Multidisciplinary Perspectives* (Wiley-Blackwell 2009).

Ping, H., 'The new weapon for combating money laundering in the EU' (2004) 8(2) *Journal of Money Laundering Control* 116.

Poland, J., *Understanding Terrorism: Groups, Strategies and Responses* (Prentice Hall 1988).

Porter, P., 'Long wars and long telegrams: containing Al-Qaeda' (2009) 85(2) *International Affairs* 285.

Powell, R., 'Zakat: drawing insights for legal theory and economic policy from Islamic jurisprudence' (2009) 7(43) *University of Pittsburgh Tax Review*, Seattle University School of Law Research Paper no. 10–17. [Online]. Available at: http://ssrn.com/abstract=1351024.

Powles, E., 'All that glisters is no gold: laundering the UK money laundering regime' (2006) 65(1) *Cambridge Law Journal* 40.

Pratt, T.C., Holtfreter, K. and Reisig, M.D., 'Routine online activity and internet fraud targeting: extending the generality of routine activity theory' (2010) 47(3) *Journal of Research in Crime and Delinquency* 267.

Preston, E., 'The USA Patriot Act: new adventures in American extraterritorially' (2002) 10(2) *Journal of Financial Crime* 105.

Rampton, S. and Stauber, J., *Weapons of Mass Deception: The Uses of Propaganda in Bush's War on Iraq* (Penguin 2003).

Rana, Muhammad Amir, 'Taliban insurgency in Pakistan: a counterinsurgency perspective' (2009) *Pakistan Institute of Peace Studies* 9. [Online]. Available at: http://www.humansecuritygateway.com/documents/PIPS_TalibanInsurgency Pakistan_CounterinsurgencyPerspective.pdf [accessed: 30 October 2009].

Rando, T.A., *Treatment of Complicated Mourning* (Research Press 1995).

Raphaeli, N., 'Financing of terrorism: sources, methods and channels' (2003) 15(4) *Terrorism and Political Violence* 59.

Rasch, W., 'Psychological dimensions of political terrorism in the Federal Republic of Germany' (1979) 2 *International Journal of Law and Psychiatry* 79.

Rashid, A., *Taliban: Militant Islam, Oil and Fundamentalism in Central Asia* (Yale University Press 2000).

—— *Taliban: The Story of the Afghan Warlords* (Pan 2001).

—— *Jihad: The Rise and Fall of Militant Islam in Central Asia* (Yale University Press 2002).

Reason, J., *UK's Oldest Investment Bank (1762 to 1995): Managing the Risks of Organizational Accidents* (Ashgate 1997).

Reeve, S., *The New Jackals: Ramzi Yousef, Osama bin Laden and the Future of Terrorism* (Andre Deutsch 1999).

Reich, W., *Understanding Terrorist Behaviour: the Limits and Opportunities of Psychological Enquiry* (Cambridge University Press 1990).

Republic of Angola, *Diamond Industry Review* (2005).

Rider, B.A.K., 'Law: The War on Terror and Crime and the Offshore Centres: The "New" Perspective?' in D. Masciandaro (ed.), *Global Financial Crime: Terrorism, Money Laundering and Offshore Centres* (Ashgate 2004).

—— 'Pursuing Corruption: Civil Weapons: Old Law in New Battles' in *Legal Studies in the Global Era: Legal Issues Beyond Borders* (Japan Chuo University Press, 2010).

—— 'Corruption, the Sharp End of Governance' in Shazzeeda, A. Ali (ed.), *Risky Business: Perspectives on Corporate Misconduct* (Caribbean Law Publishing Company 2011).

Rider, B.A.K. and Ashe, M. (eds), *Money Laundering Control* (Sweet and Maxwell 1996).

Rider, B.A.K., Alexander, K., Linklater, L. and Bazley, S. (eds), *Market Abuse and Insider Dealing* (Tottel Publishing 2009).

Rivers, G., *War against Terrorism: How to Win It?* (Charter Books 1986).

Robinson, J., *The Laundrymen: Inside the World's Third Largest Business* (Simon & Schuster 1998).

—— *The Sink: How Banks, Lawyers and Accountants Finance Terrorism and Crime and Why the Government Can't Stop Them* (Robinson 2004).

Robson, C., *Real World Research* (Blackwell 1993).

Rotberg, R.I., *Combating Maritime Piracy: A Policy Brief with Recommendations for Action* (World Peace Foundation policy brief #11 26 January 2010).

Roule, T.J. and Kinsell, J., 'Legislative and bureaucratic impediments to suspicious transaction reporting regimes' (2002) 6(2) *Journal of Money Laundering Control* 151.

Russell, C., 'Kidnapping as a Terrorist Tactic' in B.M. Jenkins (ed.), *Terrorism and Personal Protection* (Stoneham 1952).

Ryder, N., 'A false sense of security? An analysis of legislative approaches towards the prevention of terrorist finance in the US and the UK' (2007) *Journal of Business Law* 821.

Ryder, N. and Baker, A.H., 'The legal profession sighs a relief: Bowman and Fels an appropriate response to P v P?' (2005) 39(3) *The Law Teacher* 388.

Sageman, M., *Leaderless Jihad: Terror Networks in the Twenty-First Century* (University of Pennsylvania Press 2008).

—— 'Confronting al-Qaeda: understanding the threat in Afghanistan' (2009) 3(4) *Perspectives on Terrorism* 4.

Salifu, A., 'Can corruption and economic crime be controlled in developing economies – and if so, is the cost worth it?' (2008) 11(3) *Journal of Money Laundering Control* 273.

Sands, P., *Torture Team: Deception, Cruelty and the Compromise of Law* (Penguin Group 2008).

Sassen, S., *Globalization and Its Discontents* (New Press 1999).

Schmid, A.P. and Jongman, A.J., *Political Terrorism* (North-Holland Publishing 1988).

Schouten, B. and Jacobs, B., 'Biometrics and their use in e-passports' (2009) 27(3) *Image and Vision Computing, Special Issue on Multimodal Biometrics –* Multimodal Biometrics Special Issue 305.

Schroeder, R., *Possible Worlds: The Social Dynamic of Virtual Reality Technology* (Westview Press 1996).

Schwarz, P., 'Money launderers and tax havens: two sides of the same coin?' (2010) *International Review of Law and Economics*. [Online]. Available at: http://www.sciencedirect.com/science [accessed: 12 January 2011].

Sifaoui, M, *Inside Al Qaeda: How I Infiltrated the World's Deadliest Terrorist Organisation* (Granta Books 2003).

Silke, A., 'Preface' in John Horgan et al. (eds), *Terrorists, Victims and Society: Psychological Perspectives on Terrorism and its Consequences* (Wiley 2003).

Silke, A., 'Cheshire-cat logic: the recurring theme of terrorist abnormality in psychological research' (1998) 4 *Psychology, Crime and Law* 51.

—— 'The devil you know: continuing problems with research on terrorism' (2001) 13(4) *Terrorism and Political Violence* 1.

Simon, S., 'Price of the surge: how U.S. strategy is hastening Iraq's demise' (2008) 87 *Foreign Affairs* 57.

Simon, S., *The Next Attack: The Globalisation of Jihad* (Hodder & Stoughton 2005).

Simser, J., 'Money laundering and asset cloaking techniques' (2008) 11(1) *Journal of Money Laundering Control* 15.

Smith, R.G., Holmes, M.N. and Kaufmann, P. 'Nigerian advance fee fraud' (1999) Australian Institute of Criminology: Trends and Issues in Crime and Criminal Justice 121.

—— 'Cross-Border Economic Crime: The Agenda for Reform' (2001) Australian Institute of Criminology: Trends and Issues in Crime and Criminal Justice 202. [Online]. Available at: http://www.aic.gov.au/documents/5/6/E/%7B56E66958-05A3-4C6D-9048-64D5FB7B9175%7Dti202.pdf.

SOCA, *Review of the SARs Regime* (SOCA, 2006).

SOCA, *The SARs Regime Annual Report 2009* (SOCA, 2009).

Sommer, P., *Digital Footprints: Assessing Computer Evidence: Cyberspace Crime* (Ashgate 2003).

Sookhdeo, P., *Islamic Finance in Britain* (November 2004).

Sookhdeo, P., *Understanding Islamic Terrorism* (Isaac Publishing 2004).

Southwell, D., *Dirty Cash: Organised Crime in the 21st Century* (Virgin Books 2002).

Sparrow, Andrew, 'Brown Unveils National Security Strategy' *Guardian* (19 March 2008). [Online]. Available at: http://www.guardian.co.uk/politics/2008/mar/19/terrorism.uksecurity1 [accessed: 12 October 2009].

Sponsler, T.H., 'International kidnapping' (1970) 5 *International Lawyer* 24.

Sprang, G., 'The traumatic experiences inventory: a test of psychometric properties' (1997) 19(3) *Journal of Psychopathology and Behavioural Assessment* 257.

Sproat, P.A., 'Counter-terrorist finance in the UK: a quantitative and qualitative commentary based on open-source materials' (2010) 13(4) *Journal of Money Laundering Control* 315.

Srour, D., Fischer, S. and Mandell, L.L.P., 'Money laundering, terrorism financing and financial networks' (2003) 1367 PLI/Corp 411.

Stanley, C., 'Speculations on the conflict of discourses: finance, crime and regulation' (1996) 4(3) *Journal of Financial Regulation and Compliance* 239.

Stechel, I., 'Terrorist kidnapping of diplomatic personnel' (1972) 5 *Cornell International Law Journal* 189.

Stenersen, A., 'The Internet: a virtual training camp?' (2008) 20(2) *Terrorism and Political Violence* 215.

Stevenson, J., *Counter-Terrorism: Containment and Beyond* (Oxford University Press 2004).

Stewart, R.S. and Nicholls, R., 'Virtual worlds, travel and the picturesque garden' (2002) 5(1) *Philosophy and Geography* 83.

Stiglitz, J.E., *Globalization and its Discontents* (W W Norton 2002).

Stirling Assynt, *Al-Qaeda's Strategic Plan: An Overview* (Assynt Report, 30 November 2009).

Stokes, R. and Arora, A., 'The duty to report under the money laundering legislation within the UK' (2004) 3 *Journal of Business Law* 332.

Strasser, S., (ed.) *The 9/11 Investigations: The 9/11 Commission Staff Statements and Testimony: Staff Reports of the 9/11 Commission* (Public Affairs LLC, 2004).

Taheri, A., *Holy Terror: Inside the World of Islamic Terrorism* (Adler & Adler 1987).

Tang, J., Ai L., 'Combating money laundering in transition countries: the inherent limitations and practical issues' (2010) 13(3) *Journal of Money Laundering Control* 215.

Tariq, A., *The Clash of Fundamentalism* (Verso 2002).

Taylor, M., *The Terrorist* (Brassey's 1988).

Tellis, Ashley J., 'Beradar, Pakistan, and the Afghan Taliban: What Gives?' (2010) Policy Outlook, Carnegie Endownment for International Peace. [Online]. Available at: http://www.carnegieendowment.org/files/after_beradar.pdf [accessed: 25 October 2009].

Thachuk, K.L., 'Terrorism's financial lifeline: can it be severed?' (2002) 191 *Strategic Forum*.

Thanasegaran, H. and Shanmugam, B., 'Exploitation of the insurance industry for money laundering: the Malaysian perspective' (2008) 11(2) *Journal of Money Laundering Control* 135.

Thomas, R.M., *Blending Qualitative and Quantitative Research Methods in Theses and Dissertations* (Corwin Press 2003).

Thomas Viles, 'Hawala, hysteria and hegemony' (2008) 11(1) *Journal of Money Laundering Control* 25.

Thompson, E.A., *The Nexus of Drug Trafficking and Hawala in Afghanistan* (UNDC Report 'Afghanistan's Drug Industry: Structure, Functioning, Dynamics and Implications for Counter-Narcotics Policy', 2006, ch. 6).

Tinnes, J., 'Counting lives in a theater of terror: an analysis of media-oriented hostage takings in Iraq, Afghanistan, Pakistan and Saudi Arabia' (2010) 5(5) *Perspectives on Terrorism: a Journal of the Terrorism Research Initiative* 3.

Tittmar, H.G., 'Urban terrorism: a psychological interpretation' (1992) 4(3) *Terrorism and Political Violence* 64.

Trompenaars, F. and Hampden-Turner, C., *Riding the Waves of Culture: Understanding Cultural Diversity in Business* (Nicholas Brealey Publishing 1997).

Tschirhart, S.T. and Cauley, J.T., 'A theoretical analysis of transnational terrorism' (1983) 77(1) *American Political Science Review* 36.

Tuman, J.S., *Communicating Terror: The Rhetorical Dimensions of Terrorism* (Sage Publications 2003).

Tupman, W.A., *The Business of Terrorism* (Centre for Strategic and Global Studies, 1998).

Tyler, K., 'UK bank-corporate relationships: large corporates' expectations of service' (1999) 17(4) *International Journal of Bank Marketing* 158.

United Nations Office on Drugs and Crime, *2004 World Drug Report* (UNODC, 2004).

—— *Drugs and Crime Trends in Europe and Beyond* (Vienna, 29 April 2004).

—— *UN World Drug Report 2010*. [Online]. Available at: http://www.unodc.org/documents/wdr/WDR_2010/World_Drug_Report_2010_lo-res.pdf [accessed: 11 November 2010].

United States Department of Justice Office of the Inspector General, *Inspection of the FBI's security Risk Assessment Program for Individuals Requesting Access to Biological Agents and Toxins* (Evaluation and Inspections Division 1-2005-003, March 2005).

United States General Accounting Office, *Recent Estimates of Fiscal Impact of 2001 Terrorist Attack on New York* (GAO, March 2005).

US Department of State, *Patterns of Global Terrorism 2002* (April 2003).

—— *Patterns of Global Terrorism 2001 – International Narcotics Control Strategy Report 2003* (Bureau for International Narcotics and Law Enforcement Affairs, March 2004).

—— *International Narcotics Control Strategy Report: Money Laundering and Financial Crimes* (Bureau for International Narcotics and Law Enforcement Affairs, March 2004).

—— *Money Laundering and Terrorist Financing – A Global Threat 2005*. [Online]. Availableat:http://www.state.gov/p/inl/rls/nrcrpt/2005/vol2/html/42380.htm [accessed: 29 December 2009].

Varese, F., *The Russian Mafia: Private Protection in a New Market Economy* (Oxford University Press 2001).

Vaughan, P., *Early Lessons from the Deployment of M-PESA, Vodafone's Own Mobile Transactions Service* (The Policy Paper Series, 'The Transformational Potential of M-Transactions – Moving the Debate Forward' no. 6, July 2007).

Vayrynen, R., 'Some aspects of the theory and strategy of kidnapping' (1971) 1(1) *Research on Peace and Violence* 3.

Verhage, A., 'Supply and demand: anti-money laundering by the compliance industry' (2010) 12(4) *Journal of Money Laundering Control* 371.

Walker, C., *Blackstone's Guide to Anti-Terrorism Legislation* (Oxford University Press 2002).

Wallace, R., *International Law* (5th Edition, Sweet & Maxwell 2005).

Warde, I., *The Financial War on Terror* (Harvard University Press 2005).

Webb, B., *The Art of Note taking: Field Research: A Sourcebook and Field Manual* (Routledge 1982).

Webb, K.G.L., *Managing Asymmetric Threats to National Security Terrorist Information Operations* (Australian Research Council Project Report, August 2007).

Wei, J., Liu, L.C., Koong, K.S. and Li, Y., 'A risk assessment model for information security' (2011) 5(2) *International Journal of Business and Systems Research* 158.

Whittaker, D.J, *Terrorism: Understanding the Global Threat* (Pearson 2002).

Wild, C., Weinstein, S. and MacEwan, N., *Internet Law* (Old Bailey Press 2005).

Wilkinson, P., *Technology and Terrorism* (Frank Cass 1993).

—— 'The media and terrorism: a reassessment' (1997) 9(2) *Terrorism and Political Violence* 51.

—— *Aviation Terrorism and Security* (Frank Cass 1998).

Williams, Janet, talk at CONTEST conference, Defence Academy of the UK, Shrivenham, September 2004.

Williams, P.L., Al-*Qaeda: Brotherhood of Terror* (Alpha Press 2002).

—— *The al-Qaeda Connection* (Prometheus Books 2005).

Wilson, M. and Daly, M., 'Competitiveness, risk taking and violence: the young male syndrome' (1985) 6 *Ethology and Sociobiology* 59.

Winer, J. and Roule, T., 'Fighting terrorist finance' (2002) 44(3) *Survival* 89.

Wulf, W.A. and Longstaff, T.A. 'Strategic alternative response to risks of terrorism' (2003) 23(3) *Risk Analysis* 429.

Zagaris, B., 'The merging of the anti-money laundering and counter-terrorism financial enforcement regimes after September 11, 2001' (2004) 22 *Berkley Journal International Law* 123.

—— 'Problems applying traditional anti-money laundering procedures to non-financial transactions, "parallel banking systems" and Islamic financial systems' (2007) 10 (2) *Journal of Money Laundering Control* 157.

Index

For Product Safety Concerns and Information please contact our EU representative GPSR@taylorandfrancis.com Taylor & Francis Verlag GmbH, Kaufingerstraße 24, 80331 München, Germany

Batch number: 10726294

Printed by Printforce, the Netherlands